MONEY EQUALS MATHS

Books of related interest

MONEY EQUALS MATHS

John Marshall

Sydney
ALLEN & UNWIN
Wellington London Boston

First published in 1989
Allen & Unwin Australia Pty Ltd
An Unwin Hyman company
8 Napier Street, North Sydney NSW 2059 Australia

Allen & Unwin New Zealand Limited
60 Cambridge Terrace, Wellington, New Zealand

Unwin Hyman Limited
15–17 Broadwick Street, London W1V 1FP, England

Unwin Hyman Inc.
8 Winchester Place, Winchester, Mass 01890 USA

National Library of Australia
Cataloguing-in-Publication entry:
Marshall, John, 1944–
   Money equals maths.

   ISBN 0 04 340013 2.

   1. Money market—Mathematics.   2. Business mathematics.
   3. Investments—Mathematics.   I. Title.

332′.0412

Library of Congress Catalog Card Number: 88-83147
Set in 10/11 pt Times New Roman by Asco Trade Typesetting Ltd,
Hong Kong

Printed in Singapore by Kin Keong Printing Co. Pte. Ltd.

Contents

Preface

In every financial transaction there is an interest cost which may be flat interest or compound. Usually there are transaction charges such as stamp duty and administration costs which affect the return or borrowing rate. As the cash flows multiply, the choice of 'money' alternatives becomes more complex.

The purpose of this book is to give you the mathematical skills necessary to solve problems involving money, time, interest and inflation. The mathematical chapters explain the skills necessary for solving algebraic problems which occur frequently in the financial markets, particularly in the ordinary share, bond, short term money and lending markets. Each step in the calculation process is set out for you.

The procedures for computing quickly on a scientific and/or financial calculator are also explained. The emphasis throughout is on understanding the mathematics, and thus knowing which buttons to press on your calculator. The great majority of problems can be solved using an ordinary scientific calculator or using the Hewlett-Packard 12C as an ordinary calculator. In cases where a scientific calculator is not sophisticated enough to compute a problem, explanation of how to use the Hewlett-Packard's special programmes has been given.

The early chapters are designed to increase your confidence in the algebraic and computational areas. The rest of the book is concerned with applications that occur frequently in the market place such as evaluating the return on a fixed interest investment, assessing your borrowing rate allowing for all the hidden extras, calculating your loan balance, accumulating money for a holiday, pricing a share, comparing project cash flows adjusting for inflation and determining the appropriate valuation rate.

The book has arisen from the needs expressed by tertiary students but also by those attending and running professional courses. In many instances the professional who wishes to embark on solving money problems has either forgotten or not fully understood basic algebra. Further, many people have only pressed the calculator buttons on less sophisticated models. While you are working on this book you may decide to upgrade your calculator.

Several people deserve special thanks: Dianne and Tim Marshall for their patience and positive support; Nicolle Harrison for her long yet cheerful hours at the word processor; Linley Lloyd for painstakingly editing the script and checking the calculations; Sue Peatfield and Rod Crane who supported the initial idea and also provided encouragement; and finally John Iremonger, who accepted the contract, provided understanding when my mother passed away and who subsequently imposed gentle pressure with a smile and a cup of coffee. I drink to them all—not with coffee!

John Marshall,
Canberra, July 1988

1

Operations with signs

As a financial manager/officer you may often be required to perform a *chain* of calculations with varying sign and operation ($\times$, $\div$, $+$, $-$). Sometimes you will confront awkward groupings such as:

$$Q = \frac{(1 - 0.07)^3 [(1.07)^3 - 1]}{(1.07) - 1}$$

Such calculations are quite common when you have to accumulate offshore money at compound interest as well as adjust for any appreciation/depreciation of the domestic currency. A simple example is finding an equal monthly instalment sufficient to provide for your holiday in the United Kingdom. The compounding of interest on your payments and the change in value of your local currency to Sterling are key variables which can result in this awkward expression.

However before embarking on solving such complex expressions, this book will focus initially on the techniques required to master simple calculations.

This chapter will therefore help you to:
(i) sequence calculations correctly and efficiently;
(ii) compute calculations quickly on an electronic calculator—with minimum writing time.

SEQUENCE OF OPERATIONS

Can you calculate $6 - 3 \times 4 \div 2 + 3 \times 6$?
If you did not achieve a result of 18 you need to read the rest of this chapter.

The important procedure is to perform *multiplication* and *division* before addition and subtraction.

Step 1 Group the multiplications and divisions, namely:

$$6 - (3 \times 4 \div 2) + (3 \times 6)$$

Step 2   Complete the inside of each bracket, working from left to right:

$$6 - (12 \div 2) + 18$$

$$= 6 - (6) + 18$$

Step 3   Add the subtotals, working from left to right:

$$= \text{zero} + 18$$

$$= 18$$

Example 1

Find $A = 5 \times 4 - 6 \div 3 - 2 \times 5$

Step 1   Group multiplication and division first:

$$A = (5 \times 4) - (6 \div 3) - (2 \times 5)$$

Step 2   Complete the inside of each bracket working from left to right:

$$A = 20 - 2 - 10$$

Step 2   Add subtotals from left to right:

$$A = 18 - 10$$

$$= 8$$

Use of calculators

The aim of this book is to enable you to master the mathematics required for various financial calculations. A calculator can take the tedium out of many calculations but it is essential to understand the processes involved in order to know which buttons to press. Thus for most of this book we will either use an ordinary scientific calculator or use the Hewlett-Packard 12C as an ordinary calculator. Once you are familiar with the Hewlett-Packard and the financial calculations explained in this book you will be able to bypass many of the steps by using the calculator's special programmes. But those who do not have access to a Hewlett-Packard will be able to do virtually all the calculations required on their scientific calculator.

Scientific calculator

Using a calculator speeds up calculations considerably. Your calculator will automatically group the operations.

Try the previous example $6 - 3 \times 4 \div 2 + 3 \times 6$ using your calculator:

Press

Hewlett-Packard

When using the Hewlett-Packard it is essential to understand how operations are grouped.

Look again at $6 - 3 \times 4 \div 2 + 3 \times 6$

First group the multiplications and divisions:

$$6 - (3 \times 4 \div 2) + (3 \times 6)$$

Then use the calculator:

Now check Example 1 with the Hewlett-Packard:

$$A = (5 \times 4) - (6 \div 3) - (2 \times 5)$$

Note that to obtain the above results we used two processes—(1) manual computation, then (2) check with calculator. The more common order in practice is (1) use electronic calculator, then (2) check manually —exactly or by estimation.

Example 2

$$B = 15 - 3 \times 6/2 \times 3 - 21 \times 3/2$$

The slash / means division and is the symbol used in data processing. So 6/2 means '6 divided by 2'.

Step 1   Group multiplications and divisions:

$$B = 15 - (3 \times 6 \div 2 \times 3) - (21 \times 3 \div 2)$$

Step 2   Complete the inside of each bracket working from left to right with two numbers at a time:

$$B = 15 - (18 \div 2 \times 3) - (63 \div 2)$$
$$= 15 - (9 \times 3) - (31.5)$$
$$= 15 - 27 - 31.5$$
$$= -43.5$$

Using your calculator

Scientific calculator

$$B = 15 - 3 \times 6/2 \times 3 - 21 \times 3/2$$

Press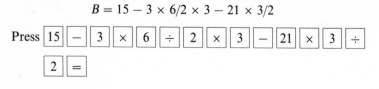

Hewlett-Packard

$$B = 15 - (3 \times 6/2 \times 3) - (21 \times 3/2)$$

Press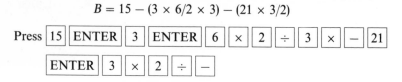

MULTIPLICATION AND DIVISION OF SIGNS

Numbers in calculations may be either positive or negative. Use the following rules to determine the correct sign when multiplying or dividing numbers.

If two numbers have the *same* sign, the answer to the multiplication or division is *positive*.

i.e. positive × positive = positive
+   ×   +   =   +

negative × negative = positive
−   ×   −   =   +

+   ÷   +   =   +
−   ÷   −   =   +

If two numbers have *different* signs, the answer to the multiplication or division is *negative*.

i.e. positive × negative = negative
+   ×   −   =   −

negative × positive = negative
−   ×   +   =   −

+   ÷   −   =   −
−   ÷   +   =   −

Note: If no sign is given, the number is positive.

You may find it helpful to think of the signs in the following way.
If 'don't' is indicated by a negative sign and 'do' by a positive sign, then:
'Don't be negative' means $(-)$ times $(-) = +$ Yes a *positive* attitude is
the key today.
Do $(+)$ be negative $(-) = (+) \times (-) =$ negative
Similarly Don't $(-)$ be positive $(+) = (-) \times (+) =$ negative

Example 3

Find C in

$$C = -32 \times -2 - 2 \times -3 + 3 \times -4 \times -5$$

Step 1   Group multiplication and division:

$$C = (-32 \times -2) - (2 \times -3) + (3 \times -4 \times -5)$$

Step 2   Determine sign in each bracket, working in pairs from left to
right:

$$C = (- \times -) - (+ \times -) + (+ \times - \times -)$$
$$\therefore C = (+) - (-) + (- \times -)$$
$$= (+) - (-) + (+)$$
$$= (+) + (+) + (+)$$

Step 3   Calculate the multiplication inside each bracket, disregarding
sign:

$$C = (32 \times 2) + (2 \times 3) + (3 \times 4 \times 5)$$
$$= \quad (64) \quad + \quad (6) \quad + \quad (60)$$

Step 4   Add correct sign as calculated in Step 2:

$$C = (+64) + (+6) + (+60)$$

Step 5   Complete the calculation from left to right:

$$C = 64 + 6 + 60$$
$$= 130$$

Using your calculator

Scientific calculator

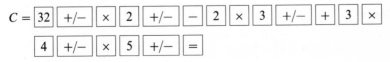

Note that the $\boxed{+/-}$ key makes the number just entered negative. e.g.
$\boxed{32}$ $\boxed{+/-}$ enters -32.

Hewlett-Packard

$\boxed{32}$ $\boxed{\text{CHS}}$ $\boxed{\text{ENTER}}$ $\boxed{2}$ $\boxed{\text{CHS}}$ $\boxed{\times}$ $\boxed{2}$ $\boxed{\text{ENTER}}$ $\boxed{3}$ $\boxed{\text{CHS}}$ $\boxed{\times}$

$\boxed{-}$ $\boxed{3}$ $\boxed{\text{ENTER}}$ $\boxed{4}$ $\boxed{\text{CHS}}$ $\boxed{\times}$ $\boxed{5}$ $\boxed{\text{CHS}}$ $\boxed{\times}$ $\boxed{+}$

Example 4

Find $D = 5 \times -4 + -2 \times -8 \div 4 - 3 + -24 \div -6 + 20$

Step 1   Group multiplication and division:

$$D = (5 \times -4) + (-2 \times -8 \div 4) - (3) + (-24 \div -6) + (20)$$

Step 2   Determine the sign in each bracket:

$$D = (+ \times -) + (- \times - \div +) - (+) + (- \div -) + (+)$$
$$= (-) + (+ \div +) - (+) + (+) + (+)$$
$$= (-) + (+) - (+) + (+) + (+)$$

Step 3   Do the numerical calculations inside each bracket:

$$D = (5 \times 4) + (2 \times 8 \div 4) - (3) + (24 \div 6) + (20)$$
$$= (20) + (4) - (3) + (4) + (20)$$

Step 4   Add the correct sign as calculated in Step 2:

$$D = (-20) + (+4) - (+3) + (+4) + (+20)$$

Step 5   Complete the calculation:

$$D = -20 + 4 - 3 + 4 + 20$$
$$= 5$$

Using your calculator

Scientific calculator

$$D = 5 \times -4 + -2 \times -8 \div 4 - 3 + -24 \div -6 + 20$$

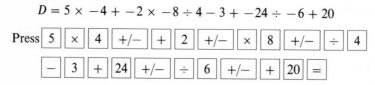

Press $\boxed{5}$ $\boxed{\times}$ $\boxed{4}$ $\boxed{+/-}$ $\boxed{+}$ $\boxed{2}$ $\boxed{+/-}$ $\boxed{\times}$ $\boxed{8}$ $\boxed{+/-}$ $\boxed{\div}$ $\boxed{4}$

$\boxed{-}$ $\boxed{3}$ $\boxed{+}$ $\boxed{24}$ $\boxed{+/-}$ $\boxed{\div}$ $\boxed{6}$ $\boxed{+/-}$ $\boxed{+}$ $\boxed{20}$ $\boxed{=}$

Hewlett-Packard

$$D = (5 \times -4) + (-2 \times -8 \div 4) - (3) + (-24 \div -6) + (20)$$

Press 5 ENTER 4 CHS × 2 CHS ENTER 8 CHS

× 4 ÷ + 3 − 24 CHS ENTER 6 CHS ÷

+ 20 +

Example 5

Calculate

$$E = \frac{2 - 3 \times 4 + 3 \times -2 \times -3}{-2 + 6 \times 4 \times -3}$$

$$= \frac{2 - (3 \times 4) + (3 \times -2 \times -3)}{-2 + (6 \times 4 \times -3)}$$

$$= \frac{2 - 12 + 18}{-2 - 72}$$

$$= \frac{8}{-74}$$

$$= -0.1081$$

Using your calculator

Scientific calculator

Using a Casio scientific calculator the steps would be:

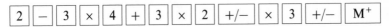

2 − 3 × 4 + 3 × 2 +/− × 3 +/− M⁺

(This calculates the numerator, 8, and stores it in memory.)

2 +/− + 6 × 4 × 3 +/−

(This calculates the denominator, −74.)

 ÷ MR   (This recalls the numerator from memory and divides by it, i.e. −74 ÷ 8)

$\frac{1}{x}$ =   (This inverts the number so it is 8 ÷ −74 instead of −74 ÷ 8. Inverting a number is called taking the *reciprocal* of the number. $\frac{1}{x}$ is the reciprocal of x and 8/−74 is the reciprocal of −74/8.)

Hewlett-Packard

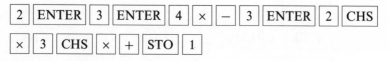

(This calculates the numerator, 8, and stores it in memory register 1.)

| 2 | CHS | ENTER | 6 | ENTER | 4 | × | 3 | CHS | × | + |

(This calculates the denominator, −74.)

| RCL | 1 | ÷ | (This recalls the number in memory register 1, and divides by it.)

    (This works out the reciprocal because we calculated −74/8 instead of 8/−74. Inverting a number is called taking the reciprocal.)

With simple calculations on the Hewlett-Packard it is not always necessary to store the numerator in memory and recall it later. However if you are not sure which calculations require memory storage and which don't, it is a good idea to get into the habit of always using the memory facility. Most of the calculations later in the book require storage and recall of the numerator.

Example 6

Calculate

$$F = \frac{1 - (1.12)(1.12)}{1 - 1.12}$$

$$= \frac{1 - 1.2544}{1 - 1.12}$$

$$= \frac{-0.2544}{-0.12}$$

$$= 2.12$$

You will be confronting this type of calculation later. A simple example of when it is used is to find an equal annual instalment sufficient to replace your car in two years' time.

Using your calculator

Scientific calculator

Try to calculate F in one process.

Press $\boxed{1}$ $\boxed{-}$ $\boxed{1.12}$ $\boxed{\times}$ $\boxed{=}$ $\boxed{\div}$ $\boxed{0.12}$ $\boxed{+/-}$ $\boxed{=}$

(Note: Some calculators have an x^2 button instead of $\boxed{\times}$ $\boxed{=}$ and some may require the number to be repeated $\boxed{1.12}$ $\boxed{\times}$ $\boxed{1.12}$ $\boxed{=}$. Not all calculators need $\boxed{=}$ to be pressed to give running totals.)

Hewlett-Packard

$$F = \frac{1 - (1.12)(1.12)}{1 - 1.12}$$

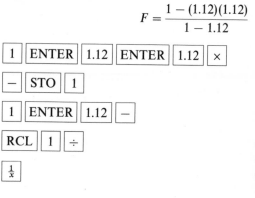

$\boxed{1}$ $\boxed{\text{ENTER}}$ $\boxed{1.12}$ $\boxed{\text{ENTER}}$ $\boxed{1.12}$ $\boxed{\times}$ (This calculates the numerator.)

$\boxed{-}$ $\boxed{\text{STO}}$ $\boxed{1}$

$\boxed{1}$ $\boxed{\text{ENTER}}$ $\boxed{1.12}$ $\boxed{-}$ (This calculates the denominator.)

$\boxed{\text{RCL}}$ $\boxed{1}$ $\boxed{\div}$ (This recalls the numerator and divides by it.)

$\boxed{\frac{1}{x}}$ (This inverts because the division was performed the wrong way round.)

Example 7

Find

$$G = \frac{-12 \div -3 \times 4 - 6 \times -3 \div -2}{-10 - (3 \times -4)}$$

Step 1   Group multiplication and division first:

$$G = \frac{(-12 \div -3 \times 4) - (6 \times -3 \div -2)}{-10 - (3 \times -4)}$$

Step 2   Find sign within each bracket:

$$G = \frac{(- \div - \times +) - (+ \times - \div -)}{-10 - (+ \times -)}$$

$$G = \frac{(+ \times +) - (- \div -)}{-10 - (-)}$$

$$G = \frac{(+) - (+)}{-10 +}$$

Step 3 $$G = \frac{+(12 \div 3 \times 4) - (6 \times 3 \div 2)}{-10 + (3 \times 4)}$$

Step 4   Find the result in each bracket, working from left to right:

$$G = \frac{16 - 9}{-10 + 12}$$

$$= \frac{7}{2}$$

$$= 3.5$$

Using your calculator

Scientific calculator

Try to calculate G in one process:

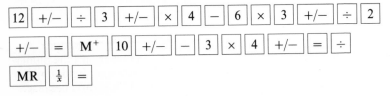

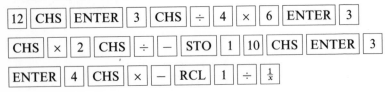

Hewlett-Packard

EXERCISES

1   Manually simplify $A = 5 - 6 \times 3 + 4 \times 2$
    Check your result using your calculator.

2   Manually simplify $B = \dfrac{12 \div (-6) + 2 - 3 \times 2}{8 \div 4 - 3}$

    Check your result on your calculator.

3   Manually solve for D in the expression

$$D = \frac{4 \times 3 - (-2) \div (-3) + 3 \times 2}{6 \div 2 + 5}$$

    Check using your calculator.

4 Manually simplify $E = \dfrac{3 \div -1 \times 4 \times 2 - 2 \times 3}{-1 - 7 \times 2}$

5 Simplify $F = \dfrac{1.912 \times 3.9 - 2.1 \times -3 \div 3}{3.8 \div 2 + 10}$

Compute F using your calculator.
Check your answer to F by manual estimation.

6 Compute $Q = \dfrac{-3 \div -2.9 + 6 \times -3 - 4.1}{-6.2 + 3.0 \times -4.9}$

Check your answer by estimation.

2

Understanding Indices

In the first chapter you learnt to sequence operations correctly and to compute them on your calculator. We are now going to launch into operations with indices so that by the end of the chapter you can compute calculations such as:

$$(1.07)^{-3} \frac{\{1 - [(1.07)^{-2}]^3\}}{1 - (1.07)^2}$$

In fact this example relates to a sum of money which is paid every two years and is accumulating at 7% compound interest. A common example is a trust established to provide a biennial research grant.

> The purpose of this chapter then is to:
> enable you to work with indices (powers) efficiently and effectively, both manually and on your calculator.

INDICES AND POWER FUNCTIONS

A shorthand way of writing a repeated multiplication is to use an index. For example,

$$2 \times 2 \times 2 \times 2 = 2^4$$

This is read as, '2 to the power 4' and 2^4 is called a power function. The '4' is called an *index* (plural, *indices*) and shows how many twos appear in the multiplication.
Similarly,

$$a \times a \times a = a^3 \quad (3 \ a\text{'s in the multiplication})$$

$$a \times a \times a \times \ldots a \ (n \text{ times}) = a^n \quad (n \ a\text{'s in the multiplication})$$

ADDITION AND SUBTRACTION WITH POWER FUNCTIONS

Power functions can only be added or subtracted when they have the same form, i.e. the same letter or number and the same index. Some examples are shown below:

$$a^2 + a^2 = 2a^2$$
$$a^2 + b^3 + 2a^2 + 3b^3 = (a^2 + 2a^2) + (b^3 + 3b^3)$$
$$= 3a^2 + 4b^3$$
$$a^2 + a^5 = a^2 + a^5 \text{ (cannot be simplified)}$$
$$a + 5a + 3a = 9a$$
$$3^4 + 2 \times 3^4 = 1(3^4) + 2(3^4)$$
$$= 3(3^4)$$
$$= 3 \times (3 \times 3 \times 3 \times 3)$$
$$= 3^5$$
$$7x^2 - 2y^2 + 4x^2 - 3y^2 = (7x^2 + 4x^2) + (-2y^2 - 3y^2)$$
$$= 11x^2 - 5y^2$$

MULTIPLICATION WITH POWER FUNCTIONS

Power functions can be multiplied when the indices are not the same.

$$a^4 \times a^2 = (a \times a \times a \times a) \times (a \times a)$$

Removing the brackets we obtain:

$$a \times a \times a \times a \times a \times a$$

As a occurs 6 times, the answer is a^6.

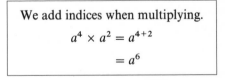

We add indices when multiplying.
$$a^4 \times a^2 = a^{4+2}$$
$$= a^6$$

Example 1

$A = 2^3 \times 2^2$

$= (2 \times 2 \times 2) \times (2 \times 2)$

$= 2 \times 2 \times 2 \times 2 \times 2$

$= 2^5 \text{ or } 2^{3+2}$

$= 32$

Example 2

$B = 7^2 \times 7^5 \times 7^3 \times 7^{10}$

$= 7^{2+5+3+10}$

$= 7^{20}$

Using your calculator
Both types of calculator have a power key $\boxed{x^y}$ or $\boxed{y^x}$. This key is used to raise a number to a particular power or index.

Scientific calculator

For $A = 2^5$, press $\boxed{2}$ $\boxed{y^x}$ $\boxed{5}$ $\boxed{=}$. This calculates '2 raised to the power 5'.

Hewlett-Packard

For $A = 2^5$, press $\boxed{2}$ $\boxed{\text{ENTER}}$ $\boxed{5}$ $\boxed{y^x}$

For 7^{20}, press $\boxed{7}$ $\boxed{\text{ENTER}}$ $\boxed{20}$ $\boxed{y^x}$. The answer will appear in standard notation because the number is too large to fit in the display. i.e. $7^{20} = 7.979226 \times 10^{16}$

Example 3

Find $(a^3)^2$

$$(a^3)^2 = (a \times a \times a) \times (a \times a \times a) \qquad \text{OR} \qquad (a^3)^2 = a^3 \times a^3$$
$$= a \times a \times a \times a \times a \times a \qquad\qquad\qquad = a^{3+3}$$
$$= a^6 \qquad\qquad\qquad\qquad\qquad\qquad\qquad = a^6$$

Example 4

Calculate $L = (2^3)^2$

$$L = (2 \times 2 \times 2) \times (2 \times 2 \times 2) \qquad \text{OR} \qquad L = 2^3 \times 2^3$$
$$= 2 \times 2 \times 2 \times 2 \times 2 \times 2 \qquad\qquad\qquad = 2^{3+3}$$
$$= 2^6 \qquad\qquad\qquad\qquad\qquad\qquad\qquad = 2^6$$
$$= 64 \qquad\qquad\qquad\qquad\qquad\qquad\qquad = 64$$

Example 5

$$(x^4)^3 = x^4 \times x^4 \times x^4$$
$$= x^{4+4+4}$$
$$= x^{12}$$

Look again at Examples 2, 3, and 4. They illustrate the following result.

When a number is raised first to one power (index), and then to another power, the indices are multiplied.

Thus in Example 4, $(x^4)^3 = x^{4 \times 3}$

$$= x^{12}$$

This is quicker than adding x^{4+4+4} especially when larger indices are involved.

Similarly, $(a^3)^2 = a^{3 \times 2}$

$$= a^6$$

Using your calculator

Scientific calculator

For $(2^3)^2$,   press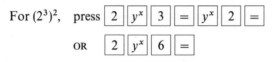

Hewlett-Packard

For $(2^3)^2$,   press   2   ENTER   3 y^x 2 y^x

OR   2   ENTER   6 y^x

Example 6

Find $A = (1.12^3)^4$ on your calculator

$$A = 1.12^3 \times (1.12)^3 \times (1.12)^3 \times (1.12)^3$$

$$A = 1.12^{3+3+3+3} = 1.12^{12}$$

OR $A = 1.12^{3 \times 4}$ $= 1.12^{12}$

$\therefore$ $A = 3.895976$

Scientific calculator

Press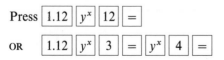

Hewlett-Packard

Press   1.12   ENTER   12 y^x

OR   1.12   ENTER   3 y^x 4 y^x

Example 7

Find $Z = (2^3 3^2)^2$

$$(2^3 3^2)^2 = (2^3 3^2) \times (2^3 3^2)$$
$$= 2^3 \times 3^2 \times 2^3 \times 3^2$$

Rearranging terms:

$$Z = 2^3 \times 2^3 \times 3^2 \times 3^2$$
$$= 2^6 \times 3^4$$
$$= 5184$$

Using your calculator

Scientific calculator

Press 2 y^x 6 = × 3 y^x 4 =

Hewlett-Packard

Press 2 ENTER 6 y^x 3 ENTER 4 y^x ×

DIVISION WITH POWER FUNCTIONS

Consider the example $F = a^5 \div a^2$

$$F = \frac{a \times a \times a \times a \times a}{a \times a}$$

Because the a's are all multiplied, this can be rewritten as:

$$F = \frac{a}{a} \times \frac{a}{a} \times a \times a \times a$$
$$= 1 \times 1 \times a \times a \times a$$
$$= a^3$$

We say the a's are *reduced*, or *cancelled*:

$$\frac{\cancel{a} \times \cancel{a} \times a \times a \times a}{\cancel{a} \times \cancel{a}} = a^3$$

Cancelling only works when the numbers in the numerator and denominator are multiplied. For example,

$$\frac{2 \times \cancel{3} \times 4 \times \cancel{5}}{\cancel{3} \times \cancel{5} \times 7} = \frac{2 \times 4}{7} = \frac{8}{7}$$

but $\dfrac{2 + 3 \times 4 - 5}{3 \times 5 + 7}$ cannot be cancelled or reduced.

Thus, returning to $a^5 \div a^2$,

$$F = a^3$$
$$= a^{5-2}$$

You should be able to see that:

> We subtract indices when dividing.

Example 8

$$Q = \frac{(1.12)^5}{(1.12)^3}$$
$$= 1.12^{5-3}$$
$$= 1.12^2$$
$$= 1.2544$$

Example 9

$$\frac{5^4 \times (5^3)^8}{(5^5)^4} = \frac{5^4 \times 5^{24}}{5^{20}}$$
$$= \frac{5^{28}}{5^{20}}$$
$$= 5^{28-20}$$
$$= 5^8$$

Example 10

$$F = \frac{(1.07)^9}{(1.02)^9 (1.07)^3}$$
$$= \frac{(1.07)^{9-3}}{(1.02)^9}$$
$$= \frac{1.07^6}{1.02^9}$$
$$= 1.2557$$

Using your calculator

Scientific calculator

Press  $\boxed{1.07}$ $\boxed{y^x}$ $\boxed{6}$ $\boxed{=}$ $\boxed{\div}$ $\boxed{1.02}$ $\boxed{y^x}$ $\boxed{9}$ $\boxed{=}$

Hewlett-Packard

Press $\boxed{1.07}$ $\boxed{\text{ENTER}}$ $\boxed{6}$ $\boxed{y^x}$ $\boxed{1.02}$ $\boxed{\text{ENTER}}$ $\boxed{9}$ $\boxed{y^x}$ $\boxed{\div}$

Example 11   **Example 12**

Find

$$M = \frac{(1.07)^3(1.12)^4}{(1.07)(1.12)^2}$$

$$M = (1.07)^{3-1} \times (1.12)^{4-2}$$

$$\quad = (1.07)^2(1.12)^2$$

$$\quad = 1.4362$$

$$Y = \frac{2a^2 \times a^8}{a^3 \times 4a}$$

$$= \frac{2 \times a^2 \times a^8}{4 \times a \times a^3}$$

$$= \frac{2a^{10}}{4a^4}$$

$$= \frac{a^{10-4}}{2}$$

$$= \frac{a^6}{2}$$

If you can agree with these results you are now well placed to test yourself on negative indices.

NEGATIVE POWERS (INDICES)

Consider the pattern below

$$10 \times 10 \times 10 = 1000 = 10^3$$

$$10 \times 10 = 100 \ \ = 10^2$$

$$10 = 10 \ \ = 10^1$$

$$1 = 1 \ \ = 10^0$$

$$\frac{1}{10} = \frac{1}{10^1} \ \ = 10^{\boxed{?}}$$

$$\frac{1}{10} \times \frac{1}{10} = \frac{1}{100} \ \ = 10^{\triangle}$$

Can you complete the pattern?
You should see that $\boxed{?} = -1$ and $\triangle = -2$

i.e. $\quad 10^{-1} = \frac{1}{10^1}; \quad 10^{-2} = \frac{1}{100} = \frac{1}{10^2}$

The negative sign simply tells you to put the expression in the denominator:

$$2^{-6} = \frac{1}{2^6} \qquad 500^{-1} = \frac{1}{500}$$

$$x^{-4} = \frac{1}{x^4} \qquad (a^3)^{-2} = \frac{1}{(a^3)^2} = \frac{1}{a^6}$$

Example 13

Find $X = 3^{-2}$

$$X = \frac{1}{3^2}$$

$$= \frac{1}{9}$$

$$= 0.111111\ldots$$

$$= 0.\dot{1} \quad \text{(the dot over the one indicates a repeating decimal)}$$

Example 14

$$F = 2^{-3}$$

$$= \frac{1}{2^3}$$

$$= \frac{1}{8}$$

$$= 0.125$$

Example 15

Find $Q = 2^{-3} \times 2^{-5}$ 　　OR　　 $Q = 2^{-3} \times 2^{-5}$

$$Q = \frac{1}{2^3} \times \frac{1}{2^5} \qquad\qquad = 2^{-3+(-5)}$$

$$= \frac{1}{2^{3+5}} \qquad\qquad\qquad = 2^{-3-5}$$

$$= \frac{1}{2^8} \qquad\qquad\qquad\quad = 2^{-8}$$

$$\qquad\qquad\qquad\qquad\qquad = \frac{1}{2^8}$$

Note that -3 added to -5 does not become positive. The following scenario may help you to understand.

Assume negative numbers occur below the water level and the water level is zero. By diving 3 metres below the water level (-3 m) and then diving a further 5 m you are 8 m below the water level, i.e. -8 m.

Using your calculator

Scientific calculator

$Q = 2^{-8}$

Press $\boxed{2}$ $\boxed{y^x}$ $\boxed{8}$ $\boxed{+/-}$ $\boxed{=}$ (calculates 2^{-8})

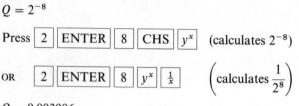

OR $\boxed{2}\ \boxed{y^x}\ \boxed{8}\ \boxed{=}\ \boxed{\frac{1}{x}}$ $\left(\text{calculates } \dfrac{1}{2^8}\right)$

$Q = 0.00390625$

Hewlett-Packard

$Q = 2^{-8}$

Press $\boxed{2}\ \boxed{\text{ENTER}}\ \boxed{8}\ \boxed{\text{CHS}}\ \boxed{y^x}$ (calculates 2^{-8})

OR $\boxed{2}\ \boxed{\text{ENTER}}\ \boxed{8}\ \boxed{y^x}\ \boxed{\frac{1}{x}}$ $\left(\text{calculates } \dfrac{1}{2^8}\right)$

$Q = 0.003906$

Example 16

Find $Y = (1.12^{-2})^4$
The index -2 tells you to put $(1.12)^2$ in the denominator.
The index 4 tells you the expression 1.12^{-2} is multiplied by itself 4 times.

$$\therefore\ Y = \frac{1}{1.12^2} \times \frac{1}{1.12^2} \times \frac{1}{1.12^2} \times \frac{1}{1.12^2} \qquad \text{OR} \qquad \begin{aligned} Y &= (1.12^{-2})^4 \\ &= 1.12^{-2 \times 4} \\ &= 1.12^{-8} \\ &= 0.403883 \end{aligned}$$

$$= \frac{1}{1.12^8}$$

$$= 1.12^{-8}$$

$$= 0.403883$$

Use your calculator in the same way as for Example 15.

INVERT AND MULTIPLY

To simplify expressions with a fraction in the denominator, we use the 'invert and multiply' tool.

For example, $\dfrac{2/3}{4/5} = \dfrac{2}{3} \div \dfrac{4}{5}$

This can be rewritten as $\dfrac{2}{3} \times \dfrac{5}{4}$. The fraction in the denominator is inverted and multiplied instead of divided. The answer is then easily computed as $\dfrac{10}{12}$ or $\dfrac{5}{6}$.

The inversion and multiplication tool is often useful in tricky calculations such as:

$$E = \frac{\dfrac{(1.07)^3}{2}}{\dfrac{2}{3}}$$

This means

$$E = \frac{1.07^3}{2} \div \frac{2}{3}$$

Invert and multiply:

$$E = \frac{1.07^3}{2} \times \frac{3}{2}$$

Example 17

$$F = \frac{\dfrac{(0.93)}{3}}{4/7} = \frac{0.93}{3} \div \frac{4}{7}$$

$$= \frac{0.93}{3} \times \frac{7}{4}$$

Example 18

$$N = \frac{[(1.09)^2]^3}{(1.02)^4} \div \frac{1}{(1.02)^2}$$

You will meet this sort of calculation later in situations involving the inflation effect of money and the compounding of the interest rate over time.

Step 1   Invert and multiply:

$$N = \frac{(1.09^2)^3}{1.02^4} \times \frac{(1.02)^2}{1}$$

$$= \frac{(1.09^2)^3 \times (1.02)^2}{(1.02)^4}$$

Step 2   Subtract indices when dividing:

$$N = (1.09^2)^3 \times 1.02^{2-4}$$

Step 3 $(a^m)^n = a^{m \times n}$

So

$$N = 1.09^{2 \times 3} \times 1.02^{-2}$$

$$N = 1.09^6 \times 1.02^{-2}$$
$$= 1.611976 \text{ or } 1.6120 \text{ to 4 decimal places}$$

Using your calculator

$$N = 1.09^6 \times 1.02^{-2}$$

Scientific calculator

Press $\boxed{1.09}$ $\boxed{y^x}$ $\boxed{6}$ $\boxed{=}$ $\boxed{\times}$ $\boxed{1.02}$ $\boxed{y^x}$ $\boxed{2}$ $\boxed{+/-}$ $\boxed{=}$

Hewlett-Packard

Press $\boxed{1.09}$ $\boxed{\text{ENTER}}$ $\boxed{6}$ $\boxed{y^x}$ $\boxed{1.02}$ $\boxed{\text{ENTER}}$ $\boxed{2}$ $\boxed{\text{CHS}}$ $\boxed{y^x}$ $\boxed{\times}$

FRACTIONAL INDICES

Can you calculate $4^{1/2}$?   Your answer should be 2.

Problems with fractional indices are common when trying to determine effective interest rates over *fractions* of a year.

How then can we determine $a^{\frac{m}{n}}$ or $a^{m/n}$?
Consider $10^{1/2}$

$$\text{Now} \quad \sqrt{10} \times \sqrt{10} = 10$$
$$\text{Let} \quad \sqrt{10} = 10^{\boxed{?}}$$
$$10^{\boxed{?}} \times 10^{\boxed{?}} = 10^1$$
$$10^{\boxed{?}+\boxed{?}} = 10^1$$
$$\boxed{?} + \boxed{?} = 1$$
$$2\boxed{?} = 1$$
$$\boxed{?} = \tfrac{1}{2}$$
$$\therefore 10^{1/2} + 10^{1/2} = 10^1$$
$$\text{i.e.} \quad \sqrt{10} = 10^{\boxed{?}} = 10^{1/2}$$
$$\text{Similarly} \quad \sqrt[3]{10} \times \sqrt[3]{10} \times \sqrt[3]{10} = 10^1$$
$$\text{Let } \sqrt[3]{10} = 10^{\triangle}$$
$$10^{\triangle} \times 10^{\triangle} \times 10^{\triangle} = 10^1$$
$$10^{\triangle+\triangle+\triangle} = 10^1$$

$$3 \triangle = 1$$
$$\triangle = \tfrac{1}{3}$$
$$\therefore \ 10^{1/3+1/3+1/3} = 10^1$$
$$\text{i.e.} \ \ 10^{1/3} = \sqrt[3]{10}$$

Can you generalise the result for $10^{1/5}$?
You should see that it is the fifth root of 10.

> In other words, a fractional index means 'find the root'. The number in the denominator of the fraction tells you which root.

Using your calculator
Find $10^{1/5}$ on your calculator.

$$10^{1/5} = 10^{0.2}$$

Scientific calculator

Press $\boxed{10}$ $\boxed{y^x}$ $\boxed{0.2}$ $\boxed{=}$

Hewlett-Packard

Press $\boxed{10}$ $\boxed{\text{ENTER}}$ $\boxed{0.2}$ $\boxed{y^x}$

Example 19

Find the fourth root of 7.

Let $B = \sqrt[4]{7}$
$$\sqrt[4]{7} \times \sqrt[4]{7} \times \sqrt[4]{7} \times \sqrt[4]{7} = 7^1$$
$$7^{\boxed{?}} \times 7^{\boxed{?}} \times 7^{\boxed{?}} \times 7^{\boxed{?}} = 7^1$$
$$7^{\boxed{?}+\boxed{?}+\boxed{?}+\boxed{?}} = 7^1$$
$$7^{1/4+1/4+1/4+1/4} = 7^1$$
$$\therefore B = 7^{1/4} = 7^{0.25}$$
$$= 1.6266 \quad \text{(to 4 decimal places)}$$

EXERCISES

1 Manually simplify:
   a) $F = 2^3 \times 2$ b) $Q = 2^2 \times 2^4 \times 2^{-3}$

2   Find $Y = 2^3 \times 2 + 3 \times 2^2 - 4 \times 2$
    Check your answer using a calculator.

3   Simplify $M = \dfrac{2^{-1} \times 2^2 \div 2^{-1} \times 2^2 + 3 \times 2}{2^3 \div 2^{-2} + 2}$
    Check your result using a calculator.

4   Use your calculator to find the following. When calculations involve brackets within brackets, always work from the inside bracket first:
    a) $\dfrac{(1.6)^3 (4.1)^2}{(2.4)^{-2}}$ b) $[(2.3)^3]^2$ c) $\sqrt[4]{1.7}$

5   Simplify $D = \dfrac{(2^3 \times \sqrt{2})^3}{\sqrt{2} \times \sqrt[3]{2^4}}$
    Check your answer with a calculator.

6   Compute $F = 1.7^{3.1} \times \sqrt[3]{1.6} - 2.1 \times \sqrt[4]{4}$

7   Compute the following:

    a) $\dfrac{1/2}{2/3}$ b) $\dfrac{(36^{1/2} - 8^{1/3})^2}{\frac{4}{5}}$ c) $2^{-2} \div \left(\dfrac{2}{3}\right)^3$

    d) $\left(\dfrac{1}{2}\right)^{-1}$ e) $\left(\dfrac{4}{5}\right)^{-2}$ f) $\dfrac{(2^4 \times 4^{-1} \times 2^{-2})^3}{3^{-2} \times 6^2}$

8   Compute $\dfrac{[1 - (1.07)^3]^2}{0.07}$

9   Compute $\dfrac{[1 - (1.09^2)^3]}{1 - 1.07} \times 41$

10 Compute $\dfrac{\left[1 - \left(\dfrac{1.07}{1.09}\right)^2\right]^3}{1 - \dfrac{1.07}{1.09}}$

11 Now see if you can compute the example from the beginning of the chapter:
    $(1.07)^{-3} \dfrac{\{1 - [(1.07)^{-2}]^3\}}{1 - (1.07)^2}$

3

Solving Equations

You are almost ready to branch into applied money mathematics. However, another necessary skill is the ability to solve linear equations, quadratic equations, and simple equations involving powers higher than two.

If you can solve x in:

(i) $$97 = \frac{3,650,000}{3,650,000 + 90x}$$ (a common money market equation)

and

(ii) $(1 + x)^{12} = 1.24$ (used to find effective interest)

then you may skip to Chapter 4.

> The objective of this chapter is to increase your capacity to solve equations and verify the result.

LINEAR EQUATIONS

In a linear equation the highest power of the unknown is unity.
Consider $3x = 6$, where the power of x (the unknown) is one (unity).
This may be simple to you, but it is important to understand the process and to check the result.
The first rule is: "whatever you do to one side, you must do to the other side".
In this case we divide both sides by 3.

$$\frac{3x}{3} = \frac{6}{3}$$

$$x = 2$$

The solution of the linear equation $3x = 6$ is $x = 2$.

Example 1

$$\frac{2x}{3} = 7$$

To remove the three (3) we multiply both sides by 3.

$$3 \times \frac{2x}{3} = 7 \times 3$$

$$2x = 21$$

Divide both sides by 2:

$$\frac{2x}{2} = \frac{21}{2}$$

$$x = 10.5$$

Check: Substitute $x = 10.5$ into $\frac{2x}{3} = 7$

$$\frac{2 \times 10.5}{3} = \frac{21}{3} = 7$$

So $\frac{2x}{3} = 7$ when $x = 10.5$

Example 2

$$-x = 4$$

Multiply both sides by -1:

$$-1(-x) = 4(-1)$$

$$x = -4$$

Example 3

$$\frac{9x}{11} = -3$$

Remove the 11 by multiplying LHS (left-hand side) and RHS (right-hand side) by 11:

$$11 \times \frac{9x}{11} = -3 \times 11$$

$$9x = -33$$

Divide LHS and RHS by 9:

$$\frac{9x}{9} = \frac{-33}{9}$$

$$x = \frac{-33}{9}$$

$$= -3.\dot{6}$$

Example 4

Solve $\qquad 3x - 6 = 12$

We need the x term only, on the LHS.

$\therefore$ Add 6 to both sides:

$$3x - 6 + 6 = 12 + 6$$

$$3x = 18$$

Divide both sides by 3:

$$\frac{3x}{3} = \frac{18}{3}$$

$$x = 6$$

Check: Substitute $x = 6$ back into $3x - 6 = 12$
i.e. $3(6) - 6 = 18 - 6 = 12 = $ RHS

Example 5

$$\frac{2x}{3} - 5 = 4$$

Add 5 to both sides:

$$\frac{2x}{3} - 5 + 5 = 4 + 5$$

$$\frac{2x}{3} = 9$$

Multiply both sides by 3:

$$3 \times \frac{2x}{3} = 9 \times 3$$

$$2x = 27$$

Divide both sides by 2:

$$\frac{2x}{2} = \frac{27}{2}$$

$$x = 13.5$$

Check: $\frac{2}{3}(13.5) - 5 = 9 - 5 = 4$

You can also use your calculator to check the result.

Example 6

Solve $\qquad \frac{-3x}{4} + 7 = -2$

Subtract 7 from both sides:

$$\frac{-3x}{4} = -2 - 7 = -9$$

Multiply both sides by -1:

$$\frac{3x}{4} = 9$$

Multiply both sides by 4:

$$3x = 36$$

$$x = 12$$

Check: $\qquad \frac{-3(12)}{4} + 7 = \frac{-36}{4} + 7$

$$= -9 + 7$$

$$= -2$$

REMOVING SINGLE BRACKETS

Consider expanding $3(x + 4)$. This means multiplying the number outside the brackets by everything inside the brackets.

$$3(x + 4)$$

So

$$3 \times x \quad + \quad 3 \times 4 = 3x + 12$$

Example 7

(i) Expand $5(x - 3)$ $= 5x - 15$
(ii) Expand $x(x + 2)$ $= (x \times x) + 2x$
                       $= x^2 + 2x$
(iii) Expand $2(12 + x)$ $= 24 + 2x$

(iv) Expand $-3(x - 2) = -3x - 3(-2)$
$$= -3x + 6$$

REMOVING DOUBLE BRACKETS

In the situation of $(a + b)(c + d)$ we can expand as follows:

$$a(c + d) + b(c + d) = ac + ad + bc + bd$$

Example 8

Expand $(x - 2)(x + 3)$
$$= x(x + 3) - 2(x + 3)$$
$$= x^2 + 3x - 2x - 6$$
$$= x^2 + x - 6$$

x can be treated as a flat rod:

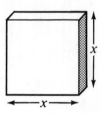

x^2 can be treated as a flat square block:

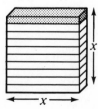

x rods fit into the flat square block:
i.e. $x \times x = x^2$

i.e. $x \times x = x^2$

x^3 can be treated as a cube:

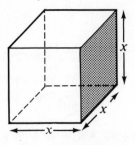

x layers of the flat square block create the cube:
i.e. $x \times x^2 = x^3$

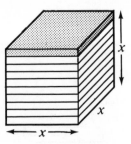

i.e. $x \times x^2 = x^3$

In the situation of $x^2 + 3x - 2x - 6$ we have:

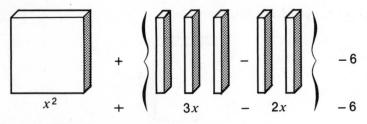

We can combine the x terms leaving:

$$x^2 + (3x - 2x) - 6 = x^2 + x - 6$$

We *cannot* combine the x^2 term(s) with the x terms.

Example 9

Expand $(2x - 3)(3x + 4)$

$$= 2x(3x + 4) - 3(3x + 4)$$
$$= 6x^2 + 8x - 9x - 12$$
$$= 6x^2 - x - 12$$

Example 10

$$(x^2 - 3)(x^3 + 2x^2)$$
$$= x^2(x^3 + 2x^2) - 3(x^3 + 2x^2)$$
$$= x^5 + 2x^4 - 3x^3 - 6x^2$$

You cannot combine any of these terms because they are all different power functions of x.

ADDING AND SUBTRACTING EQUATIONS

Equations can be added (or subtracted) by adding *like terms,* i.e. terms to the same power. For clarity, set the equations out with like terms lined up.

For example, add $2x^3 + 3x^2 - x$ to $2x^2 + x + 7$

Lining up the expressions we have:

$$\begin{array}{r} 2x^3 + 3x^2 - x \\ 2x^2 + x + 7 \quad + \text{ (add)} \\ \hline 2x^3 + 5x^2 + 0 + 7 \end{array}$$

The answer to the addition is: $2x^3 + 5x^2 + 7$

Example 11

Subtract $2x^3 - 3x^2 + 7$ from $x^3 + x^2 + 8x - 7$

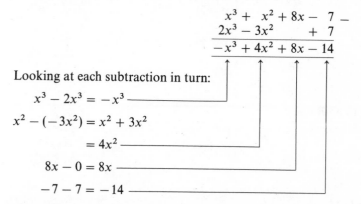

Looking at each subtraction in turn:

$$x^3 - 2x^3 = -x^3$$
$$x^2 - (-3x^2) = x^2 + 3x^2$$
$$= 4x^2$$
$$8x - 0 = 8x$$
$$-7 - 7 = -14$$

(Go below water level 7 units then dive deeper another 7 units, i.e. 14 units below the water level.)

$\therefore$ Answer $= -x^3 + 4x^2 + 8x - 14$

SOLVING WHEN THE UNKNOWN IS IN THE DENOMINATOR

Solve x in the equation:

$$\frac{2}{x} = 7$$

Multiply both sides by x. Note the use of a 'dot' to mean 'multiply'. This is a common way to represent multiplication:

$$x \cdot \frac{2}{x} = 7 \cdot x$$

$$2 = 7x \quad \text{or} \quad 7x = 2$$

Divide both sides by 7:

$$\frac{7x}{7} = \frac{2}{7}$$

$$x = \frac{2}{7}$$

Example 12

$$\frac{3}{x-2} = 4$$

Multiply both sides by $x - 2$:

$$\frac{3(x-2)}{x-2} = 4(x-2)$$

$$3 = 4(x-2)$$

$$4(x-2) = 3$$

$$4x - 8 = 3$$

Add 8 to both sides:

$$4x = 11$$

$$x = \frac{11}{4}$$

Example 13

Solve x in $97 = \dfrac{3{,}650{,}000}{36{,}500 + 90x}$

Multiply both sides by $36,500 + 90x$:

$$97(36,500 + 90x) = \frac{3,650,000 \times (36,500 + 90x)}{(36,500 + 90x)}$$

$$97(36,500 + 90x) = 3,650,000$$

$$3,540,500 + 8730x = 3,650,000$$

Subtract 3,540,500 from both sides:

$$8730x = 109,500$$

Divide both sides by 8730:

$$x = \frac{109,500}{8730}$$

$$= 12.5430$$

Check: $RHS = \dfrac{3,650,000}{36,500 + (90)(12.5430)}$

$$= 97$$

$$= LHS$$

SOLVING QUADRATIC EQUATIONS

An equation where the highest power function is 2, i.e. x^2, is called a *quadratic* equation.

Its general form is $ax^2 + bx + c = 0$

where a is the coefficient of the x^2 term

$\quad\quad$ b is the coefficient of the x term

$\quad\quad$ c is the constant term.

The coefficient b and the constant term c can equal zero. However a cannot equal zero or the x^2 term would disappear, leaving a linear equation.

Some examples of quadratic equations are:

$$2x^2 + 3x + 5 = 0 \quad\quad\quad x^2 + 7 = 0$$

$$3x^2 - 4x + 2 = 0 \quad\quad\quad x^2 - 3x = 0$$

Quadratic equations can be solved for x by using the following formulae:

(i) $x = \dfrac{-b + \sqrt{b^2 - 4ac}}{2a}$ $\quad$ and $\quad$ (ii) $x = \dfrac{-b - \sqrt{b^2 - 4ac}}{2a}$

This is known as the *Discriminant* formula, and is often written as:

$$x = \frac{-b \pm \sqrt{b^2 - 4ac}}{2a}$$

It gives two solutions for x.

A quadratic equation such as $2x^2 + 3x - 3 = 0$ will eventuate when finding an after-tax yield, allowing for a delay in the tax cash flow. For a 2-year project, the discriminant formula can be used to find the internal rate of return.

Example 14

Find the solutions for $2x^2 + 3x - 3 = 0$

Here $a = 2$ (coefficient of x^2)

$b = 3$ (coefficient of x)

$c = -3$ (constant term)

$$\therefore \text{(i) } x = \frac{-3 + \sqrt{3^2 - 4(2)(-3)}}{2(2)}$$

$$= \frac{-3 + \sqrt{33}}{4} = 0.686 \quad \text{(to 3 places)}$$

and (ii) $x = \dfrac{-3 - \sqrt{33}}{4} = -2.186$ (to 3 places)

The two solutions are $x = 0.686$ and $x = -2.186$

Using your calculator
Use your calculator to check by substituting the solutions back into the original equation.

Scientific calculator

(i) $2(0.686)^2 + 3(0.686) - 3 =$ ⬚0.686⬚ ⬚×⬚ ⬚0.686⬚ ⬚×⬚ ⬚2⬚ ⬚+⬚ ⬚3⬚

⬚×⬚ ⬚0.686⬚ ⬚−⬚ ⬚3⬚ ⬚=⬚

$$= -0.000808$$

(The slight difference from zero is caused by rounding $x = 0.686$ to 3 decimal places.)

(ii) $2(-2.186)^2 + 3(-2.186) - 3 =$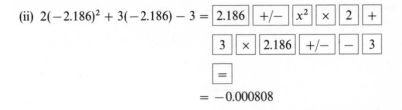

$$= -0.000808$$

Hewlett-Packard

(i) $2(0.686)^2 + 3(0.686) - 3 =$ [2] [ENTER] [0.686] [ENTER] [2]

[y^x] [×] [3] [ENTER] [0.686] [×] [+]

[3] [−]

$$= -0.000808$$

(The slight difference from zero is caused by rounding $x = 0.686$ to 3 decimal places.)

(ii) $2(-2.186)^2 + 3(-2.186) - 3 =$ [2] [ENTER] [2.186] [CHS]

[ENTER] [2] [y^x] [×] [3]

[ENTER] [2.186] [CHS] [×]

[+] [3] [−]

$$= -0.000808$$

SURDIC EQUATIONS

Equations involving a root ($\sqrt[n]{}$) sign are called *surdic* equations. These appear frequently when you are trying to convert annual interest rates to shorter periods (e.g. monthly) to determine the effective interest rate for the shorter interval.

Consider $(1 + x)^{12} - 1 = 0.24$

Add 1 to both sides:

$$(1 + x)^{12} = 1.24$$

Now take the twelfth root of both sides:

$$1 + x = 1.24^{1/12} \quad \text{(remember from Chapter 2)}$$

$$= 1.24^{0.08\dot{3}}$$

Using 0.08333333 for 0.083̇, and your calculator:

$$1.24^{0.083̇} = \boxed{1.24}\ \boxed{y^x}\ \boxed{0.0833333}\ \boxed{=}$$

$$= 1.0180876$$

$$\therefore 1 + x = 1.0180876$$

Subtract 1 from both sides:

$$x = 0.0180876$$

The interest rate x is $0.0180876 \times 100 = 1.80876\%$

Example 15

Solve for x: $(1 + x)^4 - 1 = 0.18$

Add 1 to both sides:

$$(1 + x)^4 = 1.18$$

Take the fourth root of both sides:

$$1 + x = 1.18^{1/4}$$

$$= 1.18^{0.25}$$

Using your calculator:

$$1 + x = \boxed{1.18}\ \boxed{y^x}\ \boxed{0.25}\ \boxed{=}$$

$$1 + x = 1.0422466$$

Subtract 1 from both sides:

$$x = 0.0422466$$

The interest rate x is $0.0422466 \times 100 = 4.22466\%$

EXERCISES

1   Solve the following equations and check each result:

a) $\dfrac{3x}{7} = \dfrac{2}{5}$

b) $\dfrac{-3x}{4} = -2$

c) $\dfrac{-2x}{5} + 3 = -4$

d) $2(x - 3) = 4(x - 5)$

e) $\dfrac{-3}{x} = 4$ f) $\dfrac{2}{3}(x + 6) = \dfrac{-4}{5}(2x - 10)$

g) $\dfrac{365}{365 + 4x} = -2$

2 Solve for x in the quadratic equation. Check your answer by substitution:
   a) $x^2 - 5x + 6 = 0$ b) $x^2 - 3x - 10 = 0$
   c) $2x^2 - 5x - 8 = 0$ d) $5x^2 + 2x = 0$
   e) $x^2 - 1 = 0$ f) $2x^2 - 7x + 4 = 0$

3 Simplify the following equations and solve for x:
   a) $4(x^3 + 3x^2 - 6) - 2(5x^2 + 2x^3 + x - 3) = 0$
   b) $2(x^2 - 4x - 3) - (1.4x^2 - 5x - 5.79) = 0$

4 Expand the following equations (i.e. remove the brackets):
   a) $(x - 1)(x - 2)$ b) $(x + 1)(x - 2)$
   c) $(2x - 3)(x + 5)$ d) $(3x - 7)(x^2 + 2x + 9)$

5 Solve for x in the surdic equation:
   a) $(1 + x)^3 - 1 = 0.07$
   b) $(1 + 4x)^6 - 1 = 0.12$

4

Simplifying Expressions and Equations

There will be many occasions in financial mathematics where expressions need simplification. Typical examples occur in compound interest and flat interest contracts thus:

(i) $i(1 + i) + 1 + i = (1 + i)^2$

(ii) $i(1 + i)^2 + (1 + i)^2 = (1 + i)^3$

(iii) $P + \dfrac{rn}{36{,}500} \times P = \dfrac{P(36{,}500 + rn)}{36{,}500}$

> If you cannot see how these simplifications were obtained, you need to study this chapter. By the end of the chapter you will also be able to group compound and flat interest expressions. This will facilitate your understanding of financial functions used frequently in the market place and will enable you more effectively to obtain after-tax returns on investment.

USING BRACKETS—FACTORISING

An expression can be factorised by finding the highest common factor. In the case of $ab - ac$ the common term is a. This means each distinct part of the expression contains an a. We put the a in front of a bracket thus:

$$a(\qquad)$$

The first term of the expression is $ab = a \times b$.
∴ The first term inside the bracket must be b.

$$a(b \qquad)$$

The second term of the expression is $ac = a \times c$.
∴ The second term inside the bracket must be c.

$$a(b \quad c)$$

The expression is a subtraction $ab - ac$.
∴ The bracket contains a $-$ sign:

$$a(b - c) = ab - ac$$

Alternatively, you can simplify the expression using symbols:

$$a(\boxed{?} - \triangle)$$

What do we put in the □ such that when multiplied by a it will give ab?
The answer is b.
What do we slot into the △? When multiplied by a it will equal ac. $\triangle = c$.

$$\therefore ab - ac = a(b - c)$$

Example 1

Simplify $a(1 + i) + 3(1 + i)$
In this case $(1 + i)$ is common. Put this in front of a bracket thus:

$(1 + i)(\quad)$ OR $(1 + i)(\boxed{?} + \triangle)$

The first term is $(1 + i) \times a$, so the first term inside the bracket is a.	Now $(1 + i) \times \boxed{?} = a \times (1 + i)$ $$\boxed{?} = a$$
The second term is $(1 + i) \times 3$, so the second term inside the bracket is 3.	$(1 + i) \times \triangle = 3(1 + i)$ $$\triangle = 3$$
The expression is an addition, so the bracket contains a $+$ sign.	$\therefore (\boxed{?} + \triangle) = (a + 3)$

$(1 + i)(a + 3)$

$\therefore a(1 + i) + 3(1 + i)$
$= (1 + i)(a + 3)$

$\therefore a(1 + i) + 3(1 + i)$
$= (1 + i)(a + 3)$

Example 2

Simplify $110 + 0.1(110)$
Here 110 is common.

$$\therefore 110 + 0.1(110) = 110(\boxed{?} + \triangle)$$

$$110 \times \boxed{?} = 110$$

$$\boxed{?} = 1$$

$$110 \times \triangle = 0.1(110)$$

$$\triangle = 0.1$$
$$\therefore 110 + 0.1(110) = 110(1 + 0.1)$$
$$= 110(1.1)$$
$$\text{Now} \quad 110 = (1.1)100$$
$$\therefore 110 + 0.1(110) = 110(1.1)$$
$$= (1.1 \times 100)(1.1)$$
$$= 1.1 \times 100 \times 1.1$$
$$= (1.1)^2 \times 100$$

Example 3

Simplify $(1.1)^3 + 0.1(1.1)^3$

$$(1.1)^3 + 0.1(1.1)^3 = (1.1)^3(1) + (1.1)^3(0.1)$$
$$= (1.1)^3(\boxed{?} + \triangle)$$
$$= (1.1)^3(1 + 0.1)$$
$$= (1.1)^3(1.1)$$
$$= (1.1)^4$$

FACTORISING A QUADRATIC

A quadratic is an expression of the form $ax^2 + bx + c$, e.g. $x^2 + 2x + 1$. Because the highest power of x is 2 it can be simplified into two brackets. Let us first expand two brackets.

Consider $\qquad (x + 3)(x + 2)$

This equals $\qquad x(x + 2) + 3(x + 2)$

$$= x \times x + x \times 2 + 3 \times x + 3 \times 2$$
$$= x^2 + 2x + 3x + 6$$

So $\quad (x + 3)(x + 2) = x^2 + 5x + 6$

Example 4

Expand $\quad (x - 2)(x + 4)$

$$(x - 2)(x + 4) = x(x + 4) - 2(x + 4)$$
$$= x^2 + 4x - 2x - 8$$
$$= x^2 + 2x - 8$$

The subtraction can be set out as follows:

$$\begin{array}{r} x^2 + 4x \\ -\,2x - 8 \\ \hline x^2 + 2x - 8 \end{array}$$

Example 5

Expand $(2x + 3)(4x - 7)$

$$\begin{aligned} (2x + 3)(4x - 7) &= 2x(4x - 7) + 3(4x - 7) \\ &= (2x.4x) - (2x.7) + (3.4x) + (3.-7) \\ &= 8x^2 - 14x + 12x - 21 \\ &= 8x^2 - 2x - 21 \end{aligned}$$

Factorising these quadratics requires the reverse process.
Consider $x^2 + 2x - 8$
We can put down two brackets:

$(x\quad)(x\quad)$	Each first term must be x as $x.x$ gives x^2
$(\quad 8)(\quad 1)$	The last terms can be 8 and 1
$(\quad 4)(\quad 2)$	or 4 and 2
$(\;-\;)(\;+\;)$	The signs must be negative and positive to give $+2x$ and -8. At this stage you have not worked out which bracket has a $-$ and which as a $+$.

As a first attempt, try the brackets $(x - 8)(x + 1)$.

Expanding
$$\begin{aligned} (x - 8)(x + 1) &= x(x + 1) - 8(x + 1) \\ &= x^2 + x - 8x - 8 \\ &= x^2 - 7x - 8 \end{aligned}$$

NOT THE SOLUTION

Try
$$\begin{aligned} (x - 4)(x + 2) &= x(x + 2) - 4(x + 2) \\ &= x^2 + 2x - 4x - 8 \\ &= x^2 - 2x - 8 \end{aligned}$$

NOT THE SOLUTION

Try
$$\begin{aligned} (x + 4)(x - 2) &= x(x - 2) + 4(x - 2) \\ &= x^2 - 2x + 4x - 8 \\ &= x^2 + 2x - 8 \end{aligned}$$

$$\therefore x^2 + 2x - 8 = (x + 4)(x - 2)$$

Example 6

Factorise $4t^2 - 19t - 5$

Either $(4t\quad)(1t\quad)$ or $(2t\quad)(2t\quad)$ gives $4t^2$
Either $(\quad + 5)(\quad - 1)$ or $(\quad - 5)(\quad + 1)$ gives -5

The short-cut method of determining factors is as follows.
Write the possible coefficients of the first (x^2) term vertically, and the possible constant terms vertically in a second column.
Thus one combination to test would be:

4   5   Multiply the diagonals and add to give the coefficient of the
                central (x) term.

1   −1   In this case, $4(-1) + 5(1) = -4 + 5 = 1 \neq -19$

As this is not equal to -19 we try another combination.

2 ⤫ −5 $2(1) + 2(-5) = 2 - 10 = -8$
2   1 $\neq -19$; try again!

4 ⤫ +1 $4(-5) + 1(1) = -20 + 1 = -19$
1   −5   Yes: Factors are therefore $(4t + 1)(1t - 5)$. Note that you
           read the factors horizontally.

SOLVING QUADRATIC EQUATIONS BY FACTORISING

If $(x - a)(x - b) = 0$ then there are two possible solutions.
If $(x - a) = 0$, then $(x - a)(x - b) = 0(x - b) = 0$
So one solution is given by $x - a = 0$, or $x = a$
If $(x - b) = 0$, then $(x - a)(x - b) = (x - a)0 = 0$
So the other solution is given by $x - b = 0$ or $x = b$

Example 7

Solve $3x^2 + 8x - 3 = 0$

3 ⤫ 1 $3(-3) + 1(1) = -9 + 1 = -8$ NO!
1   −3

3 ⤫ −3 $3(1) - 3(1) = 0$ NO!
1   1

3 ⤫ −1 $3(3) - 1(1) = 9 - 1 = 8$, which is the
1   3   required coefficient.

The factors are $(3x - 1)$ and $(x + 3)$.
$\therefore 3x^2 + 8x - 3 = (3x - 1)(x + 3) = 0$
This means solution 1 is given by $3x - 1 = 0$, i.e. $3x = 1$ and $x = 1/3$
Solution 2 is given by $x + 3 = 0$, i.e. $x = -3$

SOLVING QUADRATIC EQUATIONS USING THE DISCRIMINANT FORMULA

Sometimes a quadratic equation cannot be factorised. In this case, the solutions can be found using the discriminant formula.

The solutions of the general quadratic $ax^2 + bx + c = 0$ are:

$$x = \frac{-b + \sqrt{b^2 - 4ac}}{2a} \quad \text{and} \quad x = \frac{-b - \sqrt{b^2 - 4ac}}{2a}$$

If you need to remind yourself about solving a quadratic equation by using the discriminant formula, reread the last sections of Chapter 3. If you are not confident about factorising a quadratic equation, you can always use the discriminant formula.

Example 8

Find the solutions of $2x^2 + 2x - 3 = 0$
Here $a = 2, b = 2, c = -3$

$$\therefore x = \frac{-2 \pm \sqrt{4 + 24}}{4}$$

$$= \frac{-2 \pm \sqrt{28}}{4}$$

$$= 0.8229 \text{ and } -1.8229 \quad \text{(to 4 decimal places)}$$

Example 9

Solve for i in

$$\frac{1}{(1 + i)^2} - \frac{1.7}{(1 + i)} + 0.72 = 0$$

Let

$$\frac{1}{(1 + i)} = x$$

$$\therefore x^2 - 1.7x + 0.72 = 0$$

This equation can be solved either by factorising or by using the discriminant formula.

(a) factorising:

$$x^2 - 1.7x + 0.72 = (x - 0.9)(x - 0.8)$$

(Check this by expanding.)

So $x - 0.9 = 0$ and $x - 0.8 = 0$

                        $x = 0.9$ $x = 0.8$

(b) using the formula:

$$x = \frac{1.7 \pm \sqrt{(1.7)^2 - 4(1)(0.72)}}{2}$$

i.e. $x = 0.9$ and 0.8

So, in both cases, $x = 0.9$ and $x = 0.8$.

But $x = \dfrac{1}{1 + i}$

So $\dfrac{1}{1 + i} = 0.9$ and $\dfrac{1}{1 + i} = 0.8$

When $\dfrac{1}{1 + i} = 0.9$,

Multiply both sides by $1 + i$:

$$\frac{1}{1 + i} \cdot (1 + i) = 0.9(1 + i)$$

$$1 = 0.9(1 + i)$$

Divide both sides by 0.9:

$$\frac{1}{0.9} = \frac{0.9(1 + i)}{0.9}$$

$$\frac{1}{0.9} = 1 + i = 1.1111$$

Subtracting 1 from both sides:

$$i = 0.1111   \text{or}   11.11\%$$

When $\dfrac{1}{1 + i} = 0.8$,

$$1 + i = 1.25$$

$$\therefore i = 0.25 \text{ or } 25\%$$

This equation has given two solutions to rates of return and this can occur when determining the rate of return on a 2-year project where the cash flows vary in sign (i.e. there are some cash inflows and some cash outflows).

ALGEBRAIC FRACTIONS

Provided no denominator is zero, the following basic laws can be summarised:

1 $\dfrac{a}{c} + \dfrac{b}{c} = \dfrac{a + b}{c}$

2 $\dfrac{a}{c} - \dfrac{b}{c} = \dfrac{a - b}{c}$

3 $\dfrac{a}{b} \times \dfrac{c}{d} = \dfrac{ac}{bd}$

4 $\dfrac{a}{b} \div \dfrac{c}{d} = \dfrac{a}{b} \times \dfrac{d}{c} = \dfrac{ad}{bc}$

5 $a \times \dfrac{1}{b} = \dfrac{a}{1} \times \dfrac{1}{b} = \dfrac{a}{b}$

These laws are explained in the sections which follow.

ADDITIONS AND SUBTRACTIONS WITH LIKE DENOMINATORS

Find $\dfrac{1}{2} + \dfrac{3}{2}$

$$\frac{1}{2} + \frac{3}{2} = \frac{1 + 3}{2} = \frac{4}{2} = 2$$

Similarly algebraic functions can be added given the same denominator:

$$\frac{x}{3} + \frac{7x}{3} = \frac{x + 7x}{3} = \frac{8x}{3}$$

ADDITIONS AND SUBTRACTIONS WITH UNLIKE DENOMINATORS

Find $\dfrac{1}{2} + \dfrac{1}{3}$

The first step is to make the denominators the same.
Here the lowest common denominator is $2 \times 3 = 6$.

$\therefore$ to convert 1/2 to sixths we multiply the numerator and denominator by 3. Since we multiply both numerator and denominator, we are in effect multiplying by $\frac{3}{3}$ which is unity. Therefore the value of $\frac{1}{2}$ is unchanged.

$$\frac{1}{2} \cdot \boxed{\frac{3}{3}} = \frac{1}{2} \times \frac{3}{3}$$

$$= \frac{3}{6}$$

$\frac{1}{2}$ and $\frac{3}{6}$ are called *equivalent fractions*.

Similarly
$$\frac{1}{3} \cdot \boxed{\frac{2}{2}} = \frac{2}{6} \text{ which is equivalent to } \frac{1}{3}.$$

$$\therefore \frac{1}{2} + \frac{1}{3} = \frac{1}{2} \cdot \boxed{\frac{3}{3}} + \frac{1}{3} \cdot \boxed{\frac{2}{2}}$$

$$= \frac{3}{6} + \frac{2}{6}$$

$$= \frac{3 + 2}{6}$$

$$= \frac{5}{6}$$

The same principle is used with algebraic symbols.
Consider

$$\frac{x}{3} + \frac{x}{2}$$

You cannot add thirds to halves.

$$\frac{x}{3} \cdot \boxed{\frac{2}{2}} + \frac{x}{2} \cdot \boxed{\frac{3}{3}} = \frac{2x}{6} + \frac{3x}{6}$$

$$= \frac{2x + 3x}{6}$$

$$= \frac{5x}{6}$$

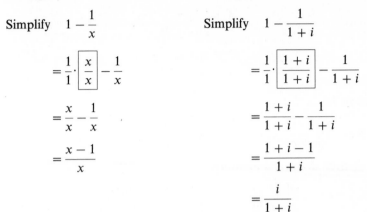

Example 10

Simplify $1 - \dfrac{1}{x}$

$$= \frac{1}{1} \cdot \boxed{\frac{x}{x}} - \frac{1}{x}$$

$$= \frac{x}{x} - \frac{1}{x}$$

$$= \frac{x-1}{x}$$

Example 11

Simplify $1 - \dfrac{1}{1+i}$

$$= \frac{1}{1} \cdot \boxed{\frac{1+i}{1+i}} - \frac{1}{1+i}$$

$$= \frac{1+i}{1+i} - \frac{1}{1+i}$$

$$= \frac{1+i-1}{1+i}$$

$$= \frac{i}{1+i}$$

Example 12

Simplify $P + \dfrac{Prn}{36{,}500}$

$$= P\left(1 + \frac{rn}{36{,}500}\right)$$

$$= P\left(\frac{36{,}500}{36{,}500} + \frac{rn}{36{,}500}\right)$$

$$= P\frac{(36{,}500 + rn)}{36{,}500}$$

This technique will be used to find the prices of bills of exchange.

MULTIPLYING AND DIVIDING ALGEBRAIC FUNCTIONS

Just as we can simplify the a's in

$$\frac{a^3}{a^2} = \frac{a \times a \times a}{a \times a} = a$$

so we can reduce bracketed terms thus:

$$\frac{(\boxed{?})}{(\triangle)(\boxed{?})} = \frac{1}{\triangle}$$

or

$$\frac{(a-b)}{(a-b)(a+b)} = \frac{1}{a+b}$$

Example 13

Simplify $\dfrac{(x + 3)^2}{(x - 2)(x + 3)} = \dfrac{(x + 3)(x + 3)}{(x - 2)(x + 3)}$

$$= \dfrac{(x + 3)}{(x - 2)}$$

Example 14

Simplify $\dfrac{a(a - b)}{b(a + b)} \div (a - b)$

For division invert and multiply:

$$\dfrac{a(a - b)}{b(a + b)} \times \dfrac{1}{(a - b)} = \dfrac{a(a - b)(1)}{b(a + b)(a - b)}$$

$$= \dfrac{a \times 1}{b(a + b)}$$

$$= \dfrac{a}{b(a + b)}$$

ADDITIONS AND SUBTRACTIONS WITH MORE THAN ONE DENOMINATOR

Consider $\dfrac{1}{x} + \dfrac{3}{x - 1}$

This is very much like the problem

$$\dfrac{1}{2} + \dfrac{3}{5}$$

where the common denominator is 2×5.
Similarly $x(x - 1)$ is the denominator required above.
What do we multiply x by to give a denominator of $x(x - 1)$? Clearly $x - 1$. We must similarly multiply the numerator by $x - 1$.

This makes the first fraction $\dfrac{1}{x} \cdot \boxed{\dfrac{x - 1}{x - 1}} = \dfrac{x - 1}{x(x - 1)}$

Now look at $\dfrac{3}{x - 1}$. We have to make the denominator the same as the denominator of the first fraction, i.e. $x(x - 1)$.

So in this case we must multiply by $\dfrac{x}{x}$.

$$\frac{3}{x-1} \cdot \boxed{\frac{x}{x}} = \frac{3x}{x(x-1)}$$

$$\therefore \frac{1}{x} + \frac{3}{x-1} = \frac{x-1}{x(x-1)} + \frac{3x}{x(x-1)}$$

$$= \frac{x-1+3x}{x(x-1)}$$

$$= \frac{4x-1}{x(x-1)}$$

Example 15

Simplify $F = 1 - \dfrac{1}{1+i} + \dfrac{i}{(1+i)^2}$

$$= \frac{1}{1} \cdot \boxed{\frac{(1+i)^2}{(1+i)^2}} - \frac{1}{1+i} \cdot \boxed{\frac{1+i}{1+i}} + \frac{i}{(1+i)^2}$$

$$= \frac{(1+i)^2}{(1+i)^2} - \frac{1+i}{(1+i)^2} + \frac{i}{(1+i)^2}$$

$$= \frac{(1+i)^2 - (1+i) + i}{(1+i)^2}$$

$$= \frac{1 + 2i + i^2 - 1 - i + i}{(1+i)^2}$$

$$= \frac{2i + i^2}{(1+i)^2}$$

$$= \frac{i(2+i)}{(1+i)^2}$$

Before leaving this chapter, make sure you now understand the three simplifications listed at the beginning of the chapter.

EXERCISES

1   Expand and simplify the following expressions:
   a) $(3x-2)(2x+3)$ b) $(2x-5)(4x-3)$
   c) $(-a+b)(-a-b)$ d) $-2x(x+3) - 3x(x-2)$

2   Factorise the following equations and solve for x:
   a) $x^2 - 4 = 0$ b) $x^2 + 4x + 4 = 0$
   c) $x^2 - 5x + 6 = 0$ d) $2x^2 + x - 6 = 0$
   c) $6x^2 - 13x + 6 = 0$ f) $3x^2 - 16x + 5 = 0$

3   Using the discriminant formula, solve for i:

   a) $3i^2 - 7i + 4 = 0$ b) $\dfrac{5}{1+i} + \dfrac{7}{(1+i)^2} - 10 = 0$

4   Simplify the following:

   a) $\dfrac{1}{2} + \dfrac{3}{8}$ b) $\dfrac{3}{4} - \dfrac{5}{12}$

   c) $\dfrac{1}{3} + \dfrac{7}{12} - \dfrac{5}{6}$ d) $\dfrac{x}{5} - \dfrac{3x}{10} + \dfrac{3x}{5}$

   e) $2 - \dfrac{i}{1+i}$ f) $\dfrac{x^2 - 4}{x + 2} + 3$

   g) $\dfrac{x+3}{x^2-9} + \dfrac{2}{x-3}$ h) $\dfrac{5}{1+i} + \dfrac{7}{(1+i)^2} - 10$

5   Solve for x in the following equations. Check your answer in each case.

   a) $\dfrac{3x}{4} - \dfrac{2}{3} = \dfrac{7}{2}$ b) $\dfrac{7}{x-2} - \dfrac{2(x^2-4)}{x-2} = 3$

   c) $\dfrac{3}{x-4} + \dfrac{2}{x-3} = -4$

5

Accumulated Value of a Single Amount

Compound interest arrangements calculate the amount of interest on the balance of both principal and interest. This causes an escalating growth in interest. Common investments of this type are interest-bearing deposits, fixed deposits, and cash management deposits, where interest is payable at a constant frequency e.g. monthly, quarterly. The interest rate may be fixed or variable.

> The aim of this chapter then is to enable you to accumulate a *single* deposit when the unknown factor is either the term, the rate, or the accumulated lump sum.

INITIAL PRINCIPAL, INTEREST AND TERM ARE GIVEN

In this case, the unknown factor is the accumulated lump sum (or accumulated value).

$100 is invested at $10\% = 0.1$ per annum compound.
The interest after 1 year $= 10\%$ of $100 = 0.1(100) = \$10$
$\therefore$ The accumulated lump sum after 1 year is $100 + \$10 = \$110$

The interest for the second year is 10% of $110 = 0.1(110) = \$11$
$\therefore$ The accumulated lump sum after 2 years is $110 + \$11 = \$121$

Mathematically the 121 can be expressed thus:

$$121 = 0.1(110) + 110$$

Now 110 is a common factor on the RHS. Factorising, we get

$$121 = 110(0.1 + 1)$$
$$= 110(1.1)$$

The 110 can be rewritten as 100(1.1).
So 110(1.1) can be rewritten as $100(1.1)(1.1) = 100(1.1)^2$

The accumulated values for years 1 to 4 can be summarised:

End of Year	Accumulated Value ($)
1	$110.00 = (1.1)(100)$
2	$121.00 = (1.1)^2(100)$
3	$133.10 = (1.1)^3(100)$
4	$146.41 = (1.1)^4(100)$

Can you see a pattern in these results?
The generated formula for accumulating $100 for n years at rate i per period compound is:

$$100(1 + i)^n$$

Similarly, to accumulate P for n years at rate i, the accumulated value (AV) is

$$AV = P(1 + i)^n \qquad (1)$$

This formula refers to n periods at rate i per period. Thus n and i can relate, for example, to quarterly, weekly, or monthly periods.

Example 1

Find the accumulated amount if $400 is invested for 10 years at 12% per annum compound.

Solution:
$$P = 400$$
$$i = 0.12$$
$$n = 10$$

Accumulated Value $(AV) = P(1 + i)^n$
$$= 400(1 + 0.12)^{10}$$
$$= 400(1.12)^{10}$$

This can be quickly computed on your calculator using the power key.

Scientific calculator: | 1.12 | | y^x | | 10 | | = | × | 400 | | = |

Hewlett-Packard: | 400 | | ENTER | | 1.12 | | ENTER | | 10 | | y^x | | × |

$$\therefore AV = 1242.34$$

The accumulated sum = 1242.34

The initial amount =   400.00

$$\therefore \text{The interest accumulated} = \overline{\$842.34}$$

Example 2

Find the accumulated value of $500 after $5\frac{1}{4}$ years at 5.2% per annum compound.

Solution:

$$P = 500, \quad n = 5\tfrac{1}{4}, \quad i = 0.052$$
$$AV = P(1 + i)^n$$
$$AV = 500(1.052)^{5.25}$$
$$= 500(1.3049)$$
$$= \$652.46$$

Using your calculator

$$AV = 500(1.052)^{5.25}$$

Scientific calculator

Press $\boxed{1.052}$ $\boxed{y^x}$ $\boxed{5.25}$ $\boxed{=}$ $\boxed{\times}$ $\boxed{500}$ $\boxed{=}$

Hewlett-Packard

Press $\boxed{500}$ $\boxed{\text{ENTER}}$ $\boxed{1.052}$ $\boxed{\text{ENTER}}$ $\boxed{5.25}$ $\boxed{y^x}$ $\boxed{\times}$

FINDING i, GIVEN n, P, AND AV

In this case the unknown factor is the interest rate, i.
Look at formula (1) again:

$$AV = P(1 + i)^n$$

$$\therefore \frac{AV}{P} = (1 + i)^n$$

Take the nth root of both sides (remember the work on fractional indices in Chapter 2):

$$\left[\frac{AV}{P}\right]^{1/n} = 1 + i$$

Subtract 1 from both sides:

$$\boxed{i = \left[\frac{AV}{P}\right]^{1/n} - 1}$$

(2)

This formula looks a little frightening. However it is not very difficult, as the following example will show.

Example 3

Find the annual compound rate at which $200 will double after 8 years.

Solution: Our equation (formula 1) is:

$$P(1 + i)^n = AV$$
$$200(1 + i)^8 = 400$$

where i is the compound rate per annum.
Divide both sides by 200:

$$(1 + i)^8 = 2$$

Now take the eighth root of both sides:

$$(1 + i) = 2^{1/8} = 2^{0.125}$$
$$2^{0.125} = 1.0905077$$
$$\therefore 1 + i = 1.0905077$$

Subtract 1 from both sides:

$$i = 0.0905077$$

So the compound rate is 9.05077% per annum.
Substituting straight into formula (2) gives:

$$i = \left(\frac{400}{200}\right)^{1/8} - 1$$
$$= 2^{1/8} - 1$$
$$= 2^{0.125} - 1$$
$$= 1.0905077 - 1$$
$$= 0.0905077$$

Example 4

$800 will accumulate to $900 after 6 quarters. Find the quarterly rate of compound interest.

Solution: $800(1 + i)^6 = 900$ where i is the compound rate per quarter.

$$(1 + i)^6 = 1.125$$

Remember that $P = (1 + i)^n$ refers to n periods at rate i per period. Thus if n is expressed in quarters, then i will be calculated as the compound rate per quarter.

Taking the sixth root of both sides:

$$(1 + i) = (1.125)^{1/6}$$

$$1 + i = 1.125^{0.1\dot{6}} = 1.01982 \text{ (to 5 places)}$$

$i = 0.01982$ or 1.982% per quarter compound.

Using your calculator

$$i = 1.125^{0.1\dot{6}} - 1$$

Scientific calculator

Press $\boxed{1.125}$ $\boxed{y^x}$ $\boxed{0.16666667}$ $\boxed{=}$ $\boxed{-}$ $\boxed{1}$

Hewlett-Packard

Press $\boxed{1.125}$ $\boxed{\text{ENTER}}$ $\boxed{0.166666667}$ $\boxed{y^x}$ $\boxed{1}$ $\boxed{-}$

FINDING n, GIVEN P, i, AND AV

In this case the unknown factor is n, the number of periods. The easiest way to solve the equation $AV = P(1 + i)^n$ for n is to use *logarithms*. If you have not learnt about logarithms before and cannot understand the explanation which follows, an alternative method is given at the end of this section.

If you have studied logarithms (logs for short) before, you may find the following reminders useful.

Logarithms

The *logarithm* of a number is the power to which the base must be raised to give that number.
We write: $\log_{10} 100$
We say: 'the log of 100 base 10'

So the log of 100 base 10 is the power to which 10 (the base) must be raised to give 100, i.e. $10^{\boxed{?}} = 100$.

$$\boxed{?} = 2 \quad \text{since} \quad 10^2 = 100$$

$$\therefore \log_{10} 100 = 2$$

Similarly $\log_2 16 = 4$ since $2^4 = 16$

$$\log_3 27 = 3 \quad \text{since} \quad 3^3 = 27$$

$$\log_5 25 = 2 \quad \text{since} \quad 5^2 = 25$$

$$\log_{10} 10 = 1 \quad \text{since} \quad 10^1 = 10$$

The general rule is:

> If $\log_b A = x$ then $A = b^x$

The following rules should be memorised to enable you to manipulate logs in calculations. The base must be the same for each log in the rule.

Rule	Examples
$\log(a \times b) = \log a + \log b$	$\log 24 = \log(6 \times 4) = \log 6 + \log 4$
	$\log 5x = \log 5 + \log x$
	$\log ab^3 = \log a + \log b^3$
$\log c^n = n \log c$	$\log 5^3 = 3 \log 5$
	$\log x^2 = 2 \log x$
	$\log 3x^2 = \log(3 \times x^2) = \log 3 + \log x^2$
	$\qquad\qquad = \log 3 + 2 \log x$
	$\log ab^3 = \log a + \log b^3$
	$\qquad\quad = \log a + 3 \log b$
$\log \dfrac{a}{b} = \log a - \log b$	$\log \dfrac{2}{3} = \log 2 - \log 3$
	$\log \dfrac{x^2}{3} = \log x^2 - \log 3$
	$\qquad\quad = 2 \log x - \log 3$

Using your calculator

To use your calculator to find logs, use the $\boxed{\ln x}$ or $\boxed{\text{LN}}$ button. This gives the Napierian logarithm of any number, i.e. the log to base e, where e stands for 'exponiential function'. We use the abbreviation 'ln' to mean 'log base e'. All the rules above apply to Napierian logs.

Scientific calculator

To find ln 45, for example, press $\boxed{45}$ $\boxed{\ln x}$ $\boxed{=}$

Hewlett-Packard

The $\boxed{\text{LN}}$ function is obtained by pressing $\boxed{\text{g}}$ $\boxed{\%\text{T}}$.
So $\ln 45 = \boxed{45}$ $\boxed{\text{g}}$ $\boxed{\%\text{T}}$

Now return to the formula

$$AV = P(1 + i)^n$$

Taking logarithms of both sides:

$$\ln AV = \ln P(1 + i)^n$$
$$= \ln P + \ln(1 + i)^n$$
$$= \ln P + n\ln(1 + i)$$
$$\ln AV = \ln P + n\ln(1 + i)$$
$$\ln AV - \ln P = n\ln(1 + i)$$

$$\boxed{\frac{\ln AV - \ln P}{\ln(1 + i)} = n} \quad \text{or} \quad \boxed{\frac{\ln\left(\dfrac{AV}{P}\right)}{\ln(1 + i)} = n} \qquad (3)$$

Example 5

With interest at 8% per annum compound, how long will it take \$100 to accumulate to \$150?

Solution:

$$100(1 + i)^n = 150$$
$$100(1.08)^n = 150$$
$$(1.08)^n = 1.5$$

Take logarithms of both sides:

$$\ln 1.08^n = \ln 1.5$$
$$n\log 1.08 = \ln 1.5$$

Divide both sides by $\ln 1.08$:

$$n = \frac{\ln 1.5}{\ln 1.08} \qquad \left[= \frac{\ln\dfrac{AV}{P}}{\ln(1 + i)} \right]$$

$$= 5.2684 \text{ (to 4 places)}$$

∴ $100 will accumulate to $150 after 5.2684 years,

i.e.   5 years and 0.2684 (365) days = 5 years and 98 days

Using your calculator

Note that $\dfrac{\ln 1.5}{\ln 1.08} = \ln 1.5 \div \ln 1.08$

This is not the same as $\ln\left(\dfrac{1.5}{1.08}\right) = \ln 1.5 - \ln 1.08$

Scientific calculator

$\ln 1.5 \div \ln 1.08 =$ | 1.5 | ln x | ÷ | 1.08 | ln x | =

Hewlett-Packard

$\ln 1.5 \div \ln 1.08 =$ | 1.5 | g | %T | 1.08 | g | %T | ÷

Now check your answer!
Are you accustomed to assuming that all your answers are correct?
Probably not! Yet do you check your results regularly?
Well, to check that last answer simply compute

$$100(1.08)^{5.2684}. \text{ You should have a result of } \$150.$$

If you cannot cope with logs, then use trial and error.
We know that $(1.08)^n = 1.5$

Try $(1.08)^2 = 1.1664.$ Too small, so try a bigger power.

$(1.08)^4 = 1.3605$

$(1.08)^5 = 1.4693$

$(1.08)^6 = 1.5869$

You can see that 1.5 lies between $(1.08)^5$ and $(1.08)^6$. Your answer lies between 5 and 6. It can be obtained by interpolation, which is covered in the next chapter.

MULTIPLE INTEREST RATES

In many cash management trusts, interest is payable on the previous balance (interest and principal) at the market rate prevailing. Since the interest rate may change from period to period, multiple rates of interest apply.
Consider $1 accumulated at 10% for 3 years and 15% for 2 years.

Year	0	1	2	3
Accumulated value @ 10%	1	1.1	$(1.1)^2$	$(1.1)^3$

Year	3	4	5
Accumulated value @ 15% if $1 is invested after 3 years	1	1.15	$(1.15)^2$

From the first number line the investment after 3 years is $(1.1)^3$—the initial $1 plus three years of interest payments.

Now Accumulated Value @ year 5 for $1 invested at year 3 $= (1.15)^2$

$\therefore$ Accumulated Value @ year 5 for $\$(1.1)^3$ invested at year 3

$$= (1.1)^3(1.15)^2$$

$$= \$1.76$$

Year	3	4	5
AV @ 15%	$(1.1)^3$	$(1.1)^3(1.15)$	$(1.1)^3(1.15)^2$

Now consider $100 invested at 10% for 3 years and 15% for 2 years. The number lines now look like this:

Year	0	1	2	3
AV at 10%	100	$100(1.1)$	$100(1.1)^2$	$100(1.1)^3$

Year	3	4	5
AV at 15%	$100(1.1)^3$	$100(1.1)^3(1.15)$	$100(1.1)^3(1.15)^2$

$\therefore$ AV at year 5 $= 100(1.1)^3(1.15)^2 = \$176$

Example 6

Find the accumulated value of $15,000 @ 12% for 2 years and 10% for the following 4 years.

$$AV = 15,000(1.12)^2(1.1)^4$$

$$= \$27,548.51$$

EXERCISES

1 Change to a decimal:
   a) 10%   b) 12%   c) $12\frac{1}{2}$%   d) 7%   e) $5\frac{1}{4}$%

2 Change to a percentage:
   a) 0.15   b) 0.185   c) 0.02   d) 0.023   e) 0.0034

3 Find the accumulated value of $25,000 after 25 quarters at a compound rate of 4% per quarter.

4 Find the annual compound rate at which $100 will triple after 15 years.

5 An investment doubles in 10 years. Find the monthly compond rate. Check your answer.

6 Calculate the following to 3 decimal places:
   a) $\ln 80$ b) $\ln(2.6)(7.4)$ c) $\ln 65^2$

   d) $\ln \dfrac{99}{4}$ e) $\ln 3(1.1)^4$ f) $\dfrac{\ln 150}{\ln 120}$

7 How long does it take to triple your money at 10% per annum compound interest? Check your answer.

8 Find the ten-year accumulated value of $20,000 at 12% for the first five years and 10% for the second five years.

9 A target retirement benefit of $200,000 is to be provided after 5 years. This benefit will be funded by an initial contribution of $80,000 and a lump sum payment after 4 years. If the fund earns 10% per annum compound, determine the capital sum required after 4 years.

10 Given the same details as in question 5 above, except that the fund earning rate is 10% for the first 2 years and 9% thereafter, determine the capital sum required after 4 years.

6

Linear Interpolation

It is very common for executives to have to estimate a particular result, e.g. an accumulated profit (*AP*), when two values (one on each side of the desired result) are known. The method they use is the *interpolation* of data. For example, assume the *AP* for an investment yielding 12% and the *AP* for an investment yielding 13% are known. It may be necessary to approximate the profit for an intervening rate such as 12.5%.

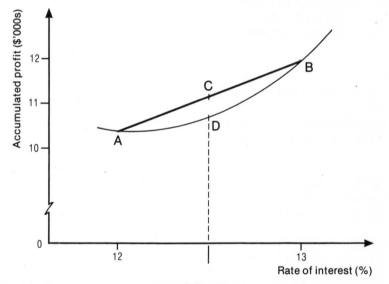

In this diagram the true profit graph relating rate of interest to *AP* is the curved line AB, and the actual profit for an interest rate of 12.5% is given by the point D. For practical purposes, however, we assume the profit graph is the straight line AB and the *AP* for 12.5% is then given by the point C. This is an approximation as it assumes that the profit growth between A and B is growing linearly. The difference between actual and estimated profit is the distance CD. The closer together the points A and B are, the smaller the difference between C and D will be, i.e. the closer to actual profit will be the approximated profit.

In this particular case,

$$\text{if the } AP \text{ for } 12\% = 10{,}400$$

$$\text{and } AP \text{ for } 13\% = 11{,}950$$

then the linear interpolation for $i = 12.5\%$ is the simple average of 10,400 and 11,950

$$\text{i.e.} \quad \frac{10{,}400 + 11{,}950}{2} = 11{,}150 \quad \text{(at point C)}$$

When the desired interpolation is not a simple average of the given data, i.e. is not half-way between the two, a weighting method must be used, as outlined in the rest of this chapter.

> By the end of this chapter you will be able to achieve
> linear interpolation between any two points and you
> will appreciate whether the error (assumed in a linear
> graph as opposed to a curved shape) is significant.

APPLYING TWO WEIGHTS

Consider Example 5 in the preceding chapter, i.e. accumulating $100 to $150 @ 8% per annum compound.

$$(1.08)^n = 1.5 \qquad \text{Find } n.$$

We know that $(1.08)^5 = 1.4693$ and $(1.08)^6 = 1.5869$
We want $(1.08)^n = 1.5$
Let $n = \triangle$ and draw a number line for $(1.08)^n$:

$(1.08)^n$	1.4693	1.5	1.5869
	A	B	C
n	$n = 5$	$n = \triangle\!\!\!\!/$	$n = 6$

Length AB $= 1.5 - 1.4693 = 0.0307$
Length BC $= 1.5869 - 1.5 = 0.0869$
Length AC $= 1.5869 - 1.4693 = 0.1176$

The ratio $\quad \dfrac{\text{AB}}{\text{AC}} = \dfrac{0.0307}{0.1176} = 0.2611$

and $\quad \dfrac{\text{BC}}{\text{AC}} = \dfrac{0.0869}{0.1176} = 0.7389 \text{ (or } 1 - 0.2611)$

Calculating these ratios is the same as converting the number line above into a strip length of unity. The distance AB is 26.11% of the total length, and BC is 73.89% of the total.

Another way of thinking of this is to regard 0.2611 and 0.7389 as weights:

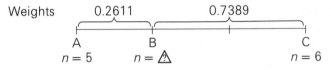

To obtain $\triangle$ we now apply one of the weights (0.2611 and 0.7389) to each end-point 5 and 6. The only question to be asked is, 'what weight?' If you consider the number line to be the plank of a seesaw, $\triangle$ is closest to 5. The greater weight should be applied to 5.

$$\therefore\ 5(0.7389) + \text{Next Step} = \triangle$$

The Next Step is simply to multiply the remaining numbers, namely 6 (0.2611):

$$\therefore\ \triangle = 5(0.7389) + 6(0.2611)$$

$$= 5.2611$$

This compares with the value of $n = 5.2684$ found by logs in the preceding chapter. The value of $\triangle = 5.2611$ will only be an approximation. Why? Because we are interpolating a function which is *not linear*. If you were to plot $(1.08)^n$ it would look like this:

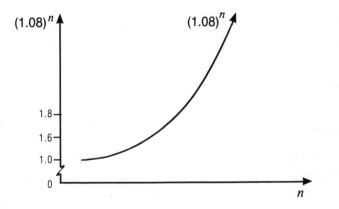

The higher the compound rate and the greater the value of n, the less accurate will be the interpolation method above, as the curvature departs more and more from linearity.

However, in practice it is a useful tool as an estimator!

Example 1

If $(1.1)^n = 2$ find n, approximately, by interpolation.

$(1.1)^7 = 1.9487$
$(1.1)^8 = 2.1436$

$(1.1)^n =$ 1.9487   2   2.1436

$n =$ 7   △   8

Place the △ approximately in the right position. It is closer to 1.9487 than to 2.1436.

$$2 - 1.9487$$
$$= 0.0513 \qquad 2.1436 - 2 = 0.1436$$

$n = 7$ $n = △$ $n = 8$

The length of the strip is $2.1436 - 1.9487 = 0.1949$.
Converting to a strip length of 1 instead of 0.1949, we have:

$$\text{first length} = \frac{0.0513}{0.1949} = 0.2632$$

$$\text{second length} = 1 - 0.2632$$

Weights   0.2632 $1 - 0.2632$

$n = 7$ $n = △$ $n = 8$

The two weights are 0.2632 and $(1 - 0.2632)$
Apply the heavier weight of $(1 - 0.2632)$ to 7 as △ is closer to 7 than to 8.
$\therefore \triangle = 7(1 - 0.2632) + 8(0.2632) = 7.2632$
$\therefore (1.1)^{7.2632}$ should be approximately equal to 2.
Check: $(1.1)^{7.2632} = 1.9982$.   A close result!
There are other methods for interpolating, but you will find this one particularly useful once you have become accustomed to it.
   Let us take another example to illustrate its attractiveness.

Example 2

Let $f(x)$ denote a function which is almost linear.

   $f(2) = 1.247$ and

   $f(6) = 0.648$

Find x approximately, using linear interpolation, if $f(x) = 1$.

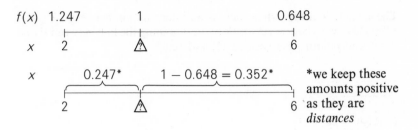

$f(x)$ 1.247   1   0.648

x 2   ⚠   6

x 0.247* $1 - 0.648 = 0.352$*   *we keep these
                                                      amounts positive
        2   ⚠   6   as they are
                                                      distances

Now $1.247 - 0.648 = 0.599$ and

$$\frac{0.247}{0.599} = 0.412$$

        0.412 $1 - 0.412 = 0.588$

x 2   ⚠   6

⚠ is closer to 2. Therefore apply the larger weight (of 0.588) to it:

$$⚠ = x = 2(0.588) + 6(0.412)$$

$$= 3.648$$

i.e. $f(3.648) \approx 1$

CHECKING FOR ACCURACY

The assumption of linearity may not hold in practice, particularly if there is an interpolation between two points which are a long distance apart.

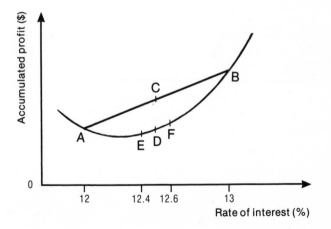

The error CD occurs when there is an interpolation between 12% and 13%. However, there is very little error in joining the line between E and F, i.e. interpolating between 12.4% and 12.6%.

EXERCISES

1 $(1.04)^n = 2.6$
   Find n by interpolation and check your estimation.

2 A lump sum of $10,000 is invested now for two years, and $20,000 is invested next year for one year. If the accumulated balance of the account is $36,000, find the compound annual rate of return by:
   (i) interpolating,
   (ii) using the quadratic (discriminant) formula.

3 $(1 + i)^{10} = 2$
   Find i by trial and error, then by interpolation. Check your result.

7

The Present Value of a Single Amount

Using compound interest it is possible to obtain a current valuation of assets (or liabilities) allowing for future cash flows and the reinvestment of such amounts at a prospective compound rate of interest.

A typical example is a zero coupon bond where no coupon or interest is paid during the term—rather, it is credited in full at maturity. The present value or price of such an instrument is found by bringing the cash flows at maturity back to now.

> The purpose of this chapter is to enable you to calculate the present value of a single cash flow in the future.

USING ALGEBRA TO FIND THE PRESENT VALUE

If the accumulated value after 2 years at 10% per annum compound is $121, what is the present value X?

Year	0	1	2
$	X		121

We know that X accumulated at 10% per annum compound will equal $121 after 2 years.
So $n = 2, i = 0.1$

$$\therefore X(1.1)^2 = 121$$

Divide both sides by $(1.1)^2$:

$$X = \frac{121}{(1.1)^2}$$

$$= \$100$$

i.e. the present value is $100.

Can you now provide a general formula for present values?
Let AV = the end benefit or accumulated value
  n = number of periods
  i = effective compound rate (as a decimal) per period.
In the previous example:

$$X = \frac{AV}{(1 + 0.1)^2}$$

In fact the general formula is:

$$\text{Present Value } (PV) = \frac{AV}{(1 + i)^n} \quad \text{or} \quad AV(1 + i)^{-n}$$

Example 1

Calculate the present value of \$20,000 payable in 4 years @ 14% per annum compound interest.

Solution: End benefit = 20,000

$$i = 0.14$$

$$n = 4$$

$$\text{Present Value} = \frac{20,000}{(1.14)^4}$$

$$= \$11,841.61$$

Using your calculator

Scientific calculator

Press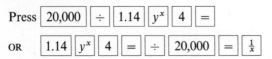

Hewlett-Packard

Press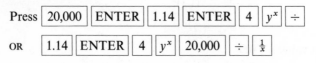

TABULAR VALUES OF $\dfrac{1}{(1 + i)^n}$

If you refer to compound interest tables such as the Present Value of a Lump Sum, you will notice a table like the one below, which calculates the Present Value of $1 for a certain number of periods at a particular rate of interest.

Period n	i 16%	i 18%	i 20%
1	0.862	0.847	0.833
2	0.743	0.718	0.694
3	0.641	0.609	0.579
4	0.552	0.516	0.482
5	0.476	0.437	0.402

Try to check some of these values.
e.g. Present Value of $1 for 4 periods @ $i = 18\%$ is $0.516.

Check:
$$n = 4$$
$$i = 0.18$$
$$\frac{1}{(1 + i)^4} = \frac{1}{(1.18)^4} = 0.516$$

Example 2

Prepare a column of present values (of $1) from $n = 1$ to $n = 4$ for $i = 16.6\%$.

Solution:

Present Value of $1

n	$\dfrac{1}{(1.166)^n}$
1	0.858
2	0.736
3	0.631
4	0.541

Example 3

Interpolate $\dfrac{1}{(1 + i)^4}$ between 16% and 18% to check your answer of 0.541 in example 2 above.

Looking back to the table, the Present Value of $1 for 4 periods at 16% is 0.552, and at 18% it is 0.516. So the number line looks like this:

Converting AB to a strip length of unity we have:

$$\text{First weight} = \frac{\text{AC}}{\text{AB}} = \frac{0.6}{2} = 0.3$$

$$\text{Second weight} = \frac{\text{CB}}{\text{AB}} = \frac{1.4}{2} = 0.7$$

The two weights are therefore 0.3 and 0.7.

Now $\triangle$ is closer to 0.552. Therefore apply the heavier weight to 0.552 and multiply the lighter weight by 0.516.

$$\therefore \frac{1}{(1 + i)^n} = 0.552(0.7) + 0.3(0.516)$$

$$\frac{1}{(1.166)^4} = 0.541$$

Example 4

Find the present value of $40,000 due in 4 years and $20,000 due in 2 years @ 16.6% per annum compound.

Solution: $$\text{Present Value} = \frac{40,000}{(1.166)^4} + \frac{20,000}{(1.166)^2}$$

$$= \$36,351.11$$

Using your calculator

Scientific calculator

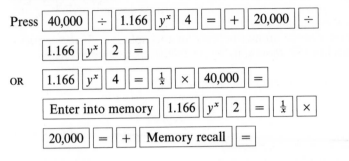

Hewlett-Packard

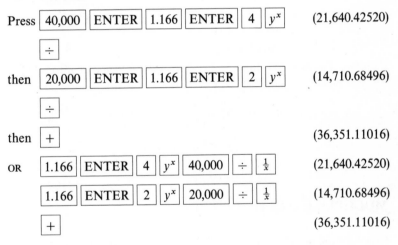

THE V FUNCTION

To save writing $\dfrac{1}{(1+i)^1}$, $\dfrac{1}{(1+i)^2}$, $\dfrac{1}{(1+i)^3}$, etc. we can abbreviate to

V^1, V^2, V^3, ... where $V = \dfrac{1}{1+i}$

$$\text{i.e.} \quad \frac{1}{(1+i)^n} = (1+i)^{-n}$$
$$= V^n$$

Example 5

Describe what $50,000\ V^6$ @ 16% means. Calculate its value.

Solution: This is the present value of $50,000 due in 6 periods @ 16% per period compound.

We cannot assume annual periods for this solution. In fact a period could be a quarter, month, half-year, biennium, triennium etc.

$$50,000\ V^6 \text{ @ } 16\% = 50,000 \times \frac{1}{(1.16)^6}$$

$$= \$20,522.11$$

Example 6

Express in terms of V the present value of the future cash flows demonstrated on the number line below. Assume rate i compound per annum.

Cash flow			$60,000		$70,000
Year	0	1	2	3	4

Solution: The $60,000 must be brought back 2 years to zero and the $70,000 must be brought back 4 years to zero.

$$\text{Present Value} = 60,000 \times \frac{1}{(1 + i)^2} + 70,000 \times \frac{1}{(1 + i)^4}$$

$$= 60,000\ V^2 + 70,000\ V^4$$

MULTIPLE RATES OF INTEREST

Consider the situation where $40,000 is payable in 4 years. However, interest will be 12% for the first 2 years and 10% thereafter.

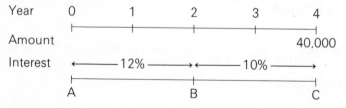

To obtain the present value bring back $40,000 to point B @ 10%,

i.e. $40,000 \dfrac{1}{(1.1)^2}$.

Now bring this amount back to A @ 12% using the function $\dfrac{1}{(1.12)^2}$ (i.e. 2 years from B to A).

Present Value of \$1 due at B $= \dfrac{1}{(1.12)^2}$.

Present Value of $40,000 \times \dfrac{1}{(1.1)^2}$ due at B $= 40,000 \times \dfrac{1}{(1.1)^2} \times \dfrac{1}{(1.12)^2}$.

$$= \$26,353.52$$

Using your calculator

$$40,000 \cdot \frac{1}{(1.1)^2} \cdot \frac{1}{(1.12)^2} \qquad \text{OR} \qquad 40,000 \,.\, (1.1)^{-2} \,.\, (1.12)^{-2}$$

Scientific calculator

For the first expression, press:

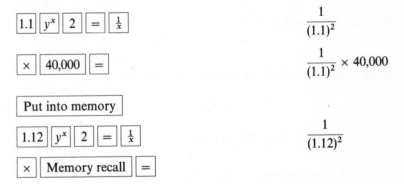

$\dfrac{1}{(1.1)^2}$

$\dfrac{1}{(1.1)^2} \times 40,000$

$\dfrac{1}{(1.12)^2}$

For the second expression, press:

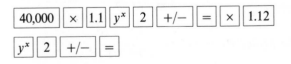

Hewlett-Packard

For the first expression, press:

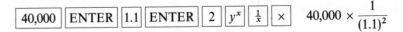 $40,000 \times \dfrac{1}{(1.1)^2}$

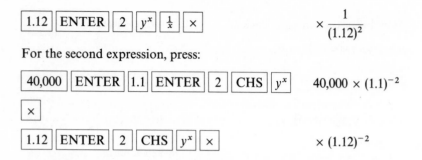

$$\times \frac{1}{(1.12)^2}$$

For the second expression, press:

| 40,000 | ENTER | 1.1 | ENTER | 2 | CHS | y^x | $40,000 \times (1.1)^{-2}$

| × |

| 1.12 | ENTER | 2 | CHS | y^x | × | $\times (1.12)^{-2}$

Example 7

Calculate the present value of $20,000 due in 8 years. Interest of 10% per annum applies for the first 3 years and 9% thereafter.

Solution:

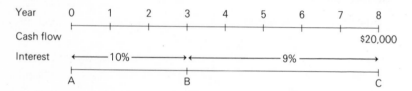

Present Value of 20,000 back to B (i.e. 5 years) @ 9%

$$= 20,000 \times \frac{1}{(1.09)^5}$$

i.e. $PV = 12,998.63$

PV of $1 due in 3 years (i.e. at B) @ 10% $= \dfrac{1}{(1.1)^3} = 0.7513$

PV of $12,998.63 due in 3 years @ 10% $= 12,998.63 \times 0.7513$
$= \$9,765.87$

This answer could be written $PV = 20,000 \cdot \dfrac{1}{(1.09)^5} \cdot \dfrac{1}{(1.1)^3}$

OR $PV = 20,000\ V_{9\%}^5 \cdot V_{10\%}^3.$

Note: When calculated in one go, the answer is $9,766.06. The previous answer contains a small error because each step in the calculation was rounded to 2 or 4 decimal places.

EXERCISES

1 Obtain the present value of \$25,000 payable in $1\frac{1}{2}$ years at 4% per quarter compound.

2 Find the present value of an estate valued at \$500,000 and payable in 7 years. Assume interest on the estate at a rate of 10% per annum compound. Assume certainty of survival.

3 A special bond pays \$70,000 in 4 years and a further \$90,000 7 years from now. If the bond earns interest at 5.5% per half-year compound, find the present value (price) of the bond.

4 Taking the details in exercise 3 above, determine the price assuming that interest is $5\frac{1}{2}$% per half-year for 4 years and 5% per half-year thereafter.

5 A bond which has a current price of \$70 will return \$100 in 5 years. Using a present value process, determine the annual compound rate earned on the bond.

6 A certain vintage car is expected to double in value in 10 years. Find the annual rate of appreciation for this vehicle.

7 A special bond pays \$100 in 4 years and 120 days. The interest on the bond is assumed to remain at 11% per annum compound. Find the price (or present value) of this security.

8 The price of a car-windscreen is expected to double after n years assuming 11% per annum compound. Find n.

8

The Present Value of an Annuity

Many situations arise in practice where a series of equal amounts occur at regular equal time intervals. This series of payments is called an *annuity*. Examples in practice are lease payments, insurance premiums, loan repayments and fixed interest coupons.

> By the end of this chapter you will be able to value an annuity from first principles. In fact you will not need to refer to a set of tables. Using your calculator you will be able to value a stream of equal cash flows, at any compound rate of interest.

THE PRESENT VALUE OF AN ORDINARY ANNUITY

In an *ordinary annuity* the cash flows occur at the *end* of each period.

Consider a series of $1 payments at the end of each year for 4 years, at 10% per annum compound.

Year	0	1	2	3	4
Amount ($) invested		$1	$1	$1	$1

The Present Value of the first $1 $= \dfrac{1}{1.1} = 0.90909$

The Present Value of the second $1 $= \dfrac{1}{(1.1)^2} = 0.82645$

The Present Value of the third $1 $= \dfrac{1}{(1.1)^3} = 0.75131$

The Present Value of the fourth $1 $= \dfrac{1}{(1.1)^4} = 0.68301$

$$\overline{3.16986}$$

∴ The total Present Value = $3.16986

This means that for an investment (loan) of $3.17 you would receive (pay) $1 per year for 4 years in arrear, at 10%. The difference of 83 cents ($4–$3.17) constitutes interest.

Example 1

Find the present value of $1 payable for 3 years, in arrear, at 10% per annum compound.

Year	0	1	2	3
Amount invested		$1	$1	$1

The Present Value of the first $1 = 0.90909
The Present Value of the second $1 = 0.82645
The Present Value of the third $1 = 0.75131
                                     2.48685

ANNUITY SYMBOL

Consider now a series of n payments of $1 per period in arrear, at rate i compound per period.

Period		1	2	3	n
Cash flow		$1	$1	$1	$1

The present value of the cash flow stream $= \dfrac{1}{1+i} + \dfrac{1}{(1+i)^2} + \cdots \dfrac{1}{(1+i)^n}$

This can be represented by the shorthand version $A_{\overline{n}|i}$ which stands for 'the present value at compound rate i of an annuity of n payments of $1 paid in arrear'.

$$A_{\overline{n}|i} = \frac{1}{(1+i)} + \frac{1}{(1+i)^2} + \cdots \frac{1}{(1+i)^n}$$

If we let $V = \dfrac{1}{1+i}$ we know that

$$V^2 = \frac{1}{(1+i)^2}$$

$$V^3 = \frac{1}{(1+i)^3}$$

and $V^n = \dfrac{1}{(1 + i)^n}$

$\therefore A_{\overline{n}|i} = V^1 + V^2 + V^3 + \ldots V^n$

ANNUITY FORMULA

$$A_{\overline{n}|i} = V^1 + V^2 + V^3 + \ldots V^n$$
$$= \frac{1}{(1 + i)} + \frac{1}{(1 + i)^2} + \frac{1}{(1 + i)^3} + \ldots \frac{1}{(1 + i)^n}$$

Multiply both sides by $(1 + i)$:

$$A_{\overline{n}|i}(1 + i) = \frac{(1 + i)}{(1 + i)} + \frac{(1 + i)}{(1 + i)^2} + \frac{(1 + i)}{(1 + i)^3} + \ldots \frac{(1 + i)}{(1 + i)^n}$$

$$= 1 + \frac{1}{(1 + i)} + \frac{1}{(1 + i)^2} + \ldots \frac{1}{(1 + i)^{n-1}}$$

$$= 1 + V^1 + V^2 + \ldots V^{n-1}$$

Lining up

$$A_{\overline{n}|i}(1 + i) = 1 + V^1 + V^2 + \ldots V^{n-1}$$
$$A_{\overline{n}|i} = \quad V^1 + V^2 + \ldots V^{n-1} + V^n$$

it is now possible to express $A_{\overline{n}|i}$ in a simpler form. Simply subtract the second equation from the first:

$$A_{\overline{n}|i}(1 + i) - A_{\overline{n}|i} = 1 - V^n \qquad \text{(all other terms disappear due to the subtraction)}$$

$$A_{\overline{n}|i} + iA_{\overline{n}|i} - A_{\overline{n}|i} = 1 - V^n$$

$$iA_{\overline{n}|i} = 1 - V^n$$

$$A_{\overline{n}|i} = \frac{1 - V^n}{i} \qquad \text{or} \qquad A_{\overline{n}|i} = \frac{1 - \dfrac{1}{(1 + i)^n}}{i}$$

Example 2

Check the answer in example 1 using the annuity formula.

The number of periods $= 3 = n$

$$i = 10\% = 0.1$$

In this case $A_{\overline{n}|i} = A_{\overline{3}|10\%}$ or $A_{\overline{3}|0.1}$

$$= \frac{1 - V^3}{0.1}$$

Now $V = \dfrac{1}{(1 + i)}$

$$V^3 = \left[\frac{1}{(1 + i)}\right]^3$$

$$= \frac{1}{(1 + i)^3}$$

$$\therefore A_{\overline{3}|10\%} = \frac{1 - \dfrac{1}{(1.1)^3}}{0.1}$$

$$= 2.486852$$

Using your calculator

Scientific calculator

$\boxed{1.1}\ \boxed{y^x}\ \boxed{3}\ \boxed{=}$	$(1.1)^3$
$\boxed{\frac{1}{x}}$	$\dfrac{1}{(1.1)^3}$
$\boxed{+/-}$	$-\dfrac{1}{(1.1)^3}$
$\boxed{+}\ \boxed{1}\ \boxed{=}$	$-\dfrac{1}{(1.1)^3} + 1,$ i.e. $1 - \dfrac{1}{(1.1)^3}$
$\boxed{\div}\ \boxed{0.1}\ \boxed{=}$	$\dfrac{1 - \dfrac{1}{(1.1)^3}}{0.1}$

OR

$$\boxed{1}\ \boxed{-}\ \boxed{1.1}\ \boxed{y^x}\ \boxed{3}\ \boxed{+/-}\ \boxed{=} \qquad 1 - (1.1)^{-3} = 1 - \frac{1}{(1.1)^3}$$

$$\boxed{\div}\ \boxed{0.1}\ \boxed{=}$$

Hewlett-Packard

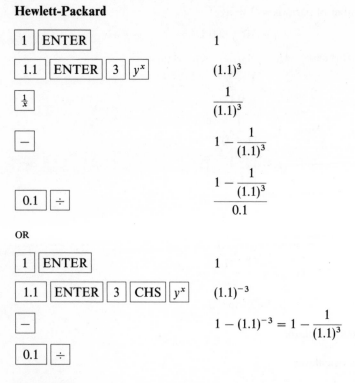

1 ENTER	1
1.1 ENTER 3 y^x	$(1.1)^3$
$\frac{1}{x}$	$\dfrac{1}{(1.1)^3}$
−	$1 - \dfrac{1}{(1.1)^3}$
0.1 ÷	$\dfrac{1 - \dfrac{1}{(1.1)^3}}{0.1}$

OR

1 ENTER	1
1.1 ENTER 3 CHS y^x	$(1.1)^{-3}$
−	$1 - (1.1)^{-3} = 1 - \dfrac{1}{(1.1)^3}$
0.1 ÷	

Example 3

Complete the following table at $i = 12\%$ per annum compound.

n (years)	$V^n = \dfrac{1}{(1 + i)^n}$	$A_{\overline{n}|i}$
① 1 2 3 4	②	③

Check your columns independently.

Solution:

$$V^1 \ @\ 12\% = \frac{1}{1.12} = 0.89286$$

$$V^2 \ @\ 12\% = \frac{1}{(1.12)^2} = 0.79719$$

$$V^3 @ 12\% = \frac{1}{(1.12)^3} = 0.71178$$

$$V^4 @ 12\% = \frac{1}{(1.12)^4} = 0.63552$$

$$
\begin{aligned}
\text{Now} \quad A_{\overline{1}|12\%} &= V^1 & &= 0.89286 \\
A_{\overline{2}|12\%} &= V^1 + V^2 & &= 0.89286 + 0.79719 \\
& & &= 1.69005 \\
A_{\overline{3}|12\%} &= V^1 + V^2 + V^3 & &= 1.69005 + 0.71178 \\
& & &= 2.40183 \\
A_{\overline{4}|12\%} &= V^1 + V^2 + V^3 + V^4 & &= 2.40183 + 0.63552 \\
& & &= 3.03735
\end{aligned}
$$

$\therefore$ The resulting table is:

n (years)	$V^n = \dfrac{1}{(1+i)^n}$	$A_{\overline{n}|i}$
1	0.89286	0.89286
2	0.79719	1.69005
3	0.71178	2.40183
4	0.63552	3.03735

Note that the entries in the third column are obtained by adding the values in the second column. Thus $A_{\overline{2}|}$ is obtained by adding V^1 and V^2, $A_{\overline{3}|} = V^1 + V^2 + V^3$, and $A_{\overline{4}|} = V^1 + V^2 + V^3 + V^4$.

If $A_{\overline{4}|}$ is checked independently using the annuity formula, and the value obtained is the same as $V^1 + V^2 + V^3 + V^4$, then the second and third columns in the table must be correct.

Check:

$$A_{\overline{4}|12\%} = \frac{1 - V^4}{i} = \frac{1 - \dfrac{1}{(1+i)^4}}{i}$$

$$= \frac{1 - \dfrac{1}{(1.12)^4}}{0.12}$$

$$= 3.03735$$

Thus the table is correct.

PRESENT VALUE OF AN ANNUITY DUE

In an *annuity due* payments are made in *advance* rather than in arrear. Common practical examples are leasing and insurance payments.

Consider now the following cash stream.

Year	0	1	2	3
Cash flow	$1	$1	$1	

The present value of the first payment = $1

The present value of the second payment $= \dfrac{1}{(1 + i)} = V^1$

The present value of the third payment $= \dfrac{1}{(1 + i)^2} = V^2$

The sum in this case can be represented by $\ddot{A}_{\overline{3}|i}$, pronounced 'A tremor 3 at rate i'. The two dots over the A tell you it is an annuity due rather than an ordinary annuity. Thus $\ddot{A}_{\overline{n}|i}$ stands for the 'the present value at compound rate i of an annuity of n payments of $1 paid in advance'.

$$\ddot{A}_{\overline{3}|i} = 1 + V^1 + V^2$$

Generating for n terms:

$$\boxed{\begin{aligned} \text{annuity due} = \ddot{A}_{\overline{n}|i} &= 1 + V^1 + V^2 + \ldots V^{n-1} \\ &= 1 + \frac{1}{1 + i} + \frac{1}{(1 + i)^2} + \ldots \frac{1}{(1 + i)^{n-1}} \end{aligned}}$$

Can you derive a formula relating the ordinary annuity to the annuity due?

$$A_{\overline{n-1}|i} = V^1 + V^2 + \ldots V^{n-1}$$

Add 1 to both sides:

$$A_{\overline{n-1}|i} + 1 = 1 + V^1 + V^2 + \ldots V^{n-1}$$
$$= \ddot{A}_{\overline{n}|i}$$

$$\boxed{\ddot{A}_{\overline{n}|i} = 1 + A_{\overline{n-1}|i}}$$

i.e. an annuity due = 1 + an ordinary annuity for one fewer period.

Consider $\ddot{A}_{\overline{4}|i}$, represented by the present value of the cash flows below:

Period	0	1	2	3	4
Cash flow	$1	$1	$1	$1	

Compare $A_{\overline{3}|i}$ = the present value of three payments in arrear:

Period	0	1	2	3	4
Cash flow		$1	$1	$1	

You can see that adding \$1 at period 0, to give $1 + A_{\overline{3}|i}$, gives the same number line as $\ddot{A}_{\overline{4}|i}$.

i.e. $\ddot{A}_{\overline{4}|i} = 1 + A_{\overline{3}|i}$

Another approach would be to multiply both sides of $A_{\overline{n}|i} = V^1 + V^2 + \dots V^n$ by $(1 + i)$:

$$(1 + i)A_{\overline{n}|i} = (1 + i)V^1 + (1 + i)V^2 + \dots (1 + i)V^n$$

$$= \frac{1 + i}{1 + i} + \frac{1 + i}{(1 + i)^2} + \dots \frac{1 + i}{(1 + i)^n}$$

$$= 1 + \frac{1}{1 + i} + \dots \frac{1}{(1 + i)^{n-1}}$$

$$= 1 + V^1 + \dots V^{n-1}$$

$$= \ddot{A}_{\overline{n}|i}$$

$$\boxed{(1 + i)A_{\overline{n}|i} = \ddot{A}_{\overline{n}|i}}$$

i.e. an annuity due = an ordinary annuity multiplied by $(1 + i)$
= an ordinary annuity compounded forward
1 period

Does this make sense?

Consider \$100 invested for 1 period at rate i:

Period	0	1
Cash flow	100	$100(1 + i)$

The accumulated lump sum at the end of period 1 is $100(1 + i)$. Similarly a lump sum of $A_{\overline{4}|i}$ accumulated forward one period becomes $A_{\overline{4}|i}(1 + i)$:

Period	0	1
Cash flow	$A_{\overline{4}|i}$	$A_{\overline{4}|i}(1 + i)$

Now $A_{\overline{4}|i}$ is represented by:

Period	0	1	2	3	4

Cash flow $\quad\longleftarrow\!\!-\$1 \qquad \$1 \qquad \$1 \qquad \$1$

$A_{\overline{4}|i}$

Accumulating $A_{\overline{4}|i}$ forward one period shifts $A_{\overline{4}|i}$ thus:

0	1	2	3	4

$\qquad\qquad\$1 \qquad \$1 \qquad \$1 \qquad \$1$

$A_{\overline{4}|i} \longrightarrow A_{\overline{4}|i}(1 + i)$

This brings the present value of the 4 payments to period 1.

You can see from the number line that this is equivalent to $\ddot{A}_{\overline{4}|i}$, with the valuation date at period 1.

i.e. $\ddot{A}_{\overline{4}|i} = A_{\overline{4}|i}(1 + i)$

The present value can be calculated at any period. Provided all cash flows are brought forward or back to the same valuation date, the present value will be the same.

DEFERRED ANNUITY

On many occasions a stream of cash flows may commence after more than one period. Ideally suited for paying bills!
e.g.

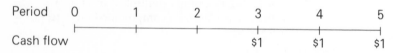

Period	0	1	2	3	4	5

Cash flow $\qquad\qquad\qquad\qquad\qquad \$1 \qquad \$1 \qquad \$1$

Present Value (N) of First Payment $= \dfrac{1}{(1 + i)^3} = V^3$

Present Value of Second Payment $= \dfrac{1}{(1 + i)^4} = V^4$

Present Value of Third Payment $= \dfrac{1}{(1 + i)^5} = V^5$

$$PV = V^3 + V^4 + V^5$$

Recall that $A_{\overline{n}|i} = V^1 + V^2 + \ldots V^n$ @ rate i compound.

$$A_{\overline{5}|i} = V^1 + V^2 + V^3 + V^4 + V^5$$

$$A_{\overline{2}|i} = V^1 + V^2$$

$$\therefore A_{\overline{5}|i} - A_{\overline{2}|i} = V^3 + V^4 + V^5$$

Recall that the subscript n in $A_{\overline{n}|i}$ refers to n payments. Similarly, $A_{\overline{5}|} - A_{\overline{2}|}$ refers to $5 - 2 = 3$ payments.

Can you think of another approach to solving this problem?

$$PV = V^3 + V^4 + V^5 = V^2(V^1 + V^2 + V^3)$$

$$PV = V^2 A_{\overline{3}|}$$

Does this make sense?
Again put the cash flows on a number line:

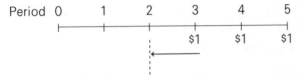

$A_{\overline{3}|}$ will present value the three cash flows back to period 2. This lump sum $(A_{\overline{3}|})$ then needs to be present valued back a further two periods (to period 0) by multiplying by $\dfrac{1}{(1 + i)^2}$ or V^2.

$$\text{i.e.} \quad PV = V^2 A_{\overline{3}|}$$

Example 4

Find the present value of $400 payable for 6 months. The first payment occurs in 5 months' time. The compound interest rate per month is 1.1%.

Solution, method 1:
Look first at payments of $1 per month.

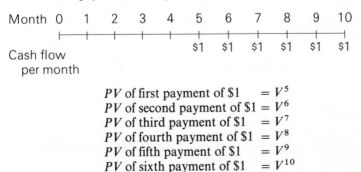

$$
\begin{aligned}
PV \text{ of first payment of } \$1 &= V^5 \\
PV \text{ of second payment of } \$1 &= V^6 \\
PV \text{ of third payment of } \$1 &= V^7 \\
PV \text{ of fourth payment of } \$1 &= V^8 \\
PV \text{ of fifth payment of } \$1 &= V^9 \\
PV \text{ of sixth payment of } \$1 &= V^{10}
\end{aligned}
$$

$$PV = V^5 + V^6 + \ldots V^{10}$$
$$= V^4(V^1 + V^2 + \ldots V^6)$$
$$= V^4 A_{\overline{6}|1.1\%}$$

Now $A_{\overline{6}|}$ is the annuity for 6 periods, beginning at period 5, present-valued back one period, to period 4:

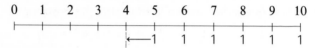

By multiplying $A_{\overline{6}|}$ by V^4 the arrow at month 4 moves back 4 periods to month zero.

$$\text{i.e.} \quad PV = V^4 A_{\overline{6}|}$$

This is the formula for payments of $1 per period. For payments of $400 per period, at rate 1.1% per period, the formula becomes:

$$PV = 400 V^4 A_{\overline{6}|1.1\%}$$

$$= 400\left(\frac{1}{(1.011)^4}\right)\left(\frac{1 - \dfrac{1}{(1.011)^6}}{0.011}\right)$$

$$= \$2,211.33$$

Using your calculator

Scientific calculator

For $400\left(\dfrac{1}{(1.011)^4}\right)$, which can be written $400(1.011)^{-4}$ or $\dfrac{400}{(1.011)^4}$:

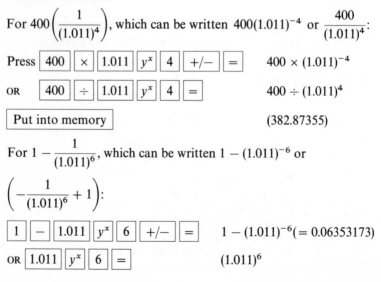

Press | 400 | | × | | 1.011 | | y^x | | 4 | | +/− | | = | $400 \times (1.011)^{-4}$

OR | 400 | | ÷ | | 1.011 | | y^x | | 4 | | = | $400 \div (1.011)^4$

| Put into memory | (382.87355)

For $1 - \dfrac{1}{(1.011)^6}$, which can be written $1 - (1.011)^{-6}$ or

$\left(-\dfrac{1}{(1.011)^6} + 1\right)$:

| 1 | | − | | 1.011 | | y^x | | 6 | | +/− | | = | $1 - (1.011)^{-6}(= 0.06353173)$

OR | 1.011 | | y^x | | 6 | | = | $(1.011)^6$

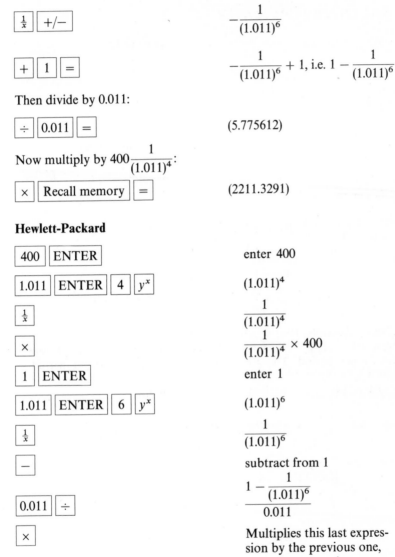

$\boxed{\tfrac{1}{x}}\ \boxed{+/-}$ $-\dfrac{1}{(1.011)^6}$

$\boxed{+}\ \boxed{1}\ \boxed{=}$ $-\dfrac{1}{(1.011)^6} + 1$, i.e. $1 - \dfrac{1}{(1.011)^6}$

Then divide by 0.011:

$\boxed{\div}\ \boxed{0.011}\ \boxed{=}$ (5.775612)

Now multiply by $400\dfrac{1}{(1.011)^4}$:

$\boxed{\times}\ \boxed{\text{Recall memory}}\ \boxed{=}$ (2211.3291)

Hewlett-Packard

$\boxed{400}\ \boxed{\text{ENTER}}$ enter 400

$\boxed{1.011}\ \boxed{\text{ENTER}}\ \boxed{4}\ \boxed{y^x}$ $(1.011)^4$

$\boxed{\tfrac{1}{x}}$ $\dfrac{1}{(1.011)^4}$

$\boxed{\times}$ $\dfrac{1}{(1.011)^4} \times 400$

$\boxed{1}\ \boxed{\text{ENTER}}$ enter 1

$\boxed{1.011}\ \boxed{\text{ENTER}}\ \boxed{6}\ \boxed{y^x}$ $(1.011)^6$

$\boxed{\tfrac{1}{x}}$ $\dfrac{1}{(1.011)^6}$

$\boxed{-}$ subtract from 1

$\boxed{0.011}\ \boxed{\div}$ $\dfrac{1 - \dfrac{1}{(1.011)^6}}{0.011}$

$\boxed{\times}$ Multiplies this last expression by the previous one, i.e. by $400 \times \dfrac{1}{(1.011)^4}$

Alternatively, the *PV* expression can be written with negative indices:

$$PV = 400(1.011)^{-4}\left(\dfrac{1 - (1.011)^{-6}}{0.011}\right)$$

The calculator sequence then becomes:

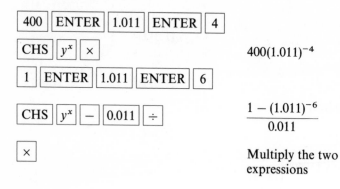

$$400(1.011)^{-4}$$

$$\frac{1 - (1.011)^{-6}}{0.011}$$

Multiply the two expressions

Solution, method 2:

$$PV = V^5 + V^6 + V^7 + V^8 + V^9 + V^{10}$$

Now $A_{\overline{10}|} = V^1 + V^2 + V^3 + V^4 + \dots V^{10}$

$$A_{\overline{4}|} = V^1 + V^2 + V^3 + V^4$$

$$A_{\overline{10}|} - A_{\overline{4}|} = V^5 + V^6 + V^7 + V^8 + V^9 + V^{10}$$

Check subscripts: $10 - 4 = 6$ payments.

Now $PV = A_{\overline{10}|} - A_{\overline{4}|}$ represents the present value when payments are \$1 per period. The PV when payments are \$400 per period $= 400(A_{\overline{10}|} - A_{\overline{4}|})$.

$\therefore PV$ of \$400 per month at rate 1.1% per month is

$$PV = 400(A_{\overline{10}|1.1\%} - A_{\overline{4}|1.1\%})$$

Recall that $A_{\overline{n}|i} = \dfrac{1 - \dfrac{1}{(1 + i)^n}}{i}$

$$\therefore A_{\overline{10}|1.1\%} = \frac{1 - \dfrac{1}{(1.011)^{10}}}{0.011} = 9.4207$$

$$A_{\overline{4}|1.1\%} = \frac{1 - \dfrac{1}{(1.011)^4}}{0.011} = 3.8924$$

$$\therefore PV = 400(9.4207 - 3.8924)$$

$$= \$2{,}211.32$$

EXERCISES

1   Complete the following table at 10% per annum compound:

Year	$(1 + i)^n$	V^n	$A_{\overline{n}|i}$
1			
2			
3			
4			

2   Check your answer to $A_{\overline{4}|10\%}$ using $A_{\overline{n}|i} = \dfrac{1 - V^n}{i}$

3   Total the $A_{\overline{n}|i}$ column in the table above and check your answer independently.
(Hint: $A_{\overline{n}|} = V^1 + V^2 + V^3 + \ldots V^n$)

4   Find the present value of the cash flows indicated on the number line below. Use 11% per annum compound interest.

Year	0	1	2	3	4	5	6
Cash flow (in 000's)				40	40	40	40 / 30

5   Show that $\ddot{A}_{\overline{n}|} = A_{\overline{n-1}|} + 1$

6   An estate pays an annuity certain (i.e. cash is payable whether or not the annuitant survives) of $50,000 per annum in arrear for 5 years. From the sixth year until the tenth year this annual payment doubles. Determine the present value of the estate assuming 12% per annum compound.

7   Find the present value of the cash flows indicated on the number line:

Month	0	1	2	3	4	5	6	7	8
Cash flow (in 000's)		20	20	20			20	20	20

Assume 1.2% per month compound.

8   Determine the present value of the cash flows in exercise 7 above assuming 1.2% per month compound for the first 6 months and 1% per month compound thereafter.

9

Geometric Progressions

In the last chapter we confronted several progressions involving $V^1 + V^2 + \ldots V^n$ or $\dfrac{1}{(1+i)^1} + \dfrac{1}{(1+i)^2} + \dfrac{1}{(1+i)^3} + \ldots \dfrac{1}{(1+i)^n}$. These are in fact *geometric progressions* as each term is obtained by multiplying the previous term by a fixed factor (r). The second term is $\dfrac{1}{1+i}$ times the first term. The third term is $\dfrac{1}{1+i}$ times the second term, i.e. $r = \dfrac{1}{1+i}$. This progression can be used to simplify annuity cash flows from $V^1 + V^2 + \ldots V^n$ into the form $A_{\overline{n}|i} = \dfrac{1 - V^n}{i}$.

Another example of a geometric progression is $x^1 + x^2 + x^3 + x^4$. The second term is obtained by multiplying the first term by x. The third term = second term $\times$ x, the fourth term = third term $\times$ x.

In many financial problems these progressions may occur, for a finite period or in perpetuity (forever). An example in the latter case is a stream of company dividends which are assumed to be infinite.

> By the end of this chapter you will be able to sum a finite or infinite geometric progression. You will be able to apply both techniques to practical problem solving.

A FINITE GEOMETRIC PROGRESSION

Consider the progression:

$$S_n = a + ar + ar^2 + ar^3 + \ldots + ar^{n-1}$$

The first term $= a$

Note that: $\dfrac{\text{2nd term}}{\text{1st term}} = \dfrac{ar}{a} = r$

$\dfrac{\text{3rd term}}{\text{2nd term}} = \dfrac{ar^2}{ar} = r$

and the $\dfrac{n\text{th term}}{(n-1)\text{th term}} = r$

This is a geometric progression as the $\dfrac{n\text{th term}}{(n-1)\text{th term}}$ is a fixed value, r.

How do you simplify S_n?
Clue: Multiply S_n by r.
Let us see if you were correct!

Now $\quad S_n = a + ar + ar^2 + \ldots ar^{n-1}$

$\qquad rS_n = ar + ar^2 + \ldots ar^{n-1} + ar^n$

(Remember $ar^{n-1} \times r = ar^{n-1+1} = ar^n$)

$$\therefore S_n - rS_n = a - ar^n$$

$$= a(1 - r^n)$$

$$S_n(1 - r) = a(1 - r^n)$$

$$\boxed{S_n = \frac{a(1 - r^n)}{1 - r}}$$

This is the formula for the sum of a geometric progression where:

$$a = \text{first term}$$

$$n = \text{number of terms}$$

$$r = \frac{\text{Term } n}{\text{Term } n-1} = \frac{T_n}{T_{n-1}}$$

Example 1

Sum the following series:

$$S_{40} = (1.12)^1 + (1.12)^2 + (1.12)^3 + \ldots + (1.12)^{40}$$

Solution:

$$\text{The first term } a = 1.12$$

$$n = 40 \text{ terms}$$

$$r = \frac{\text{2nd term}}{\text{1st term}} \quad \text{or} \quad \frac{T_n}{T_{n-1}}$$

$$= \frac{(1.12)^2}{1.12} = 1.12$$

$$S_n = \frac{a(1 - r^n)}{1 - r}$$

$$= \frac{1.12[1 - (1.12)^{40}]}{1 - 1.12}$$

If $\dfrac{1 - x}{1 - y}$ is multiplied by $\boxed{\dfrac{-1}{-1}}$ we obtain $\dfrac{x - 1}{y - 1}$

$$\therefore S_n = \frac{1.12[(1.12)^{40} - 1]}{1.12 - 1}$$

$$= \frac{1.12[(1.12)^{40} - 1]}{0.12}$$

$$= 859.14$$

Using your calculator

$$\frac{1.12[(1.12)^{40} - 1]}{0.12}$$

It is usually easier to work any brackets first, i.e. in this case $(1.12)^{40} - 1$.

Scientific calculator

Hewlett-Packard

Example 2

Find the sum of

$$\frac{1}{(1.11)^3} + \frac{1}{(1.11)^5} + \frac{1}{(1.11)^7} + \cdots \frac{1}{(1.11)^{21}}$$

Solution:

the first term $a = \dfrac{1}{(1.11)^3}$

$$r = \frac{\text{2nd term}}{\text{1st term}} = \frac{1}{(1.11)^5} \div \frac{1}{(1.11)^3}$$

$$= \frac{1}{(1.11)^5} \times \frac{(1.11)^3}{1}$$

$$= \frac{1}{(1.11)^2}$$

Another way of looking at it is to ask—what do you need to multiply the first term by to obtain the second term?

$$\frac{1}{(1.11)^3} \times \boxed{?} = \frac{1}{(1.11)^5}$$

$$\frac{1}{(1.11)^3} \times \boxed{\frac{1}{(1.11)^2}} = \frac{1}{(1.11)^5}$$

$$\therefore r = \frac{1}{(1.11)^2}$$

How many terms are there? i.e. what does n equal?
A little tricky—so try a simple model.

Take: $\dfrac{1}{(1.11)^3} + \dfrac{1}{(1.11)^5} + \dfrac{1}{(1.11)^7}$

When the highest power is 7, the lowest power is 3 and there are three terms.

Now $\dfrac{7-3}{2} + 1 = 3$

i.e. $\dfrac{\text{highest power} - \text{lowest power}}{2} + 1$

gives the number of terms (3).

Similarly for $\dfrac{1}{(1.11)^3} + \dfrac{1}{(1.11)^5}$ the highest power (5) relates to two terms.

i.e. $\dfrac{\text{highest power} - \text{lowest power}}{2} + 1 = \dfrac{5-3}{2} + 1$

$$= 2$$

So when the highest power is 21, the number of terms is found by:

$$\frac{21-3}{2} + 1 = 10$$

An alternative method is to find a relationship between the number of terms in the progression and the highest power at that point.

Number of terms	Highest power
1	3
2	5
3	7
⋮	⋮
n	$2n + 1$
⋮	⋮
?	21

When the highest power is 21, $2n + 1 = 21$

$$2n = 20$$

$$n = 10$$

i.e. there are 10 terms in the progression given.
Recapping:

$$a = \frac{1}{(1.11)^3}$$

$$r = \frac{1}{(1.11)^2}$$

$$n = 10$$

$$S_n = \frac{a(1 - r^n)}{1 - r}$$

$$= \frac{\dfrac{1}{(1.11)^3} \left\{ 1 - \left[\dfrac{1}{(1.11)^2} \right]^{10} \right\}}{1 - \dfrac{1}{(1.11)^2}}$$

$$= \frac{\dfrac{1}{(1.11)^3} \left[1 - \dfrac{1}{(1.11)^{20}} \right]}{1 - \dfrac{1}{(1.11)^2}}$$

$$= 3.4$$

Using your calculator

Scientific calculator

Rewrite the expression as: $(1.11)^{-3}[1 - (1.11)^{-20}] \div [1 - (1.11)^{-2}]$
Then work the square bracket first:

Continue with the calculation of the numerator:

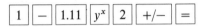

| Put numerator into memory |

Calculate the denominator:

$$\boxed{1}\ \boxed{-}\ \boxed{1.11}\ \boxed{y^x}\ \boxed{2}\ \boxed{+/-}\ \boxed{=}$$

Divide by memory recall (i.e. denominator ÷ numerator), then take reciprocal:

$$\boxed{\div}\ \boxed{\text{Memory recall}}\ \boxed{=}\ \boxed{\tfrac{1}{x}}$$

Alternatively, if you are not confident about negative indices, use positive indices and take reciprocals. In this case you need to work the part being subtracted first, then make it negative and add one, i.e. $-\dfrac{1}{(1.11)^{20}} + 1$ for $1 - \dfrac{1}{(1.11)^{20}}$:

$$\boxed{1.11}\ \boxed{y^x}\ \boxed{20}\ \boxed{=}\ \boxed{\tfrac{1}{x}}\ \boxed{+/-}\ \boxed{+}\ \boxed{1}\ \boxed{=}\ \boxed{\text{STO}}$$

Calculate $\dfrac{1}{(1.11)^3}$ and multiply by what you just stored:

$$\boxed{1.11}\ \boxed{y^x}\ \boxed{3}\ \boxed{=}\ \boxed{\tfrac{1}{x}}\ \boxed{\times}\ \boxed{\text{RCL}}\ \boxed{=}$$

| Store numerator in memory |

Calculate the denominator:

$$\boxed{1.11}\ \boxed{y^x}\ \boxed{2}\ \boxed{=}\ \boxed{\tfrac{1}{x}}\ \boxed{+/-}\ \boxed{+}\ \boxed{1}\ \boxed{=}$$

Then divide by memory recall and take the reciprocal:

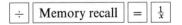

Hewlett-Packard

Two methods are shown below. The first works from left to right, numerator to denominator:

Numerator:

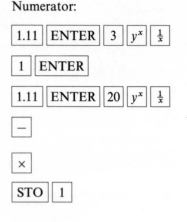

1.11 ENTER 3 y^x $\frac{1}{x}$	$\dfrac{1}{(1.11)^3}$
1 ENTER	enter 1
1.11 ENTER 20 y^x $\frac{1}{x}$	$\dfrac{1}{(1.11)^{20}}$
−	Subtract previous two terms
×	Multiply by earlier term
STO 1	Store numerator in memory

Denominator:

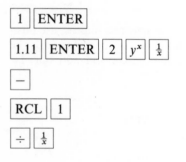

1 ENTER	enter 1
1.11 ENTER 2 y^x $\frac{1}{x}$	$\dfrac{1}{(1.11)^2}$
−	Subtract
RCL 1	Recall the numerator
÷ $\frac{1}{x}$	Divide denominator by numerator, then take reciprocal to make the division the right way round

The second method calculates the denominator first:

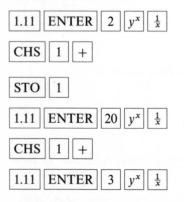

1.11 ENTER 2 y^x $\frac{1}{x}$	$\dfrac{1}{(1.11)^2}$
CHS 1 +	Make negative and add to one, i.e. subtract from 1
STO 1	Store the denominator
1.11 ENTER 20 y^x $\frac{1}{x}$	$\dfrac{1}{(1.11)^{20}}$
CHS 1 +	Subtract from 1
1.11 ENTER 3 y^x $\frac{1}{x}$	$\dfrac{1}{(1.11)^3}$

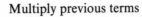

| | Multiply previous terms |

$\boxed{\text{RCL}}\ \boxed{1}\ \boxed{\div}$ Recall the denominator and divide by it

Example 3

A wealthy retired doctor wishes to establish a trust fund to provide a biennial annuity of $30,000. The first payment occurs after 3 years. Six payments of $30,000 will occur. Interest is 10.5% per annum compound. What lump sum should the doctor pay to establish the fund?

Solution:

The cash flows are:

Year	0	1	2	3	4	5	6	7	8	9	10	11	12	13
Cash flow (000's)				30		30		30		30		30		30

The Present Value (in 000's) $= \dfrac{30}{(1+i)^3} + \dfrac{30}{(1+i)^5} + \dfrac{30}{(1+i)^7} + \cdots \dfrac{30}{(1+i)^{13}}$

$$= 30V^3 + 30V^5 + \ldots + 30V^{13}$$

$$a = 30V^3$$

$$r = \frac{30V^5}{30V^3} = V^2$$

$$n = 6$$

$$S_n = \frac{a(1 - r^n)}{1 - r}$$

$$S_6 \text{ (in 000's)} = \frac{30V^3[1 - (V^2)^6]}{1 - V^2}$$

$$= \frac{30V^3(1 - V^{12})}{1 - V^2}$$

Now $V = \dfrac{1}{1+i} = \dfrac{1}{1.105}$

$$V^3 = \frac{1}{(1.105)^3}$$

$$V^{12} = \frac{1}{(1.105)^{12}}$$

$$V^2 = \frac{1}{(1.105)^2}$$

$$\text{Sum} \quad S_6 = \frac{30\left[\dfrac{1}{1.105^3}\right]\left[1 - \dfrac{1}{(1.105)^{12}}\right]}{1 - \dfrac{1}{(1.105)^2}}$$

$$= \frac{15.525409}{0.181016}$$

$$= 85.768159$$

Therefore this is the sum required in thousands.
Therefore Required Capital Outlay = \$85,768.16

AN INFINITE GEOMETRIC PROGRESSION (IGP)

The sum of n terms $= a + ar + \ldots ar^{n-1}$

$$= \frac{a(1 - r^n)}{1 - r}$$

As n tends to infinity (∞), r^n will approach zero if r is positive but less than one,   i.e. $0 < r < 1$.

$$\text{e.g.} \quad \text{if } r = \frac{1}{1.1}, \quad r^n = \frac{1}{(1.1)^n}$$

$$\text{Now if} \quad n = 40,000, \quad r^n = r^{40,000} = \frac{1}{(1.1)^{40,000}}$$

This result will be very small indeed.

$$\text{Hence} \quad \frac{1}{1.1^n} \to \text{zero} \quad \text{as } n \to \infty$$

r^n can be set at zero if $0 < r < 1$.

$$\therefore \text{Sum } S_n = \frac{a(1 - 0)}{1 - r}$$

$$= \frac{a(1)}{1 - r}$$

$$= \frac{a}{1 - r}$$

$$\boxed{\text{The sum of an IGP} = \frac{a}{1 - r}; \quad 0 < r < 1}$$

Example 4

A wealthy woman wishes to establish a leukaemia research grant of $250,000, payable triennially (every three years) in perpetuity. The first payment will occur two (2) years from now. Interest on the fund is assumed to be reinvested at 10% per annum compound.
Find the amount needed to establish the research fund.

Solution:
The present value $= 250,000V^2 + 250,000V^5 + 250,000V^8 + \ldots$

$$a = 250,000V^2$$

$$= \frac{250,000}{(1.1)^2} = 206,611.5702$$

$$r = \frac{250,000V^5}{250,000V^2}$$

$$= V^3$$

$$= \frac{1}{(1.1)^3}$$

$$= 0.751315$$

$$\therefore 0 < r < 1$$

$$\therefore \text{Sum} = \frac{a}{1-r}$$

$$= \frac{206,611.5702}{1 - 0.751315}$$

$$= \$830,816.38$$

Thus $830,816.38 invested now at 10% per annum compound will provide triennial payments of $250,000, starting in two years' time.

EXERCISES

1   Find the sum of the following geometric progressions from first principles and check your answer:

a) $4 + 8 + 16 + 32 = S_4$

b) $\dfrac{1}{1.1} + \dfrac{1}{(1.1)^2} + \dfrac{1}{(1.1)^3} = A_{\overline{3}|10\%}$

2   Use the formula $\dfrac{a(1 - r^n)}{1 - r} = S$ to find the sum of the following progressions.

In each case simplify the expression before using your calculator:

a) $1.05 + (1.05)^3 + (1.05)^5 + \ldots (1.05)^{19}$

b) $\dfrac{1}{(1.04)^3} + \dfrac{1}{(1.04)^4} + \dfrac{1}{(1.04)^5} + \ldots \dfrac{1}{(1.04)^{10}}$

c) $\dfrac{1}{(1.04)^3} + \dfrac{1}{(1.04)^6} + \ldots \dfrac{1}{(1.04)^{24}}$

3   Find the sum of the following infinite geometric progressions. Simplify the expressions before computing:

a) $\dfrac{1}{(1.05)} + \dfrac{1}{(1.05)^2} + \dfrac{1}{(1.05)^3} + \ldots$

b) $\dfrac{1}{(1.05)^3} + \dfrac{1}{(1.05)^6} + \dfrac{1}{(1.05)^9} + \ldots$

4   Determine the initial deposit required to establish a biennial research grant of \$20,000. The first payment commences in 2 years' time and interest on the fund is assumed to compound at 10% per annum.

5   A company is projected to have annual after-tax cash earnings of \$400,000 in perpetuity after the tenth year (first payment of \$400,000 occurs at the end of year 11). Earnings prior to year 10 are projected to be \$800,000 per annum. If the valuation rate is 10% per annum compound find the estimated value of the firm.

(Hint: Present value the future cash flows)

10

The Accumulation of an Annuity

After reading Chapter 8 (hopefully not too many times) you were able to bring a string of equal cash flows back to a common point in time.

Let us now consider a terminal valuation i.e. accumulating cash flows forward to one point in time.

A common application is simply accumulating an annuity (equal periodical amount) in an interest-bearing deposit.

> By the end of this chapter you will be able to accumulate such cash flows allowing for different payment frequencies. A fixed interest rate is assumed.

ACCUMULATION OF AN ORDINARY ANNUITY

Consider a cash flow stream of equal payments in arrear:

Year	0	1	2	3
Cash flow		$1	$1	$1

Cash is accumulated to ⟶ Valuation date

Assume compound interest of 10%.

The accumulated value of the first $1 = $(1.1)^2$
(i.e. the $1 is accumulated 2 periods from year 1 to year 3)

The accumulated value of the second $1 = $(1.1)^1$
(this $1 is accumulated 1 period from year 2 to year 3)

The accumulated value of the third $1 = 1$
(since the valuation date is year 3)

Total Accumulated Value $(AV) = 1 + (1.1)^1 + (1.1)^2$

$$= 3.31$$

i.e. by the end of year 3, there have been three payments of $1 plus 31 cents interest.

Example 1

Accumulate an annuity of $1 payable monthly in arrear (ordinary annuity) for 5 months @ 1% compound per month.

Month	0	1	2	3	4	5
Cash flow		$1	$1	$1	$1	$1

→ Valuation date

$$\text{Accumulation of first \$1} = (1.01)^4$$
$$\text{Accumulation of second \$1} = (1.01)^3$$
$$\text{Accumulation of third \$1} = (1.01)^2$$
$$\text{Accumulation of fourth \$1} = (1.01)^1$$
$$\text{Accumulation of fifth \$1} = 1$$

$$AV = 1 + (1.01)^1 + \ldots (1.01)^4$$

This is a geometric progression:

$$a = 1$$

$$r = \frac{1.01}{1} = 1.01$$

$$n = 5$$

$$\text{Sum} = \frac{a(1 - r^n)}{1 - r}$$

$$= \frac{1[1 - (1.01)^5]}{1 - 1.01}$$

$$= \frac{(1.01)^5 - 1}{1.01 - 1}$$

$$= \$5.10$$

After five months the accumulated sum is $5.10. Interest of $0.10 has accumulated in the account and $5 principal was invested in five payments of $1.

$$AV = 1 + (1.01)^1 + \ldots (1.01)^4$$

This can be symbolised by $S_{\overline{5}|1\%}$
In general terms

$$\boxed{S_{\overline{n}|i} = 1 + (1 + i)^1 + (1 + i)^2 + \ldots (1 + i)^{n-1}}$$

Example 2

Complete the following table where $i = 10\% = 0.1$:

n	$(1 + i)^n$	$S_{\overline{n}|i}$
1		
2		
3		
4		

Solution:

$$i = 0.1$$
$$1 + i = 1 + 0.1$$
$$= 1.1$$

n	$(1 + i)^n$
1	$(1.1)^1 = 1.1$
2	$(1.1)^2 = 1.21$
3	$(1.1)^3 = 1.331$
4	$(1.1)^4 = 1.4641$

Use these values to calculate the entries in the $S_{\overline{n}|i}$ column:

$$S_{\overline{1}|} = 1$$
$$S_{\overline{2}|} = 1 + (1.1) = 2.1$$
$$S_{\overline{3}|} = 1 + (1.1) + (1.1)^2$$
$$= S_{\overline{2}|} + (1.1)^2$$
$$= 2.1 + 1.21$$
$$= 3.31$$
$$S_{\overline{4}|} = 1 + (1.1) + (1.1)^2 + (1.1)^3$$
$$= S_{\overline{3}|} + (1.1)^3$$
$$= 3.31 + 1.331$$
$$= 4.641$$

The table can now be completed:

n	$(1 + i)^n$	$S_{\overline{n}|i}$
1	1.1000	1.000
2	1.2100	2.100
3	1.3310	3.310
4	1.4641	4.641

THE FORMULATION OF $S_{\overline{n}|i}$

Recall that $S_{\overline{n}|i} = 1 + (1 + i)^1 + (1 + i)^2 + \ldots (1 + i)^{n-1}$

Using the standard GP formula:

$$\text{Sum} = \frac{a(1 - r^n)}{1 - r}$$

$$a = 1$$

$$r = 1 + i$$

$$n = n$$

$$\therefore S_{\overline{n}|i} = \frac{1[1 - (1 + i)^n]}{1 - (1 + i)}$$

$$= \frac{(1 + i)^n - 1}{(1 + i) - 1} \quad \left(\text{multiplying by} \boxed{\frac{-1}{-1}} \right)$$

$$\boxed{S_{\overline{n}|i} = \frac{(1 + i)^n - 1}{i}}$$

Example 3

Find the accumulated value of \$1000 per quarter payable in arrear for 8 quarters. Assume compound interest of 3% per quarter.

Solution:

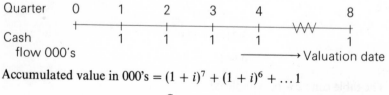

Accumulated value in 000's $= (1 + i)^7 + (1 + i)^6 + \ldots 1$

$$= S_{\overline{8}|3\%}$$

$$\text{Now} \quad S_{\overline{n}|i} = \frac{(1+i)^n - 1}{i}$$

$$\therefore S_{\overline{8}|3\%} = \frac{(1.03)^8 - 1}{0.03}$$

$$= 8.892336$$

Accumulated Value $= \$8{,}892.34$

The principal invested was \$8000 and interest of \$892.34 accumulated.

ACCUMULATION OF AN ANNUITY DUE

We now consider the situation where payments occur in advance:

Period   0   1   2   3   4

Cash flow   \$1   \$1   \$1   \$1

$\longrightarrow$ Valuation date

The accumulated value (AV) of first \$1 $= (1+i)^4$
The accumulated value of the second \$1 $= (1+i)^3$
The accumulated value of the third \$1 $= (1+i)^2$
The accumulated value of the fourth \$1 $= (1+i)^1$

$$\text{Total } AV = (1+i) + (1+i)^2 + (1+i)^3 + (1+i)^4$$

$$= (1+i)[1 + (1+i) + \dots (1+i)^3]$$

$$= (1+i)S_{\overline{4}|}$$

$$= \ddot{S}_{\overline{4}|} \quad \text{(The tremor or two dots above } S_{\overline{n}|} \text{ represents}$$
$$\text{payments in advance)}$$

$\therefore$ the general formula for n payments in advance is

$$\ddot{S}_{\overline{n}|} = (1+i)S_{\overline{n}|}$$
$$= (1+i) + (1+i)^2 + \dots (1+i)^n$$

Now try to use another approach to obtain a generalised equation involving $S_{\overline{n}|}$ and $\ddot{S}_{\overline{n}|}$.
Consider a simple model:

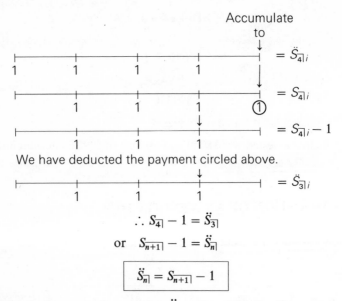

We have deducted the payment circled above.

$$\therefore S_{\overline{4|}} - 1 = \ddot{S}_{\overline{3|}}$$

$$\text{or} \quad S_{\overline{n+1|}} - 1 = \ddot{S}_{\overline{n|}}$$

$$\boxed{\ddot{S}_{\overline{n|}} = S_{\overline{n+1|}} - 1}$$

This is another way of expressing $\ddot{S}_{\overline{n|}} = (1 + i)S_{\overline{n|}}$. See if you can prove this yourself.

Example 4

An investor wishes to invest \$400 per month for 18 months in advance. Assume interest @ 1.1% per month compound.
Find: the accumulated value after 18 months, and the accumulated interest.

Solution:

$$AV = 400\ddot{S}_{\overline{18|}1.1\%}$$

$$= 400(S_{\overline{19|}} - 1)$$

$$\text{Now} \quad S_{\overline{n|}} = \frac{(1 + i)^n - 1}{i}$$

$$S_{\overline{19|}1.1\%} = \frac{(1 + 0.011)^{19} - 1}{0.011}$$

$$= 21.003583$$

$$\therefore AV = 400(21.003583 - 1)$$

$$= \$8001.43$$

The accumulated value after 18 months is \$8001.43
Principal = 400 × 18 = \$7200
Accumulated Interest = \$8001.43 − \$7200 = \$801.43

ACCUMULATION OF A DEFERRED ANNUITY

In this case the annuity payments are delayed as in the situation below:

Period	0	1	2	3	4	5
Cash flow				1	1	1

The accumulated value $= (1 + i)^2 + (1 + i)^1 + 1$

$$= S_{\overline{3}|}$$

The accumulation then, simply uses the standard $S_{\overline{n}|}$, where n is the number of payments made, not the period of accumulation.

ACCUMULATION OF AN ANNUITY WHERE FINAL PAYMENTS HAVE BEEN DELETED

Consider a cash stream where cash flows are accumulated to period 5:

	0	1	2	3	4	5
Cash flow	\$1	\$1	\$1			

The accumulated value (AV) at period 5 is:

$$(1 + i)^5 + (1 + i)^4 + (1 + i)^3 = (1 + i)^3 + (1 + i)^4 + (1 + i)^5$$
$$= (1 + i)^3[1 + (1 + i) + (1 + i)^2]$$
$$= (1 + i)^3 S_{\overline{3}|}$$

Remember: $S_{\overline{n}|} = 1 + (1 + i) + \ldots (1 + i)^{n-1}$

first term $= 1$ \qquad last term $= (1 + i)^{n-1}$

The result $(1 + i)^3 S_{\overline{3}|}$ can be seen from the number line below:

	0	1	2	3	4	5
	1	1	1			

$$AV = S_{\overline{3}|}$$

Now accumulate the lump sum $S_{\overline{3}|}$ forward to period 5 by multiplying by $(1 + i)^3$.

Another way to solve this problem is by subtracting the $S_{\overline{n}|}$ functions.

$$AV = (1 + i)^3 + (1 + i)^4 + (1 + i)^5$$

Now $1 + (1 + i) + (1 + i)^2 + (1 + i)^3 + (1 + i)^4 + (1 + i)^5 = S_{\overline{6}|i}$

$1 + (1 + i) + (1 + i)^2 \qquad\qquad\qquad\qquad = S_{\overline{3}|i}$

$$\therefore S_{\overline{6}|i} - S_{\overline{3}|i} = (1 + i)^3 + (1 + i)^4 + (1 + i)^5$$
$$= AV$$

Check subscripts: $6 - 3 = 3$ payments of $1.

EXERCISES

1 Find the accumulated value of the following cash flows at $i = 10\%$. Check your answer using a geometric progression.

	Year	0	1	2	3	4
a)	Cash flow		4	4	4	4 Valuation date

	Year	0	1	2	3	4
b)	Cash flow	4	4	4	4	Valuation Date

	Year	0	1	2	3	4
c)	Cash flow			4	4	4 Valuation date

2 Find the accumulated value of an annuity of $20,000 payable half-yearly in arrear for 10 years, at 6% per half-year compound.

3 What would be your result in exercise 2 if payments were in advance?

4 Find the accumulated value, at year 32, of $10,000 payable triennially. The first payment occurs in 2 years and the last payment occurs at the end of year 32. Assume $i = 10\%$.

5 Find the accumulated value of the cash flows in the number line below:

Year	0	1	2	3	4	5	6	7
Cash flow (000's)		40	40	40	40			Valuation date

Assume $i = 10\%$.
Use an advance and arrear function and check your answer using first principles by applying the geometric progression formula.

11

Introductory Equations of Value

An Equation of Value represents the valuation of inflows at a given point in time equated to the valuation of outflows at the *same* point in time. The valuation date may be at the outset (resulting in the use of present values) or at the application of accumulated values. In fact an intermediate period would give the same results, provided all cash flows are valued at the same point in time.

Equations of value occur continually in practice—in life assurance, leasing, banking. In fact in all financial institutions they are used to calculate premium rates, loan repayments, loans outstanding, lease repayments, terminal values on leases, life assurance, superannuation and other finance contracts. These examples indicate only a small subset of the possible occurrences of such equations.

> By the end of this chapter you will be able successfully to formulate and solve equations of value involving certain cash flows.

LOAN REPAYMENTS WHEN INSTALMENTS ARE EQUAL

Consider a 7-year personal loan of $40,000 repayable quarterly in arrear by equal instalments. The loan is subject to a compound rate of 4% per quarter. Find the quarterly loan repayment $= \$X$.

From the bank's viewpoint the inflows are the loan repayments whilst the outflow is the $40,000. The 28 equal repayments in arrear represent an annuity.

Quarter	1	2	3	28
Cash inflows	$X	$X	$X	$X
Cash outflow				
$40,000				

Valuing at outset, the present value of inflows $= XA_{\overline{28}|4\%}$

109

Remember $XV^1 + XV^2 + \dots XV^{28} = XA_{\overline{28}|4\%}$
The equation of value therefore is:

Present Value of inflows = Present Value of outflows

$$XA_{\overline{28}|4\%} = 40{,}000$$

$$X = \frac{40{,}000}{A_{\overline{28}|4\%}}$$

Now $\quad A_{\overline{n}|i} = \dfrac{1 - V^n}{i}$

$$= \frac{1 + \left(\dfrac{1}{(1+i)^n}\right)}{i}$$

So $\quad A_{\overline{28}|4\%} = \dfrac{1 - \dfrac{1}{(1.04)^{28}}}{0.04}$

$$= 16.663$$

$$\therefore X = \frac{40{,}000}{16.663}$$

$$= \$2{,}400.52$$

Thus the quarterly loan repayment = $2,400.52.

Example 1

Establish an equation of value for the previous personal loan example; however, set the valuation date at quarter number 3. Find X.

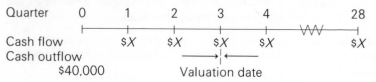

Quarter   0   1   2   3   4   28

All cash flows up to period 3 must be accumulated forward to period 3, and cash flows after period 3 must be present-valued back to period 3.

Value at period 3 of cash inflow occurring at period $\quad 1 = X(1.04)^2$
Value at period 3 of cash inflow occurring at period $\quad 2 = X(1.04)^1$
Value at period 3 of cash inflow occurring at period $\quad 3 = X$
Value at period 3 of cash inflow occurring at period $\quad 4 = XV^1$
Value at period 3 of cash inflow occurring at period $\quad 5 = XV^2$
$$\vdots$$
Value at period 3 of cash inflow occurring at period $28 = XV^{25}$

Total Value of Inflows at period 3

$$= X(1.04)^2 + X(1.04) + X + XV^1 + XV^2 + \ldots XV^{25}$$
$$= X[(1.04)^2 + (1.04) + 1] + X(V^1 + V^2 + \ldots V^{25})$$
$$= XS_{\overline{3}|4\%} + XA_{\overline{25}|4\%}$$

Recall that $S_{\overline{n}|i} = \dfrac{(1+i)^n - 1}{i}$ and $A_{\overline{n}|i} = \dfrac{1 - \dfrac{1}{(1+i)^n}}{i}$

$$S_{\overline{3}|4\%} = \frac{(1.04)^3 - 1}{0.04} \qquad\qquad A_{\overline{25}|4\%} = \frac{1 - \dfrac{1}{(1.04)^{25}}}{0.04}$$

$$= 3.1216 \qquad\qquad\qquad\qquad = 15.62208$$

Total Value $= X(3.1216) + X(15.62208)$

$$= X(18.74368)$$

Now the value at period 3 of the outflow of \$40,000 $= 40{,}000(1.04)^3$

$$= 44{,}994.56$$

$\therefore$ The equation of value is

$$(18.74368)X = 44{,}994.56$$
$$\therefore X = \$2400.53$$

LOAN REPAYMENTS WHEN INSTALMENTS ARE UNEQUAL

Since the de-regulation of the banking sector, loans (among other instruments) have been subjected to greater variation such as deferred repayments and increasing inflation-linked repayments (balloon repayments).

Assume a loan of \$40,000 has the following repayments over 28 quarters:

Quarter	0	1	2	3	4	5	6		28
Repayment		\$2X	\$2X	\$2X	\$X	\$X	\$X	...	\$(X + 2000)
Loan	\$40,000								

If the valuation date is period 0, the present value of inflows @ 4% per quarter compound is

$$PV = 2XV^1 + 2XV^2 + 2XV^3 + XV^4 + XV^5 + \ldots (X + 2000)V^{28}$$
$$= 2XV^1 + 2XV^2 + 2XV^3 + XV^4 + XV^5 + \ldots XV^{28} + 2000V^{28}$$

$$= X[V^1 + V^2 + V^3 + V^1 + V^2 + V^3 + V^4 + \ldots V^{28}]$$
$$+ 2000V^{28}$$
$$= X[A_{\overline{3}|4\%} + A_{\overline{28}|4\%}] + 2000V^{28}$$

The present value of outflows is

$$PV = 40,000$$

The equation of value is:

$$X[A_{\overline{3}|4\%} + A_{\overline{28}|4\%}] + 2000V^{28} = 40,000$$
$$X[A_{\overline{3}|4\%} + A_{\overline{28}|4\%}] = 40,000 - 2000V^{28}$$
$$= 40,000 - \frac{2000}{(1.04)^{28}}$$
$$= 40,000 - 666.954943$$
$$= 39,333.04506$$
$$X = \frac{39,333.04506}{A_{\overline{3}|4\%} + A_{\overline{28}|4\%}}$$
$$= \frac{39,333.04506}{2.775091 + 16.663063}$$
$$\therefore X = \$2023.50$$

i.e. The repayments for periods 1, 2 and 3   = \$4047.00 (i.e. 2X)
    The repayments for periods 4 to 27 inclusive = \$2023.50
    The repayment for period 28   = \$4023.50

REPAYMENT OF A LOAN OUTSTANDING

An equation of value at the date of loan termination will facilitate the calculation of a loan outstanding.

Consider the loan in the previous example. Immediately after the fourth (4th) payment has been made, the borrower wishes to pay off his loan. What is the loan outstanding?

From the borrower's viewpoint, the cash flows are:

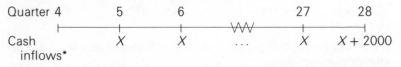

*These cash flows are inflows to the borrower as they are future savings that will no longer need to be paid.

Cash outflow $= Y =$ the loan outstanding which will be paid at period 4. Recall that the fourth payment has just been made.

The present value of inflows at period 4 is

$$PV = XV^1 + XV^2 + \ldots XV^{23} + XV^{24} + 2000V^{24} \text{ @ } 4\%$$

This is the same as the present value of the outflow, since the loan is to be repaid in full at this point.

$$\therefore Y = X(V^1 + \ldots V^{24}) + 2000V^{24}$$

Now $X = 2023.50$

$$\therefore Y = 2023.50(A_{\overline{24}|}) + 2000V^{24} \text{ @ } 4\%$$

$$= (2023.50 \times 15.246963) + (2000 \times 0.390121)$$

$$= \$31,632.47$$

SINKING FUND

A sinking fund is the accumulation of money to achieve a given terminal lump sum. A typical example is where money is required to replace old machinery. To ensure that the money is available at replacement time, instalments are accumulated in an interest-bearing deposit (sinking fund).

Consider a $100,000 machine which will be replaced in 3 years. Equal instalments are invested monthly in advance @ 4% per month compound. Determine the monthly instalment (B) that will provide a lump sum of $100,000 after 36 months.

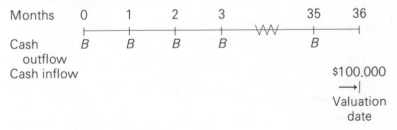

The accumulated value of outflows is

$$AV = B(1 + i)^{36} + B(1 + i)^{35} + \ldots B(1 + i)$$

$$= B[(1 + i)^1 + (1 + i)^2 + \ldots (1 + i)^{36}]$$

$$= B\ddot{S}_{\overline{36}|4\%}$$

$$= B(S_{\overline{37}|4\%} - 1)$$

The accumulated inflow = 100,000
The equation of value is therefore:

$$B(S_{\overline{37}|4\%} - 1) = 100,000$$

$$S_{\overline{n}|} = \frac{(1 + i)^n - 1}{i}$$

$$\text{So} \quad S_{\overline{37}|4\%} = \frac{(1.04)^{37} - 1}{0.04}$$

$$= 81.702246$$

$$\therefore \ B(81.702246 - 1) = 100,000$$

$$B = \$1,239.12$$

i.e. an advance payment of \$1,239.12 will be sufficient to provide \$100,000 after 36 months.

EXERCISES

1   A ten-year loan of \$70,000 is repayable by equal monthly instalments in arrear @ 1.2% per month compound. Develop an equation of value and find the monthly instalment.

2   A project involves an outlay of \$600,000 and inflows after tax (in arrear) of \$40,000 for 4 years and \$X for the following 4 years. The final residual value of the project is \$60,000. Find X by using an equation of value. Assume $i = 0.1$.

3   A home unit is purchased for \$210,000 and then rented out. Rent is estimated to be \$200 per week and outgoings are projected to be \$30 per week (in arrear). The estimated market value of the unit after 12 months is \$240,000 and legal costs on purchase and sale amount to \$1000 in each case. Stamp duty on purchase is assumed to be \$2000. Write down an equation of value at rate i compound per week.

4   You wish to go on a camel ride in 12 months. The cost of this trip is estimated to be \$3000 and it will be provided by accumulating equal monthly instalments in arrear @ $i = 0.01$. Using an equation of value find the monthly instalment.

5   A tractor valued at \$120,000 is to be replaced in 4 years by equal quarterly instalments in advance. Assuming $i = 2.5\%$ per quarter, find the quarterly instalment.

6 A female pensioner secures an annuity certain (payable whether she lives or dies) of $2000 payable monthly in arrear for 5 years. Find the capital sum required to fund the annuity. Assume $i = 1\%$ per month.
   (Hint: Use an equation of value.)

12

Multiple Interest Rates

There are many situations where a future rate of interest is assumed to be a variable rate. This may be due to the need to set more conservative interest rates with the passage of time, or to adjust for rising/falling interest rates in the future.

An example is a superannuation scheme where the earning rate on the fund is assumed to be 13% for the first year reducing each year by 1% per annum, to a minimum of 10% per annum.

There are also many floating rate instruments which have variable interest components.

> This chapter will therefore enable you to value cash flows involving variable payments and interest rates.

ACCUMULATION OF A SINGLE AMOUNT

Consider the accumulation of $100 for 3 years at 12% per annum compound and for the following two years at 10% per annum compound.

Years	0	1	2	3	4	5

Cash invested $100

Compound per annum rate ←——— 12% ———→|←——— 10% ———→|

The accumulation of $100 for 3 years @ 12% $= P(1 + i)^n$

$$= 100(1.12)^3$$

The accumulation of $1 at 10% from years 3–5 $= (1 + i)^n$

$$= (1.1)^2$$

The accumulation of $100(1.12)^3$ from years 3–5 $= 100(1.12)^3(1.1)^2$

$$= 169.996288$$

$$= \$170$$

116

Example 1

Accumulate $400 for 3 years @ $8\frac{1}{2}\%$, 2 years @ 7% and 5 years @ $6\frac{1}{2}\%$.

The accumulated value $= (400)(1.085)^3(1.07)^2(1.065)^5$

$$= \$801.43$$

Using your calculator

Scientific calculator

Hewlett-Packard

| 400 | ENTER | 1.085 | ENTER | 3 | y^x | × | 1.07 | ENTER | 2 |

| y^x | × | 1.065 | ENTER | 5 | y^x | × |

ACCUMULATION OF AN ANNUITY

Consider the following cash flows and interest rates:

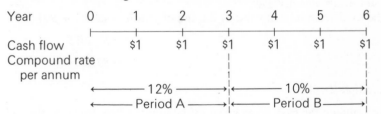

Accumulation of cash flow in period A:
The accumulation of $1 @ 12% to end of year 3 $= (1.12)^2 + (1.12)^1 + 1$

$$= S_{\overline{3}|} @ 12\%$$

$$= \frac{(1.12)^3 - 1}{0.12}$$

$$= \$3.3744$$

Year   0   1   2   3

             $1 $1 $1

                    Accumulated
                 value = \$3.3744

Now accumulate the \$3.3744 forward, from year 3, @ 10% per annum compound, to the end of year 6. At this stage ignore the cash flows in period B, and simply accumulate the single amount \$3.3744.

$$
\begin{array}{ccc}
4 & 5 & 6
\end{array}
$$

3.3744 @ 10%

$$
= 3.3744(1.1)^3
$$
$$
= 4.4913
$$

∴ The cash flows in period A accumulated to the end of year 6 = \$4.4913

Accumulation of cash flows in period B:

←Period B (10%)→

$$
\begin{array}{ccc}
4 & 5 & 6
\end{array}
$$

Cash flow   \$1   \$1   \$1

The accumulated value of the cash flows in period B

$$
= (1.1)^2 + (1.1)^1 + (1.1)^0
$$
$$
= S_{\overline{3}|} \ @ \ 10\%
$$
$$
= \$3.31
$$

Total Accumulated Value:
The total accumulated value at the end of year 6 = 4.4913 + 3.31

$$
= \$7.8013
$$
$$
= \$7.80
$$

Example 2

Accumulate the cash flows given in the number line below, to the end of year 6:

Year

$$
\begin{array}{cccccc}
1 & 2 & 3 & 4 & 5 & 6
\end{array}
$$

500   500   500   600   600   600

Compound rate
per annum   ←12%→|←   10%   →
            ←Period A→|←   Period B   →

Accumulation of cash flows in period A:
Accumulated value to end of year 2 = $500(1.12)^1 + 500 \ @ \ 12\%$

$$
= 500 S_{\overline{2}|} \ @ \ 12\%
$$
$$
= 1060
$$

Now accumulate $1060 to the end of year 6 @ $10\% = (1060)(1.1)^4$

$$= 1551.95$$

∴ The cash flows in period A accumulated to the end of year 6 = $1551.95

Accumulation of cash flows in period B:

Year	3	4	5	6
Cash flow	600 −100	600	600	600
Compound interest rate	←————————— 10% —————————→			

The accumulation of the above cash flows to end of year 6 is

$$AV = (600 - 100)(1.1)^3 + 600(1.1)^2 + 600(1.1) + 600$$

$$= 600(1.1)^3 + 600(1.1)^2 + 600(1.1) + 600 - 100(1.1)^3$$

$$= 600S_{\overline{4}|10\%} - 100(1.1)^3$$

$$= 2784.60 - 133.10$$

$$= \$2651.50$$

The Total Accumulated Value:
Combining the cash flows in periods A and B we have
1551.95 + 2651.50 = $4203.45

Example 3

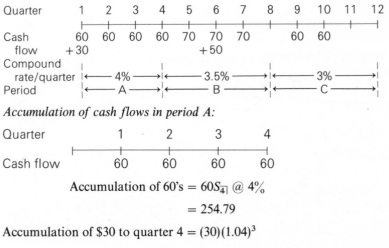

Accumulation of cash flows in period A:

Quarter	1	2	3	4
Cash flow	60	60	60	60

$$\text{Accumulation of 60's} = 60S_{\overline{4}|} @ 4\%$$

$$= 254.79$$

Accumulation of $30 to quarter 4 $= (30)(1.04)^3$

$$= 33.75$$

Total accumulation to quarter 4 = 254.79 + 33.75

$$= \$288.54$$

Now accumulate \$288.54 to quarter 8 @ 3.5%:

Quarter   5   6   7   8

$288.54 —————————————————→ $= (288.54)(1.035)^4$

$$= \$331.11$$

Now accumulate \$331.11 to quarter 12 @ 3% $= 331.11(1.03)^4$

$$= \$372.67$$

The total cash flows in period A accumulated to the end of period 12 are \$372.67.

Accumulation of cash flows in period B:

4   5   6   7   8

       70   70   70
              50

The accumulation of the 70s to period 8 is:

$$AV = 70(1.035)^3 + 70(1.035)^2 + 70(1.035)$$

$$= 70\ddot{S}_{\overline{3}|}$$

An alternative method of calculating the AV of the 70s is first to accumulate them to period 7:

$$AV = 70(1.035)^2 + 70(1.035) + 70$$

$$= 70S_{\overline{3}|}$$

Now accumulate this lump sum to period 8:

$$AV = 70S_{\overline{3}|}(1.035)^1$$

$$= 70\ddot{S}_{\overline{3}|}$$

$$= \$225.05$$

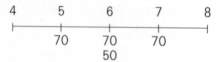

Quarter   5   6   7   8

                   70   70   70
                          ——————→
                          $= 70S_{\overline{3}|}$

                          ————————————→ $= 70S_{\overline{3}|3·5\%}(1.035)^1$
                                        $= \$225.05$

The accumulation of \$50 to period 8 @ $3.5\% = 50(1.035)^2$

$$= \$53.56$$

∴ The total AV of the cash flows in period B $= 225.05 + 53.56$

$$= \$278.61$$

The accumulation of \$278.61 to period 12 @ $3\% = (278.61)(1.03)^4$

$$= \$313.58$$

The total cash flows in period B accumulated to the end of period 12 are \$313.58.

Accumulation of cash flows in period C:

Quarter	8	9	10	11	12
Cash flow		60	60		
Compound rate			3%		

Accumulation of 60's to quarter 10 $= 60S_{\overline{2}|}$

Now accumulate $60S_{\overline{2}|}$ to quarter 12 @ $3\% = 60S_{\overline{2}|}(1.03)^2$

$$= 129.22$$

The cash flows in period C accumulated to the end of period 12 are \$129.22.

Total accumulation:

Accumulation to period 12 for cash flows in A $= 372.67$
Accumulation to period 12 for cash flows in B $= 313.58$
Accumulation to period 12 for cash flows in C $= \underline{129.22}$
$$\$815.47$$

PRESENT VALUE OF A SINGLE AMOUNT

Now that you have mastered pushing money forward in time, it will be easy for you to bring it back in time.
Consider \$100 due in 5 years at the following rates:

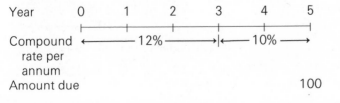

The present value of \$100 back to year 3 $= \dfrac{100}{(1.1)^2}$ or $100V^2_{10\%}$

$$= \$82.6446$$

The present value of \$82.6446 brought back to inception @ 12%

$$= \dfrac{82.6446}{(1.12)^3} \quad \text{or} \quad 82.6446V^3_{12\%}$$

$$= \$58.82$$

Check: \$58.82 invested for 3 years @ 12% and two years thereafter @ 10% $= (58.82)(1.12)^3(1.1)^2 = \$100$.

PRESENT VALUE OF AN ANNUITY

The accumulation technique applies exactly to present-valuing across differing interest bands.
The following two examples will demonstrate this.

Example 4

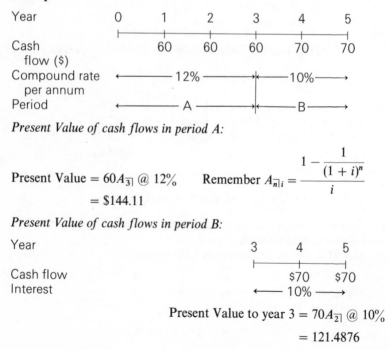

Present Value of cash flows in period A:

Present Value $= 60A_{\overline{3}|}$ @ 12%   Remember $A_{\overline{n}|i} = \dfrac{1 - \dfrac{1}{(1 + i)^n}}{i}$

$$= \$144.11$$

Present Value of cash flows in period B:

Year	3	4	5
Cash flow		\$70	\$70
Interest		←—— 10% ——→	

Present Value to year 3 $= 70A_{\overline{2}|}$ @ 10%

$$= 121.4876$$

Now Present Value $121.4876 back to year 0 @ $12\% = \dfrac{121.4876}{(1.12)^3}$

$$= 86.47$$

Total Present Value (PV):

PV of Period A flows = 144.11
PV of Period B flows =   86.47

Total *PV* $230.58

Example 5

Determine the *PV* of the following cash flows:

Half-year	0	1	2	3	4	5	6	7	8	9	10
Cash flow ($)			50	50	50			60	60	60 30	60
Half-yearly compound rate		← 6% →			←		5%			→	
Period		← A →			←		B			→	

PV of cash flows in period A:

Half-year	0	1	2	3	4
Cash flow ($)			50	50	50
Half-yearly compound rate		←	6%	→	

Present Value at Half-year $1 = 50A_{\overline{3}|}$ @ 6%

$$= \$133.6506$$

Now *PV* the $133.6506 back to inception:

$$= \dfrac{133.6506}{(1.06)^1}$$

$$= \$126.09$$

PV of cash flows in period B:

Half-year	4	5	6	7	8	9	10
Cash flow ($)				60	60	60 30	60
Half-yearly compound rate	←			5%			→

PV of 60's back to half-year 6 $= 60A_{\overline{4}|} @ 5\%$

PV of 60's back to half-year 4 $= 60A_{\overline{4}|5\%} V_{5\%}^2$

$$= \frac{60A_{\overline{4}|}}{(1.05)^2}$$

$$= \$192.98$$

PV of 60's back to inception @ 6% $= 192.98 V_{6\%}^4$

$$= \frac{192.98}{(1.06)^4}$$

$$= \$152.86$$

PV of \$30 back to half-year 4 @ 5% $= \dfrac{30}{(1.05)^5}$

$$= \$23.51$$

PV of \$23.51 back to inception @ 6% $= 23.51 V_{6\%}^4$

$$= \frac{23.51}{(1.06)^4}$$

$$= \$18.62$$

Total Present Value:
PV of cash flows in period A $= 126.09$
PV of cash flows in period B $= 152.86$
$$\underline{ 18.62}$$
$$\underline{\underline{\$297.57}}$$

EXERCISES

1 Find the accumulation of \$40,000 at 10% per annum compound for the first 10 years and 9% for the next 5 years.

2 Find the present value of \$50,000 due in 25 years. Assume interest of 12% for the first 4 years, 11% for the next 2 years, and 10% thereafter. Each of these rates is compounded per annum.

3 A loan of \$40,000 is provided over 15 years on the basis of 4% per quarter for the first 5 years and 4.3% per quarter thereafter. The loan has initial fees of \$300 due to the borrower and quarterly administration charges of 2% of the quarterly instalment in arrear. Write down an equation of value. Let X be the quarterly loan instalment in arrear.

4 A loan of $60,000 is payable by equal annual instalments in arrear over a 7-year term. If $i = 0.11$ for the first 2 years and 0.12 thereafter, find the annual instalment.

5 You have been asked to advise a prospective pensioner. She expects to collect a lump sum retirement benefit of $300,000 in 5 years. Calculate the monthly instalment payable in advance necessary to provide her with a total capital sum (including the $300,000) of $500,000. Assume $i = 1.2\%$ per month compound for the first 2 years and 1% per month compound thereafter.

6 Find the present value of the cash flows in the number line below:

Half-year	0	1	2	3	4	5	6	7	8
Cash flow		50	50	50	50	60	60	60	60
Half-yearly compound rate				10					20

$\longleftarrow$———————6%———————$\longrightarrow\!\longleftarrow$———5%———$\longrightarrow$

13

Effective Versus Nominal Rates of Interest

There will be many occasions where you will need to compare instruments which are quoted in differing interest rate terms. An example is the comparison of Commonwealth bonds with money market bills of exchange. Commonwealth bonds quote interest rates in half-yearly rests and money market bills of exchange invariably quote in terms of 90-day rollover periods. To compare each security effectively it is necessary to determine the effective annual return of each, adjusted for transaction expenses.

> By the end of this chapter you will be able to determine the effective return for any instrument, given a nominal rate of interest. Adjustments for transaction costs will be examined in the following chapter.

NOMINAL AND EFFECTIVE RATES OF INTEREST

If a security has a return of 12% per annum nominal convertible monthly, the effective return per month is 1% compound.

Similarly, an effective return of j% per period, where there are m periods in the year, will give a nominal annual return of jm% per annum convertible m times each year.

Example 1

A Commonwealth bond yields 12% per annum nominal convertible half-yearly. Find the effective half-yearly rate.

The answer is simply $\dfrac{12\%}{2} = 6\%$ per half-year

EFFECTIVE ANNUAL RATE OF RETURN

To derive the effective annual return it is necessary to invest $1 principal, rollover the interest, and then deduct the principal.

Consider 12% per annum nominal convertible monthly. This constitutes 1% per month effective.

Month 0   1   2   12

Invest $1

After 1 month the investment is worth 1.01
After 2 months the investment is worth $(1.01)^2$
After 12 months the investment is worth $(1.01)^{12}$

The interest earned after 12 months is therefore $(1.01)^{12} - 1$
(i.e. deducting the original principal of $1)

Thus the effective annual return on $1 = 0.126825

and the effective annual rate = 12.6825%

Example 2

A certain bankcard rate quotes 22.5% per annum nominal convertible monthly.

Find the effective annual cost on bankcard assuming the interest is accumulated on a compound basis (i.e. there were no monthly bankcard payments).

$$\text{The effective rate per month} = \frac{22.5\%}{12} = 1.875\%$$

Assuming a principal of $1
the amount owing after 12 months $= (1.01875)^{12}$

$= 1.249716$

Deduct Principal of $1 $= 0.249716$

The effective annual interest rate
(i.e. the cost) $= 24.9716\%$

Example 3

An Australian Savings Bond quotes a yield of 14%. Find the effective annual return.

All Australian Savings Bonds and Commonwealth Bonds are quoted on a nominal rate convertible half-yearly.

∴ The 14% is in fact a nominal rate convertible half-yearly, i.e. 7% per half-year.

The effective return $= (1.07)^2 - 1$

$$= 14.49\%$$

Example 4

A Commonwealth bond yielding 14% per annum nominal convertible half-yearly is to be compared with a bill of exchange yielding 13.9% per annum nominal convertible every 90 days. The bill is assumed to be rolled over for more than 360 days.
Which instrument is superior?

Solution:
The effective annual return on the bond = 14.49% (as in example 3)
To find the effective 90-day return on the bill of exchange, you must first calculate how many 90-day periods are in a year $\left(\dfrac{365}{90}\right)$, and then divide by this number.

i.e. the effective return every 90 days on the bill $= 13.9\% \div \dfrac{365}{90}$

$$= 13.9 \times \frac{90}{365}$$

$$= 3.427397\%$$

Invest $1

The accumulated investment of $1 after 90 days $= 1.03427397$
The accumulated investment of $1 after 360 days $= (1.03427397)^4$
The accumulated investment of $1 after 365 days $= (1.03427397)^{4.0\dot{5}}$

since $\dfrac{365}{90} = 4.0\dot{5}$

$$= 1.146451$$

Deduct $1 = 0.146451$

The effective annual rate on the bill $= 14.6451\%$

The bill is therefore superior as 14.6451 exceeds the 14.49% effective return on the bond.

CONVERSION FROM EFFECTIVE TO NOMINAL RATES

Sometimes a client is accustomed to working in nominal rates and may not understand the effective rate or how it is determined. You may be required to convert your effective rate into a nominal rate.

Consider a break-even effective annual return of 14% obtained from the short-term money market. What nominal yield convertible half-yearly will equate with the 14%, such that the dealer is indifferent between bonds and money market instruments?

Let the nominal rate % per annum convertible half-yearly = $\boxed{?}$

The effective rate % per half-year $= \dfrac{\boxed{?}}{2}$

The effective rate % per half-year as a decimal $= \dfrac{\boxed{?}}{200}$

Half-year	0	1	2
Principal	$1		
Accumulated value		$1 + \dfrac{\boxed{?}}{200}$	$\left(1 + \dfrac{\boxed{?}}{200}\right)^2$

The effective interest after one year is 14%.
But from the number line above, the effective interest is

$$\left(1 + \frac{\boxed{?}}{200}\right)^2 - 1.$$

$$\therefore \left(1 + \frac{\boxed{?}}{200}\right)^2 - 1 = 0.14$$

Add 1 to both sides:

$$\left(1 + \frac{\boxed{?}}{200}\right)^2 = 1.14$$

Take square root of both sides:

$$1 + \frac{\boxed{?}}{200} = \sqrt{1.14}$$

$$= 1.14^{0.5}$$

$$= 1.067708$$

$$\frac{\boxed{?}}{200} = 0.067708$$

$$\boxed{?} = (200)(0.067708)$$

$$= 13.541567\%$$

The nominal annual break-even bond yield is therefore 13.541567%.
A bond with the same term as the money market security will therefore be chosen if the nominal yield convertible half-yearly on the bond exceeds 13.541567%.

Example 5

A debenture is quoted at 15% per annum nominal convertible quarterly. As a director you are considering the conversion of this rate to a nominal per annum convertible monthly basis. What is the proposed rate?

Effective rate/quarter $= \dfrac{15\%}{4} = 3.75\%$

Remember to subtract the $1:

Effective return per annum $= [(1.0375)^4 - 1] \times 100\%$

$\qquad\qquad\qquad\qquad\quad = 15.8650\%$

Let $\boxed{?}$ = the nominal rate % per annum convertible monthly.

The effective return per month as a decimal $= \dfrac{\boxed{?}}{1200}$

The effective return per annum $= \left(1 + \dfrac{\boxed{?}}{1200}\right)^{12} - 1$

Now $\left(1 + \dfrac{\boxed{?}}{1200}\right)^{12} - 1 = 0.15865$

i.e. $\left(1 + \dfrac{\boxed{?}}{1200}\right)^{12} = 1.15865$

$1 + \dfrac{\boxed{?}}{1200} = 1.15865^{1/12}$

$\qquad\qquad\quad = 1.15865^{0.08\dot{3}}$

$\qquad\qquad\quad = 1.012347$

$\dfrac{\boxed{?}}{1200} = 0.012347$

$\boxed{?} = (1200)(0.012347)$

$\quad = 14.816275$

The proposed rate is therefore 14.816275% nominal per annum convertible monthly.

Using your calculator

Scientific calculator

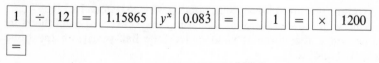

Hewlett-Packard

| 1.15865 | ENTER | 1 | ENTER | 12 | $\div$ | y^x | 1 | $-$ | 1200 | $\times$ |

EFFECTIVE ANNUAL RETURN IF INVESTMENT/ BORROWING IS LESS THAN ONE YEAR

Invariably in the money market, investments such as bills of exchange are rolled over for periods less than 365 days. It is therefore necessary to adjust the rate of return to a 365-day basis.
Consider a nominal rate of 14% convertible every 90 days.

$$\text{The effective rate per 90 days} = 14 \div \frac{365}{90}$$

$$= 14 \times \frac{90}{365}$$

$$= 3.452055\%$$

Assume this is compounded for 3 periods of 90 days.
Again, invest \$1 as principal.

$$\text{The accumulated value after 270 days} = (1.03452055)^3$$

$$= 1.107178$$

$$\therefore \text{ The effective return for 270 days} = (1.107178 - 1) \times 100$$

$$= 10.7178\%$$

As the investment is not compounded back into similar securities, a simple pro-rata 365-day adjustment is required, to give an effective annual rate.

$$\text{i.e.} \quad 10.7178 \times \frac{365}{270} = 14.488878$$

(Dividing by 270 gives the daily rate, and then multiplying by 365 gives the annual rate.)
This is slightly lower than the return achieved if the bills were rolled over for more than 365 days. In that case the effective annual rate of return is found by compounding over the 365 days thus:

$$(1.03452055)^{365/90} - 1 = 1.14756 - 1$$

$$= 14.756\%$$

EFFECTIVE RETURN MUST MATCH CASH FLOW FREQUENCY

A very simple rule when valuing cash flows is to match the effective rate per period with the frequency of the cash flows. Thus, for example, if cash is rolling over quarterly, an effective quarterly rate is required for valuation purposes.

Example 6

A cancer research fund has been established to provide 10 biennial payments of $10,000. The first payment occurs in 4 years' time. The anticipated future average earning rate on the fund is 11% per annum effective. What initial capital sum is required to establish the research grant scheme?

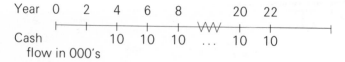

```
Year  0   2    4    6    8          20   22
      ├───┼────┼────┼────┼──WW──┼────┼───────┤
Cash           10   10   10   ...   10   10
  flow in 000's
```

This may be converted to periods of *two years* as the cash is turning over biennially:

```
Two-year
  periods  0   1    2    3    4    5    6         10   11
           ├───┼────┼────┼────┼────┼────┼──WW──┼────┤
Cash            10   10   10   10   10   ...   10   10
  flow (000's)
```

The effective rate every 2 years $= [(1.11)^2 - 1] \times 100$

$$= 23.21\%$$

The two-yearly effective rate matches the two-yearly cash flow frequency.

The number line represents an annuity due of 10 payments in advance, each of $10,000, beginning at the second two-year period. To find the capital sum required to set up the research grant scheme means finding the present value of the annuity due.

The *PV* of 10 payments in advance (in '000s) of $1 $= \ddot{A}_{\overline{10}|23.21\%}$

$\therefore$ The *PV* when payments (in '000s) are $10 $= 10\ddot{A}_{\overline{10}|23.21\%}$

This formula gives the present value at the first two-year period, when the first payment is made.

$\therefore$ To find the capital sum required now, the amount $10\ddot{A}_{\overline{10}|23.21\%}$ must be present-valued back two more periods, to 0.

i.e. $\quad PV = 10\ddot{A}_{\overline{10}|23.21\%} \times V^2$

$$= 10\ddot{A}_{\overline{10}|23.21\%} \times \frac{1}{(1+i)^2}$$

Now $\quad \ddot{A}_{\overline{10}|} = (1+i)A_{\overline{10}|}$

$$\therefore PV = \frac{10(1+i)A_{\overline{10}|}}{(1+i)^2}$$

$$= \frac{10A_{\overline{10}|}}{(1+i)}$$

$$A_{\overline{10}|23.21\%} = \frac{1 - \dfrac{1}{(1.2321)^{10}}}{0.2321}$$

$$= 3.774089$$

$$\therefore PV = \frac{10 \times 3.774089}{1.2321}$$

$$= 30.631354$$

The required capital outlay is therefore \$30,631.35.

EXERCISES

1 What is the effective rate per annum if the nominal rate per annum convertible quarterly is 12%?

2 12% per annum nominal convertible monthly = $\boxed{?}$% per annum nominal convertible quarterly.

3 16% per annum nominal convertible half-yearly = $\boxed{?}$% per annum nominal convertible monthly.

4 A quarterly fixed interest security is quoted at a rate of 12% per annum nominal convertible half-yearly. Another instrument with the same characteristics and term to maturity is quoted on the basis of 11.6% per annum nominal convertible monthly. Determine the superior instrument.

5 A triennial research grant provides \$20,000 in perpetuity. The first payment occurs in 4 years. Interest is quoted on the basis of 12% per annum nominal convertible monthly. Determine the capital sum required for the perpetuity.

6 A unit is purchased for \$250,000 and then rented out. Rent is \$200 per week (in advance) whilst levies of \$200 per quarter (in arrear) are paid. Insurance and rates of \$600 are paid half-yearly in advance. The estimated market value of the unit after 12 months is \$260,000 after legal costs and commission. Given a 12 months' horizon, write down an equation of value.

(Hint: use the effective rate to match cash flows and base your answer on rate i effective/week)

7 A retirement adviser has been asked to quote on the quarterly instalment (in advance) required to accumulate a target benefit of \$200,000 after 5 years. Additional payments of \$10,000 are paid at the end of the first and second years. Interest is assumed to be 12% per annum nominal convertible half-yearly. Find the quarterly instalment.

8 A certain cash management trust projects an earning rate of 10.7% per annum convertible daily. Find the initial investment required to provide a target benefit of \$50,000 after 5 years assuming one-half of the initial investment is withdrawn after 3 years. (Ignore leap years.)

14

Net Present Value and Net Terminal Value

Within some stage of your financial career you will be required to assess the feasibility of a project.

This can be achieved by obtaining the Net Present Value (NPV) which is

> the present value of project inflows adjusted for tax

minus

> the present value of outflows at the cost of funds appropriate to the organisation.

Alternatively, the same decision will be derived by accumulating project inflows and outflows to the end of the period. The Net Terminal Value (NTV) =

> the accumulated value of after-tax inflows

minus

> the accumulated value of the outflows.

> By the end of this Chapter you will be able effectively to compute NPV's and NTV's allowing for variable cash flows and interest rates. In a later chapter you will compare this outcome with the internal rate of return.

NPV USING ONE INTEREST RATE

Consider a project with the following cash flows:

Year	0	1	2	3	4	5
After-tax inflows (000's)		40	46	46	46	46
Outflows	120		40			

The after-tax cost of capital is projected to be 10% per annum compound.

PV of inflows $= 46A_{\overline{5}|} - 6V^1$ @ 10%   (taking a stream of 46 and deducting 6 at year 1)

$$= 174.376191 - 5.454545$$

$$= 168.92$$

PV of outflows $= 120 + \dfrac{40}{(1.1)^2}$

$$= 153.06$$

$NPV = PV$ of inflows $- PV$ of outflows

$$= 168.92 - 153.06$$

$$= 15.86$$

As the $NPV > 0$ it is feasible.

Using your calculator

Inflows: $46A_{\overline{5}|10\%} - 6V^1_{10\%} = 46\left[\dfrac{1 - \dfrac{1}{(1.1)^5}}{0.1}\right] - \dfrac{6}{1.1}$

$$= 46\left[\dfrac{1 - (1.1)^{-5}}{0.1}\right] - \dfrac{6}{1.1}$$

Scientific calculator

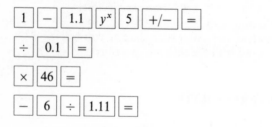

$1 - (1.1)^{-5}$

$46A_{\overline{5}|10\%}$

Remember your calculator automatically performs the division before the subtraction

These steps have calculated the PV of the inflows. Now subtract the PV of the outflows:

$\boxed{-}\ \boxed{120}\ \boxed{=}\ \boxed{-}\ \boxed{40}\ \boxed{\div}\ \boxed{1.1}\ \boxed{y^x}\ \boxed{2}\ \boxed{=}$ $-\left(120 + \dfrac{40}{(1.1)^2}\right)$

Note: for a more complicated calculation of the PV of outflows, it may be necessary to store the PV of inflows and recall it later, i.e. store inflows, calculate outflows, change sign of outflows, recall inflows and add (inflows − outflows = −outflows + inflows). This method will be illustrated in the next section.

Hewlett-Packard

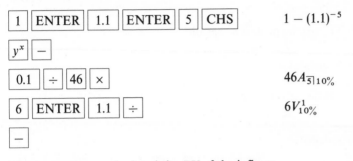

| 1 | ENTER | 1.1 | ENTER | 5 | CHS | $1 - (1.1)^{-5}$

| y^x | − |

| 0.1 | ÷ | 46 | × | $46A_{\overline{5}|10\%}$

| 6 | ENTER | 1.1 | ÷ | $6V^1_{10\%}$

| − |

These steps have calculated the *PV* of the inflows.
Now subtract the *PV* of the outflows:

| 120 | − | -120

| 40 | ENTER | 1.1 | y^x | 2 | ÷ | − | $-\dfrac{40}{(1.1)^2}$

Note: for a more complicated calculation of the *PV* of the outflows, it may be necessary to store the *PV* of inflows and recall it later, i.e. store inflows, calculate outflows, change sign of outflows, recall inflows and add (inflows − outflows = −outflows + inflows). This method will be illustrated in the next section.

NTV USING ONE INTEREST RATE

Take the preceding example.
The accumulated inflows to year 5 are:

$$AV = 46S_{\overline{5}|} - 6(1.1)^4 \ @ \ 10\%$$

   (taking a stream of 46 and deducting 6 at year 1)

$$= 280.8346 - 8.7846$$

$$= 272.05$$

The accumulated value of the outflows is:

$$AV = 120(1.1)^5 + 40(1.1)^3$$

$$= 193.2612 + 53.24$$

$$= 246.50$$

$$NTV = \text{Accumulated Inflows} - \begin{array}{l}\text{Accumulated Outflows} \\ \text{to end of project period}\end{array}$$

$$= 272.05 - 246.50$$

$$= 25.55$$

As the $NTV > 0$ the project is feasible.

Using your calculator

Inflows: $46S_{\overline{5}|10\%} - 6(1.1)^4 = 46\left[\dfrac{(1.1)^5 - 1}{0.1}\right] - 6(1.1)^4$

Scientific calculator

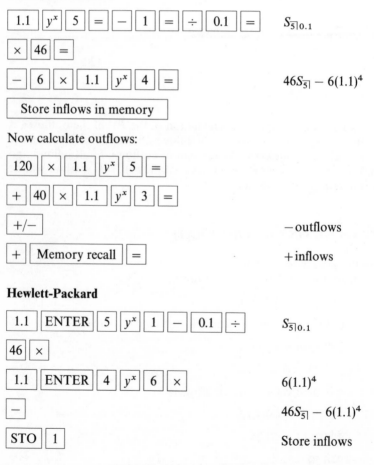

| 1.1 | y^x | 5 | = | − | 1 | = | ÷ | 0.1 | = | $S_{\overline{5}|0.1}$

| × | 46 | = |

| − | 6 | × | 1.1 | y^x | 4 | = | $46S_{\overline{5}|} - 6(1.1)^4$

| Store inflows in memory |

Now calculate outflows:

| 120 | × | 1.1 | y^x | 5 | = |

| + | 40 | × | 1.1 | y^x | 3 | = |

| +/− | − outflows

| + | Memory recall | = | + inflows

Hewlett-Packard

| 1.1 | ENTER | 5 | y^x | 1 | − | 0.1 | ÷ | $S_{\overline{5}|0.1}$

| 46 | × |

| 1.1 | ENTER | 4 | y^x | 6 | × | $6(1.1)^4$

| − | $46S_{\overline{5}|} - 6(1.1)^4$

| STO | 1 | Store inflows

Now calculate outflows:

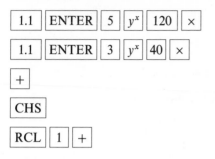

| | −outflows |
| | +inflows |

RELATIONSHIP BETWEEN *NPV* AND *NTV*

If the *NPV* is accumulated to the end of the period at the valuation rate the result will be the *NTV*.

$$\text{i.e.} \quad \boxed{NPV(1 + i)^n = NTV}$$

In the previous example, the $NPV = 15.86$

$$NTV = 25.55$$

Check: $(15.86)(1.1)^5 = 25.54$ (slight rounding error)

NPV USING MULTIPLE INTEREST RATES

If you mastered chapter 12 you will find this very easy. Essentially you must move through each interest band separately.

Taking the same cash flows as before but with two interest rates the number line is as follows. Note that outflows can be represented by a bracketed number on the inflows line:

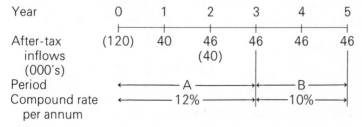

Period A cash flows:

Year	0	1	2	3
Cash inflows		46	46	46
		−6		
Interest		←——12%——→		

PV of inflows @ $12\% = (46 - 6)V^1 + 46V^2 + 46V^3$

$$= 46(V^1 + V^2 + V^3) - 6V^1$$

$$= 46A_{\overline{3}|12\%} - \frac{6}{1.12}$$

$$= 110.48 - 5.36$$

$$= 105.12$$

	0	1	2	3
Outflows	120		40	
Interest		←——12%——→		

PV of outflows $= 120 + \dfrac{40}{(1.12)^2}$

$$= 151.89$$

Period B cash flows:

Year	3	4	5
Cash inflows		46	46
Interest		←—10%—→	

PV of inflows back to period 3 @ $10\% = 46A_{\overline{2}|10\%}$

$$= 79.834711$$

Now present value the \$79.834711 back to period 0 @ 12% $= \dfrac{79.834711}{(1.12)^3}$

$$= 56.82$$

$$NPV = 56.82 + 105.12 - 151.89$$

$$= 10.05$$

As the $NPV > 0$ the project is feasible.

NTV USING MULTIPLE INTEREST RATES

Use the simple check procedure to calculate the expected *NTV* in the previous example.

Solution:

$$NTV = NPV(1.12)^3(1.1)^2$$

i.e. accumulate the *NPV* through period A @ 12% (for 3 years) then period B @ 10% (for 2 years)

$$\therefore NTV = 10.05(1.12)^3(1.1)^2$$

$$= 17.08$$

The *NTV* can, of course, also be calculated on the basis of cash flows, as follows.

Period A cash flows:

Year	0	1	2	3
Cash inflows		46	46	46
		-6		
Interest		$\longleftarrow$ 12% $\longrightarrow$		

Accumulated Value (AV) to year 3 @ 12% $= 46S_{\overline{3}|} - 6(1.12)^2$

$$= 147.696$$

Now accumulate 147.696 through to year 5 @ 10% $= (147.696)(1.1)^2$

$$= 178.71$$

Year	0	1	2	3
Cash outflow	120			
			40	
Interest		$\longleftarrow$ 12% $\longrightarrow$		

The accumulated outflow to end of period 3 $= 120(1.12)^3 + 40(1.12)^1$

$$= 213.39136$$

Now accumulate 213.39136 to period 5 @ 10% $= 213.39136(1.1)^2$

$$= 258.20$$

Period B cash flows

Year	3	4	5
Cash inflow		46	46
Interest		$\longleftarrow$ 10% $\longrightarrow$	

AV of cash inflows to year 5 = $46S_{\overline{2}|}$ @ 10%

$$= 96.6$$

Total NTV

The total NTV = 178.71 + 96.6 − 258.20

$$= 17.11 \quad \text{(slight rounding difference)}$$

EXERCISES

1 A project has the following after-tax cash flows:

Year	0	1	2	3	4	5
Outflows (in 000's)	80			20		
Inflows (in 000's)		30	30		30	30

Find (a) the net present value (NPV) @ $i = 10\%$
     (b) the net terminal value (NTV) @ $i = 10\%$.
Check your answer to (b) using your answer to (a).

2 Find the NPV and NTV for the cash flows above, assuming $i = 10\%$ for the first 2 years and 11% thereafter. Check your result.

3 A property was purchased for a tax-free superannuation fund. The purchase plus transaction costs amounted to $280,000 with rent of $900 per month (in advance), maintenance and levies of $200 per quarter (in arrear), water and sewerage rates of $350 per quarter (in arrear), and insurance of $300 per annum (in advance). The estimated net sale price (after legal costs and commission) of the property in 2 years is $350,000. If the cost of borrowing is 12% per annum nominal convertible monthly, determine the Net Present Value.

4 You borrow $100,000 to purchase a Commonwealth bond. The interest payable on the bond is $6,000 per half-year in arrear and the forecast sale price in 3 years is $106,000 (excluding the last interest payment). The borrowing rate is 12% per annum nominal convertible quarterly. The investment and borrowing are within a tax-free superannuation fund. Calculate the NPV.

5 Using the same information as in exercise 4, determine the NTV, given that the borrowing rate is 12% per annum nominal convertible quarterly in the first 2 years and 14% per annum convertible quarterly thereafter.

15

The Internal Rate of Return

An alternative measure for investment feasibility is the *internal rate of return* (*IRR*) which equates the present value of inflows with the present value of outflows (or the future value of inflows with the future value of outflows). The unknown rate of interest solving the equation is the internal rate of return. This measure can give conflicting results to the *NPV/NTV* approach and may suffer from a reinvestment and/or multiple solution problem.

> By the end of this chapter you will understand how to obtain the *IRR* and you will be able to explain the strengths and weaknesses of this measure.

USING THE EQUATION OF VALUE

Consider the stream of cash flows below:

Year	0	1	2
After-tax inflows (000's)		20	20
Outflows	36		

The equation of value as at year 0 is:

$$PV \text{ of inflows} = PV \text{ of outflows}$$

$$\text{i.e.} \quad 20A_{\overline{2}|i} = 36$$

The unknown in this equation is the *IRR* or rate i. The computed value for the *IRR* tells you the interest rate at which the initial capital is borrowed and interim payments are reinvested to give break-even point (*PV* of inflows = *PV* of outflows). If in fact the cost of capital is greater than the computed *IRR*, then the project will not be feasible. In other words, the *IRR* must be greater than the cost of funds for a project to be feasible.

143

Since this project is a 2-year project, a quadratic equation can be solved for $i = IRR$. First rewrite the equation as:

$$20V^1 + 20V^2 = 36 \qquad @ \text{ rate } i$$

This is a quadratic which can be rearranged thus:

$$20V^2 + 20V^1 - 36 = 0$$

or $\qquad\qquad 5V^2 + 5V^1 - 9 = 0$

Recall the solution to a quadratic! For $ax^2 + bx + c = 0$,

$$x = \frac{-b \pm \sqrt{b^2 - 4ac}}{2a}$$

In the equation $5V^2 + 5V^1 - 9 = 0$,

$$a = 5, \quad b = 5, \quad c = -9$$

$$V = \frac{-5 + \sqrt{5^2 - (4)(5)(-9)}}{2(5)} \quad \text{and} \quad V = \frac{-5 - \sqrt{25 + 180}}{10}$$

$$V = \frac{-5 + \sqrt{25 + 180}}{10} \qquad\qquad\qquad = \frac{-5 - \sqrt{205}}{10}$$

$$V = 0.931782 \qquad\qquad\qquad\qquad = -1.931782$$

Now $V = \dfrac{1}{1 + i}$
$\qquad\qquad\qquad\qquad \dfrac{1}{1 + i} = -1.931782$

$\therefore \dfrac{1}{1 + i} = 0.931782$
$\qquad\qquad\qquad 1 + i = -0.517657$

$\qquad\qquad\qquad\qquad\qquad\qquad i = -1.517657$

$1 + i = \dfrac{1}{0.931782}$

$\qquad = 1.073212$

$\therefore i = 0.073212$

$\qquad = 7.3212\%$

As this gives a negative rate of return, this solution can be ignored. It is not always the case that you will have only one positive solution. Where cash flows change in sign, e.g. an outlay in years 0 and 2 with an inflow in year 1, two positive solutions are possible.

Check:
The accumulation of the inflows should equal the accumulated outflow at 7.3212%.

$$\text{i.e.} \quad 20(1.073212) + 20 = 36(1.073212)^2$$

$$41.464 = 41.464$$

In this simplified model you should have observed two very important aspects of the IRR.

Firstly, there were two solutions (admittedly in this case one was a negative solution).

Secondly, in the check procedure the cash flows assumed a particular future investment rate of 7.3212% (i.e. the first $20 was accumulated at 7.3212% and the $36 was accumulated for two years at that rate).

This raises two problems with the IRR, namely:

(i) there may be multiple solutions;
(ii) the reinvestment rate assumed by the IRR may not necessarily be that which applies in practice. In this example, if the actual reinvestment rate is less than 7.3212%, the project is feasible. This is because the cost of funds would then be less than the IRR. (Check this by substituting $i = 5\%$ into $20(1 + i) + 20 = 36(1 + i)^2$. You will find that at this rate, which is less than the IRR, the AV of the inflows exceeds the AV of the outflows. Also, the NPV @ 5% is positive.)

Example 1

A project has an initial outlay of $20,000 and an after-tax return after one year of $54,000. After the second year it costs $35,000 to dismantle the project. What is (are) the internal rate(s) of return?

Year	0	1	2
Outflows (000's)	20		35
Inflows (000's)		54	

Using an equation of value at year 2:

$$20(1 + i)^2 + 35 = 54(1 + i) \quad \text{where } i = IRR$$

$$20(1 + i)^2 - 54(1 + i) + 35 = 0$$

Using the quadratic formula:

$$a = 20$$
$$b = -54$$
$$c = 35$$

$$\therefore 1 + i = \frac{-(-54) \pm \sqrt{(-54)^2 - 4(20)(35)}}{2(20)}$$

$$= \frac{54 \pm \sqrt{2916 - 2800}}{40}$$

$$= \frac{54 \pm 10.77}{40}$$

$$= \frac{64.77}{40} \quad \text{and} \quad \frac{43.23}{40}$$

$$1 + i = 1.61925 \quad \text{and} \quad 1.08075$$

$$\text{i.e.} \quad i = 61.93\% \quad \text{and} \quad 8.08\%$$

In this situation two solutions for the *IRR* exist, ranging from a low to a very high return.

In this situation therefore the *NPV* (or *NTV*) should be used, valuing the cash flows at the cost of capital associated with the project.

Consider a cost of capital of 10%.

The $NTV = AV$ of inflows $- AV$ of outflows

$$= 54(1.1) - 20(1.1)^2 - 35$$

$$= 59.4 - 24.2 - 35$$

$$= 0.2$$

The $NPV = PV$ of inflows $- PV$ of outflows

$$= \frac{54}{1.1} - 20 - \frac{35}{(1.1)^2}$$

$$= 49.09 - 20 - 28.93$$

$$= 0.16$$

In both cases the *NPV* and *NTV* exceed zero. The project is marginally feasible. In practice the qualitative factors could well swing this decision into the negative zone.

This example does reinforce the reinvestment aspect, particularly using the *NTV*. Money is accumulated at 10%. For example, the inflow of 54 is assumed to be invested at 10%. If, in practice, the total inflow is not reinvested, then it is less likely that a project will be feasible.

INTERPOLATING THE *IRR*

Example 2

An investor has an opportunity to purchase a home unit for $90,000. He would like a return of 13.5% per annum compound. He expects to be able to sell it after 5 years for $105,000 and anticipates the following cash flows (ignoring tax):

Year	0	1	2	3	4	5

Cash flows
(000's)

Rent minus expenses		4	4	4	4	5
Sale of unit						105
Purchase price	90					

Using the *NPV* approach,

$$NPV = 4A_{\overline{5}|} + 1V^5 + 105V^5 - 90 \quad @ \ 13.5\%$$
$$= 13.90 + 0.53 + 55.75 - 90$$
$$= -19.82$$

The project is therefore not feasible, as the return is less than the required rate of return. The required rate of return relates to the cost of borrowing to fund the project.

Using the *IRR* approach means calculating the *IRR*. The *IRR* can be calculated by computer or your Hewlett-Packard. If you possess neither it can be achieved by interpolation.

What is the first trial rate for the *IRR*?
A first approximation can be found as follows:

approximate *IRR* = accounting return + capital accretion return

(a) accounting return:
There is an accounting rate of return of approximately $4,000 per year for an outlay of $90,000,

$$\text{i.e.} \quad \frac{4,000}{90,000} \times 100 = 4.44\%$$

(b) capital accretion return:
There is a capital accretion of approximately (105,000 − 90,000) over the 5 years,

i.e. $\dfrac{105,000 - 90,000}{5}$ per year = $3,000   (this is an estimate and ignores the time value aspect)

The capital accretion *return per annum* for an outlay of 90,000 is:

$$\frac{3,000}{90,000} \times 100 = 3.33\%$$

(c) approximate IRR:

The total approximate annualised return $= \dfrac{\text{accounting}}{\text{return}} + \dfrac{\text{capital}}{\text{accretion}}$
return

$$= \quad 4.44 \quad + \quad 3.33$$

$$= \quad 7.77\%$$

The first approximation to the *IRR* is thus 7.77%. If we now interpolate between 7% and 8% we will obtain a more accurate approximation to the *IRR*.

First substitute 7% and 8% into the formula for *NPV*, i.e. into
$4A_{\overline{5}|} + 106V^5 - 90 = NPV$

At 7% $NPV = 1.977$

At 8% $NPV = -1.887$

Now interpolate between these values of the *NPV*, putting the *IRR* at zero (break-even *NPV*):

NPV	1.977	0	−1.887

i	7%	*IRR*	8%

$\longleftarrow$ 3.864 $\longrightarrow$

The strip lengths are:

1.977   1.887

IRR

The total length is 3.864.

Therefore the weights are $\dfrac{1.977}{3.864} = 0.512$ and $\dfrac{1.887}{3.864} = 0.488$.

Remember the weights add up to unity.

Weights: 0.512   0.488

7%   *IRR*   8%

As *IRR* is closer to 8%, the heavier (0.512) is applied to 8% and the lighter weight (0.488) is applied to 7%.

$$\text{i.e.}\quad IRR = 8(0.512) + 7(0.488)$$

$$= 7.512\%$$

This interpolated value for the *IRR* is not far off the more accurate version obtained from the Hewlett Packard, i.e. 7.505%.

Using the Hewlett-Packard

If you have a Hewlett-Packard, refer to the section on *IRR* in your manual. The short-cut method below is only recommended after you have mastered the processes explained in your manual.

The necessary keystrokes are:

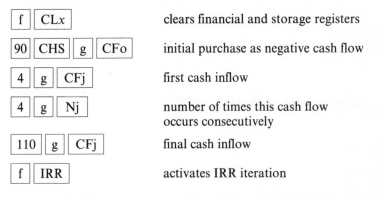

f CLx	clears financial and storage registers
90 CHS g CFo	initial purchase as negative cash flow
4 g CFj	first cash inflow
4 g Nj	number of times this cash flow occurs consecutively
110 g CFj	final cash inflow
f IRR	activates IRR iteration

The rate of return on the project is 7.505%. This assumes that future cash flows are reinvested at 7.505%. As the project return is less than the borrowing rate of 13.5%, the project is not feasible. There is in fact a negative margin of $13.500 - 7.505 = 7.995\%$.

EXCESSIVE IRR

In some projects the resulting *IRR* can be far in excess of reasonable levels of future cash investment rates.
Consider the following cash flows:

Year	0	1	2	3	4	5
Outflow (000's)	28					
After-tax annual inflows (000's)		10	10	10	10	10

Assuming a cost of capital of 10%, the $NPV = 10A_{\overline{5}|} - 28$ @ 10%

$$= 9.908$$

Alternatively, the *IRR* is 23% (as found by computer or the Hewlett-Packard).

If the *NPV* were ignored and a decision made purely on the basis of the *IRR* it is assumed that future cash is invested at 23%. Can you be confident that future rates will be at such high levels? The 10% used in the *NPV* is a much more realistic reinvestment assumption.

HORIZON RATE OF RETURN AT SPECIFIC REINVESTMENT RATE

The *IRR* result assumes that future cash flows are reinvested at that rate. This may be an unrealistic assumption if the *IRR* is high.

A more conservative approach is to adopt a lower reinvestment rate and use it to calculate a lower rate of return, called the horizon rate of return.

Consider the cash flows in the number line below:

Year	0	1	2	3	4
Cash flows	(40)	10	20	20	20

Using the Hewlett-Packard, the computed $IRR = 24.026\%$

Check: $NTV = 20S_{\overline{4}|0.24026} - 10(1.24026)^3 - 40(1.24026)^4 = 0$

i.e. obtain an *NTV* (or *NPV*) at 24.026%. The *NTV* (or *NPV*) should equal zero, since the *IRR* is the rate at which *AV* (or *PV*) of inflows = *AV* (or *PV*) of outflows.

These cash flows assume reinvestment at 24.026%. If you have a more conservative view of future interest rates, say 10% per annum compound, then the accumulated inflows become:

$$AV = 10(1.1)^3 + 20S_{\overline{3}|0.1}$$

$$= 79.51$$

Let $j =$ the horizon return per annum.

The outlay of 40 accumulated at this horizon return is equated with the inflows accumulated at 10%,

$$\text{i.e.} \quad 40(1 + j)^4 = 79.51$$

$$(1 + j)^4 = 1.98775$$

$$1 + j = 1.98775^{1/4}$$

$$= 1.98775^{0.25}$$

$$1 + j = 1.18738$$

$$j = 18.738\%$$

Thus a more conservative reinvestment rate of 10% reduces the return for the period to the more realistic value of 18.738%. This reduced return is called the gross horizon rate of return before tax.

INCREMENTAL ANALYSIS OF MUTUALLY EXCLUSIVE PROJECTS

The XYZ company wishes to choose between two mutually exclusive investments, A and B. Details are:

	Project A I	Project B II	Incremental Amount (II-I)
Cost (000's)	28	100	72
Annual after-tax cash inflows (000's)	10	30	20
Life (years)	5	5	—
NPV @ 11% (in 000's)	8.96	10.9	1.94
IRR%	23	15	12.05

Comparing the *IRRs*, project A is superior whilst using the *NPV* approach, project B is preferred. The *IRR* of 23% for project A assumes that the after-tax cash flows are reinvested at 23%. This may not be a realistic assumption. Nevertheless an 11% reinvestment rate gives a positive contribution to the investor of $8,960. Project B has an inferior *IRR* but superior *NPV*. It in fact contributes a higher level of wealth to the investor.

The conflict between A and B can be overcome by examining the incremental cash flows:

Year	0	1	2	3	4	5
Incremental outflow (000's)	72					
Inflows		20	20	20	20	20

i.e. for an additional $72,000 outlay, an annuity of 5 payments of $20,000 is received.

The *IRR* for the incremental cash flows can be determined thus:

$$20A_{\overline{5}|IRR} = 72$$

$$IRR = 12.05\%$$

The return obtained from paying an extra $72,000 is 12.05%. This exceeds the company's required rate of return (11%) to cover all of its borrowings.

∴ The incremental outlay of $72,000 is feasible.

This concept can be easily demonstrated by the following example. If you borrowed $300,000 @ 14% to purchase a motel and the interest on the loan after tax was 8.54% (i.e. approximately 14% × (1 − the tax rate, assumed to be 39%). You would need an *IRR* in excess of your cost of funds of 8.54% to make the motel a viable project. The 8.54% is in fact the required minimum rate of return. Alternatively, it can be called the cost of capital.

EXERCISES

1   A project has the following cash flows:

Year	0	1	2
Outflow	40		
Inflows		30	20

Find the *IRR*. State the assumed reinvestment rate, giving reasons for your answer.

2   A fixed interest security is purchased for $92 and pays annual interest amounts of $12 for 5 years in arrear. At the end of the term, $100 is paid (in addition to the last payment of interest). Estimate the *IRR* and thus obtain a 'first guess' for the *IRR*. Obtain the *IRR* by interpolation. Check your answer using the Hewlett-Packard, if you have one.

3   A project has the following cash flows:

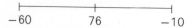

$$-60 \qquad 76 \qquad -10$$

Determine the *IRR* using the quadratic formula.

4   A parcel of shares is purchased for $55,000. During each year dividends of $2,000 are paid half-yearly in arrear. The estimated sale price after 2 years is $56,000. Assuming it is a tax-free fund, determine the *IRR*, by interpolation. Check your answer if possible using an appropriate calculator.

5   Given the following cash flows on the number line, determine the *IRR* using a Hewlett-Packard calculator. Check your result by a *NTV*.

Year	0	1	2	3
Cash flows	−60	30	30	30
(000's)		10		

What is the assumed reinvestment rate? Can this rate be maintained?

6   If cash inflows in exercise 5 are reinvested at 10%, find the annual effective rate of return, i.e. the horizon rate of return.

16

Perpetuities

Recall from Chapter 9 that the sum of a geometric progression (GP) is:

$$S_n = \frac{a(1 - r^n)}{1 - r}$$

where a = first term

$$r = \frac{T_n}{T_{n-1}} = \frac{\text{Term } n}{\text{Term } n - 1}$$

n = the number of terms

As $n \to \infty$, $S_n \to \frac{a(1 - 0)}{1 - r}$ if $0 < r < 1$

i.e. $S = \frac{a}{1 - r}$

There will be occasions when this simple formula $\frac{a}{1 - r}$ proves to be very useful in determining the cost of perpetual grants/ cash flows or when you are required to compare mutually exclusive projects with different lives.

> The objective of this chapter is therefore to enable you to solve financial problems involving perpetual cash flows.

PROJECTS WITH UNEQUAL LIVES

When you are comparing mutually exclusive investments with unequal lives it is necessary to replicate each project, such that there is a common project period e.g. a 2-year project and a 3-year project can be compared over 6 years.

Consider the two projects below.

Project A

Year	0	1	2	3

Annual after-tax
  cash inflows
  (000's)   10   10   10
Outflow (000's)   24

Project B

Year	0	1	2

Annual after-tax
  cash inflows
  (000's)   15   15
Outflow
  (000's)   25.2

If the required rate of return in each case is 10%:

$$NPV_A \text{ in (000's)} = 10A_{\overline{3}|} - 24 = 0.87$$

$$NPV_B \text{ in (000's)} = 15A_{\overline{2}|} - 25.2 = 0.83$$

The Net Terminal Value for A and B in (000's) would be:

$$NTV_A = NPV_A(1.1)^3 = 1.160$$

$$NTV_B = NPV_B(1.1)^2 = 1.004$$

If the projects were simply compared on the basis of their NPV's or NTV's for their actual lives, then project A would be chosen. However this decision ignores the fact that the NTV of the shorter project can be reinvested up to the life of the longer project. Thus in this case the NTV_B can be reinvested for a further year at 10%, in which case it would accumulate to $1.004(1.1) = 1.1044$. This figure is still below the NTV for project A, hence project A should be chosen.

Another way of comparing the projects is to replicate them over the period of lowest common life.

REPLICATION OVER LOWEST COMMON LIFE

If the projects were compared over a 6-year life, project A would be replicated twice and project B, three times.
The number lines would be as follows:

Project A

Year	0	1	2	3	4	5	6

Annual after-tax
cash inflow
(000's)   10   10   10   10   10   10
Outflow   24   24

The $NPV_A = 10A_{\overline{6}|} - 24 - 24V^3$ @ 10%

$\qquad = 1.52$

Check:

Year	0	1	2	3	4	5	6

NPV_A 0.87   0.87

NPV_A for 6 years $= 0.87 + \dfrac{0.87}{(1.1)^3}$

$\qquad\qquad\qquad = 1.52$

Project B

Year	0	1	2	3	4	5	6

Annual after-tax
cash inflows
(000's)   15   15   15   15   15   15
Outflows
(000's)   25.2   25.2   25.2

$NPV_B = 15A_{\overline{6}|} - 25.2 - \dfrac{25.2}{(1.1)^2} - \dfrac{25.2}{(1.1)^4}$

$\qquad = 65.33 - 25.2 - 20.83 - 17.21$

$\qquad = 2.09$

or

NPV_B for 6 years can be found by replicating the NPV_B for 2 years, i.e.

Year	0	1	2	3	4	5	6

NPV_B 0.83   0.83   0.83

NPV_B for 6-year life $= 0.83 + \dfrac{0.83}{(1.1)^2} + \dfrac{0.83}{(1.1)^4}$

$$= 0.83 + 0.69 + 0.57$$

$$= 2.09$$

$\therefore$ In this example, although the $NPV_A > NPV_B$ in the short term, for periods 6 years or longer the $NPV_B > NPV_A$ and project B is superior.

REPLICATION OVER HIGHEST COMMON LIFE— PERPETUITY

Mutually exclusive projects with different lives can be compared under a common life of perpetuity, i.e. replicate the NPV infinitely in both cases.

Year	0	1	2	3	4	5	6	7	8	9
NPV_A	0.87			0.87			0.87			0.87
NPV_B	0.83		0.83		0.83		0.83		0.83	

The infinite NPV can be defined as ∞NPV and written:

$$\infty NPV_A = 0.87 + \frac{0.87}{(1.1)^3} + \frac{0.87}{(1.1)^6} + \ldots$$

This is an infinite geometric progression where

$$a = 0.87$$

$$r = \frac{0.87}{(1.1)^3} \div 0.87$$

$$= \frac{1}{(1.1)^3}$$

$$n \to \infty$$

Similarly,

$$NPV_B = 0.83 + \frac{0.83}{(1.1)^2} + \frac{0.83}{(1.1)^4} + \ldots$$

where $a = 0.83$

$$r = \frac{0.83}{(1.1)^2} \div 0.83$$

$$= \frac{1}{(1.1)^2}$$

$$n \to \infty$$

Since $0 < r < 1$ the infinite GP sum of $\dfrac{a}{1-r}$ is approximately:

$$\infty NPV_A = \frac{0.87}{1 - \dfrac{1}{(1.1)^3}}$$

$$= 3.50$$

$$\infty NPV_B = \frac{0.83}{1 - \dfrac{1}{(1.1)^2}}$$

$$= 4.78$$

Since $NPV_B > NPV_A$, project B is superior.

COMPARISON USING THE EQUIVALENT ANNUAL ANNUITY (*EAA*) APPROACH

Look again at the sum of ∞NPV_A:

$$\infty NPV_A = \frac{0.87}{1 - \dfrac{1}{(1.1)^3}}$$

This can be expressed as:

$$\infty NPV_A = \frac{NPV_A}{1 - \dfrac{1}{(1+i)^n}}$$

where i = required rate of return as a decimal
n = project life

Thus in general terms:

$$\infty NPV = \frac{NPV}{1 - \dfrac{1}{(1+i)^n}}$$

$$= NPV \div \left[1 - \frac{1}{(1+i)^n} \right]$$

Multiply the denominator by $\boxed{\dfrac{i}{i}}$, i.e. unity. Remember this does not change its value, since multiplying by unity leaves a number or expression unchanged:

$$\infty NPV = NPV \div \left[1 - \frac{1}{(1+i)^n} \right] \times \boxed{\frac{i}{i}}$$

$$= NPV \div \frac{\left[1 - \frac{1}{(1+i)^n} \right] i}{i}$$

$$= NPV \div [A_{\overline{n}|i} \times i]$$

$$\boxed{\therefore \ \infty NPV = \frac{NPV}{iA_{\overline{n}|i}}}$$

Taking the previous example,

$$\infty NPV_A = \frac{NPV_A}{(0.1)A_{\overline{3}|0.1}}$$ (Check your result against $\infty NPV_A = 3.5$)

$$\infty NPV_B = \frac{NPV_B}{(0.1)A_{\overline{2}|0.1}}$$ (Check your result against $\infty NPV_B = 4.78$)

In this case, $\infty NPV_B > \infty NPV_A$

$$\therefore \ \frac{NPV_B}{0.1A_{\overline{2}|0.1}} > \frac{NPV_A}{0.1A_{\overline{3}|0.1}}$$

Multiply the inequality by 0.1 on both sides:

$$\frac{NPV_B}{A_{\overline{2}|0.1}} > \frac{NPV_A}{A_{\overline{3}|0.1}}$$

What do you notice about this result?

Quite simply that projects with unequal lives can be compared by dividing the NPV by the annuity function for the project life. This is called the Equivalent Annual Annuity (EAA) approach.

You should now also be able to see that:

$$\boxed{\infty NPV = \frac{EAA}{i}}$$

Using the EAA approach, project B is superior.

Example 1

Consider the two mutually exclusive projects below.

Project A:

Year	0	1	2

Annual cash
   inflows (000's)   24   24
Outflow (000's)   30

Project B:

Year	0	1	2	3	4

Annual cash
   inflow (000's)   14   14   14   14
Outflow (000's)   30

Using a required rate of return, determine the superior project.

Solution:
There are three different methods which can be used to determine the superior project.

Method 1: the EAA approach

$$NPV_A = 24A_{\overline{2|}} - 30 \quad \text{in (000's) @ 10\%}$$

$$= 11.653$$

$$NPV_B = 14A_{\overline{4|}} - 30 \quad \text{in (000's) @ 10\%}$$

$$= 14.378$$

The Equivalent Annual Annuities are:

$$EAA_A = \frac{NPV_A}{A_{\overline{2|}}} \qquad EAA_B = \frac{NPV_B}{A_{\overline{4|}}}$$

$$= \frac{11.653}{1.7355} \qquad = \frac{14.378}{3.1699}$$

$$= 6.714 \qquad = 4.536$$

Since $EAA_A > EAA_B$, project A is superior.

Method B: the perpetuity approach
Using an infinite geometric progression:

$$\infty NPV_A = 11.653 + \frac{11.653}{(1.1)^2} + \frac{11.653}{(1.1)^4} + \dots$$

Now use $\dfrac{a}{1-r}$ where $a = 11.653$ and $r = \dfrac{1}{(1.1)^2}$:

$$\infty NPV_A = \frac{11.653}{1 - \dfrac{1}{(1.1)^2}}$$

$$= 67.14$$

Alternatively,

$$\infty NPV_A = \frac{NPV_A}{iA_{\overline{2}|}}$$

$$= \frac{EAA}{i}$$

$$= \frac{6.714}{0.1}$$

$$= 67.14$$

In the same way,

$$\infty NPV_B = 14.378 + \frac{14.378}{(1.1)^4} + \frac{14.378}{(1.1)^8} + \ldots$$

Using $\dfrac{a}{1-r}$ where $a = 14.378$ and $r = \dfrac{1}{(1.1)^4}$

$$\infty NPV_B = \frac{14.378}{1 - \dfrac{1}{(1.1)^4}}$$

$$= 45.36$$

Check using $\dfrac{EAA}{i}$: $\dfrac{4.536}{0.1} = 45.36$

Since $\infty NPV_A > \infty NPV_B$, project A is superior.

Method 3: the NPV approach
Replicate project A once so that it too runs over 4 years:

Year	0	1	2	3	4
Cash inflows (000's)		24	24	24	24
Outflows (000's)	30		30		

$$NPV_A \text{ over 4 years} = NPV_A + \frac{NPV_A}{(1.1)^2}$$

$$= 11.653 + \frac{11.653}{(1.1)^2}$$

$$= 21.284$$

$$NPV_B \text{ over 4 years} = 14.378$$

Since $NPV_A > NPV_B$, project A is superior.

You can use any one of these three methods. Each gives the same decision. You should now be able to see clearly that the perpetuity method of $\frac{a}{1-r}$ (provided $0 < r < 1$) explains NPV and the EAA approach.

PERPETUAL GRANTS/SCHOLARSHIPS

A common perpetuity is a research scheme which pays a biennial/triennial grant in perpetuity.

Consider a fund which is expected to earn 10% per annum compound. An amount of $20,000 is paid triennially. The first payment occurs in four years' time. What initial capital sum is required to establish the fund?

Solution:

Year	0	1	2	3	4	5	6	7	8	9	10
Grant (000's)					20			20			20

The Present Value in Perpetuity $= \dfrac{20}{(1.1)^4} + \dfrac{20}{(1.1)^7} + \dfrac{20}{(1.1)^{10}} + \cdots$

$$\text{Here} \quad a = \frac{20}{(1.1)^4}$$

$$r = \frac{1}{(1.1)^3} \quad (0 < r < 1)$$

$$\therefore \frac{a}{1-r} \text{ can be used.}$$

$$PV = \frac{20}{(1.1)^4} \div \left(1 - \frac{1}{(1.1)^3}\right)$$

$$= \frac{13.660269}{0.248685} = 54.929964$$

The initial capital required = $54,929.96

Example 2

A cancer research grant is established with an initial outlay of $250,000. Grants are to occur biennially. The first payment (P) occurs in 3 years. If the fund is expected to earn 11% per annum compound, determine the biennial payment (P).

Year   0   1   2   3   4   5   6   7
            ├───┼───┼───┼───┼───┼───┼───┤
                        $P $P $P

Outflow $250,000

The equation of value can be found thus:

$$PV \text{ of inflows} = \frac{P}{(1.11)^3} + \frac{P}{(1.11)^5} + \frac{P}{(1.11)^7} + \cdots$$

$$= \frac{P}{(1.11)^3} \div \left(1 - \frac{1}{(1.11)^2}\right) \qquad a = \frac{P}{(1.11)^3}$$

$$r = \frac{1}{(1.11)^2}$$

$$= \frac{P}{(1.11)^3} \div 0.188378$$

$$= \frac{P}{(1.11)^3(0.188378)}$$

$$= \frac{P}{0.257631}$$

$$= P \times \frac{1}{0.257631}$$

$$= 3.88152P$$

$$PV \text{ of outflow} = 250,000$$

$$\therefore 250,000 = 3.88152P$$

$$P = \$64,407.75$$

EXERCISES

1 Compare the two mutually exclusive projects below:

Project A	Year	0	1	2		
	Cash flow	−80	49	49		

Project B	Year	0	1	2	3	4
	Cash flow	−82	28	28	28	28

Use two methods to confirm your result. Assume $i = 10\%$.

2 A firm is valued for acquisition by taking the present value of its annual after-tax cash inflow of $520,000 for a horizon of 10 years and present valuing subsequent after-tax cash inflows of $300,000 in perpetuity. If the valuation rate is 10% per annum compound, determine the value of the firm.

3 An arthritis research grant is established in perpetuity, providing $20,000 biennially, with the first payment occurring in 3 years' time. Interest is assumed to be 10% per annum compound for the first two years and 9% per annum compound thereafter. Find the capital sum required to establish the perpetuity.

4 The market value of an ordinary share is $5. The share pays dividends of $0.40 payable half-yearly in arrear adjusted for inflation by $2\frac{1}{2}\%$ per half-year, i.e. the first dividend $= (0.4)(1.025)$. Write down an equation of value expressing the market price equal to the present value of the dividends adjusted for growth. The present value rate (IRR) is j per half-year.

Using the infinite geometric progression find j and hence the effective rate per annum.

5 Using a geometric progression, show that the present value of a stream of P payable annually in arrear, in perpetuity, at rate i is $\dfrac{P}{i}$.

6 A cancer fund is established in perpetuity by a grant of $1 m. The first payment of $10,000 is payable in 2 years' time. Subsequent payments of $X are made quarterly in arrear in perpetuity. The interest rate is assumed to be 10% per annum nominal convertible half-yearly. Find X.

17

Inflation

You are now in a position to examine the impact of inflation on cash flows. Inflation has a compounding effect and must be considered in cases where there is an erosion of income/capital, where benefits are inflation-linked (such as index-linked bonds where the interest payments on the security are adjusted according to a price index e.g. consumer price index) or where project cash flows are affected by differing inflation rates.

> By the end of this chapter you will be able correctly and efficiently to adjust your analysis for inflation.

NET PRESENT VALUE

Assume a project with the following cash flows (not adjusted for inflation):

Year	0	1	2	3	4
After-tax net inflows (000's)		18	18	18	18
Outflow (000's)	72				

The net inflows are expected to increase by 9% per annum from the first year, and the nominal required rate of return = 10%.

The after-tax annual inflows, adjusted for inflation, become:

$$
\begin{array}{ccccc}
0 & 1 & 2 & 3 & 4 \\
& 18 & 18\,(1.09) & 18\,(1.09)^2 & 18\,(1.09)^3 \\
(72) & & & &
\end{array}
$$

$$
\text{The } NPV = \frac{18}{1.1} + \frac{(18)(1.09)}{(1.1)^2} + \frac{(18)(1.09)^2}{(1.1)^3} + \frac{(18)(1.09)^3}{(1.1)^4} - 72
$$

$$
= \frac{18}{1.09}\left[\frac{1.09}{1.1} + \frac{(1.09)^2}{(1.1)^2} + \frac{(1.09)^3}{(1.1)^3} + \frac{(1.09)^4}{(1.1)^4}\right] - 72
$$

164

Let $\dfrac{1}{1+i} = \dfrac{1.09}{1.1}$

$\therefore NPV = \dfrac{18}{1.09}\left[\dfrac{1}{1+i} + \dfrac{1}{(1+i)^2} + \dfrac{1}{(1+i)^3} + \dfrac{1}{(1+i)^4} \right] - 72$

$\qquad = \dfrac{18}{1.09} A_{\overline{4}|i} - 72$

Now $\dfrac{1}{1+i} = \dfrac{1.09}{1.1}$

$\qquad 1 + i = \dfrac{1.1}{1.09} \quad \text{(taking reciprocals)}$

$\qquad\quad i = \dfrac{1.1}{1.09} - 1$

$\qquad\quad\, = 0.009174$

$A_{\overline{4}|0.009174} = \dfrac{1 - \dfrac{1}{(1.009174)^4}}{0.009174}$

$\qquad\qquad\quad = 3.909917$

$\therefore NPV = \dfrac{18}{1.09}[3.909917] - 72$

$\qquad\quad = -7.43$

$\therefore$ Even allowing for inflows to increase with inflation, the project is not feasible (since the NPV is negative).

Example 1

Calculate the NPV for a 5-year project with after-tax annual cash flows of \$50,000. Inflation of 8% per annum will affect the cash flows as follows:

Year	0	1	2	3	4	5
Inflation-adjusted annual cash flow (000's)		$50(1.08)$	$50(1.08)^2$	$50(1.08)^3$	$50(1.08)^4$	$50(1.08)^5$

If the nominal rate of return is 10% determine the breakeven outlay for the project. Use an adjusted annuity function.

Solution:
In order to break even, PV of outflows $= PV$ of inflows.

$$\therefore \text{Outlay} = \frac{50(1.08)}{1.1} + \frac{50(1.08)^2}{(1.1)^2} + \dots \frac{50(1.08)^5}{(1.1)^5}$$

$$= 50 \left[\frac{1}{(1+i)} + \frac{1}{(1+i)^2} + \dots \frac{1}{(1+i)^5} \right]$$

$$= 50 A_{\overline{5}|i}$$

where $\quad \dfrac{1}{1+i} = \dfrac{1.08}{1.1}$

$$1 + i = \frac{1.1}{1.08}$$

$$i = \frac{1.1}{1.08} - 1$$

$$= 1.8519\%$$

$A_{\overline{5}|1.8519\%} = 4.733788$

$\therefore$ Project breakeven price $= 50 A_{\overline{5}|}$

$$= 50 \times 4.733788 \text{ (in 000's)}$$

$$= \$236,689.41$$

If the initial outlay required to set up the project is more than \$236,689 then the project is not feasible.

NOMINAL AND REAL RATES OF RETURN

The real rate of return r is *approximately* the nominal (or gross) rate of return g minus the rate of inflation j.

For example, consider a nominal rate of 13% and inflation of 9%.
The real rate intuitively and approximately is $13 - 9 = 4\%$.
The accurate result is obtained from the formula:

$$(1 + r)(1 + j) - 1 = g$$

$$(1 + r)(1 + j) = 1 + g$$

$$(1 + r) = \frac{1 + g}{1 + j}$$

$$\boxed{\therefore r = \frac{1 + g}{1 + j} - 1}$$

In the above example, therefore, the real rate of return r is:

$$r = \frac{1 + 0.13}{1 + 0.09} - 1$$

$$= \frac{1.13}{1.09} - 1$$

$$= 0.036697$$

$$= 3.6697\%$$

The error increases as interest and/or inflation increase.

Look back to the previous two calculations of NPV and see that the rate i was calculated according to this formula for r.

LUMP SUM EROSION

A significant problem for retirees is the erosion of a lump sum payable on retirement or ill-health. Often this amount is the largest encountered in one's lifetime. If it is invested in non-inflation proofing assets it can erode quickly, particularly if the lump sum is drawn upon for normal living requirements.

Consider a lump sum of $250,000 payable at age 55. The interest earned on the fund is assumed to be 12% per annum compound. Inflation is assumed to be 8% per annum compound. An amount of $20,000 is withdrawn for living at the end of the first year, $20,000(1.08) at the end of the second year and $20,000(1.08)^{n-1}$ at the end of the nth year.

The following calculations show the various cash flows involved in such a situation.

At end of year 1:

Balance including interest	$= (250,000)(1.12)$
	$= 280,000$
Deduct first withdrawal	$= \underline{20,000}$
Gross balance	$= 260,000$
Real balance (maintaining purchasing power)	$\dfrac{260,000}{1.08}$

(i.e. the gross balance reduced by one year of inflation at 8%)

$$= \$240,740.74$$

At the end of year 2:

Balance including interest $= 260,000(1.12)$
$= 291,200$

Deduct second withdrawal
    i.e. 20,000 × 1.08 = 21,600
Gross balance   = 269,600

Real balance $= \dfrac{269,600}{(1.08)^2}$

            = \$231,138.55

At the end of year 3:

Balance including interest = (269,600)(1.12)
                = 301,952
Deduct third withdrawal
    i.e. 20,000 × (1.08)² = 23,328
Gross balance   = 278,624

Real balance $= \dfrac{278,624}{(1.08)^3}$

            = \$221,180.71

The following examples show how to calculate the life of such a fund.

Example 2

Jim Smith retires on \$300,000. He can be confident of earning 9% per annum after tax. Inflation is assumed to be conservatively 8% per annum and Jim is going to withdraw \$30,000 per annum in arrear. How long will it take the fund to be zero?

Figures in (000's)

At the end of Year 1:

Balance in fund after 1 year = 300(1.09)   = 327
Withdrawal   30
∴ Balance   = 300(1.09) − 30 = 297

Real value of fund $= \dfrac{297}{1.08}$ = 275

At the end of Year 2:

Balance in fund   = (297)(1.09)   = 323.73
Withdrawal   30.00
∴ Balance   = [300(1.09) − 30]1.09 − 30 = 293.73

Real value of fund $= \dfrac{293.73}{(1.08)^2}$ = 251.83

At the end of Year 3:

Balance in fund $= \{[(300)(1.09) - 30]1.09 - 30\}1.09 - 30$

$$= [(300)(1.09)^2 - (30)(1.09) - 30]1.09 - 30$$

$$= (300)(1.09)^3 - 30(1.09)^2 - 30(1.09) - 30$$

$$= 300(1.09)^3 - 30S_{\overline{3}|9\%}$$

At end of year n, the balance of the fund is $300(1.09)^n - 30S_{\overline{n}|9\%}$
To achieve a zero balance,

$$300(1.09)^n - 30S_{\overline{n}|9\%} = 0$$

i.e. $\quad 300(1.09)^n = 30S_{\overline{n}|9\%}$

$$10(1.09)^n = S_{\overline{n}|9\%}$$

$$10 = \frac{1}{(1.09)^n} \cdot S_{\overline{n}|9\%}$$

$$= \frac{1}{(1.09)^n}\left[\frac{(1.09)^n - 1}{0.09}\right]$$

$$= \frac{\dfrac{(1.09)^n}{(1.09)^n} - \dfrac{1}{(1.09)^n}}{0.09}$$

$$= \frac{1 - \dfrac{1}{(1.09)^n}}{0.09}$$

$$= \frac{1 - V^n}{0.09}$$

$$= A_{\overline{n}|9\%}$$

[In other words, $\dfrac{1}{(1.09)^n} \cdot S_{\overline{n}|9\%} = V^n \cdot S_{\overline{n}|9\%} = A_{\overline{n}|9\%}$

Intuitively this is confirmed, as the present value of an accumulation of
$1 in arrear for n years is the same as the present value of a stream of
$1 in arrear for n years.]

This equation $10 = A_{\overline{n}|9\%}$ can be solved for n by using logs or by using
the special programmes in the Hewlett-Packard.

(1) using logs:

$$10 = \frac{1 - \dfrac{1}{(1.09)^n}}{0.09}$$

$$10 \times 0.09 = 1 - \frac{1}{(1.09)^n}$$

Add $\dfrac{1}{(1.09)^n}$ to both sides:

$$\frac{1}{(1.09)^n} + 0.9 = 1$$

Subtract 0.9 from both sides:

$$\frac{1}{(1.09)^n} = 1 - 0.9$$

$$= 0.1$$

Take the reciprocal of both sides:

$$(1.09)^n = \frac{1}{0.1}$$

$$= 10$$

$$\log(1.09)^n = \log 10 \qquad \text{(reread Chapter 5 if you need reminding about logs)}$$

$$n \log 1.09 = \log 10$$

$$n = \frac{\log 10}{\log 1.09}$$

$$= 26.72$$

$$\therefore n = 27 \text{ years}$$

(2) using the Hewlett-Packard:

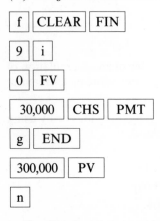

f · CLEAR · FIN	clears the financial registers
9 · i	enters 9% annual interest rate
0 · FV	enters zero balance in the future
30,000 · CHS · PMT	enters payments of $30,000 a year
g · END	sets payments at the end of each year
300,000 · PV	enters the initial $300,000
n	calculates $n = 27$

$\therefore$ It will take 27 years to have zero balance.

Example 3

Taking the data in Example 1, determine the real value of the $300,000 after 8 years. After n years the balance in the fund is $300(1.09)^n - 30S_{\overline{n}|9\%}$.
$\therefore$ After 8 years,

$$\text{balance} = 300(1.09)^8 - 30S_{\overline{8}|9\%}$$

The real value of the fund, however, has been eroded by 8 years of inflation at 8% per annum, i.e. $(1.08)^8$ where $(1.\underline{08})^{8\}=8\text{ years}}$

$= 8\%$ inflation rate

$$\therefore \text{ real value (in 000's)} = \frac{300(1.09)^8 - 30S_{\overline{8}|9\%}}{(1.08)^8}$$

$$= \frac{597.7688 - 30(11.0285)}{1.8509}$$

$$= 144.207575$$

$$= \$144,207.58$$

The value of the retiree's fund has more than halved in 8 years owing to the inflation erosion, the impact of tax, and the withdrawal of living expenses.

Example 4

Now look at Jim Smith's data again. This time assume he withdraws an amount adjusted for inflation, i.e. his first withdrawal is $30,000, his second withdrawal is $30,000(1.08)$, his third withdrawal is $30,000(1.08)^2$, and his n^{th} withdrawal is $30,000(1.08)^{n-1}$. How long does it now take for his fund to be zero?

A similar formula can be derived, but complicated by the inflation-increased withdrawals.

Working in (000's), the balance in the fund is found as follows.

At the end of year 1:

Balance in fund $= 300(1.09) - 30$

At the end of year 2:

Balance $= \underbrace{[300(1.09) - 30]1.09}_{\substack{\text{previous balance} \\ \text{increased by 9\%}}} - \underbrace{30(1.08)}_{\substack{\text{withdrawal} \\ \text{increased by 8\%}}}$

$$= 300(1.09)^2 - 30(1.09) - 30(1.08)$$

$$= 300(1.09)^2 - 30(1.09 + 1.08)$$

At the end of year 3:

$$\text{Balance} = [300(1.09)^2 - 30(1.09 + 1.08)]1.09 - 30(1.08)^2$$
$$= 300(1.09)^3 - 30(1.09)^2 - 30(1.08)(1.09) - 30(1.08)^2$$
$$= 300(1.09)^3 - 30[(1.09)^2 + (1.08)(1.09) + (1.08)^2]$$

At the end of year n:

$$\text{Balance} = 300(1.09)^n - 30[(1.09)^{n-1} + (1.09)^{n-2}(1.08)$$
$$+ (1.09)^{n-2}(1.08)^2 + \ldots (1.09)(1.08)^{n-2} + (1.08)^{n-1}]$$

Divide each term inside the square brackets by $(1.08)^{n-1}$ and multiply the square brackets by $(1.08)^{n-1}$ $\left(\text{i.e. multiply by } \boxed{\dfrac{1.08^{n-1}}{1.08^{n-1}}} \text{ which is unity} \right)$:

$$\text{Balance} = 300(1.09)^n - 30(1.08)^{n-1} \left[\frac{(1.09)^{n-1}}{(1.08)^{n-1}} + \frac{(1.09)^{n-2}}{(1.08)^{n-2}} + \ldots \frac{1.09}{1.08} + 1 \right]$$
$$= 300(1.09)^n - 30(1.08)^{n-1} S_{\overline{n}|r}$$

where $r = $ real rate of return

$$= \frac{1.09}{1.08} - 1$$

Check the value of r by looking at the GP inside the square brackets.

Instead of $1 + (1 + r) + (1 + r)^2 + \ldots (1 + r)^{n-1}$

we have $1 + \dfrac{1.09}{1.08} + \dfrac{1.09^2}{1.08^2} + \ldots \dfrac{(1.09)^{n-1}}{(1.08)^{n-1}}$

$$\therefore \frac{1.09}{1.08} = 1 + r$$

$$r = \frac{1.09}{1.08} - 1$$

$$= 0.009259$$

$$\therefore \text{Balance} = 300(1.09)^n - 30(1.08)^{n-1} S_{\overline{n}|r}$$
$$= 300(1.09)^n - 30(1.08)^{n-1} S_{\overline{n}|0.009259}$$

The value of n is found by trial and error (or computer). We know that when Jim withdraws $30,000 each year it takes 27 years for the fund to be depleted.

So try $n = 20$ in the formula above.

$n = 20$,   balance $= -\$1,149.03$ in (000's)

$n = 15$,   balance $= -\$\ \ 318.19$ in (000's)

$n = 12$,   balance $= -\$\ \ \ 39.68$ in (000's)

$n = 11$,   balance $=\ \ \ \$\ \ \ 27.77$ in (000's)

$\therefore$ When Jim withdraws an annual amount adjusted for inflation, the fund is depleted before 12 years have elapsed.

EXERCISES

1   If the nominal rate of interest is 18% per annum compound with inflation assumed to be 11% per annum compound, determine the real rate of return.

2   The nominal and inflation rates (per annum compound) are provided for 10-year fixed interest securities for three countries as follows:

	Japan	Australia	U.K.
Nominal rate % per annum	4.1	11	7.2
Inflation rate % per annum	0.9	6.2	3

Assuming that each instrument has the same security rating, determine the superior bond, based on the real rate of return.

3   A biennial perpetuity pays an inflation-linked research grant. The first payment, occurring 3 years from now, is $30,000. Future payments will be increased according to an inflation index, assumed to be 7% per annum compound. If the fund is assumed to earn 10% per annum compound, determine the capital sum required to establish the perpetuity.

4   A 5-year project has an after-tax cash inflow of $250,000 at the end of the first year. Future after-tax inflows are assumed to inflate at 6% per annum compound. The nominal desired minimum rate of return is 12% per annum compound. Find the maximum project outlay required.

5   A retiree leaves service with a lump sum of $300,000. Forty per cent is invested in shares with an assumed capital growth of 4% per annum (which is reinvested in shares) and annual dividend yield $\left(\dfrac{\text{dividend}}{\text{market price}} \times \dfrac{100}{1} \right)$ is 6%. The remaining 60% is invested in interest-bearing deposits (IBDs) earning 10% per annum compound. Withdrawals of $20,000, $20,000(1 + g), \ldots$ are assumed to occur annually in arrear ($g = 7\%$) and are taken from the IBDs. The share dividends and the interest on the IBDs are spent by the retiree.

a) Determine the balance of the fund after 3 years.

b) Try to express the balance in terms of a compound interest formula.

c) Generalise the formula for the balance of the fund after n years.

6   A 10-year loan of $100,000 is repayable by monthly instalments (in arrear) linked to an inflation factor of $\frac{1}{2}\%$ per month. The rate of interest on the loan is 12% per annum nominal convertible monthly.
Determine the first monthly instalment.

7   A widow wishes to go overseas in 5 years' time. She projects that $20,000 will be needed and decides to pay monthly instalments in advance. After each 12 months, monthly instalments for the following year will be equal, however they will be 6% higher than in the preceding year. If her investments are assumed to earn 12% per annum nominal convertible monthly, determine the first monthly instalment.

18

Taxation Effects

All of the cash flows to date have not been exposed to taxation, either on income or capital gains.

> This chapter will give you the financial mathematical methodology to adjust for tax using present or accumulated cash flows.

THE IMPACT OF DEPRECIATION

The existence of depreciation as an allowable deduction for taxation purposes will reduce the tax payable.

Consider a corporate income before tax and depreciation of $100,000. With company tax (t) at 49%,

the tax payable is $t \times 100,000 = (0.49)100,000 = \$49,000$

the after-tax income is $100,000 - 49,000 = \$51,000$

Another way of writing this is:

$$\text{after-tax income} = (100,000)(1 - t)$$

$$= (100,000)0.51$$

$$= \$51,000$$

If the company acquires additional capital equipment with straight line depreciation (D) of $10,000 per annum, the assessable income for corporate tax becomes $90,000. The tax payable is then 49% of 90,000 i.e. $44,100.

The after-tax cash flow is $100,000 - 44,100 = \$55,900$

Another way of expressing this is the after-tax income, ignoring depreciation, plus the tax remission (or tax saving) on depreciation.

i.e. After-tax cash inflow $= 100,000(1 - t) + tD$

$$= 100,000(1 - 0.49) + (0.49)(10,000)$$

175

$$= 51{,}000 + 4{,}900$$

$$= \$55{,}900$$

Example 1

A new truck worth \$300,000 has an expected life of 5 years with no salvage. The truck is depreciated on a straight line basis (i.e. \$60,000 each year) and corporate tax is 49%. The annual expected income before tax and depreciation is \$130,000. If the required cost of capital is 10% per annum compound, determine whether the project is feasible.

Income before tax and depreciation	130,000
Annual depreciation (300,000 ÷ 5)	60,000
Assessable income (130,000–60,000)	70,000
Tax payable (49% of 70,000)	34,300
After-tax cash flow (130,000–34,300)	
or (130,000)(1 − 0.49) + 0.49(60,000)	95,700

$$NPV = PV \text{ of inflows} - PV \text{ of outflows}$$

$$= 95{,}700A_{\overline{5}|10\%} - 300{,}000$$

$$= 362{,}778.29 - 300{,}000$$

$$= \$62{,}778.29$$

The project is therefore feasible.

Using your calculator

Scientific calculator

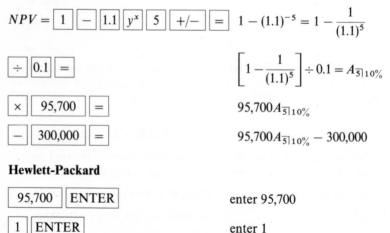

$NPV = \boxed{1}\ \boxed{-}\ \boxed{1.1}\ \boxed{y^x}\ \boxed{5}\ \boxed{+/-}\ \boxed{=}$ $\quad 1 - (1.1)^{-5} = 1 - \dfrac{1}{(1.1)^5}$

$\boxed{\div}\ \boxed{0.1}\ \boxed{=}$ $\qquad\qquad \left[1 - \dfrac{1}{(1.1)^5}\right] \div 0.1 = A_{\overline{5}|10\%}$

$\boxed{\times}\ \boxed{95{,}700}\ \boxed{=}$ $\qquad\quad 95{,}700A_{\overline{5}|10\%}$

$\boxed{-}\ \boxed{300{,}000}\ \boxed{=}$ $\qquad\quad 95{,}700A_{\overline{5}|10\%} - 300{,}000$

Hewlett-Packard

$\boxed{95{,}700}\ \boxed{ENTER}$ $\qquad$ enter 95,700

$\boxed{1}\ \boxed{ENTER}$ $\qquad$ enter 1

1.1 ENTER 5 CHS y^x	$1.1^{-5} = \dfrac{1}{(1.1)^5}$
−	subtract from 1, i.e. $1 - \dfrac{1}{(1.1)^5}$
0.1 ÷	divide by 0.1
×	multiply result by 95,700
300,000 −	subtract 300,000

Alternatively, the Hewlett-Packard can be used as follows:

f CLEAR FIN	clear financial registers
10 i	enter $i = 10\%$ p.a.
5 n	enter $n = 5$ years
95,700 PMT	enter inflows of 95,700 at
g END	end of each year
PV	calculate $PV = 95,700 A_{\overline{5}|10\%}$
300,000 −	subtract 300,000

Another way of presenting the cash flows is as follows:

(figures in '000s)

Year	0	1	2	3	4	5
Outflow	(300)					
Depreciation tax saving $\dfrac{300}{5} \times 0.49$		29.4	29.4	29.4	29.4	29.4
After-tax income $130(1 - 0.49)$		66.3	66.3	66.3	66.3	66.3
Net cash flow	(300)	95.7	95.7	95.7	95.7	95.7

$$NPV = (95.7 A_{\overline{5}|10\%} - 300)1000$$

INFLATION ADJUSTMENTS

Assume that the before tax and depreciation cash inflow is subject to 7% inflation per annum. All other details in example 1 apply. How would you adjust the cash flows for inflation?

The projected before tax and depreciation inflow (F_n) is:

$$F_1 = 130,000(1.07) \qquad \text{for year 1}$$
$$F_2 = 130,000(1.07)^2 \qquad \text{for year 2}$$
$$F_n = 130,000(1.07)^n \qquad \text{for year } n$$

The after-tax cash inflow for year n, ignoring depreciation, is M_n:

$$M_n = F_n(1 - t)$$
$$= 130,000(1.07)^n(1 - t)$$

e.g. for year 3 the after-tax cash inflow ignoring depreciation is

$$M_3 = (130,000)(1 - t)(1.07)^3$$

On account of depreciation, there is a tax remission tD of $(0.49)(60,000)$ each year.

The after-tax cash inflow for year n is

$$\boxed{M_n = F_n(1 - t)(1.07)^n + tD}$$

e.g.

$$M_1 = 130,000(1 - 0.49)(1.07) + (0.49)(60,000) = 100,341$$
$$M_2 = 130,000(1 - 0.49)(1.07)^2 + (0.49)(60,000) = 105,307$$

Similarly:

$$M_3 = 130,000(1 - 0.49)(1.07)^3 + (0.49)(60,000) = 110,620$$
$$M_4 = 130,000(1 - 0.49)(1.07)^4 + (0.49)(60,000) = 116,306$$
$$M_5 = 130,000(1 - 0.49)(1.07)^5 + (0.49)(60,000) = 122,389$$

The Net Present Value $= \dfrac{100,341}{1.1} + \dfrac{105,307}{(1.1)^2} + \dfrac{110,620}{(1.1)^3} + \dfrac{116,306}{(1.1)^4}$

$$+ \frac{122,389}{(1.1)^5} - 300,000$$

$$= 416,793 - 300,000 \quad \text{(to nearest dollar)}$$

$$= 116,793$$

Can you abbreviate the method above?

The $NPV = \dfrac{(130,000)(1 - t)(1.07)^1}{1.1} + \dfrac{(0.49)(60,000)}{1.1}$

$\qquad + \dfrac{(130,000)(1 - t)(1.07)^2}{(1.1)^2} + \dfrac{(0.49)(60,000)}{(1.1)^2}$

$\qquad + \dfrac{(130,000)(1 - t)(1.07)^3}{(1.1)^3} + \dfrac{(0.49)(60,000)}{(1.1)^3}$

$\qquad + \dfrac{(130,000)(1 - t)(1.07)^4}{(1.1)^4} + \dfrac{(0.49)(60,000)}{(1.1)^4}$

$\qquad + \dfrac{(130,000)(1 - t)(1.07)^5}{(1.1)^5} + \dfrac{(0.49)(60,000)}{(1.1)^5} - 300,000$

$\qquad = (130,000)(1 - t)\left[\dfrac{1.07}{1.1} + \dfrac{(1.07)^2}{(1.1)^2} + \cdots \dfrac{(1.07)^5}{(1.1)^5}\right]$

$\qquad\quad + (0.49)(60,000)\left[\dfrac{1}{1.1} + \dfrac{1}{(1.1)^2} + \cdots \dfrac{1}{(1.1)^5}\right] - 300,000$

Let $\dfrac{1}{1 + k} = \dfrac{1.07}{1.1}$

$\qquad NPV = (130,000)(1 - t)\left[\dfrac{1}{1 + k} + \dfrac{1}{(1 + k)^2} + \cdots \dfrac{1}{(1 + k)^5}\right]$

$\qquad\quad + (0.49)(60,000)A_{\overline{5}|0.1} - 300,000$

$\qquad = (130,000)(1 - t)A_{\overline{5}|k} + (0.49)(60,000)A_{\overline{5}|0.1} - 300,000$

Recall that $\dfrac{1}{1 + k} + \dfrac{1}{(1 + k)^2} + \cdots \dfrac{1}{(1 + k)^5} = A_{\overline{5}|k}$

$$\text{and} \quad \dfrac{1}{1 + k} = \dfrac{1.07}{1.1}$$

$$\therefore 1 + k = \dfrac{1.1}{1.07}$$

$$k = \dfrac{1.1}{1.07} - 1$$

$$= 0.028037$$

$$= 2.8037\%$$

$\therefore NPV = (130,000)(0.51)A_{\overline{5}|2.8037\%} + (0.49)(60,000)A_{\overline{5}|10\%} - 300,000$

$$NPV = 305,343.93 + 111,449.13 - 300,000$$

$$= \$116,793 \quad \text{(to nearest dollar)}$$

You can see from this example that:

$$NPV = F_n(1 - t)A_{\overline{n}|k} + tDA_{\overline{n}|i} - \text{outflow}$$

where $\quad i = $ cost of capital

and $\quad k = \dfrac{1 + i}{1 + \text{inflation rate}} - 1$

Another way of presenting the cash flows is as follows:

(Figures in '000s)

Year	0	1	2	3	4	5
Outflow	(300)					
Depreciation tax saving		29.4	29.4	29.4	29.4	29.4
After-tax income inflated @ 7%		$66.3(1.07)$	$66.3(1.07)^2$	$66.3(1.07)^3$	$66.3(1.07)^4$	$66.3(1.07)^5$

$$NPV \text{ (in '000s)} = 29.4A_{\overline{5}|10\%} + 66.3\left[\frac{1.07}{1.1} + \frac{(1.07)^2}{(1.1)^2} + \ldots \frac{(1.07)^5}{(1.1)^5}\right] - 300$$

$$= 29.4A_{\overline{5}|10\%} + 66.3A_{\overline{5}|r} - 300$$

$$\text{where real rate } r = \frac{1.1}{1.07} - 1$$

$$= 29.4A_{\overline{5}|10\%} + 66.3A_{\overline{5}|2.8037\%} - 300$$

$$= 116.793$$

$$\therefore NPV = \$116,793$$

AFTER-TAX INTERNAL RATE OF RETURN

If a before-tax rate of return is $i\%$ per annum effective, the after-tax yield or cost of funds is often quoted as $i(1 - t)$. This assumes that tax remissions are *not* deferred. In practice, deferral periods of at least six months can make a considerable difference to the after-tax yield.

Consider a borrowing of $100 with an interest payment of $14 payable at the end of each year for 5 years. On maturity (after 5 years) a capital sum of $100 is payable (together with the final interest payment). Assuming tax at 49% and a tax deferment period of one year the following cash flows apply:

Year	0	1	2	3	4	5	6
Cash inflows							
Loan receipt	100						
Tax remission on interest payment			(14) (0.49) = 6.86	6.86	6.86	6.86	6.86
Cash Outflows							
Loan interest		14	14	14	14	14	
Principal						100	

Combining these cash flows and using a negative sign to indicate money paid out we have:

Year	0	1	2	3	4	5	6
Inflows	+100						
Outflows		−14	−7.14	−7.14	−7.14	−107.14	+6.86

NET $IRR = 7.6261\%$ (calculated on the Hewlett-Packard)

Intuitively the cost of funds is greater than $14(1 - t)$ as the benefit of the tax remission is deferred for 12 months. If the tax benefit applied earlier, the cost of funds would be less.

The same after-tax IRR would be obtained by taking only one year's interest and remission on the loan with the return of the principal after one year.

Year		1	2
Loan receipt	+100		
Interest payment		−14	—
Tax remission on interest		—	+6.86
Payment of principal		−100	

The equation of value at year 0 is:

$$PV \text{ of inflows} = PV \text{ of outflows}$$

$$100 + 6.86V^2 = 114V^1$$

$$6.86V^2 - 114V^1 + 100 = 0$$

Solving this quadratic for V:

$$a = 6.86$$

$$b = -114$$

$$c = 100$$

$$\therefore V = \frac{-(-114) \pm \sqrt{(-114)^2 - (4)(6.86)(100)}}{(2)(6.86)}$$

$$= \frac{114 \pm \sqrt{12{,}996 - 2{,}744}}{13.72}$$

$$= \frac{114 \pm \sqrt{10{,}252}}{13.72}$$

$$\therefore V = \frac{114 + 101.252161}{13.72} \quad \text{and} \quad V = \frac{114 - 101.252161}{13.72}$$

$$= 15.688933 \qquad\qquad\qquad = 0.929143$$

$$= \frac{1}{1+i} \qquad\qquad\qquad\quad = \frac{1}{1+i}$$

$$\therefore 1 + i = \frac{1}{15.688933} \qquad\qquad 1 + i = \frac{1}{0.929143}$$

$$= 0.063739 \qquad\qquad\qquad = 1.076261$$

$$i = 0.063739 - 1 \qquad\qquad i = 0.076261$$

$$= -0.936261 \qquad\qquad IRR = 7.6261\%$$

Ignore this negative solution

CAPITAL GAINS TAX

If an investment incurs a capital gains tax at rate b and an income tax at rate t the deferral of both tax payments should be included in any NPV or IRR calculations.

Consider an investment in a Commonwealth bond for $96 with interest payments of $6 each half-year and a return of $100 at the end of one year. Assume a tax deferral period of twelve months with income tax @ 49% and capital gains tax at 30%. The investment occurred on the 30th June.

The cash flows are:

Half-Year	0	1	2	3	4

Outflow	−96				
Interest inflow		6	6		
Return of capital			100		
Tax on interest					− (6 + 6) (0.49)
Tax on capital gain					− (100 − 96) 0.30

The internal rate of return can be found by equating the present value of inflows with outflows thus:

$$96 + \frac{(12)(0.49) + (4)(0.3)}{(1 + i)^4} = \frac{6}{(1 + i)^1} + \frac{106}{(1 + i)^2}$$

where i is the effective half-yearly after-tax yield.

$$96 + \frac{7.08}{(1 + i)^4} = \frac{6}{(1 + i)} + \frac{106}{(1 + i)^2}$$

$i = 5.020847\%$ (by interpolation, computer, or Hewlett-Packard)

The effective annual compound rate is

$$(1 + i)^2 - 1 = 1.102938 - 1$$

$$= 10.2938\%$$

or a nominal rate convertible half-yearly of $(5.02) \times 2$, i.e. 10.04%. (Reread Chapter 13 if you have forgotten this.)

Using the Hewlett-Packard

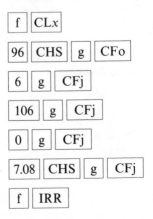

INTERNAL RATE OF RETURN WITH QUARTERLY TAX

Due to corporate and provisional tax, the tax cash flows may occur quarterly. This can create problems if all other cash is given annually or semi-annually.

Consider the previous example of an investment in a Commonwealth bond for $96 with interest payments of $6 each half-year and a return of $100 at the end of one year. Tax on income and capital gain = 39%.

$$\text{Tax on income and capital gain} = 0.39(-96 + 6 + 106)$$

$$= 6.24$$

Quarter	Assumed tax for quarter		Comment
5	125% of 6.24 =	7.80	Tax is paid in full plus next quarter's provisional tax
6	25% of 6.24 =	1.56	Next quarter's tax due
7	25% of 6.24 =	1.56	Next quarter's tax due
8	75% remission on 6.24 =	−4.68	Refund of 75% of tax overpaid
		6.24	

Summary of cash flows:

Quarter	0	1	2	3	4	5	6	7	8
Cash flow before tax	−96		6		106				
Tax						−7.80	−1.56	−1.56	4.68
Cash flow after tax	−96		6		106	−7.80	−1.56	−1.56	4.68

The internal rate of return per quarter can be found by equating the present value of inflows with the present value of outflows thus:

$$96 + \frac{7.8}{(1+j)^5} + \frac{1.56}{(1+j)^6} + \frac{1.56}{(1+j)^7} = \frac{6}{(1+j)^2} + \frac{106}{(1+j)^4} + \frac{4.68}{(1+j)^8}$$

where j = the after-tax quarterly effective rate of return
By interpolation or an iterative process,

$$j = 2.508521\%$$

The annual after-tax effective rate of return is:

$$(1.02508521)^4 - 1 = 10.418\%$$

EXERCISES

1   A 5-year project costs $1 million and may be depreciated on a straight line basis (i.e. $200,000 per year). The before-tax cash flows, ignoring depreciation, are $400,000 per annum in arrear and tax is assumed to be 49% with no deferral of tax remission. Determine the NPV assuming a required rate of return of 10% per annum compound.

2   Use the same information as in exercise 1, but inflate the before-tax cash flows by 6% per annum. Determine the NPV assuming a 10% per annum required nominal rate of return. Assume that the before-tax inflow (ignoring depreciation) is $400,000 \times 1.06$.

3   Using the information in exercise 2, determine the NPV assuming tax remissions are deferred 12 months.

4   A share is purchased for $8 and 3 years later is sold for $20. Capital gains tax @ 49% is assumed to be paid at the end of the fourth year. Dividends of 50 cents are payable each half-year in arrear and yearly tax of 49% of two dividends is paid one year after the receipt of the end of the year's dividends. Determine the after-tax effective annual IRR. Check your answer approximately, explaining any resulting differences.

5   Given the same information as in exercise 4, determine the IRR assuming tax is paid immediately you receive the dividends and capital gain.

6   A certain security pays interest of $1.50 quarterly in arrear for 10 years. This quarterly interest is taxed one year later @ 40% and the face amount payable on maturity is $100. Capital gains are taxed at 20% (assume one year deferral of tax again). Determine the purchase price to give an after-tax yield of 10% per annum effective.

19

Loan Applications

Generally at least 30% of our pay-packet is absorbed in loan repayments, particularly on our home and/or vehicle.

You now have the skill to calculate your own loan repayment, schedule your loan and determine a more favourable repayment system that could be presented to your bank, building society or credit union manager.

For accounting/tax purposes you may also be required to determine the interest and principal contained in your loan repayments for the financial year.

> The purpose of this chapter is therefore to equip you with the essential skills in loan mathematics, involving compound interest contracts.

LOANS REPAYABLE BY EQUAL ANNUAL INSTALMENTS—INTEREST CHARGED ON LOAN OUTSTANDING

The equal instalment loan repayment covers the interest due up to the date of payment plus the balance to be repaid on the principal.

Consider a 4-year loan of $10,000 repayable by equal annual instalments in arrear. The interest rate is 10% per annum compound.

Our equation of value is:

$$PA_{\overline{4}|10\%} = 10,000$$

where P is the required annual loan repayment.

$$P = \frac{10,000}{A_{\overline{4}|10\%}}$$

$$= \$3,154.708$$

If the repayment is rounded to $3154.71 the repayment schedule would be:

Year number	Principal outstanding at beginning of year	Interest due at 10%	Principal contained in payment	Principal outstanding at end of year
	A	B	C	D
1	10,000.00	1000.00	2154.71	7845.29
2	7,845.29	784.53	2370.18	5475.11
3	5,475.11	547.51	2607.20	2867.91
4	2,867.91	286.79	2867.92	−0.01*

*Slight error due to rounding of annual repayment.

Column B = Column A × the interest rate

Column C = Repayment − Column B

Column D = Column A − Column C

Column A for year n = Column D for year $n − 1$

CHECKING THE INTEREST AND PRINCIPAL WITHOUT A SCHEDULE

The loan outstanding can be found by simply taking the present value of payments yet to be made.

For example, find the loan outstanding immediately after the second payment in the preceding example.

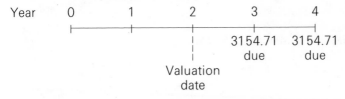

Loan outstanding = present value (at valuation date)
of payments 3 and 4

$= $ annual repayment $\times A_{\overline{2}|10\%}$

$= 3154.71 A_{\overline{2}|10\%}$

$= 5475.12$ (slight rounding difference)

The interest contained in the 3rd repayment

$= 5475.12 \times 0.1$

$$= \text{Interest rate} \times \text{Loan outstanding immediately after the second payment}$$

$$= 547.51$$

Example 1

A loan of \$40,000 @ 14% compound interest will be repaid by 20 equal annual payments. Find, without preparing a schedule:

(a) the principal outstanding immediately after the 14th payment has been made;
(b) the interest and principal contained in the 15th payment.

The annual instalment P is found thus:

$$PA_{\overline{20}|14\%} = 40,000$$

$$P = \frac{40,000}{A_{\overline{20}|14\%}}$$

$$A_{\overline{20}|14\%} = \frac{1 - \dfrac{1}{(1.14)^{20}}}{0.14}$$

$$= 6.623131$$

$$P = 6039.44$$

(a) Immediately after the 14th payment, six instalments are outstanding. The present value of these instalments is

$$PV = (6039.44)A_{\overline{6}|} \ @ \ 14\%$$

$$= \$23,485.37$$

(b) The interest contained in the 15th payment

$$= (0.14)(23,485.37)$$

$$= \$3,287.95$$

The principal content $=$ repayment $-$ interest

$$= 6039.44 - 3287.95$$

$$= \$2,751.49$$

MULTIPLE INTEREST RATE LOAN

Quite a common occurrence is to have stepped increases in the loan interest rate. A simple model can demonstrate the mechanics.

Assume a loan of $10,000 repayable by 4 equal annual instalments. Interest is 10% in the first 2 years and 11% for the final 2 years.

Year	0	1	2	3	4
Interest		←——10%——→	←——11%——→		
Repayment		P	P	P	P

The repayment (P) is found thus:

$$10{,}000 = PA_{\overline{2}|10\%} + PA_{\overline{2}|11\%} V^2_{10\%}$$

$PA_{\overline{2}|10\%}$ present values the first 2 payments at 10%.
$PA_{\overline{2}|11\%}$ brings the last 2 payments back to year 2. Multiplying by V^2 @ 10% brings $PA_{\overline{2}|11\%}$ back to inception.

$$\therefore P(1.735537) + P(1.712523)\left(\frac{1}{(1.1)^2}\right) = 10{,}000$$

$$P(1.735537 + 1.415308) = 10{,}000$$

$$P = \$3173.75$$

Let us now examine the loan schedule to check our answer.

Year number	Interest rate applied %	Principal outstanding at beginning of year	Interest due	Principal contained in payment
1	10	10,000.00	1000.00	2173.75
2	10	7,826.25	782.63	2391.12
3	11	5,435.13	597.86	2575.89
4	11	2,859.24	314.52	2859.23
5		0.01*		

*Slight rounding error.

Example 2

Independently check the loan outstanding immediately after the first payment in the preceding problem.

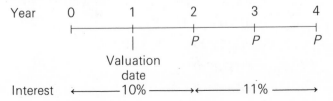

Year	0	1	2	3	4
		Valuation date	P	P	P
Interest		←——10%——→	←——11%——→		

The loan outstanding $= \dfrac{P}{1.1} + \dfrac{PA_{\overline{2}|11\%}}{1.1}$

$$= 3173.75 \left[\frac{1}{1.1} + \frac{A_{\overline{2}|11\%}}{1.1} \right]$$

$$= \$7826.25$$

LOAN WITH DEFERRED PAYMENTS

The ideal loan is to have all the payments deferred. However you will not be so fortunate. One form of loan is to have the first few payments deferred to give the borrower some initial relief.

Assume a $50,000 loan for 6 years, repayable by 70 equal monthly payments (P). The first two months of the loan will incur no loan repayments. Interest on the loan is @ 12% per annum nominal convertible monthly.

The equation of value is:

$$50,000 = PA_{\overline{70}|1\%}V^2$$

$$= 49.179996P$$

$$P = \$1016.67$$

Example 3

Determine the loan repayment for the loan details below:

Months		1	2	3	4	5	6		96
Repayment ($)		—	—	P	P	P	P	...	P
Loan	50,000					P	P	...	P

$$i = 1\%/\text{month compound.}$$

In the above case the repayments double from month 5 to month 96 inclusive. The equation of value is:

$$50,000 = \frac{PA_{\overline{94}|1\%}}{(1.01)^2} + \frac{PA_{\overline{92}|1\%}}{(1.01)^4}$$

$$= P(59.557308) + P(57.625737)$$

$$50,000 = P(117.183045)$$

$$P = \$426.68$$

Example 4

Determine the loan repayment in example 3 assuming interest of 1% per month for the first 6 months and 1.1%/month thereafter.

Month	0	1	2	3	4	5	6	7		96
Repayment	—	—	P	P	$2P$	$2P$	$2P$	...		$2P$

Interest $\longleftarrow$ 1% $\longrightarrow$ $\longleftarrow$ 1.1% $\longrightarrow$

Calculate the PV of the repayments in three steps.

(1) First look at the two repayments of P:

$$0 \quad 1 \quad 2 \quad 3 \quad 4$$
$$P \quad P$$
$$\longleftarrow 1\% \longrightarrow$$

$$PV = PA_{\overline{2}|1\%}V^2_{1\%}$$
$$= \frac{PA_{\overline{2}|1\%}}{(1.01)^2}$$

(2) Now calculate the PV of the two repayments of $2P$ @ 1%:

$$0 \quad 1 \quad 2 \quad 3 \quad 4 \quad 5 \quad 6$$
$$2P \quad 2P$$
$$\longleftarrow 1\% \longrightarrow$$

$2PA_{\overline{2}|1\%}$ brings the payments back to month 4.
Multiplying by $V^4_{1\%}$ brings the payments back to inception.

$$\therefore PV = \frac{2PA_{\overline{2}|1\%}}{(1.01)^4}$$

(3) Calculate the PV of the payments of $2P$ @ 1.1%:

$$0 \quad 1 \quad 2 \quad 3 \quad 4 \quad 5 \quad 6 \quad 7 \quad \quad 96$$
$$2P \quad \quad 2P$$
$$\longleftarrow 1\% \longrightarrow \longleftarrow 1.1\% \longrightarrow$$

$2PA_{\overline{90}|1.1\%}$ brings the payments back to month 6.
Multiplying by V^6 @ 1% brings the payments back to inception.

$$\therefore PV = \frac{2PA_{\overline{90}|1.1\%}}{(1.01)^6}$$

Thus the equation of value is:

$$50,000 = \frac{PA_{\overline{2}|1\%}}{(1.01)^2} + \frac{2PA_{\overline{2}|1\%}}{(1.01)^4} + \frac{2PA_{\overline{90}|1.1\%}}{(1.01)^6}$$

$$= \frac{P(1.970395)}{1.020100} + \frac{2P(1.970395)}{1.040604} + \frac{2P(56.946305)}{1.06152}$$

$$= P\left[\frac{1.970395}{1.0201} + \frac{2(1.970395)}{1.040604} + \frac{2(56.946305)}{1.06152}\right]$$

$$= P[113.010598]$$

$$\therefore P = \$442.44$$

INTEREST FREQUENCY NOT MATCHING PAYMENT FREQUENCY

Can you recall the key fact that the effective interest rate must match the payment frequency? e.g. if payments are quarterly, a quarterly effective rate is required.

Consider a $20,000 5-year loan with an effective annual rate of 16%. Payments are quarterly.

A quarterly effective rate (j) is needed.

$$(1 + j)^4 - 1 = 16\%$$

$$(1 + j)^4 = 1.16$$

Taking the fourth root of both sides:

$$1 + j = (1.16)^{1/4}$$

$$= 1.16^{0.25}$$

$$= 1.037802$$

$$j = 3.7802\%$$

The equation of value therefore is:

$$20,000 = PA_{\overline{20}|3.7802\%}$$

$$= P\left(\frac{1 - \dfrac{1}{(1.037802)}}{0.037802}\right)$$

$$= P(13.858714)$$

$$P = \frac{20,000}{13.858714}$$

$$= \$1443.14$$

INFLATION-LINKED LOAN REPAYMENTS

This form of loan makes sense in that payments are to some extent geared to salary increases.

Assume a $20,000 loan repayable by 5 annual instalments. The first payment is P. Thereafter P will increase by 7% compound per annum. The interest rate is 14% on the loan.

Year	0	1	2	3	4	5
Annual payment		P	$P(1.07)$	$P(1.07)^2$	$P(1.07)^3$	$P(1.07)^4$

The equation of value becomes:

$$20,000 = \frac{P}{1.14} + \frac{P(1.07)}{(1.14)^2} + \frac{P(1.07)^2}{(1.14)^3} + \frac{P(1.07)^3}{(1.14)^4} + \frac{P(1.07)^4}{(1.14)^5}$$

$$= \frac{P}{1.07}\left[\frac{1.07}{1.14} + \frac{(1.07)^2}{(1.14)^2} + \frac{(1.07)^3}{(1.14)^3} + \frac{(1.07)^4}{(1.14)^4} + \frac{(1.07)^5}{(1.14)^5}\right]$$

Let $\quad \dfrac{1}{1+i} = \dfrac{1.07}{1.14}$

$$1 + i = \frac{1.14}{1.07}$$

$$i = 6.5421\%$$

$$20,000 = \frac{P}{1.07} A_{\overline{5}|6.5421\%}$$

$$= \frac{P}{1.07}(4.150962)$$

$$\therefore P = \frac{20,000 \times 1.07}{4.150962}$$

$$= \$5155.43$$

EXERCISES

1 Determine the monthly loan repayment on a 20-year first mortgage of $50,000 with interest of 18% per annum nominal convertible monthly.

2 Given the loan in exercise 1, find the balance of the loan outstanding immediately after the fourth payment. Check your answer using a loan schedule.

3 A personal 7-year loan of $30,000 is obtained for a swimming pool. The interest rate is 18% per annum nominal convertible monthly for the first three years and 19.2% per annum nominal convertible monthly for the next four years. Find the equal monthly instalment and calculate the loan outstanding immediately after the 20th payment.

4 A five-year loan of $100,000 is granted on the basis of 15% per annum compound for the first 2 years and 16% per annum compound thereafter. Annual payments on the loan are in arrear and are equal for the first four years. However in the final year there is a payment of $20,000.
   a) Determine the value of the first loan repayment.
   b) Calculate the loan outstanding immediately after the 2nd payment and check your answer with a loan schedule.
   c) Determine the interest contained in the 3rd payment and check your answer against the loan schedule.

5 An index-linked loan is offered for an amount of $72,000. This is repaid over 10 years by quarterly payments in arrear. Payments inflate at the rate of $1\frac{1}{2}$% per quarter and interest on the loan is 14% per annum nominal convertible quarterly.
   a) Find the first quarterly instalment.
   b) Determine the loan outstanding immediately after the 15th payment has been made.

6 You have been asked to compare two loans. Loan A is quoted on the basis of 14% per annum nominal convertible monthly and loan B is quoted at 14.4% per annum nominal convertible half-yearly. Which loan is superior?

20

Fixed Interest Investments

Commonwealth bonds, semi-government securities and local government securities are forms of fixed interest investments. Trading of such securities comprises a substantial portion of portfolio management both for individual holders and for large financial institutions.

> By the end of this chapter you will be able to:
> (i) explain the advantages and disadvantages of a fixed interest security;
> (ii) solve the major pricing and interest rate problems confronting an investment manager/adviser.

COUPON SECURITIES

Fixed interest investments are called coupon securities and zero coupon securities. The coupon represents the interest paid in cash (often half-yearly). This interest is fixed over the life of the investment or may be linked to an inflation index. The various types of fixed interest instruments are discussed below.

Commonwealth bonds

Coupons on these bonds are payable half-yearly on the 15th of the month. They are highly secure, as coupons and principal are guaranteed by the Federal Government.

Consider now the retail market on the stock exchange as at 22 April 1988—look at Table 1. The bond marked *, namely a 7% July 1991 principal (face amount) has a *coupon* of 7, i.e. for each $100 principal (face amount), $3.50 is paid in interest on the 15th of July and 15th of January each year, the final coupon/interest payment occurring on 15 July 1991. The market price of this bond (per $100 face amount) is $92.07. The yield of 10.65% reflects the running yield on the coupon,

$$\text{i.e. } \frac{\text{coupon}}{\text{price}} \times \frac{100}{1} = \frac{7}{92.07} \times \frac{100}{1} = 7.60\%,$$

Table 1   Bonds on the retail market (from *Financial Review* 22 April 1988)

THE RETAIL MARKET

Smaller parcels of bonds are usually traded on the stock exchanges or are reported to the exchanges by brokers. The following rates are indicative prices for smaller parcels of stock.

Issue	Maturing Date		Market Price	Redeem Yield	Issue	Maturing Date		Market Price	Redeem Yield
12.5	May	1988	105.52	10.50	9.5	Nov	1994	92.97	12.00
9.1	July	1988	102.10	10.30	10.2	Nov	1994	97.03	11.85
9.2	July	1988	102.10	10.50	13.0	Feb	1995	106.88	12.00
12.0	July	1988	103.52	10.30	14.0	Mar	1995	110.58	12.00
13.5	Aug	1988	103.35	10.35	12.5	Apr	1995	102.52	12.00
13.0	Sept	1988	102.16	10.55	13.5	June	1995	111.26	12.10
8.8	Oct	1988	99.32	10.55	13.0	July	1995	108.16	12.00
9.0	Oct	1988	99.41	10.55	13.0	Nov	1995	111.26	11.85
12.0	Nov	1988	105.94	10.60	13.5	Mar	1996	108.06	12.15
13.0	Jan	1989	104.93	10.80	12.5	Jun	1996	106.63	12.05
9.0	Feb	1989	100.08	11.00	12.5	July	1996	105.34	12.10
12.5	Feb	1989	103.37	11.00	13.0	July	1996	108.29	12.05
11.5	Mar	1989×	101.55	11.00	9.1	Oct	1996	84.74	12.05
7.0	May	1989×	99.15	11.15	9.2	Oct	1996	85.26	12.05
9.7	May	1989×	102.78	11.15	10.2	Oct	1996	90.26	12.10
12.5	June	1989	105.70	10.20	10.5	Oct	1996	91.83	12.10
12.5	July	1989	104.75	11.20	12.0	Nov	1996	104.66	12.10
13.0	Oct	1989	102.47	11.30	12.0	Dec	1996	104.69	12.10
13.5	Oct	1989	103.01	11.40	9.0	Feb	1997	85.31	12.05
13.0	Nov	1989	108.07	11.25	12.5	Mar	1997	103.92	12.00
13.5	Jan	1990	107.32	11.40	13.5	May	1997	112.85	12.20
14.0	Mar	1990×	106.48	11.55	8.8	July	1997	84.50	12.05
5.4	May	1990×	90.98	11.75	13.5	Aug	1997	108.95	12.30
11.7	June	1990	105.46	10.95	12.5	Sept	1997	104.00	12.00
13.5	Dec	1990	109.14	11.50	12.5	Jan	1998	107.57	11.75
13.0	Jan	1991	107.32	11.30	13.0	Apr	1998	105.94	12.00
12.0	Apr	1991×	101.67	11.40	13.5	July	1998	111.34	12.15
13.0	May	1991	110.45	11.10	14.5	Sept	1998	115.09	12.15
6.7	July	1991	89.83	11.20	14.0	Mar	1999	112.39	12.15
7.0	July	1991*	92.07	10.65	14.0	Apr	1999	111.61	12.10
6.0	Oct	1991	84.92	11.40	5.4	Feb	2000	60.27	11.90
12.0	Dec	1991	105.47	11.55	13.0	Feb	2000	107.57	12.15
13.0	Feb	1992	107.95	11.15	13.0	May	2000	110.93	12.15
12.0	Mar	1992	104.28	11.00	13.0	July	2000	108.43	12.20
15.0	Mar	1992	111.09	11.85	13.0	Dec	2000	109.27	12.25
12.5	May	1992	108.42	11.55	7.0	Feb	2001	68.69	12.05
12.5	July	1992	106.40	11.55	12.0	Nov	2001	105.19	12.00
6.0	Oct	1992	82.77	11.00	6.5	July	2003	64.13	11.90
12.5	Dec	1992	107.68	11.55	5.4	May	2004	57.39	11.65
13.5	Jan	1993	109.03	11.95	6.0	July	2005	59.00	11.85
13.0	May	1993	110.87	11.60	7.0	July	2005	65.51	12.05
13.0	June	1993	109.43	11.70	5.25	July	1988	100.22	10.30
13.0	Aug	1993	106.96	11.80	5.25	July	1989	95.35	10.60
14.0	Sept	1993	109.98	11.90	5.25	Feb	1990	91.91	10.85
6.5	Oct	1993	80.00	11.55	5.25	July	2001	61.54	11.05
8.5	Oct	1993	87.27	11.75	5.25	July	2003	59.09	11.05
13.5	Jan	1994	109.01	12.15	5.25	Feb	2004	58.02	11.05
10.2	Feb	1994	94.63	11.95					
13.5	May	1994	111.30	12.20					
12.5	July	1994	105.00	12.10					
12.5	Sept	1994	103.86	11.90					
13.5	Oct	1994	107.31	11.90					
5.4	Nov	1994	75.68	11.25					

r — Tax rebate allowed
Market price is approximate.
Redemption yield is quoted as a percentage.

and the capital gain acquired on maturity, i.e. $100 - 92.07 = \$7.93$ expressed as an annual rate of capital accretion. From April 1988 to July 1991 there are approximately $3\frac{1}{4}$ years. If the capital gain 7.93 is spread over $3\frac{1}{4}$ years there is an approximate annual gain of \$2.44. If this is expressed as a percentage of the outlay \$92.07, then

$$\begin{array}{c}\text{the annual capital accretion}\\ \text{rate of return}\end{array} \approx \frac{2.44}{92.07} \times \frac{100}{1} \quad \begin{array}{l}\text{(to convert to}\\ \text{a percentage)}\end{array}$$

$$\approx 2.65\%$$

The overall yield is therefore approximately $2.65\% + 7.60\%$, i.e. 10.25%.

The actual yield of 10.65% more accurately reflects the accounting return (i.e. the running yield) and the annual capital accretion. The discrepancy of $10.65\% - 10.25\%$ is caused by ignoring the half-yearly compounding and the time value aspect when dividing by $3\frac{1}{4}$ years (strictly an annuity for $6\frac{1}{2}$ half-years should have been used).

You will note that the yields vary for each security, e.g. 10.5% yield for the 12.5% May 1988. Yields vary each day according to demand and supply (just as prices for shares, gold, and other commodities vary). In fact, transactions in the Australian fixed interest market are based on yield not price.

Consider the April 1991 bond listed for an issue (coupon) of 12.0 or \$6 per half-year per \$100 at redemption (or \$100 face value).

The cash flows are:

Half-year	15/10/88	15/4/89	15/10/89	15/4/90	15/10/90	15/4/91
Coupon	6	6	6	6	6	6
Face value						100

The yield quoted is 11.4% or 5.7% per half-year.

The price of this bond on 15/4/88 @ 11.4% per annum nominal convertible half-yearly is:

$$6A_{\overline{6}|5.7\%} + 100V^6 \text{ @ } 5.7\% = 101.489$$

The price listed on 22 April 1988 is 101.67. The difference is due to the fact that we assumed complete half-years when setting a pricing date of 15/4/88. In practice the pricing allows for the exact number of days.

If the yield were to decrease on the same day, to 11%, the price would be:

$$6A_{\overline{6}|i} + 100V^6 \text{ @ } \frac{11}{2}\% = 102.498$$

Note that when 'yield' falls, price rises (from 101.489 to 102.498).

Sale by tender

Commonwealth bonds are sold by tender. In 1986 and 1987 this occurred approximately five times each year. In 1987 approximately \$5.5

billion were raised by the Federal Government to finance its deficit on balance of payments (to cover balance of trade losses, interest on debt, insurance, freight and other invisibles) and to meet budget expenditures for social service payments, public service salaries and capital work costs.

The tender is bid on a yield basis (the lower yield bidders are more likely to win the stock). Consider a $400 m issue of 14% April, 90's. In this case the bond has a coupon of 14% ($7 paid half-yearly per $100 at maturity which is 15th April 1990). Financial institutions who would like to take up these bonds (for strategic or capital ratio purposes) put in a bid in terms of the face amount required, the yield and the name of their institution. The lowest yield is taken first (the lower the yield, the higher the price). Obviously the Reserve Bank will take the highest-priced offer first.

The following is a simple model of offers:

Institution	Yield bid %	Face amount bid (million) $
A	14	300
B	13.9	100
C	13.87	150
D	13.86	200

C and D would win the tender as they offered the higher prices (lower yields). B would be entitled to the remaining $50 million as $350 million were granted to C and D. A was unsuccessful.

Consider the cash flows for D as an example. D wins $200 million face amount at 13.86% yield (this is a nominal rate convertible half-yearly).

The cash flows per $100 face amount are:

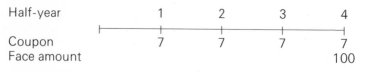

Half-year	1	2	3	4
Coupon	7	7	7	7
Face amount				100

The price $= 7A_{\overline{4}|i} + 100V^4$ @ $i = \dfrac{13.86}{2}\%$, i.e. 6.93%

$= \$100.237$

i.e. D pays $100.237 per $100 face amount.
For an issue of $200 million face amount, D would therefore pay

$$200\ m \times \frac{100.237}{100} = \$200.474\ \text{million}.$$

Small investors can apply for Commonwealth bonds in multiples of $1,000 to a maximum of $200,000 and are allocated bonds at the average tender rate. Coupon rates are fixed at tender.

Australian Savings Bonds

These are available to small investors as well as large investors through banks and post offices. The minimum investment is $100 and the maximum is $200,000. The rate of interest is fixed for the term of the bond and interest is paid every six months. ASB's are redeemable at one month's notice to the Reserve Bank and may be bought or sold on the secondary market through stockbrokers.

Hence in government securities (as in many fixed interest securities) there is a primary market and a secondary market. If interest rates go up the bonds can be redeemed at face value with the Reserve Bank and the money reinvested in higher rate bonds. If rates fall they can be held to maturity or sold at a profit on the secondary market (provided there is a buyer) through the stock exchange, via a broker.

If the bonds have been held for less than six months, a penalty charge on sale is usually levied.

Semi-government bonds

These are bonds issued by organisations associated with but not part of the Federal and State governments. As well as obtaining funds from the Commonwealth government, States also borrow indirectly via semi-government institutions which they control.

Semi-government institutions are agencies of government either Federal or State which are organised as a business unit (i.e. a separate entity) rather than as a government department. Examples are Telecom (a Federal government agency) and the Electricity Commissions (State government agencies). The institutions issue securities which are backed by their respective governments, although this backing is not always necessarily an explicit guarantee of repayment in the event of default by the institutions. These securities range from short term to long term, with a slight premium over government securities. Interest is generally paid half-yearly. Small parcels may from time to time suffer from marketability problems.

Local government bonds

These are usually less marketable and carry higher risk than similar term government and semi-government bonds. They are often issued through private placements to insurance offices and pension funds, but are also periodically available through public issues in the same way as semi-government bonds.

Company debentures

Companies raise debentures to finance expansion. The interest payable by the company to debenture holders is tax deductible. This makes debentures an attractive form of finance (share dividends payable by a company are not tax deductible).

Debentures are issued by both financial companies and industrial companies. Terms usually range from 3 months to 5 years. Debentures purchased on the primary market are obtained by submitting applications from the *current* prospectus.

Prospectuses must be renewed every six months, but are often renewed earlier when interest rates change. An abridged form of a prospectus (called a short-term prospectus) is often used in these circumstances, or sometimes a changed insert suffices.

Some debentures (but certainly not all) are listed on the stock exchange after the issue closes. This is an important benefit. An investor always needs to make sure he has the current rates, as a seemingly current prospectus may have out-of-date rates.

Debentures may be secured by a fixed charge with a particular set of assets as security. Alternatively security may be by a floating charge in which no specific assets are specified. The trust deed usually has a number of limitations on the financial affairs of the borrowing company.

Holders of first-ranking debentures (i.e. those which rank before other fixed interest securities) are paid ahead of any other creditors on wind-up (with the exception of salaries, wages and taxes). Points to consider when analysing debentures include whether they will be listed, frequency of interest payments, term, interest level and yield curve, if applicable deferred interest debentures or compound interest debentures (enabling postponement of the receipt of income which may help reduce taxation), whether investors are able to redeem their funds early with an adjustment of the interest rate, and whether there are floating rate debentures.

Unsecured notes

These notes are issued by finance companies at a rate higher than debentures since they do not offer the level of security. In some cases the parent (borrower) guarantees the unsecured notes. Hence the local issuer and its parent would both be in trouble on default.

Index-linked securities

The coupons and/or face amount vary according to an inflation index (often the C.P.I.).

Consider a 2-year bond with coupon 4% ($2 per half-year) linked to a 3% per half-year inflation index. The nominal redemption yield is assumed to be 10% per annum. The face value is also inflation-linked @ 3% per half-year compound.

The cash flows are:

Half-year	1	2	3	4
Inflation-adjusted coupon	$2(1.03)$	$2(1.03)^2$	$2(1.03)^3$	$2(1.03)^4$
Inflation-adjusted face amount				$100(1.03)^4$

$$\text{The price} = \frac{2(1.03)}{1.05} + \frac{2(1.03)^2}{(1.05)^2} + \ldots \frac{2(1.03)^4}{(1.05)^4} + \frac{100(1.03)^4}{(1.05)^4}$$

$$= 2A_{\overline{4}|j} + 100V^4 \ @ \ j = \frac{1.05}{1.03} - 1$$

MARKETABILITY

Marketability is concerned with your ability to sell a security at short notice. Although fixed interest securities, if held to maturity, provide a full redemption value (face value), the market value of the fixed interest securities changes at any time with overall changing level of yields in the market place.

For example if a market yield (redemption yield) increases by 1% for a fixed interest security, the only way a new investor can achieve the higher return is for the price to drop (as the maturity value is fixed at face value). A drop in the purchase price means there is a capital return as well as an income return if held to maturity.

As yields rise, prices fall. There is therefore a chance of capital loss on forced sale.

A RECAP OF PRICING

Consider a 12% coupon 2-year bond yielding 14% per annum nominal convertible half-yearly.

The cash flows per $100 face value are:

Half-year	1	2	3	4
Coupon	6	6	6	6
Face value				100

The price = present value of coupons + present value of face amount

$$= 6A_{\overline{4}|} + 100V^4 \ @ \ 7\%$$

$$= 20.323 + 76.290$$

$$= 96.613$$

VOLATILITY

Volatility expresses the extent to which a bond price responds to a change in the market yield.

For an upward movement in yield volatility is expressed as:

$$\frac{\text{Change in price for a 1\% change in yield}}{\text{Original price}} \times \frac{100}{1}$$

This rate is usually expressed as a positive percentage. It still indicates a loss if yields are rising. It can also be expressed for a 0.1% or 0.01% change in yield.

Similarly, when yields are falling the volatility can be found from the same expression.

Example 1

Calculate the volatility of the 2-year bond above.

Price at a yield of 14% (i.e. 7% per half-year) = \$96.61

Price at a yield of one percent more (i.e. $i = 15\% = 7\frac{1}{2}\%$ per half-year) is:

$$\text{Price} = 6A_{\overline{4}|} + 100V^4 \ @ \ 7\tfrac{1}{2}\%$$

$$= 20.096 + 74.880$$

$$= \$94.98$$

$$\text{Volatility} = \frac{96.61 - 94.98}{96.61} \times \frac{100}{1}$$

$$= 0.016872 \times 100$$

$$= 1.69\%$$

EFFECT OF TERM ON VOLATILITY

If the term of the bond is increased, keeping the yield and coupon the same, what is the effect on volatility?

Let us take a 5-year bond coupon 12%, yield 14%.

$$\text{Price} \ @ \ 14\% \ \text{yield} = 6A_{\overline{10}|} + 100V^{10} \ @ \ 7\%$$

$$= \$92.98$$

$$\text{Price} \ @ \ 15\% \ \text{yield} = 6A_{\overline{10}|} + 100V^{10} \ @ \ 7.5\%$$

$$= \$89.70$$

$$\text{Volatility} = \frac{92.98 - 89.70}{92.98} \times \frac{100}{1}$$

$$= 0.035276 \times 100$$

$$= 3.53\%$$

Compare this result with the volatility calculated for the 2-year bond coupon 12%, yield 14%.

What is your observation?
Yes, volatility increases with term.
In this case, the volatility has increased from 1.69% to 3.53% by increasing the term of the bond from 2 years to 5 years.

Example 2

A client holds $250,000 (market price) of 10-year bonds with a volatility of 6.8%. If interest rates are expected to rise by 1.6% determine the approximate interest exposure or dollar loss.

The 6.8% volatility refers to a 1% upward movement in yield.

$$\text{The expected loss for a 1\% movement} = 0.068 \times 250,000$$

$$= \$17,000$$

$$\text{The expected loss for a 1.6\% movement} = 1.6 \times 17,000$$

$$= \$27,200$$

EFFECT OF COUPON ON VOLATILITY

What is the effect on volatility if the coupon is reduced?

Taking a 2-year bond yielding 14% with coupon 4%, the volatility can be found thus:

$$\text{Price @ 14\% yield} = 2A_{\overline{4}|} + 100V^4 \text{ @ 7\%}$$

$$= 83.064$$

$$\text{Price @ 15\% yield} = 2A_{\overline{4}|} + 100V^4 \text{ @ } 7\tfrac{1}{2}\%$$

$$= 81.579$$

$$\text{Volatility} = \frac{83.064 - 81.579}{83.064} \times \frac{100}{1}$$

$$= 1.79\%$$

Compare this result with the volatility calculated for the 2-year bond yielding 14% with coupon 12%.

What is your conclusion?
Yes, volatility increases as coupon reduces. In this case the volatility increased from 1.69% to 1.79% when the coupon reduced from 12% to 4%.

EFFECT OF YIELD ON VOLATILITY

If yield rises would you expect volatility to rise?

Example 3

Taking the 2-year 4% coupon bond, calculate the volatility for a yield of 25%.

$$\text{Price @ } 25\% = 2A_{\overline{4}|} + 100V^4 \text{ @ } 12\tfrac{1}{2}\%$$

$$= 68.441$$

$$\text{Price @ } 26\% = 2A_{\overline{4}|} + 100V^4 \text{ @ } 13\%$$

$$= 67.281$$

$$\text{Volatility} = \frac{68.441 - 67.281}{68.441} \times \frac{100}{1}$$

$$= 1.69\%$$

The volatility calculated for the 2-year bond coupon 4% yield 14% was 1.79%.
Thus you can see that as yield rises volatility generally falls.

HORIZON ANALYSIS

If a bond is purchased and later sold, a frequent problem is to determine the return on the investment. Consider a 9% 2-year bond purchased @ $89.18, with market yield 15.45%.
Remember that yield is changing constantly due to differences in demand and supply. If, based on an economic projection of interest rates, the bond is anticipated to be sold @ 15% yield in one year, the one-year horizon return is calculated thus:

$$\frac{\text{horizon}}{\text{return}} = \frac{\substack{\text{Anticipated} \\ \text{sale price}} + \substack{\text{Accumulated} \\ \text{coupons}} - \substack{\text{Purchase} \\ \text{price}}}{\text{Purchase price}} \times \frac{100}{1}$$

Selling at the end of 1 year (with 1 year to run) gives the following cash flows:

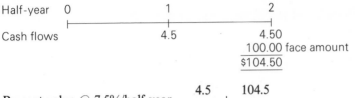

Half-year	0	1	2
Cash flows		4.5	4.50

100.00 face amount
$104.50

Present value @ 7.5%/half-year $= \dfrac{4.5}{1.075} + \dfrac{104.5}{(1.075)^2}$

$$= \$94.61$$

In other words, the anticipated sale price is $94.61.

While the bond is being held in the first year a coupon is received after a half-year. This is assumed to be reinvested conservatively at 10% per annum.

$\therefore$ income from first coupon = coupon of 4.5 + interest on reinvestment

$$= \text{coupon of } 4.5 + \frac{10}{100} \times 4.5 \times \frac{1}{2}$$

$$= 4.5 + 0.225$$

$$= 4.725 \quad \text{or} \quad 4.73$$

The coupon received at date of sale = 4.5

$\therefore$ Accumulated coupons after one year = 4.5 + 4.73

$$= \$9.23$$

After one year the asset proceeds from the bond are $9.23 (the accumulated coupons) plus the anticipated sale price of 94.61, i.e. $103.84.

For an outlay of $89.18 the gross holding period return:

$$= \frac{103.84 - 89.18}{89.18} \times \frac{100}{1}$$

$$= 16.44\%$$

This answer looks reasonable considering that the bond was sold for a profit.
If the marginal rate of tax were $t = 60\%$ on the coupons and capital gain, the proceeds after one year would be:

$$\text{proceeds} = 103.84 - 60\% \text{ tax on } 9.23$$

$$- 60\% \text{ tax on profit } (94.61 - 89.18)$$

$$= 103.84 - 5.54 - 3.26$$
$$= 95.04$$

For an outlay of \$89.18 the holding period return after tax is approximately:

$$= \frac{95.04 - 89.18}{89.18} \times \frac{100}{1}$$

$$= 6.57\% \text{ (or 40\% of the gross yield 16.44\%)}$$

The short-cut method of multiplying the gross holding period return (i.e. the before-tax yield) by $(1 - t)$ is an approximation only. It assumes that there is no tax deferral period.

The after-tax holding period return is also only an approximation because:

  (i) future sale yields are unknown
 (ii) tax payments may be deferred
(iii) coupons may be reinvested at rates variant from those assumed
(iv) allowance for exact days may not be made.

COMPARATIVE YIELDS

While changes in market yield affect all fixed interest securities to different degrees, the absolute level of interest (or yield) depends on the general ranking within the market of different securities. This ranking is according to:

* type of customer
* credit worthiness
* general risk and return associated with the investment
* the length of the investment period
* marketability of security.

THE YIELD CURVE

Major differences in rates are also attributable to different maturities. Usually long-term investments demand higher rates as the risk is greater and the investor forfeits access to money. If yield rates are plotted against maturities, the resulting curve—the yield curve—would normally be rising as maturity increases. There are often periods when this normal condition does not apply. Four examples of yield curves are given below.

1. The normal yield curve is a positive, upward-sloping yield curve, reflecting higher interest rates for longer periods:

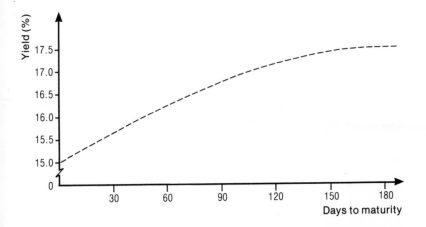

Normal yield curve

2. The inverse yield curve is a downward, negative-sloping yield curve which suggests uncertainty with high short-term rates and lower rates for long periods (resulting possibly from tight current liquidity and an expectation of general falling market rates in the future):

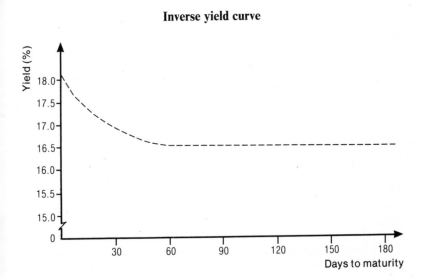

Inverse yield curve

3. The humped yield curve is a hump-backed or humped curve which reflects perceptions of interest rates peaking in the medium term and then declining.

Consider the yield curve as at 22 April 1988. Look back to Table 1 on page 000 and the bonds marked x.

Term to maturity (years)	Yield at 22/4/88
1 (i.e. April '89)	11.1 (average of March '89 and May '89 yields)
2 (i.e. April '90)	11.65 (average of March '90 and May '90 yields)
3 (i.e. April '91)	11.40 (April '91 yield)

The yield curve is humped thus:

Humped yield curve

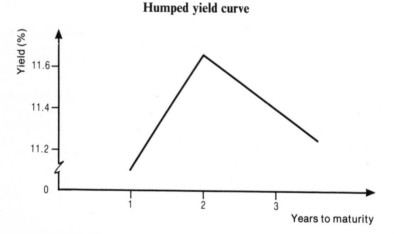

4. The flat yield curve is a flat, horizontal yield curve which suggests interest rates will remain the same:

Flat yield curve

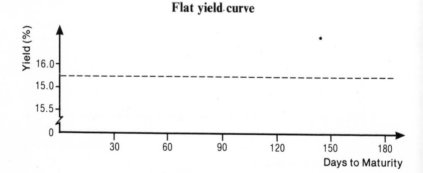

Short-term rates are influenced by immediate seasonal and liquidity conditions, and general day-to-day cash movements within the financial system. If companies are draining their cash to pay short-term commitments (e.g. provisional tax) the lower money supply will cause short interest rates to rise.

In addition the major longer-term forces such as economic, monetary and international events influence the structure of interest rates at the longer end. Such forces include worsening balance of trade (exports less imports), increasing inflation, deteriorating employment and productivity, a weakening of the Australian dollar and a deterioration in the size of our overseas debt.

Fixed interest profit can therefore be enhanced by trading on favourable interest rate movements. Managers of pooled investments with underlying fixed interest securities are usually active traders attempting to derive capital yields as well as interest yields. Current yields on certain investments are either on, above or below the yield curve. The particular position will determine (along with other conditions) whether the security is sold, bought, held, or swapped for another security considered to have a better yield or swap maturity. Managers no longer buy securities and hold them to maturity. They now tend to trade the securities actively taking a view on the direction of interest rates and riding the yield curve, buying in and selling out when rates and timing look right. Additionally the manager must look for a balance between accounting effects, taxation effects, and the investment effects of any trading or investment decision. It is essential that the manager's and the client's objectives are common in these considerations.

ZERO COUPON BOND

This instrument provides face value at maturity. However, no interest (coupon) is paid prior to redemption.

Consider a 5-year 'zero' yielding 10% (per annum nominal convertible half-yearly).

The price per $100 face amount $= 100V^{10}$ @ 5%

$$= \$61.39$$

It is possible to strip the coupons from a coupon bond. Each stripped coupon represents a 'zero'.

Assume that a 12% one-year bond yields 11% and a 6-month bond with coupon 12% yields 10%. At what yields can the coupons on the one-year bond be stripped?

For the six-month bond,

$$\text{price} = 6V^1 + 100V^1 \text{ @ } 5\%$$

For the one-year bond,

$$\text{price} = 6V^1 + 6V^2 + 100V^2 \text{ @ } 5\tfrac{1}{2}\%$$
$$= 100.923$$

If the face amount and the two coupons for the one-year bond are sold separately at yields $y\%$ and $z\%$, then:

$$\text{the sale proceeds} = 6V^1 \text{ @ yield } y\% + (6V^2 + 100V^2) \text{ @ } z\%$$
$$= 100.923$$

Now the 6-month yield is given, i.e. 10%.

$$\therefore 100.923 = \frac{6}{1.05} + \frac{106}{(1+z)^2}$$

$$100.923 - \frac{6}{1.05} = \frac{106}{(1+z)^2}$$

$$95.2087 = \frac{106}{(1+z)^2}$$

$$(1+z)^2 = \frac{106}{95.2087}$$

$$= 1.1133$$

$$1 + z = \sqrt{1.1133}$$

$$= 1.05515$$

$$z = 0.055151$$

$$= 5.5151\% \text{ per half-year}$$

$$\therefore z = 11.0302\% \text{ nominal per year}$$

Thus the one-year bond can be 'stripped' as follows:

Sell first coupon now @ 10% for $\dfrac{6}{1.05}$ $= 5.71429$

Sell second coupon now @ 11.0302% for $\dfrac{6}{\left(1 + \dfrac{11.0302}{200}\right)^2}$ $= 5.38917$

Sell face amount now @ 11.0302% for $\dfrac{100}{\left(1 + \dfrac{11.0302}{200}\right)^2}$ $= \dfrac{89.81953}{100.92299}$

The first six-month coupon is sold at a 6-month yield of 10% and second coupon and face amount (each a 'zero' in its own right) are sold at zero one-year yields of 11.0302%. The total proceeds of 100.923 equal the conventional price of the one-year bond.

If zero coupon yields are sold for less than the above yields (e.g. if the first six-month coupon is sold at a yield less than 10%), then profits accrue to the bond 'stripper'.

ADVANTAGES AND DISADVANTAGES OF FIXED INTEREST SECURITIES

Advantages
1. They are generally marketable.
2. Interest stream is predictable.
3. They are low risk securities (except for poor ranking debentures, unsecured notes, or local government authority securities).
4. Short securities are not volatile to interest rate changes.

Disadvantages
1. They can be eroded by inflation if not inflation-linked.
2. They can be volatile, the longer the term and the lower the coupon.
3. The holder may be forced to sell at a loss.
4. The after-tax real return may be low.
5. Interest income and capital gain are generally liable to tax.

EXERCISES

1 Taking the 14% April 1999 bond in the table on page 000, calculate the price at a yield of 12.1%. Assume a valuation date of 15 April 1988. State the reason(s) for the discrepancy in your solution. (The table has an answer of $111.61.)

2 Assume that you hold the bond in exercise 1 and that you sell this after one year at a yield of 11% with coupons reinvested at 5% per half-year. Find the horizon rate of return.

3 Calculate the volatility of the bond in exercise 1. Assume that interest rates will rise.

4 A client holds $200,000 market value of 5-year bonds with volatility 3%. Estimate the likely loss if interest rates are projected to rise by 1.6%.

5 A 4-year quarterly debenture has a coupon of 14% per annum and yields 12% per annum nominal convertible quarterly. Find the purchase price.

6   A 4-year index-linked bond pays a first coupon of $3. Subsequent half-yearly coupons are indexed (inflated) at $2\frac{1}{2}\%$ per half-year and the nominal rate per annum convertible half-yearly is 10%. The face value is not inflation-linked. Find the price of the bond.

7   A six-month bond yields 10%.
    A 12-month bond yields 11%.
    An 18-month bond yields 12%.
    The coupon on each bond is 12%. Find the zero coupon yields for 12 and 18 months.

8   Two debentures are quoted on the basis of 14% per annum nominal convertible monthly and 14.6% per annum nominal convertible half-yearly. Which debenture would you prefer?

21

Valuing Simple Interest Bills of Exchange, Promissory Notes and Treasury Notes

Commercial bills generally mature after not more than 180 days and are normally struck for periods of 30, 60, 90, 120, 150 or 180 days. In return for a purchase price of P, the face value is payable after n days at a yield (annual interest) of $r'\%$. Commercial bills in Australia normally have face values in multiples of $100,000.

The parties to a bill of exchange include the drawer (borrower), the Acceptor who agrees to pay the final holder, and the endorser(s) who agree(s) to meet any default of the drawer and/or Acceptor. Any holder of the bill may discount (sell) the bill on the open market.

Treasury Notes are issued by tender by the Reserve Bank of Australia (RBA) and are used to finance short-term Commonwealth debt. The Notes are 13 weeks or 26 weeks and are bid on a yield basis. Treasury notes can be sold back to the RBA at the rediscount rate, defined by the RBA.

Promissory notes are issued by one name e.g. Wheat Board and are a promise by the authority to pay the face amount after a period in days.

> By the end of this chapter you will understand how to price and to calculate the return on both yield and discounted instruments.

PRICE BASED ON YIELD

If the face value is $100, the purchase price can be determined as follows:

$$\text{Price} + \text{Interest} = \text{Face Value}$$

Now Interest on $1 = r'\%$ per annum

$$= \frac{r'}{100}$$

213

$$\therefore \text{ Interest on \$1 for 1 day} = \frac{r'}{100} \div 365$$

$$= \frac{r'}{100} \times \frac{1}{365}$$

$$\text{Interest on \$1 for } n \text{ days} = \frac{r'}{100} \times \frac{n}{365}$$

$$\text{Interest on \$}P \text{ for } n \text{ days} = P \times \frac{r'}{100} \times \frac{n}{365}$$

Substitute this in the equation

$$\text{Price} + \text{Interest} = \text{Face Value}$$

$$P + \left(P \times \frac{r'}{100} \times \frac{n}{365} \right) = 100$$

$$P \left(1 + \frac{r'n}{36{,}500} \right) = 100$$

$$P = \frac{100}{1 + \dfrac{r'n}{36{,}500}}$$

$$= 100 \div 1 + \frac{r'n}{36{,}500}$$

$$= 100 \div \frac{36{,}500 + r'n}{36{,}500}$$

$$= 100 \times \frac{36{,}500}{36{,}500 + r'n}$$

$$\boxed{\therefore P = \frac{3{,}650{,}000}{36{,}500 + r'n}}$$

Example 1

Calculate the purchase price on a 180-day bill yielding 17% per annum.

Solution:

$$r' = 17, \quad n = 180$$

$$\therefore P = \frac{3{,}650{,}000}{36{,}500 + (17)(180)}$$

$$= 92.2649$$

$$\therefore \text{ Price} = \$92.26$$

Check:

92.26 + 180 days' interest on 92.26 @ 17%

$$= 92.26 + \frac{180}{365} \times 92.26 \times .17$$

$$= 92.26 + 7.734674$$

$$= 99.995 \quad \text{(slight rounding error)}$$

HOLDING PERIOD RETURN

Assume that the 180-day bill in Example 1 is sold after 10 days for a yield of 17%. What is the holding period return annualised, i.e. the effective annual return?

The bill now has 170 days to run.

$$\therefore \text{Selling Price } (SP) = \frac{3,650,000}{36,500 + (17)(170)}$$

$$= \$92.6631$$

$$\text{The return for 10 days} = \frac{\text{selling price} - \text{purchase price}}{\text{purchase price}} \times 100$$

$$= \frac{92.6631 - 92.2649}{92.2649} \times \frac{100}{1}$$

$$= 0.4316\%$$

The holding period return is 0.4316%.

There are $\dfrac{365}{10}$ 10-day periods in a year.

$\therefore$ The annualised holding period return is $\dfrac{365}{10}$ times greater than the holding period return.

$$\text{The return for 365 days} = 0.4316 \times \frac{365}{10}$$

$$= 15.7528\%$$

Example 2

If the 180-day bill in Example 1 is sold after 100 days for a yield of 17%, what is the annualised holding period return?

$$\text{The } SP = \frac{3,650,000}{36,500 + (17)(80)}$$

$$= \$96.4078$$

$$\text{The return for 100 days} = \frac{96.4078 - 92.2649}{92.2649} \times \frac{100}{1}$$

$$= 4.4902\%$$

$$\text{The return for 1 day} = \frac{4.4902}{100}$$

$$\text{The return for 365 days} = \frac{4.4902}{100} \times 365$$

$$= 16.3893\%$$

Note that if you buy and sell a bill, treasury note or promissory note for the same yield, before maturity, the holding period return will be less than the yield at purchase. But the holding period return approaches the purchase yield as the holding date approaches maturity.

TREASURY NOTE TENDER

Assume that on a particular Wednesday the RBA offers a $300 million tender of 13-week (90-day) treasury notes.
The yields and face amounts are assumed to be bid as follows:

Institution bidding	Yield bid (r')	Face amount bid (millions)	Price of note per $100 face value $P = \dfrac{3,650,000}{36,500 + 90r'}$
A	13	50	96.894080
B	12.9	50	96.917235
C	12.8	100	96.940402
D	12.7	100	96.963579
E	12.6	100	96.986767

The institutions winning the treasury notes will be C, D and E as they offered the lowest yields/highest prices.
The price paid would be:

$$\text{For A,} \quad \text{Price} = \frac{3,650,000}{36,500 + 90(13)}$$

$$= 96.894080 \text{ per } \$100 \text{ face value}$$

$$\therefore \text{ price} = 0.96894080 \text{ per } \$1 \text{ face value}$$

$$= 0.96894080 \times 50\text{m per 50m face value}$$

$$= \$48,447,040$$

For B,   Price $= \dfrac{3,650,000}{36,500 + 90(12.9)}$

$= 96.917235$ per \$100 face value

$= \$48,458,618$ per 50m face value

For C,   Price $= \dfrac{3,650,000}{36,500 + (90)(12.8)}$

$= 96.940402$ or \$96,940,402 for a face amount of \$100m.

For D,   Price $= \dfrac{3,650,000}{36,500 + (90)(12.7)}$

$= 96.963579$ or \$96,963,579 for a face amount of \$100m.

For E,   Price $= \dfrac{3,650,000}{36,500 + (90)(12.6)}$

$= 96.986767$ or \$96,986,767 for a face amount of \$100m.

BILLS PURCHASED AT A DISCOUNT

If bills are trading at a discount ($d\%$) the price is determined as follows:

Price = Face Amount − Discount

$= 100 - (d\%$ of face amount for relevant time period)

$= 100 - \left(\dfrac{d}{100} \times \dfrac{n}{365} \times 100 \right)$

$= 100 \left(1 - \dfrac{dn}{36,500} \right)$

$= 100 - \dfrac{dn}{365}$

$$\boxed{P = 100 - \dfrac{dn}{365}}$$

Example 3

Consider a 180-day bill bought and sold after 10 days at a discount of 17%.

$$\text{Purchase Price} = 100 - \frac{(17)(180)}{365}$$

$$= 91.6164$$

$$\text{Sale Price} = 100 - \frac{(17)(170)}{365}$$

$$= 92.0822$$

$$\text{Annualised Holding Period Yield} = \frac{92.0822 - 91.6164}{91.6164} \times 100 \times \frac{365}{10}$$

$$= 0.005084 \times 3650$$

$$= 18.557485$$

$$= 18.56\%$$

Now the yield at purchase can be determined from the cash flows on the number line:

Days   0   180

Purchase price = 91.6164
Maturity value   100

$$\text{Holding Period Yield} = \frac{100 - 91.6164}{91.6164} \times 100 \times \frac{365}{180}$$

$$= 18.555715$$

$$= 18.56\%$$

What can you conclude from this?
Yes! When you buy and sell a bill at the same discount your annualised holding period return is equal to the *yield* at purchase.

CONVERTING FLAT RATES TO COMPOUND RATES

Consider a 5-year loan of $100,000 at a flat rate of 10% per annum payable annually in arrear. Equal annual payments of principal are made.

$$\text{The annual principal repayment} = \frac{100,000}{5} \qquad = 20,000$$

$$\text{The annual interest repayment} = \frac{10}{100} \times 100,000 = \underline{10,000}$$

$$\text{Total annual repayment} \qquad\qquad\qquad = \underline{30,000}$$

Now a *credit foncier* arrangement is a loan L based on compound interest i which is charged on the reducing principal. The interest content therefore diminishes where equal repayments P apply.

$$\text{Thus} \quad PA_{\overline{n}|i} = L$$

For repayment $P = 30,000$ and a loan L of $100,000$ on a credit foncier arrangement for 5 years:

$$30,000 A_{\overline{5}|i} = 100,000$$

i.e. the present value of $30,000 a year for 5 years at a compound rate i equals the loan.

Solving this equation for i gives the compound rate i equivalent to the flat rate of 10% per annum.

$$i = 15.238\%$$

Thus an annual compound rate of 15.238% is equivalent to a flat rate of 10% per annum.

Example 4

A 5-year personal loan of $30,000 for a swimming pool has been granted at a flat rate of 12% per annum. Equal payments of principal and interest are made, monthly in arrear.

Required: (i) Find the equivalent monthly compound rate.
(ii) Convert this rate to an effective annual compound rate.

Solution:

(i) Monthly repayment of principal $= \dfrac{30,000}{60} = 500$

$\qquad$ Monthly interest payment $= 1\%$ of $30,000 \ = \underline{300}$

$\qquad\qquad\qquad$ Total monthly payment $= \underline{800}$

$$\therefore \ 800 A_{\overline{60}|i} = 30,000$$

$$i = 1.6925\%$$

The equivalent monthly compound rate is 1.6925%.

(ii) The annual effective rate $= (1.016925)^{12} - 1$

$$= 22.31144\%$$

EXERCISES

1 A 90-day bill of exchange is bought and sold for a yield of 12%. Determine the annualised holding period return assuming a holding period of a) 10, b) 50 and c) 90 days. What do you conclude from these results?

2   A 180-day bill is purchased at a yield of 13% and sold after 50 days for a yield of 15%. Find the annualised holding period return.

3   A 90-day discount security is purchased and sold at a discount rate of 12%. Find the annualised holding period returns assuming holding periods of 10, 50 and 90 days. What do you conclude from these results?

4   A 150-day bill is purchased for a yield of 12% and funded over 2 days at a cost of 11% per annum simple interest. Determine the break-even selling *yield*, sufficient to cover the purchase price plus the interest on the borrowed funds.

5   A one-year 12% coupon bond is purchased for a yield of 13%. After 6 months (assume 183 days) the bond is sold for a yield of 12.6%. Determine the break-even yield on a '183'-day bill of exchange. Assume that bonds with 6 months or less to maturity are priced on a compound basis (though in Australia bonds with 6 months or less to maturity are actually priced on a bill of exchange basis, i.e. (face value + coupon)/$(1 + nr/36,500)$.)

6   Develop a formula expressing yields in terms of discounts. Make the discount rate d the subject of the formula. Check your result using your answer to exercise 3 above.

22

The Cost of Capital

The weighted average required rate of return or weighted average cost of capital reflects both the explicit and implicit costs of financing and should be used in project evaluation i.e. in the net present value calculation.

To determine the *WACC* (weighted average cost of capital) it is necessary to find the cost of capital for each component of the capital structure and then weight according to market value.

> By the end of this chapter you will be able to compute the weighted average cost of capital for a net present value calculation.

COST OF DEBT

The cost of debt can be found using an *IRR* approach to the cash flows. Assume debt raised at a discount of $98 per $100 face amount. The debt matures after 4 years and interest is payable half-yearly equal to $7 per half-year. The $14 interest per annum acquires a tax remission of $(14)(0.49) = $6.86 at the end of each 12 months on average. The capital gain of $2 is tax deductible at the conclusion of the debenture.
The cash flows are:

Half-year	0	1	2	3	4	5	6	7	8	9	10
Inflow to company	98										
Interest payments by company		(7)	(7)	(7)	(7)	(7)	(7)	(7)	(7)		
Face amount outflow									(100)		
Tax remission on interest					6.86		6.86		6.86		6.86
Tax remission on capital gain											2(0.49)

Let i = the half-yearly after-tax cost of debt.

221

The equation of value is:

$$98 = 7A_{\overline{8}|} - 6.86(V^4 + V^6 + V^8 + V^{10}) - 0.98(V^{10}) + 100V^8$$

Using the Hewlett-Packard

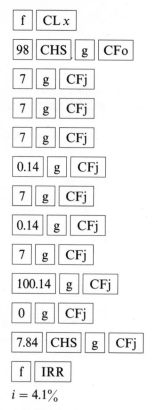

$i = 4.1\%$

4.1% is the half-yearly rate.
The annual rate is therefore $(1.041)^2 - 1 = 0.083681$

The annual effective after-tax cost of debt = 8.37%.

COST OF EQUITY

If the current market price per share = \$2 and dividends are projected
to be   0.2, 0.2(1 + g), 0.2(1 + g)^2 + ...
then the equation of value is:

$$\$2 = \frac{0.2}{1 + k_e} + \frac{0.2(1 + g)}{(1 + k_e)^2} + \frac{0.2(1 + g)^2}{(1 + k_e)^3} + ...$$

where k_e is the cost of equity, i.e. the company's cost of paying dividends, bonus issues, and rights issues expressed as a rate of interest. This constitutes an infinite geometric progression.

$$\text{The sum} = \frac{a}{1 - r} \quad 0 < r < 1$$

$$a = \frac{0.2}{1 + k_e}$$

$$r = \frac{1 + g}{1 + k_e}$$

$$\text{Sum} = \frac{0.2}{1 + k_e} \div \left[1 - \frac{1 + g}{1 + k_e} \right]$$

$$= \frac{0.2}{1 + k_e} \div \left[\frac{1 + k_e - 1 - g}{1 + k_2} \right]$$

$$= \frac{0.2}{1 + k_e} \div \frac{k_e - g}{1 + k_e}$$

$$= \frac{0.2}{1 + k_e} \times \frac{1 + k_e}{k_e - g}$$

$$= \frac{0.2}{k_e - g}$$

$$\text{Now} \quad 2 = \frac{0.2}{1 + k_e} + \frac{0.2(1 + g)}{(1 + k_e)^2} + \frac{0.2(1 + g)^2}{(1 + k_e)^3} + \cdots$$

$$\therefore 2 = \frac{0.2}{k_e - g}$$

$$2k_e - 2g = 0.2$$

$$2k_e = 2g + 0.2$$

$$k_e = \frac{2g}{2} + \frac{0.2}{2}$$

$$k_e = g + \frac{0.2}{2}$$

$$\therefore k_e = \text{growth} + \frac{\text{dividend}}{\text{market price}}$$

$$= \text{growth} + \text{dividend yield}$$

where dividend yield = dividend ÷ market price

Example 1

Consider a company with market price per share = \$4. The dividend yield = 10% and dividends are expected to grow at 4% for the first 2 years and 8% thereafter. Show how to find the cost of equity k_e.

The equation of value is:

$$4 = \frac{0.4}{1 + k_e} + \frac{0.4(1.04)}{(1 + k_e)^2} + \frac{0.4(1.04)^2}{(1 + k_e)^3} + \frac{(0.4)(1.04)^2(1.08)}{(1 + k_e)^4}$$

$$+ \frac{(0.4)(1.04)^2(1.08)^2}{(1 + k_e)^5} + \cdots$$

$$4 = \frac{0.4}{1 + k_e} + \frac{(0.4)(1.04)}{(1 + k_e)^2} + \frac{(0.4)(1.04)^2}{(1 + k_e)^3}$$

$$+ \frac{(0.4)1.04^2}{(1 + k_e)^3}\left[\frac{1.08}{1 + k_e} + \frac{1.08^2}{(1 + k_e)^2} + \cdots\right]$$

$$= \frac{0.4}{1 + k_e} + \frac{(0.4)(1.04)}{(1 + k_e)^2} + \frac{(0.4)(1.04)^2}{(1 + k_e)^3}$$

$$+ \frac{(0.4)(1.04)^2}{(1 + k_e)^3}\left[\frac{(1.08)}{(k_e - 0.08)}\right]$$

Note:

$$\frac{1.08}{1 + k_e} + \frac{(1.08)^2}{(1 + k_e)^2} + \cdots = \frac{a}{1 - r}$$

$$a = \frac{1.08}{1 + k_e}$$

$$r = \frac{1.08}{1 + k_e}$$

$$\frac{a}{1 - r} = \frac{1.08}{1 + k_e} \div \left[1 - \frac{1.08}{1 + k_e}\right]$$

$$= \frac{1.08}{1 + k_e} \div \frac{1 + k_e - 1.08}{1 + k_e}$$

$$= \frac{1.08}{1 + k_e} \div \left[\frac{1 + k_e}{1 + k_e} - \frac{1.08}{1 + k_e}\right]$$

$$= \frac{1.08}{1 + k_e} \times \frac{1 + k_e}{k_e - 0.08}$$

$$= \frac{1.08}{k_e - 0.08}$$

The value of k_e must now be solved by computer *iteration* until the left-hand side of $4 is obtained.

An alternative approach to finding the cost of equity is by Beta where

$$k_e = r_f + \beta(r_m - r_f)$$

where r_f is the risk-free rate. A proxy for r_f would be a Commonwealth Bond for a term equal to the project length.

r_m = return on the market. A proxy for r_m is the return on the All Ordinaries index, which would be extrapolated from past returns.

$$\beta = \frac{\sum_{t=1}^{n} (r_{st} - \bar{r}_s)(r_{mt} - \bar{r}_m)}{\sum_{t=1}^{n} (r_{mt} - \bar{r}_m)^2}$$

$$= \frac{\text{covariance } (r_{mt}, r_{st})}{\text{variance } (r_{mt})}$$

where r_{st} is the return on a stock for day t, found by

$$\frac{\text{Price for day } t - \text{Price for day } (t-1)}{\text{Price for day } (t-1)}$$

$\bar{r}_s$ is the mean stock return, found by averaging the r_{st} values

r_{mt} is the return on the All Ords for day t, found by

$$\frac{\text{All Ords for day } t - \text{All Ords for day}(t-1)}{\text{All Ords for day } (t-1)}$$

$\bar{r}_m$ is the average market return, found by averaging the r_{mt} values

$\sum_{t=1}^{n}$ is the sum of all values from day 1 to day n

In order to understand how to calculate β, you need to understand some simple statistics.

Sigma

The summation symbol $\sum$ is called sigma. It is used to abbreviate the addition of a series.

Consider $1 + 2 + 3 + 4 + 5$.

This can be represented by:

$$\sum_{i=1}^{i=5} i$$

$\displaystyle\sum_{i=1}$ The notation below the $\sum$ represents the starting point for the variable (in this case the starting point is $i = 1$).

$\displaystyle\sum^{i=5}$ The notation above the $\sum$ represents the last addition (in this case, $i = 5$).

Similarly, $1 + 2 + 3 \ldots + n$ starts at $i = 1$ and finishes at $i = n$. Therefore the addition of the series can be represented by the notation:

$$\sum_{i=1}^{i=n} i$$

You could select any variable name. Thus:

$$\sum_{i=1}^{i=n} i = \sum_{q=1}^{q=n} q = \sum_{r=1}^{r=n} r = 1 + 2 + 3 \ldots + n$$

Consider $\displaystyle\sum_{r=1}^{r=6} \boxed{r}$

Starting with $r = 1$ you then substitute 1 for r within the box.

     Add

Move to $r = 2$. Substitute 2 for r in the box.

     Add

Move to $r = 3$. Substitute 3 for r in the box.

     Add

Keep going up by one and substitute for r in the box.

     Add

The last addition will be $r = 6$.

$$\sum_{r=1}^{r=6} r = 1 + 2 + 3 + 4 + 5 + 6$$
$$= 21$$

Similarly, $\displaystyle\sum_{r=3}^{r=8} r = 3 + 4 + 5 + 6 + 7 + 8$
$$= 33$$

Consider the following examples.

$$\sum_{r=1}^{r=4} r^2 = 1^2 + 2^2 + 3^2 + 4^2$$
$$= 1 + 4 + 9 + 16$$
$$= 30$$

$$\sum_{r=4}^{r=6} r(r-1) = 4(4-1) + 5(5-1) + 6(6-1)$$
$$= 4(3) + 5(4) + 6(5)$$
$$= 12 + 20 + 30$$
$$= 62$$

$$\sum_{m=2}^{m=4} m^3 = 2^3 + 3^3 + 4^3$$
$$= 8 + 27 + 64$$
$$= 99$$

$$\sum_{r=1}^{r=n} 1 = 1 + 1 + 1 + 1 + \dots 1 \quad (n \text{ times})$$
$$= 1 \times n$$
$$= n$$

Expressing series in sigma notation

Now we shall try to work in reverse.

Simplify: $x_1 + x_2 + x_3 + x_4$

The fixed expression is x whilst the subscript i in x_i varies. In fact i starts at 1 and finishes at 4.

$$\therefore \sum_{i=1} \quad \text{and} \quad \sum^{i=4}$$

$$\text{i.e.} \sum_{i=1}^{i=4}$$

Now x is fixed and i is variable.

$$\therefore \sum_{i=1}^{i=4} x_i = x_1 + x_2 + x_3 + x_4$$

Example 2

Simplify $r^2 + r^3 + r^4 + r^5$

Here r is fixed. Put the fixed expression into the sigma.

$$\sum r^{\square}$$

The variable component starts at $l = 2$ (we can say $f = 2, t = 2$, or any other symbol except $r = 2$).

$$\text{i.e.} \sum_{l=2}$$

The variable component ends at $l = 5$.

$$\text{i.e.} \quad \sum_{}^{l=5}$$

Now put the variable symbol into the box:

$$\text{i.e.} \quad r^2 + r^3 + r^4 + r^5 = \sum_{l=2}^{l=5} r^l = \sum_{m=2}^{m=5} r^m = \sum_{s=2}^{s=5} r^s$$

Example 3

Simplify $2s^3 + 3s^4 + 4s^5 + 5s^6$
Here s is fixed but there are two variables, represented below by a box and a triangle:

$$\sum \square s^{\triangle}$$

Call the variable in the box t, say, and put t into the sigma:

$$\sum_{t=2}^{t=5} t s^{\triangle}$$

Notice that the variable in the $\triangle$ is one more than the variable in the box, i.e. one more than t.

$$\therefore \sum_{t=2}^{t=5} t s^{t+1} = 2s^3 + 3s^4 + 4s^5 + 5s^6$$

Example 4

Simplify $(x_1 - \bar{x})^2 + (x_2 - \bar{x})^2 + (x_3 - \bar{x})^2$
The fixed items are:

$$(\quad)^2 \qquad - \qquad x \quad \bar{x}$$

Now put these fixed terms back into the sigma:

$$\text{i.e.} \quad \sum (x_\square - \bar{x})^2$$

Within $\square$ the starting point is 1 and the final point is 3.

$$\therefore \sum_{i=1}^{i=3}$$

Now put i back into the $\sum$.
The simplification becomes:

$$\sum_{i=1}^{i=3} (x_i - \bar{x})^2$$

Variance

The variance is the average of the squared dispersions from the mean. Consider three share returns as follows:

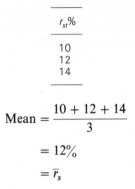

$$\text{Mean} = \frac{10 + 12 + 14}{3}$$

$$= 12\%$$

$$= \bar{r}_s$$

The dispersions from the mean are:

$r_{st} - \bar{r}_s$
$10 - 12 = -2$
$12 - 12 = 0$
$14 - 12 = 2$

The squared dispersions are:

$(r_{st} - \bar{r}_s)^2$
4
0
4

Note that the squared dispersions make all the distances from the mean positive.

The average of the squared dispersions is:

$$\text{average} = (4 + 0 + 4) \div 3$$

$$= \frac{8}{3}$$

$$= 2.\dot{6}\%$$

$$\therefore \text{ The variance} = 2.\dot{6}\%$$

Standard deviation

The square root of the variance gives a measure of dispersion from the mean called the standard deviation. The standard deviation of a rate of return represents the swing (volatility) of returns around the average. The higher the value of the standard deviation the more risky is the security (i.e. its returns are more volatile).

Covariance

This measure is used to describe the relationship of one variable with another. If the two variables are moving together the covariance is positive.

The covariance is the average of the cross-products.

A cross-product is the dispersion from the mean for the first variable multiplied by the dispersion from the mean for the second variable.

Consider the returns on a share and on a market index (e.g. 'All-Ords'):

Share price returns $(r_{st}\%)$	Market returns $(r_{mt}\%)$
10	14
12	16
14	18

$\therefore$ The means are $\bar{r}_s = 12$ and $\bar{r}_m = 16$

Dispersions from the mean for shares	Dispersions from the mean for 'All Ords'
$10 - 12 = -2$	$14 - 16 = -2$
$12 - 12 = 0$	$16 - 16 = 0$
$14 - 12 = 2$	$18 - 16 = 2$

Now obtain the cross-products and add them up:

$$(-2 \times -2) + (0 \times 0) + (2 \times 2) = 8$$

The average of the cross-products is therefore:

$$8/3 = 2.\dot{6}\% = \text{covariance} (r_{mt}, r_{st})$$

Beta

β measures the market risk of a portfolio. Market risk is non-diversifiable risk comprising factors that cannot be minimised by spreading shares across sectors/industries and companies. Non-diversifiable (or systematic) risk covers sociological, political, and economic factors.

β measures the relationship between changes in share or portfolio returns with changes in the return for a market index.

$$\beta = \frac{\text{covariance } (r_{mt}, r_{st})}{\text{variance } (r_{mt})}$$

Taking the above simple example where the covariance was $2.\dot{6}\%$, and

$$\text{variance of the market returns} = \frac{(14 - 16)^2 + (16 - 16)^2 + (18 - 16)^2}{3}$$

$$= 2.\dot{6}\%,$$

$$\beta = \frac{2.\dot{6}\%}{2.\dot{6}\%}$$

$$= 1$$

When $\beta = 1$ the stock returns move in sympathy with the market.

Now try

$r_{st}\%$	$r_{mt}\%$
10	14
13	16
19	18

$$\bar{r}_s = \frac{42}{3} = 14$$

$$\bar{r}_m = \frac{48}{3} = 16$$

Intuitively β should exceed 1 as the share price returns are moving faster than the market.

The dispersions are:

$r_{st} - \bar{r}_s$	$r_{mt} - \bar{r}_m$	Cross-products
$10 - 14 = -4$	$14 - 16 = -2$	$-4 \times -2 = 8$
$13 - 14 = -1$	$16 - 16 = 0$	$-1 \times 0 = 0$
$19 - 14 = 5$	$18 - 16 = 2$	$5 \times 2 = 10$
		$\overline{18}$

$$\text{Covariance } (r_{mt}, r_{st}) = \frac{18}{3} = 6$$

$$\beta = \frac{6}{2.\dot{6}} = 2.25$$

If $\beta = 0$ what would be your conclusion?
r_{st} would be constant.

Consider

r_{st}	Dispersion $r_{st} - \bar{r}_s$	r_{mt}
10	10 − 10	14
10	10 − 10	16
10	10 − 10	18

Mean = 10

Since the cross-products are zero, $\beta = 0$. Thus a zero β has a share/portfolio with a constant return.

Example 5

Consider the following small sample of prices and 'All Ords' indices. Calculate the β.

Day	Price	Return on stock r_{st}	All Ords index	Return on market r_{mt}
1	2		1900	
2	2.1	5	1920	1.05
3	2.4	14.29	1960	2.08
4	2.2	−8.33	1950	−0.51
5	2.3	4.55	1970	1.03

$$\bar{r}_s = \frac{5 + 14.29 - 8.33 + 4.55}{4}$$

$$= 3.88$$

$$\bar{r}_m = \frac{1.05 + 2.08 - 0.51 + 1.03}{4}$$

$$= 0.91$$

Day	$r_{st} - \bar{r}_s$	$r_{mt} - \bar{r}_m$	$(r_{st} - \bar{r}_s)(r_{mt} - \bar{r}_m)$	$(r_{mt} - \bar{r}_m)^2$
2	5 − 3.88 = 1.12	1.05 − 0.91 = 0.14	0.1568	.0196
3	14.29 − 3.88 = 10.41	2.08 − 0.91 = 1.17	12.1797	1.3689
4	−8.33 − 3.88 = −12.21	−0.51 − 0.91 = −1.42	17.3382	2.0164
5	4.55 − 3.88 = 0.67	1.03 − 0.91 = 0.12	0.0804	0.0144
			29.7551	3.4193

$$\beta = \frac{29.7551}{3.4193} = 8.702$$

Beta is obviously spurious given such a small sample of data, but for more data, the same basic method would apply. However, adjustment for dividends, rights issues and stock splits would be necessary. e.g. if a dividend of 0.1 were declared on day 3 the return would be

$$\frac{(2.4 + 0.1 - 2.1)}{2.1} \times 100 = 19.05$$

Example 6

If Beta for a similar industry $= 1.8$, $r_f = 11\%$ and $r_m = 14\%$ find the cost of equity.

$$k_e = r_f + \beta(r_m - r_f)$$
$$= 11 + 1.8(14 - 11)$$
$$= 11 + 5.4$$
$$= 16.4\%$$

COST OF RETAINED EARNINGS

There is an opportunity cost that retained earnings achieve at least the return allocated for equity. Therefore the cost of retained earnings $= k_e$.

Under current legislation dividends paid with tax already deducted are not taxed again under dividend imputation. Retained earnings are taxed at the same rate so there is an incentive to distribute retained earnings. Dividends in fact cost the same as retained earnings.

COST OF PREFERENCE SHARES

If preference shares (i.e. shares ranking before ordinary shares with dividends paid out of net profit) have a market price of $4 and dividends are 0.4 per annum, the equation of value is:

$$4 = \frac{0.4}{1 + k_p} + \frac{0.4}{(1 + k_p)^2} + \dots$$

where k_p is the cost of preference shares (i.e. the cost $\%$ to the company of paying future dividends). The right-hand side is an infinite geometric progression $\dfrac{a}{1 - r}$.

$$\text{RHS} = \frac{a}{1 - r}; \qquad a = \frac{0.4}{1 + k_p}$$

$$r = \frac{1}{1 + k_p}$$

$$\therefore \frac{a}{1 - r} = \frac{0.4}{1 + k_p} \div \left[1 - \frac{1}{1 + k_p} \right]$$

$$= \frac{0.4}{1 + k_p} \div \frac{1 + k_p - 1}{1 + k_p}$$

$$= \frac{0.4}{1 + k_p} \div \frac{k_p}{1 + k_p}$$

$$= \frac{0.4}{1 + k_p} \times \frac{1 + k_p}{k_p}$$

$$= \frac{0.4}{k_p}$$

Now   LHS $= 4$

and   LHS $=$ RHS

$$\therefore 4 = \frac{0.4}{k_p}$$

$$\therefore k_p = \frac{0.4}{4}$$

$$= 0.1$$

$$= 10\%$$

COST OF TERM LOANS

If there exist term loans with monthly payments and the interest is tax deductible, then the cost of the loan on a monthly basis (k_L) can be found thus:

$$\text{Loan} = \frac{\text{Present Value of}}{\text{monthly repayments}} - \frac{\text{Present Value of tax}}{\text{remissions on interest}}$$

The k_L can be found the same way as an *IRR*.
The effective annual cost $= (1 + k_L)^{12} - 1$.

Example 7

Consider a 6-month term loan of \$6m repayable by instalments of \$1m per month in arrear and simple interest of 1% per month on the loan outstanding. The total tax remission on interest is assumed to be received 12 months from now. Tax is 49%.

The cash flows are:

Month	0	1	2	3	4	5	6	12
Principal payment (m)		(1)	(1)	(1)	(1)	(1)	(1)	
Interest		(.06)	(0.05)	(0.04)	(0.03)	(0.02)	(0.01)	
Tax remission								$+(0.21)(0.49)$
Loan receipt (m)	6							

The equation of value is:

$$PV \text{ of outflows} = PV \text{ of inflows}$$

$$1A_{\overline{6}|k_L} + (0.06V^1 + 0.05V^2 + \ldots 0.01V^6) = 6 + (0.21)(0.49)V^{12} \ @ \ k_L\%$$

$$\text{or} \quad 6 = A_{\overline{6}|k_L} + (0.06V^1 + 0.05V^2 + \ldots 0.01V^6) - (0.21)(0.49)V^{12}_{k_L\%}$$

i.e.   Loan = PV of monthly repayments − PV of tax remission
on interest

Using the Hewlett-Packard,

$$k_L = 0.533766\%$$

The effective after-tax rate per annum $= (1.00533766)^{12} - 1$

$$= 6.60\%$$

THE WEIGHTED AVERAGE COST OF CAPITAL

To find the weighted average cost of capital (WACC), simply multiply each cost of capital by the market value weights.
Consider the following example.

Capital	Cost of capital	Assumed market value proportions (millions)
Equity (shares)	$k_e = 15$	30
Retained earnings	$k_e = 15$	10
Debentures	$k_d = 9$	30
Preference	$k_p = 16$	10
Term loans	$k_l = 10$	20
		100

$$WACC = \left(\frac{30}{100} \times 15\right) + \left(\frac{10}{100} \times 15\right) + \left(\frac{30}{100} \times 9\right)$$

$$+ \left(\frac{10}{100} \times 16\right) + \left(\frac{20}{100} \times 10\right)$$

$$= 12.3\%$$

The value of 12.3% assumes that the market value proportions will remain constant in the future. If there is an intended change in the proportions, target weights should be used. An example is shown in exercise 8 below, where the WACC is used to assess a project's feasibility.

EXERCISES

1   A company raises debentures at a price of $100 per $100 face amount. The company pays interest quarterly @ 3% and the term of the debenture is 8 years. Tax of 49% is assumed to be remitted immediately on payment of the interest. Find the effective annual after-tax cost of debt.

2   Given the same information as in exercise 1, except that quarterly tax remissions are deferred 12 months, find the effective annual after-tax cost of debt.

3   A share has a market price of $2 and a first half-yearly dividend of 20 cents. Thereafter dividends will increase by 3% compound per half-year in perpetuity. Find the effective annual internal rate of return (or cost of equity in this case), by equating the market value of the share with the present value of future dividends in perpetuity.

4   A share in XYZ PTY LTD has the following prices:

Week	Share price
1	10
2	14
3	16
4	18
5	21

The corresponding 'All Ords' weekly figures are:

Week	All Ords index
1	1000
2	1200
3	1300
4	1500
5	1600

The risk-free rate on a 15-year Commonwealth bond is 11% and the market return is 14%. Estimate the cost of equity and discuss the shortcomings in the resulting rate.

5 An 8-month loan for $2m has been raised. Interest at 12% flat together with the principal are due after 8 months and the tax remission on interest is assumed to be paid one year from now. Assume tax = 49%. Determine the annual effective after-tax cost of the term loan.

6 Find: (a) $\displaystyle\sum_{i=4}^{i=7} (i^2 - 1)$

   (b) $\displaystyle\sum_{t=2}^{t=4} (3t + 2)(t - 1)$

   (c) $\displaystyle\sum_{t=1}^{t=3} (t^3 - 2)$

7 Simplify, using i as the variable in Σ:
   (a) $x_3^2 + x_4^2 + x_5^2$
   (b) $(x_3 - \bar{x})^2 + (x_4 - \bar{x})^2 + (x_5 - \bar{x})^2$
   (c) $(r_{1s} - \bar{r}_s) + (r_{2s} - \bar{r}_s) + (r_{3s} - \bar{r}_s)$
   (d) $(r_{3s} - \bar{r}_s)(r_{3m} - \bar{r}_m) + (r_{4s} - \bar{r}_s)(r_{4m} - \bar{r}_m) + (r_{5s} - \bar{r}_s)(r_{5m} - \bar{r}_m)$

8 A company has the following capital structure and costs of capital:

Capital	Cost of capital (adjusted for tax if appropriate)	Market value (millions)
Debentures	9.2%	20
Term loans	8.7%	20
Ordinary shares	14.6%	50
Retained earnings	14.6%	10
		100

The company is considering undertaking a project with Beta 1.7, $r_m = 14\%$ and $r_f = 11\%$. The market value of the project is $30m to be financed by raising ordinary shares.

The after-tax inflows on the project are projected to be:

Year	0	1	2	3	4	5
After-tax cash flow (m)		5	5	5	5	20

Find the *NPV* of the project using the appropriate weighted average cost of capital.

23

The Effect of Transaction Costs

When you apply for a loan it is not uncommon to be quoted the borrowing rate exclusive of transaction costs. This can considerably understate the real position when such things as legal expenses, stamp duty, bank charges, and valuation expenses are taken into account.

It is desirable therefore to calculate a return adjusted for transaction expenses.

> The purpose of this chapter is to enable you to calculate investment and borrowing rates adjusted for transaction expenses.

COMPOUND INTEREST LOAN WITH EXPENSES

Consider a 15-year first mortgage for $40,000 based on a compound rate of 13.8% per annum convertible monthly. Loan application and valuation fees amount to $300 and legal charges by the lender's solicitors amount to $400. Costs for the borrower's legal services resulting from the mortgage amount to $250.

There is a final bank charge of $250 at the expiration of the mortgage.

Expenses which do not arise as a result of the mortgage (e.g. stamp duty on purchase) have been ignored.

Required: Determine the borrowing rate (i) adjusted for transaction costs.

Solution: The equation of value becomes:

$$40,000 = PA_{\overline{180}|i} + 950 + 250V^{180} \quad @ \ i$$

where P = monthly repayment.

To determine the monthly repayment P, use the equation:

$$40,000 = PA_{\overline{180}|1.15\%}$$

$$\therefore P = \$527.33$$

$$\therefore 40,000 = 527.33A_{\overline{180}|i} + 950 + 250V^{180}$$

239

The cash flows are:

Month	0	1	2	3		179	180
Cash flows	40,000 (950)	(527.33)	(527.33)	(527.33)		(527.33)	(527.33) (250.00)

You need to use a computer or Hewlett-Packard to find the *IRR*. Using an iterative process, the Hewlett-Packard is limited as it allows for only 99 repeated cash flows. Therefore we will present-value 99 lots of 527.33 then a further 80 lots. The final payment of $527.33 is added to the $250 final bank charge. Thus:

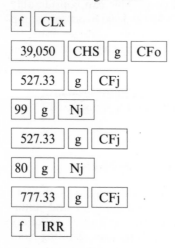

$i = 1.191\%$ per month or 14.292% per annum nominal.

The transaction expenses have increased the borrowing rate by 0.492%.

The borrowing rates as effective rates of interest are 15.266% after transaction expenses [i.e. $(1.01191)^{12} - 1$] and 14.707% excluding transaction costs. (Using the Hewlett-Packard and ignoring transaction costs, the *IRR* is 1.149992% per month or $1.01149992^{12} - 1 = 14.707\%$ per annum effective.)

BILL OF EXCHANGE TRANSACTION COST EFFECTS

Consider the situation where you wish to build a home in Canberra and sell it shortly after. The bank offers you a $70,000 (face value) bill of exchange for 180 days @ 16% per annum. A bank establishment fee of $755 is charged. No stamp duty will apply to this bill of exchange established in Canberra.

The annualised borrowing rate adjusted for transaction expenses

$$= \frac{\text{Repayment after 180 days} - (\text{loan} - 755)}{(\text{loan} - 755)} \times \frac{36{,}500}{180}$$

Now, Price per $100 face value $= \dfrac{3{,}650{,}000}{36{,}500 + (180)(16)}$

$$= \$92.686643$$

$$\text{Loan} = \frac{70{,}000}{100} \times 92.686643$$

$$= \$64{,}880$$

Thus the effective annualised borrowing rate adjusted for transaction

$$\text{costs} = \frac{70{,}000 - (64{,}880 - 755)}{64{,}880 - 755} \times \frac{36{,}500}{180}$$

$$= 18.578$$

The transaction charges have therefore increased the annualised borrowing rate by 2.578%.

TRANSACTION EFFECT ON INVESTMENT RETURNS

A certain capital-guaranteed insurance bond offers a minimum return of 10% per annum compound (convertible quarterly). Outlay on the bond is assumed to be $20,000 and 5% initial commission/administration fees are deducted. The bond is assumed to be held for 10 years upon which interest income is offered free of tax.

The guaranteed minimum return (j) adjusted for transaction costs can be found from the equation:

$$[20{,}000 - 0.05(20{,}000)](1.025)^{40} = 20{,}000(1 + j)^{40}$$

$$(1 + j)^{40} = 2.550811$$

$$(1 + j) = (2.550811)^{1/40}$$

$$= 2.550811^{0.025}$$

$$j = 2.3686\% \text{ quarterly}$$

$$= 9.4744\% \text{ per annum}$$

An example in life assurance

A 5-year endowment assurance provides a return of premiums paid (plus interest) on death with a benefit of $40,000 on maturity. Premiums are annual in advance based on 10% per annum compound. Initial commission amounts to $800. Initial administration expenses are 6% of the total premium. Renewal expenses (for the second and subsequent premiums) amount to 2% of each premium. There is a charge on maturity of $300.

Required: Determine the total annual premium.

Solution:

In most life assurance problems the probability of surviving to pay premiums and collect the end benefit must be included in the equation of value. In the above example, there is no death risk assumed. We can therefore use straight compound interest.

The inflows and outflows to the life office, assuming a total (gross) annual premium (P) which includes all expenses, are:

Year	0	1	2	3	4	5
Inflows						
Gross premiums	P	P	P	P	P	
Outflows						
Maturity value						40,000
Initial commission	800					
Administration fee	$0.06P$					
Renewal fees		$0.02P$	$0.02P$	$0.02P$	$0.02P$	
Maturity fee						300

The equation of value is therefore:

$$P\ddot{A}_{\overline{5}|10\%} = 40{,}300V^5 + 800 + 0.06P + 0.02PA_{\overline{4}|10\%} \text{ @ } 10\%$$

$$P\ddot{A}_{\overline{5}|10\%} - 0.02PA_{\overline{4}|10\%} - 0.06P = 40{,}300V^5 + 800$$

$$P(\ddot{A}_{\overline{5}|10\%} - 0.02A_{\overline{4}|10\%} - 0.06) = 40{,}300V^5 + 800 \text{ @ } 10\%$$

$$P(4.169865 - 0.063397 - 0.06) = 25{,}823.12932$$

$$P(4.046468) = 25{,}823.12932$$

$$\therefore P = \$6{,}381.65 \quad \text{(rounding up)}$$

The gross annual premium is therefore $6,381.65.

DELAYS IN REMITTING INTEREST

On some occasions interest, particularly on cash, may be received several days after the date that interest is calculated and principal refunded. An example would be $1m deposited for 7 days at a flat rate of 10% per annum. The principal is refunded at the end of 7 days, however interest of $\frac{10}{100} \times 1m \times \frac{7}{365}$, i.e. $1,917.81, is payable at the end of the month. Assume that the principal is refunded 23 days before the interest is received.

The cash flow diagram is therefore:

Days	0	7		30
Cash flow	($1m)	$1m		1917.81

Assume the interest forgone on $1917.81 is at 10% per annum simple.

$$\text{The present value of } \$1917.81 \text{ at day } 7 = \frac{1917.81}{1 + 0.1 \times 23/365}$$

$$= \$1905.8008$$

$$\text{The annualised } \textit{flat} \text{ rate of return} = \frac{1,001,905.8008 - 1m}{1m} \times \frac{36,500}{7}$$

$$= 9.9374\%$$

The effect of a 23-day deferral in receiving the interest has reduced the rate of return on cash by 0.0626%. This can make a substantial difference on multi-million dollar deposits.

CONCLUSION

When negotiating loan or investment contracts the true rate of interest should reflect:
  (i) all charges associated with the contract;
 (ii) a consistent timing of principal with the interest (e.g. interest deferments should be compensated for the loss of 'interest on the interest';
(iii) the effective annualised rate.

EXERCISES

1   A 10-year first mortgage for $50,000 is repayable monthly @ 1% per month compound. Associated loan expenses are:
   a) initial legal fee $500
   b) initial bank charges $400
   c) bank charge on maturity $200.
   Find the nominal and effective annual borrowing rates adjusted for transaction expenses.

2   A 90-day bill of exchange at 14% for $60,000 face value has an assumed bank charge of $600. Find the annualised borrowing rate.

3   A 5-year pure endowment policy for $50,000 is payable by half-yearly premiums in advance. Expenses amount to $500 commission, 7% of initial half-yearly premium and $1\frac{1}{2}$% of subsequent half-yearly premiums. Interest is assumed to be 5% compound per half-year. Find the half-yearly premium.

4   A 7-year investment of $30,000 guarantees a return of 10% per annum compound. The interest is reinvested back into the same investment. Three per cent of the deposit is deducted for commission and administration and there is a 0.1% annual charge (on the $30,000) for the second and subsequent years. Find the effective return after transaction costs.
(Tax is assumed to be ignored.)

5   Take the same details as in exercise 4, except that 20% of the interest is taxed in full at maturity (a 29% rebate of tax is assumed), with a 12-month deferment of tax payment. Find the after-tax rate of return adjusted for transaction costs.

6   A certain money market fund pays flat interest on cash (held for at least one day) on the 15th of the month. A deposit of $10m has been made on 3 May 1988 at 11.2% per annum (simple). The deposit has been held for 4 days. Principal is returned on the morning of 8 May 1988 (4 days assumed) and the interest is paid on 15 May 1988. Find the annualised *flat* return on cash, adjusted for the deferment of interest and state any assumption(s).

24

Foreign Exchange Mathematics

Whenever you go overseas you are faced with the problem of selecting the currency that will not only be readily convertible to meet day-to-day expenses but will also offer a reasonable return.

Whilst you are abroad, any strengthening of that local currency against the home currency will mean increased home dollars on your return.

Against this, a borrowing in an overseas currency will have an increased cost of funds if the overseas currency strengthens, relative to the home economy.

> By the end of this chapter you will:
> (i) appreciate how foreign exchange rates impact on interest rates;
> (ii) understand the mathematics of protecting against adverse currency movements.

SPOT

A spot transaction is the purchase or sale of foreign exchange with delivery and settlement to be completed normally on the second following business day.

A spot of $US/$A means the number of $US required to buy/sell one $A. For example, a spot of $US/$A = S($US/$A) = 0.75 means 0.75$US are needed to buy each $A1, or each $US buys $(1 \div 0.75)$A = $A1.33.

A bid (buy) and a sell is always viewed from the FX (foreign exchange) dealer's viewpoint. Suppose you wish to repay a loan denominated in $US with $A. You owe $US 1.1m. You must use your $A to buy the $US, i.e. the FX dealer, say a bank, *sells* $US to you, the borrower. At a spot ($US/$A) = 0.75, you must buy $US 1.1m with $A(1.1m \div 0.75) = $A1.47m.

FORWARD RATE

A forward transaction calls for delivery at a fixed future date of a specified amount of one currency for a specified amount of another currency. The exchange rate is established at the time the contract is agreed, but payment and delivery are not required until maturity. Forward rates are normally quoted for fixed periods of 1, 2, 3 and 6 months. One can buy or sell forward.

A *prospective weakening* of the home currency denotes a *forward premium*.

A *prospective strengthening* of the home currency denotes a *forward discount*.

A change of 1 point means a change in the forward rate of 0.0001. Thus a change of 100 points means a change in the forward rate of 0.01.

For example, if there is a forward 30-day premium of 100 points with spot ($US/$A) = 0.75, then the exchange rate in 30 days will be 0.7400. Similarly, a forward discount of 100 points would change the forward exchange rate to 0.7600.

BORROWING IN EURODOLLARS

Consider a $10m 90-day loan borrowed in the Euro-$US market. (These are $US borrowed outside the US. Similarly, Euroyen means that yen are raised outside Japan.)

The borrowing rate is assumed to be 8% per annum (on a 360-day basis).

Spot $US/$A = 0.7500

The 'locked-in' (or hedged) exchange rate in 90 days using the forward market is assumed to be 0.7400. The difference between spot and forward is $0.7500 - 0.7400 = 0.0100$. This is called a forward premium (meaning that extra·$A or a 'premium' of $A is required to offset the future weakening·of $A against $US). If the forward rate were 0.7600 there would be a discount of 0.0100 or 100 points, if spot were 0.7500.

The principal and interest are hedged in 90 days at the exchange rate of 0.7400. This means that the borrower buys $US in 90 days to repay the loan + interest at a fixed exchange rate of 0.7400, using the forward market.

At the inception of the loan, the borrower receives $US 10m. As the $US are then sold by the borrower for $A, *buy* rate is appropriate, as the bank is buying the $US.

$$\text{\$A received by borrower} = \frac{10m}{0.75}$$

$$= 13.\dot{3}m$$

After 90 days, one-quarter of the US financial 360-day year interest of 2% ($\frac{1}{4}$ of 8%) is charged.

The principal + interest due after 90 days = $US 10.2m

Here the borrower must buy $US. As the bank is selling $US, a bank forward sell rate of 0.7400 is locked in, by contract.

The \$A due after 90 days $= \dfrac{10.2}{0.74}$

$= 13,783,783.78$

The cost of funds for 90 days $= \dfrac{13,783,783.78 - 13,333,333.33}{13,333,333.33}$

$= \dfrac{13,783,783.78}{13,333,333.33} - \dfrac{13,333,333.33}{13,333,333.33}$

$= \dfrac{13,783,783.78}{13,333,333.33} - 1$

$= 3.37838\%$

The annualised cost of funds $= 3.37838 \times \dfrac{365}{90}$
(for 365 days)

$= 13.7012\%$

WEAKENING OF SPOT

If the spot rate reduced to 0.7468 and the forward premium remained at 100 points, what would be the effect on the annualised cost of funds, assuming that all the other factors in the above example are constant?

\$A receipts $= \dfrac{10\text{mUS}}{0.7468}$

$= \$A13,390,465.99$

\$A due after 90 days $= \dfrac{\$10.2\text{mUS}}{0.7368}$

$= 13,843,648.21$

Cost of funds for 90 days $= \dfrac{13,843,648.21 - 13,390,465.99}{13,390,465.99}$

$= \dfrac{13,843,648.21}{13,390,465.99} - 1$

$= 3.384365\%$

The annualised cost of funds
(for 365 days) $= 13.72548\%$

A 32-point drop in spot with all other factors constant caused the landed cost to rise from 13.7012% to 13.7255%.

CHANGE IN DISCOUNT OR PREMIUM

What would be the effect of changing the forward premium, holding all other factors constant?

i.e. Spot $US/$A $= 0.7500$

Forward premium $= 132$ points (remember we changed spot by 32 points)

End hedge or forward exchange rate $= 0.7500 - 0.0132$

$= 0.7368$

$A receipts $= \dfrac{10m}{0.75}$

$= 13,333,333.33$

$A due after 90 days $= \dfrac{\$10.2mUS}{0.7368}$

$= 13,843,648.21$

Cost of funds for 90 days $= \dfrac{13,843,648.21}{13,333,333.33} - 1$

$= 3.82736\%$

Annualised cost of funds $= 15.5221\%$

The effect of a 32-point change in the forward premium (from 100 points to 132 points) has increased the annualised cost of funds from 13.7012% to 15.5221%.

EQUILIBRIUM WITH DOMESTIC RATES

The landed cost is the rate at which funds can be borrowed offshore, fully hedged. Take the last example of 15.5221%. If $10m can be borrowed in Australia for 16%, the demand for borrowing in $US will increase (since the rate is cheaper in the US). This demand for $US will weaken the $A relative to the $US causing the landed cost to rise in line with higher domestic rates. Eventually the landed cost moves into equilibrium with domestic borrowing rates.

From the preceding two examples a weakening in the spot $A or forward $A against another currency will increase landed costs. If overseas borrowings are heavily weighted in that currency domestic rates for the same term will rise.

Hence a reaction in the money market that $US/$A has fallen generally causes an upward reaction in domestic interest rates.

PURCHASE PRICE PARITY (PPP)

Assume two countries produce the same product (say rubber bands) and for the sake of this simple model this is the only product to be considered.

Country A sells rubber bands in $A

Country B sells rubber bands in $B

Buyer C pays the same amount $C for identical volume/quality of rubber bands from each producer.

Country A, unfortunately, is starting to face rampant inflation.

Inflation in A is 12% per annum compound.
Inflation in country B is only 1%.

Country B, having the lower inflation rate, will have more attractive product prices.

Country C, in demanding $B for country B products, will push up the value of $B, relative to $A.

Conversely, $A will fall (relative to $B) due to the reduced demand for $A denominated products.

Country C's outlay for the rubber bands will therefore remain the same. Inflation is offset by currency depreciation.

Intuitively the $B will appreciate approximately 11% (12% − 1%) against the $A. More accurately, this relationship can be developed as follows:

Let $S(\$A/\pounds)$ = number of $A required for £1.

Assume $S(\$A/\pounds) = 2.4000$

If a man's coat in the UK cost £100(P_{UK}), the equivalent price in Australia would be $240A($P_A$).

$$(100)(2.4000) = 240$$

i.e. $P_{UK} \cdot [S(\$A/\pounds)] = P_A$　　　　　　　(1)

Let the inflation rate per annum in UK $= j_{UK}$
Let the inflation rate per annum in Australia $= j_A$
The position in one year would be:

$$P_{UK}(1 + j_{UK})F(\$A/\pounds) = P_A(1 + j_A)\qquad(2)$$

where $F(\$A/\pounds)$ = the forward spot rate in one year.
Dividing equation (2) by equation (1), we get:

$$\frac{F(\$A/\pounds)}{S(\$A/\pounds)} \cdot (1 + j_{UK}) = (1 + j_A)$$

$$F(\$A/\pounds) = \frac{S(\$A/\pounds)(1 + j_A)}{(1 + j_{UK})}$$

Assume inflation in Australia = 6% and in the UK = 4%.

$$F(\$A/\pounds) = \frac{2.4000(1.06)}{1.04}$$

$$= 2.4462$$

In other words, based on a spot of $2.4000A to the £1, the forecast exchange rate in one year, using PPP, is $2.4462A to the £1.

This theory ignores withholding taxes, transaction costs, relative political, economic and sociological factors, and may suffer from inconsistencies in the nature of the inflation indices (e.g. in Australia, inflation can be measured against wages or consumer prices. The overseas measure would require the same inflation basis.)

Example 1

West Germany has a spot of 1.2000 Dm to the $A. Forecasted inflation in West Germany for the next six months is 0.4% and in Australia is 3%. Find the forecasted Dm/$A in six months.

Intuitively, the $A will weaken (higher inflation) by approximately 2.6% (3%–0.4%).

i.e. $1.2000 - 2.6\%$ of $1.2000 = 1.1688$

$$P_{WG} = P_A \cdot S(Dm/\$A) \qquad (3)$$

$$P_{WG}(1 + j_{WG}) = P_A F(Dm/\$A)(1 + j_A) \qquad (4)$$

Dividing equation (4) by equation (3) we get:

$$(1 + j_{WG}) = \frac{F(Dm/\$A)}{S(Dm/\$A)} \cdot (1 + j_A)$$

$$F(Dm/\$A) = \frac{(1 + j_{WG})}{(1 + j_A)} \cdot S(Dm/\$A)$$

$$= \frac{1.004}{1.03} \cdot (1.2000)$$

$$= 1.1697$$

In crude terms, however, if a home country's inflation is worsening relative to another's, it is one sign of a weakening in the home currency, relative to the other currency.

If there is high consumer demand in the home country with imports outstripping exports, imports become more expensive due to the weakening of the home currency. This may further add to inflation (and higher interest rates).

INTEREST RATE PARITY

If $100A are borrowed in $US and invested in the USA at US rates then the maturing proceeds converted to $A should equal the accumulation of $100A in Australia for the same term.

Interest rate parity therefore means that a domestic investment accumulated at the domestic rate will equal the accumulated value offshore, at the offshore rate, converted back to the domestic currency (at the forward rate). Each investment will involve the same initial outlay in terms of the domestic currency.

This result can be used to find the forward exchange rate, as follows.

$$\$100A(1 + r_A) = \frac{100 \cdot S(\$US/\$A)(1 + r_{US})}{F(\$US/\$A)}$$

where r_A = the Australian rate for n days
and r_{US} = the US rate for n days

$$\therefore \frac{1 + r_A}{1 + r_{US}} = \frac{S(\$US/\$A)}{F(\$US/\$A)}$$

$$F(\$US/\$A) = \frac{S(\$US/\$A)(1 + r_{US})}{(1 + r_A)}$$

Example 2

Find the forward premium given the following:

$r_A = 11\%$ per annum (365-day basis)
$r_{US} = 7\%$ per annum (360-day basis)
Investment period = 90 days
Investment = $100A
Spot ($US/$A) = 0.7500

$$100\left(1 + \frac{0.11 \times 90}{365}\right) = \frac{75\left(1 + \dfrac{0.07 \times 90}{360}\right)}{F(\$US/\$A)}$$

$$F(\$US/\$A) = \frac{75\left(1 + \dfrac{0.07 \times 90}{360}\right)}{100\left(1 + \dfrac{0.11 \times 90}{365}\right)}$$

$$= \frac{76.3125}{102.7123}$$

$$= 0.7430$$

The forward premium $= 0.7500 - 0.7430$

$$= 0.0070 \text{ or } 70 \text{ points}$$

Example 3

Given example 2 above, derive an equation for the forward premium in relation to $S(\$US/\$A)$, r_A, r_{US}, and n, the investment period in days.

$$100\left(1 + \frac{r_A \cdot n}{365}\right) = \frac{100[S(\$US/\$A)]\left(1 + \dfrac{r_{US} \cdot n}{360}\right)}{F(\$US/\$A)}$$

$$F(\$US/\$A) = \frac{S(\$US/\$A)\left(1 + \dfrac{r_{US} \cdot n}{360}\right)}{\left(1 + \dfrac{r_A \cdot n}{365}\right)}$$

forward premium $= S(\$US/\$A) - F(\$US/\$A)$

$$= S(\$US/\$A) - \frac{S(\$US/\$A)\left(1 + \dfrac{r_{US} \cdot n}{360}\right)}{\left(1 + \dfrac{r_A \cdot n}{365}\right)}$$

$$= \frac{S(\$US/\$A)\left[1 - \left(1 + \dfrac{nr_{US}}{360}\right)\right]}{1 + \dfrac{nr_A}{365}}$$

$$= S(\$US/\$A)\left[\frac{1 + \dfrac{nr_A}{365} - 1 - \dfrac{nr_{US}}{360}}{1 + \dfrac{nr_A}{365}}\right]$$

$$\therefore \text{ Forward premium} = \frac{S(\$US/\$A)n\left(\dfrac{r_A}{365} - \dfrac{r_{US}}{360}\right)}{1 + \dfrac{nr_A}{365}}$$

In the case of the \$A against the £, since each financial year is 365 days,

$$\text{the forward premium} = \frac{S(£/\$A)\dfrac{n}{365}(r_A - r_{UK})}{1 + \dfrac{nr_A}{365}}$$

The approximate formula often used for rough margin calculations (i.e. calculations of premium or discount) is:

$$\text{Forward margin} \approx \text{Spot} \times \frac{\text{Interest}}{\text{Differential}} \times \text{Time fraction}$$

This formula ignores the denominator $\left(1 + \dfrac{nr_A}{365}\right)$ above and also assumes the same number of days in the financial year for the two countries involved.

Example 4

Assuming Spot (Dm/\$A) = 1.2

$$r_{WG} = 4\%$$
$$r_A = 10\%$$
$$n = 90 \text{ days}$$

find the *approximate* forward margin using the approximate equation above.

Solution: Estimated forward margin $= 1.2000 \times 0.06 \times \dfrac{90}{365}$

$$= 0.0178, \quad \text{i.e. } 178 \text{ points}$$

EUROBONDS

Eurobonds are bonds in currency X available outside country X. Coupon interest is generally annual and pricing is based on the present value of future coupons and the face amount.

Companies wishing to raise debt finance may issue Eurobonds off-shore. This may have the attraction to the Eurobond investor and borrower that yields are attractive.

Consider a 10-year Eurosterling bond, issue yield 5%, purchased by an Australian investor at Spot ($A/£) = 2.4000.

The coupon on the issue is 4.6% per annum.

After 12 months the Eurobond is estimated to be sold for a yield of 4.8%. Inflation in the UK is projected to be 3.5% and 8% in Australia.

Find the estimated horizon return for the year assuming the sale proceeds are converted at a future exchange rate based on PPP.

Solution:

$$\text{Purchase price in £} = 4.6 A_{\overline{10}|5\%} + 100V^{10} \text{ @ } 5\%$$

$$= 96.9113$$

$$\text{Purchase price in \$A} = 232.5871$$

$$\text{Sale price in £} = 4.6 A_{\overline{9}|4.8\%} + 100V^9 \text{ @ } 4.8\%$$

$$= 98.5657$$

$$\text{Sale proceeds + coupon in £} = 98.5657 + 4.6$$

$$= 103.1657$$

Using PPP, the forecasted exchange rate in one year

$$= 2.4000 \frac{(1.08)}{(1.035)}$$

$$= 2.5044$$

Sale proceeds of bond + coupon in $A

$$= (103.1657)2.5044$$

$$= 258.3682$$

$$\text{Horizon rate of return} = \frac{258.3682 - 232.5871}{232.5871} \times \frac{100}{1}$$

$$= 11.0845\%$$

OTHER SIGNS OF A WEAKENING HOME CURRENCY

The following signs would bring about a worsening of one's own currency against currency X:
 (1) worsening inflation relative to X;
 (2) worsening exports minus imports (balance of trade);
 (3) credit rating deteriorating relative to X;
 (4) $\dfrac{\text{interest on foreign debt}}{\text{Gross National Product}}$ deteriorating relative to X;
 (5) $\dfrac{\text{interest on foreign debt}}{\text{exports}}$ deteriorating relative to X;
 (6) forward rates deteriorating relative to X;
 (7) employment deteriorating relative to X;
 (8) political, economic, sociological instability increasing relative to X;
 (9) import growth outstripping exports relative to X;
 (10) housing starts and investment deteriorating relative to X.

Example 5

An oil explorer is considering exploration overseas. Export prices from the host country will be linked to the $US.
 List the problems associated with calculating an *NPV*.

 A non-exhaustive set of problems could be:
 (1) determining the project risk;
 (2) determining the return on the market overseas;
 (3) forecasting cash flows and adjusting for future political, seasonal, economic and sociological impacts;
 (4) estimating future exchange rates;
 (5) estimating possible oil strike dates, volume and oil prices;
 (6) allowing for world demand for oil and adjusting for cartel manipulation;
 (7) estimating future inflation rates;
 (8) adjusting for changes in world growth, importers' demands and general domestic, importers' and world interest trends.

CONCLUSION

Decision-making involving offshore cash flows involves a cobweb of intertwining threads—interest rates affecting currency and vice-versa; relative inflation impacting on imports, currency and interest; currency influencing imports, exports, the balance of trade, inflation and interest rates; growth drying up money supply, lifting interest rates domestically, possibly raising imports and worsening the balance of payments.

A never-ending cycle! And often these threads can significantly affect an *NPV*, even if the quantifiable *NPV* looks reasonable.

EXERCISES

1 A Eurodollar 90-day loan of $10 mUS is obtained at spot $US/$A = 0.7000. The forward exchange rate is 0.6900 and the interest on the Eurodollar loan is 8% (on 360-day basis). Find the cost of hedging the principal and interest expressed on a 365-day basis.

2 If the forward exchange rate in exercise 1 reduces to 0.6875, find the amended landed cost. What do you notice when forward exchange rates worsen?

3 The spot $US/$A exchange rate is assumed to be 0.7000. If inflation for the next year is anticipated to be 6.5% in Australia and 4.5% in the USA, determine the projected exchange rate 12 months from now, assuming that Purchase Price Parity (PPP) prevails.

4 A project is assumed to derive after-tax cash flows in the UK equal to £200,000 per annum for 3 years. Spot ($A/£) = 2.4000. Inflation in the UK is projected to be 4% per annum compound and in Australia 6.5%.
   Required: Determine the break-even purchase price (in $A) of the project, assuming a required rate of return of 10% per annum compound. Assume that the yearly after-tax cash flows are invested in Australia and that PPP prevails.

5 Using Interest Rate Parity and given
$$r_A = 12\%$$
$$r_{US} = 7\%$$
Spot ($US/$A) = 0.7000,
derive the forward exchange rate after 90 days.

6 A 10-year sterling Eurobond is issued by an Australian company. The bond coupon (paid annually) is 5% per annum and face amount is £50 million. The Spot ($A/£) = 2.4000. The yield on which the bond is sold is 6% per annum and there is an establishment fee of 0.2% of the face amount. The fee is in sterling. *Required:* Determine the Australian company's $A receipts.

25

Financial Futures

Interest rate futures were introduced into the Australian market in October 1979 to add a new dimension to financing strategies adopted by corporate treasurers, investment managers and money market dealers. Increased usage by money market dealers and other corporate entities is evident in the expanding volume of business being transacted.

> By the end of this chapter you will be able to apply futures contracts to the hedging (locking-in) of future borrowing and investment requirements, allowing for all transaction charges and interest forgone on capital outlay.

BABF CONTRACTS

The *bank-accepted bill futures* (BABF) contract is quoted in an index derived by deducting the yield rate per cent per annum from 100. A futures contract is a binding obligation to deliver a specific quantity of a specific grade of good at an agreed price, place and rate. Actual deliveries of the good occur infrequently in relation to total contract turnover, since the legal and institutional framework within which futures trading is conducted provides that a party may liquidate a delivery obligation by entering into an offsetting arrangement. In other words, an opposite futures position is obtained, and the cash settlement represents the difference between these two positions.

If one examines the BABF contract specifications, it is clear that the contract is for certain types of securities for which value or settlement price is synonymously determined by yield rate. Specifically, the Sydney Futures Exchange Ltd By-Laws provide that:

> In the fulfilment of every contract the seller must deliver $500,000 face value of bank-accepted bills of exchange comprising five bills each having a face value of $100,000.

Each bill comprising a tender shall:
- have been accepted by the same approved acceptor
- have been drawn by the same drawer
- have the same maturity date
- be payable at the same city branch of an approved acceptor in an Australian state capital
- bear the open endorsement of the person entitled to proceeds at settlement.

The maturity date on each bill will be not less than 85 days and not more than 95 days from the date of settlement. The signature of the acceptor and the last endorser appearing on the bill shall be registered with the approved settlement facility before 3.00 p.m. on the final day of trading.

Numerous strategies can be devised to maximise yield over an investment period or to hedge an investment or to improve financial planning by reducing borrowing costs.

Consider the Futures Market release from the *Financial Review* dated 26 May 1988 (Table 2).

Recall that the pricing formula for a bill with n days to maturity, yielding $r\%$, is:

$$P = \frac{3,650,000}{36,500 + nr}$$

The price P + interest for the fraction of a year $\frac{n}{365}$ = the face value of 100.

i.e. $P + \left(\frac{n}{365} \times \frac{r}{100} \times P \right) = 100$

$$P\left(1 + \frac{nr}{36,500}\right) = 100$$

$$P\left(\frac{36,500 + nr}{36,500}\right) = 100$$

$$\therefore P = \frac{3,650,000}{36,500 + nr}$$

The previous price beside June 88 under Bank Bills (i.e. the first row) is 87.45. This constitutes a yield of $100 - 87.45$ or 12.55%. In fact the opening or previous price, high and low, are all three indices expressing yield where

$$100 - \text{the index} = \text{yield}$$

FUTURES MARKETS

The SFE futures and options trading data as detailed below does not include the night trading
session in the financial contracts on May 25th because of deadline requirements.

	Prev. Price	Opening Range		High	Low	Settlement Price	Change	$ Value of Chg	Volume	Open Pos.

**BANK BILLS—$A500,000 face value, 90-day bank bills; quotes
are an index derived by deducting yield rate per cent per annum from 100.**

Jun 88	87.45	87.45	87.50	87.56	87.41	—	—		10964	39376
Sep 88	87.37	—	—	87.45	87.34	—	—		1308	10306
Dec 88	87.12	—	—	87.15	87.08	—	—		▲123	5415
Mar 89	86.94	—	—	86.97	86.90	—	—		106	3340
Jun 89	86.73	—	—	86.82	86.75	—	—		9	2310
Sep 89	86.73	—	—	86.82	86.80	—	—		7	1319
Dec 89	86.73	—	—	86.82	86.80	—	—		13	953
Mar 90	86.73	—	—	86.85	86.80	—	—		10	709

TOTALS: **Volume** 12540 **Open Position (previous day):** 63728.

ALL ORDINARIES SHARE PRICE INDEX—dollar value of 100 times index.

Jun 88	1479.0	1490.0	1495.0	1516.0	1490.0	—	—		1607	5220
Sep 88	1495.0	—	—	1534.0	1530.0	—	—		27	101
Dec 88	1525.0	—	—	—	—	—	—		0	0
Mar 89	1555.0	—	—	—	—	—	—		0	0
Jun 89	1585.0	—	—	—	—	—	—		0	0
Sep 89	1615.0	—	—	—	—	—	—		0	0

TOTALS: **Volume** 1634 **Open Position (previous day):** 5321.

**TEN YEAR COMMONWEALTH TREASURY BOND—$A100,000 face value;
quotes are an index derived by deducting yield rate per cent
per annum from 100.**

Jun 88	87.915	87.920	87.940	87.985	87.920	—	—		15166	62507
Sep 88	87.815	—	—	87.900	87.840	—	—		143	3123
Dec 88	87.715	—	—	—	—	—	—		0	7
Mar 89	87.615	—	—	—	—	—	—		0	0

TOTALS: **Volume** 15309 **Open Position (previous day):** 65637.

LIVE CATTLE—10,000 kilos; cents per kilo.

Jul 88	120.0	119.0	122.5	121.0	121.0	121.0	+1.0	100.00	1	22
Dec 88	111.8	114.0	121.0	112.5	112.5	112.3	+.5	50.00	1	10

TOTALS: **Volume** 2 **Open Position (previous day):** 215.

WOOL (CASH SETTLEMENT)—2,500 kilos 22 micron; cents per kilo.

Jun 88	1300	1200	1400	—	—	1300	—	.00	0	11

TOTALS: **Volume** 0 **Open Position (previous day):** 95.

**AUSTRALIAN DOLLAR—$A100,000 face value;
quotes in US dollars per Australian dollars.**

Jun 88	.7840	.7826	.7835	.7875	.7846	—	—		61	1011
Sep 88	.7748	—	—	—	—	—	—		0	8

TOTALS: **Volume** 61 **Open Position (previous day):** 1019.

**THREE YEAR COMMONWEALTH TREASURY BOND—$A100,000 face value;
quotes are an index derived by deducting yield rate per cent
per annum from 100.**

Jun 88	87.89	87.91	87.93	87.94	87.86	—	—		4486	10468
Sep 88	87.73	—	—	—	—	—	—		0	0

TOTALS: **Volume** 4486 **Open Position (previous day):** 10468.

COMEX GOLD CONTRACT—100 troy ounces; US cents per ounce.

May 88	462.2	—	—	—	—	460.6	−1.6	−160.00	0	8
Jun 88	463.0	460.8	461.3	—	—	461.1	−1.9	−190.00	0	39419
Jul 88	464.9	—	—	—	—	463.7	−1.2	−120.00	0	0
Aug 88	466.4	—	—	—	—	465.4	−1.0	−100.00	0	28462
Oct 88	471.1	—	—	—	—	470.3	−.8	−80.00	0	11606
Dec 88	476.3	—	—	—	—	475.4	−.9	−90.00	0	22766
Feb 89	481.3	—	—	—	—	480.7	−.6	−60.00	0	9651
Apr 89	486.7	—	—	—	—	486.2	−.5	−50.00	0	6888
Jun 89	492.2	—	—	—	—	491.8	−.4	−40.00	0	9638
Aug 89	498.1	—	—	—	—	497.8	−.3	−30.00	0	5887
Oct 89	504.3	—	—	—	—	504.1	−.2	−20.00	0	7217
Dec 89	510.6	—	—	—	—	510.5	−.1	−10.00	0	5523
Feb 90	516.9	—	—	—	—	516.9	—	.00	0	1593

TOTALS: **Volume** 0 **Open Position (previous day):** 148658.

Table 2 (cont.)

U.S. T-BONDS—$US100,000 face value; quotes are in $US per $US100 face value minimum fluctuation is $US1/32.									
Jun 88	85-10	85-08	85-22	—	—	85-15	+ −05	156.25	0	6579
Sep 88	84-21	—	—	—	—	84-17	− −04	−125.00	0	574
Dec 88	83-23	—	—	—	—	83-19	− −04	−125.00	0	0

TOTALS: Volume 0 Open Position (previous day): 7153.

EURO DOLLAR INTEREST RATES—$US1m 3-month time deposit; quotes are an index derived by deducting yield rate per cent per annum from 100.

Jun 88	92.32	92.25	92.39	—	—	92.36	+.04	100.00	0 19271
Sep 88	91.79	—	—	—	—	91.81	+.02	50.00	0 12978
Dec 88	91.46	—	—	—	—	91.46	—	.00	0 9435
Mar 89	91.26	—	—	—	—	91.26	—	.00	0 1580
Jun 89	91.07	—	—	—	—	91.07	—	.00	0 229
Sep 89	90.92	—	—	—	—	90.92	—	.00	0 37
Dec 89	90.78	—	—	—	—	90.78	—	.00	0 18
Mar 90	90.65	—	—	—	—	90.65	—	.00	0 9

TOTALS: Volume 0 Open Position (previous day): 43557.

On 25 May one could buy a bill from a low index (high yield → low price) @ $100 - 87.41$, i.e. 12.59% to a high index (low yield → high price) of $100 - 87.56$, i.e. 12.44%.

The price per contract (based on $500,000 face value) would therefore range from:

$$\frac{3,650,000}{36,500 + (90)(12.59)} \times \frac{500,000}{100} \quad \text{to} \quad \frac{3,650,000}{36,500 + (90)(12.44)} \times \frac{500,000}{100}$$

or $484,945   to $485,119

The transaction costs amount to a deposit of approximately $1,100 refundable on delivery plus Clearing House fees to cover other overheads (say a fixed per 'deal' charge).

Thus at 25 May 1988 a contract is entered into to buy a bill in June 1988 (on the Wednesday preceding the second Friday). Assuming a yield of 12.59%, the purchase price would be $484,945. Ninety days later $500,000 would be collected.

The investor has therefore hedged against falling interest rates and has locked in a forward 90-day investment return of slightly less than 12.59% (adjusting for transaction costs).

Alternatively, a borrower may sell a bill in the future. He/she has a bill in the portfolio. When this is delivered (sold) the raising of cash constitutes a borrowing.

In order to protect against default the Clearing House requires a deposit and margins. 'Default' means the failure of one party (buyer or seller) to meet his/her obligation.

Suppose under a buy contract at 88 (yield 12%) the proposed purchaser fails to buy and current yields are 13%. The Clearing House would buy at the contracted rate of 12%. If it then onsold the bill at the market rate of 13% it would realise a loss. This loss (expressed as the difference between the contract price and current price) is called day by day and is expressed as a margin.

Margins accrue interest and for large portfolios positive margins are often offset by negative margins. For the purpose of simplicity, we will assume a balanced portfolio where the margin balance is zero.

CASH AND CARRY

The object of this exercise is to achieve the highest annualised yield (r_h) available over an investment period of 90 days or less, which is the term of the BABF contract.

$$r_h = \left(\frac{S - P}{P}\right)\frac{36{,}500}{n}$$

where S = sale price

P = purchase price

n = days held.

Example 1

A firm has the opportunity of investing \$500,000 for 60 days. This may be achieved either (a) by purchasing 60-day *bank-accepted bills* (BABs) at 13.1%, or (b) by purchasing 150-day BABs at 15.5% (maturity being an acceptable delivery date in terms of the futures contract) and selling the last 90 days of this paper on the futures exchange at 16.25%.

The set of transactions (b) would earn a yield determined as follows:

$$r_h = \left(\frac{(S - P)}{P}\right)\frac{365}{n} \times 100$$

where

$$S \text{ and } P = \left(\frac{3{,}650{,}000}{36{,}500 + r'n}\right) \cdot \frac{500{,}000}{100}$$

$$\therefore P = \left(\frac{3{,}650{,}000}{36{,}500 + (15.5)(150)}\right)5000$$

$$= \$470{,}057.95$$

$$\therefore S = \left(\frac{3,650,000}{36,500 + (16.25)(90)}\right)5000$$

$$= \$480,737.57$$

$$\therefore r_h = \left(\frac{480,737.57 - 470,057.95}{470,057.95}\right)\frac{365}{60} \times 100$$

$$= 13.821\% \text{ per annum}$$

Thus, an annualised yield of 13.82% could be achieved for a 60-day investment by utilising the futures market. This is more attractive than the 13.1% available in the physical market, even after allowing for a 10 points (in yield) futures transaction cost. (Note that a one-point change in yield = 0.01% change, and thus a 10-point change = 0.1%.)

BREAK EVEN

Example 2

Given that a firm has the option of investing for 120 days at 15.4%, an investment manager should consider the potential benefits of purchasing 30-day physical paper at 12.5% and covering the last 90 days of the investment period through a futures contract. The question becomes: at what level must BABF trade in order to achieve the same yield as available on 120-day physical paper? This is determined as follows.

Determine the yield on physical paper for 120 days and 30 days respectively.

$$r_{120} = 15.4 \times \frac{120}{365} = 5.06301\%$$

$$r_{30} = 12.5 \times \frac{30}{365} = 1.02740\%$$

The yield on the 120-day paper must be equivalent to the yield on the 30-day paper and the futures yield (R_F), as follows:

$$1 + r_{120} = (1 + r_{30})\left(1 + \frac{R_F}{100} \times \frac{90}{365}\right)$$

$$1 + 0.0506301 = 1 + 0.0102740\left(1 + \frac{R_F}{100} \times \frac{90}{365}\right)$$

$$\frac{1.0506301}{1.0102740} = 1 + \frac{R_F}{100} \times \frac{90}{365}$$

$$\frac{1.0506301}{1.0102740} - 1 = \frac{R_F}{100} \times \frac{90}{365}$$

$$\therefore R_F = \left(\frac{1.0506301}{1.0102740} - 1\right) \cdot \frac{365}{90} \cdot \frac{100}{1}$$

$$= 16.2\% \text{ per annum}$$

Therefore, BABF would have to trade at 16.2% or better in order to achieve the same yield available on a 120-day physical paper. This does not take into account brokerage, other sundry costs, or accrued interest on futures contracts' deposits.

BOND FUTURES

The *Treasury-bond (T-bond) futures contract* was introduced in Australia on 21 February 1984. This contract has been designed to complement the bank-bill futures market by providing the hedge vehicle to 'lock in' a future investment and/or borrowing rate, as well as providing another investment opportunity for speculators.

The following sections will demonstrate the potential of the hedging arm of the bond futures contract, such that an organisation may improve its prospective returns. The techniques will also be applied to the US bond futures contract, together with an introductory consideration of Chicago options on bond futures.

THE NATURE AND PRICING OF CONTRACTS

Contract specifications
Australian Three- and Ten-Year Treasury Bond futures contracts have face values of $100,000. The US bond futures contract is expressed as $US100,000. Each contract is based on a standard. The Australian contract uses a 3-year or 10-year, 12% per annum coupon (with no tax rebate), with coupons assumed paid half-yearly. The US Treasury Note is based on a $6\frac{1}{2}$- to 10-year maturity, with an 8% coupon 10-year standard futures contract. For terms in excess of 15 years, a Treasury Bond is offered. The standard contract is a 20-year 8% coupon bond. Conversion factors are provided daily to convert the price of the standard contract to the deliverable contract required.

Delivery dates generally occur quarterly. In Australia these are the 15th day of March, June, September, and December. The delivery months can extend out to 2 years; however, the Australian contract is currently *non*-deliverable. This means there is no delivery of physical paper, unlike with a bill of exchange contract which can range from 85 to 90 days, certified on a piece of paper. Every bond may have a different coupon, making the delivery of physical paper impractical.

An initial deposit is required, and Clearing House fees are due on the closing out of the contract. The Clearing House generally pays interest on the deposit and any other excess cash, denoted by margins. Margins are needed to counteract a loss arising from adverse price movements. Conversely, the Clearing House will charge interest on negative balances.

Pricing the standard contract

The price of a $100 face amount standard contract is given by:

$$P = \frac{C}{2} A_{\overline{2n}|i} + 100V^{2n}$$

where i = the yield per compound period

n = term in years

C = annual coupon per $100 face value

m = number of compound periods per year

r = annual yield %

and $i = \frac{r}{m}$

Example 3

Assume that the contract is selling for a yield of 12%, term 3 years, and coupon 12%. What is the price per $100?

$$P = 6A_{\overline{6}|6} + 100V^6$$

$$= 100$$

i.e. in this case, the price = face amount. The price will always equal the face amount if coupon = yield and the valuation falls on a coupon date.

Quotations

The contract can be quoted in terms of *price* or *yield*. In Australia the price is based on an index derived by deducting the yield rate per cent per annum from 100. Therefore, a bid quote of 88 for a September contract means a purchase yield of 12% (i.e. 100 − 88%).

In the USA, prices are quoted on the Chicago Board of Trade in terms of points. Each point is worth $US1,000, and prices are expressed in 32nds of a point. Each 32nd is worth $US31.25 (i.e. $1,000/32). Therefore, a price of $81–12, which means 81 points plus twelve 32nds of a point, carries a price of:

$$(81 \times 1000) + (12 \times 31.25) = \$US81,375$$

OPERATION OF A BORROWING HEDGE

For an organisation to enter the futures market (i.e. to sell contracts) it must identify a borrowing need at some time in the future. If interest rates increase from the date of entering the futures market to the date of borrowing in the cash market, the extra interest incurred will be offset by a *gain* in the futures market. This gain occurs on offset when identical futures contracts are purchased at a reduced price at the time of borrowing. Conversely, a *reduction* in interest rates will be offset by a *loss* in the financial futures market.

In a *perfect hedge* the increase/reduction in interest rates should be identical to a gain/loss in the futures market. It is highly unlikely that a perfect hedge would be achieved in practice.

Let us examine a *borrowing hedge*, first using bank bill futures, and then apply a similar strategy to T-bond futures.

Locking in a borrowing rate using bank bills

Example 4

Assume that a local authority wishes to borrow $971,260 for 90 days in 6 months' time. It wishes to 'lock in' a future borrowing rate of 12% p.a. This rate is the current forward bill rate, 6 months hence.

Let the current date be indicated by the beginning of the time line, as follows:

Month	0	6
	It is necessary to sell bank bill futures contracts forward at 12% at price of $97.126.	Current 90-day bill rate is 14% (Price = $96.663.) The effect of selling a bill here at 12% will mean a borrowing rate of 12%. Notionally a bill can be purchased here at 14% and sold for 12%. The profit would reduce the loan amount.

The cash profit (or *hedged profit*) on the sell/buy of the bill futures arm per \$100 face value is

$$97.126 - 96.663 = \$0.463$$

$$\text{or } \$4630 \text{ per } \$1m.$$

The funds required in 6 months are therefore made up as follows:

$$\$971,260 = 4630 + 966,630$$

Thus, by borrowing in 6 months at 14%, the local authority receives \$966,630.

That, together with the cash profit on the sell/buy futures of \$4630, constitutes a *hedged borrowing rate* of 12%, given a repayment of \$1m in 90 days. This can be demonstrated as follows:

$$P = \frac{3,650,000}{36,500 + r'n}$$

$$97.126 = \frac{3,650,000}{36,500 + r'(90)}$$

$$\therefore r' = 12.00\%$$

Effect of transaction costs   The borrowing rate is not *exactly* 'locked in', as *transaction costs* and *interest forgone* on the deposit and *margins* have been ignored. If we assume a delivery fee of \$40, commission of \$131 and interest forgone on a deposit of \$1600 at 5%, we can utilise the above procedure to determine the borrowing rate. These costs total \$191, thereby reducing the hedged profit to \$4439 (i.e. \$4630 − 191). The hedged borrowing rate can be determined as follows. First we convert the \$191 of costs to a \$100-face-amount basis (i.e. to \$0.0191); then let

$$P = 97.126 - 0.0191$$

$$= \$97.1069$$

Since

$$P = \frac{3,650,000}{36,500 + r'n}$$

we have

$$97.1069 = \frac{3,650,000}{36,500 + r'(90)}$$

$$\therefore r' = 12.08\%$$

It is common practice to allow for a margin of approximately 10 points in yield for transaction costs, i.e. a change of 0.1% in yield.

Assumptions   The calculations make these assumptions:

1 The close-out date on the futures transaction coincides with the borrowing date.
2 The local authority is definite about its borrowing requirements. If the authority finds that at the close-out date it no longer requires to borrow the funds, it must close out the contract.

Example 5

Consider the following set of circumstances:

Cash transaction		Futures transaction	
June	$	*June*	$
Corporate treasurer of Harjoh Ltd is notified of a borrowing require- ment of $1m for 90 days in September			
Pays 2 deposits of $800 for futures contracts	1,600	Sells 2 September BABF contracts at 12% (S_F)[a]	971,261.31
September		*September*	
Draws down $1m for 90 days at 12.75%	969,519.89	Closes hedge by buying 2 BABF contracts at 12.6% (P_F)[a]	969,876.67
plus Net futures cash flow	1,263.60		
Net receipts	970,783.49	Gross profit $(S_F - P_F)$	1,384.64
		less Brokerage and fees	109.20
		less Opportunity cost[b]	11.84
		Net futures cash flow	1,263.60

Notes: a Determined by $\left(\dfrac{3,650,000}{36,500 + r'n}\right)10,000.$
    b Say 3% on $1600 futures deposits for 90 days June to September

The *effective hedged borrowing rate* can be determined as follows:

$$P = \frac{3,650,000}{36,500 + r'n}$$

$$97.078349 = \frac{3,650,000}{36,500 + r'(90)}$$

$$\therefore r' = 12.2055\%$$

This compares to an original borrowing rate of 12.75% and an original hedge rate of 12%. The difference of 0.2055% between the original and actual hedge rate is due to *basis risk* and reflects the fact that the actual debt cost of 12.75% is higher than the close-out futures rate of 12.6%.

Locking in a borrowing rate using bonds

Example 6

Let us assume that a company wishes to lock in a 3-year borrowing rate in 6 months. The borrowing rate in this instance is assumed to be *geared to the bond rate*. Hence, bond futures will be used instead of bill futures.

Assume that the 6-month forward bond rate is 13%. The strategy therefore is to sell a bond contract forward at 13% and, at the close-out date, buy against the sale at the expected higher rate. Assume that bond rates in 6 months move to 14%. Recall that the standard coupon on the 3-year contract is 12%.

At the close-out date, then, per $100 face value:

sale price of bond at 13% is

$$P_S = 6A_{\overline{6}|6.5\%} + 100V^6 \ @ \ 6\tfrac{1}{2}\%$$
$$= \$97.5795$$

purchase price of bond at 14% is

$$P_P = 6A_{\overline{6}|7\%} + 100V^6 \ @ \ 7\%$$
$$= \$95.2335$$

cash profit is

$$P_S - P_P = 97.5795 - 95.2335$$
$$= 2.3460 \text{ per } \$100 \text{ face value}$$

If the future loan is $1m, repayable by a target half-yearly rate of 13%, then any profit on the buy/sell hedge will compensate for the higher interest due on the loan.

Now, 10 contracts will be required for a $1m loan, since each bond future contract has a face value of $100,000. (It is based on a 3-year standard 12% coupon, non-deliverable bond.) Hence,

$$\text{Profit on buy/sell hedge} = 2.346 \times \frac{1,000,000}{100}$$

$$= 23,460$$

$$\text{Loan funds required} = 1,000,000 - 23,460$$

$$= \$976,540$$

The interest payment on this loan will be

$$976,540 \times \frac{0.14}{2} = \$68,358 \text{ per half-year}$$

The principal to be repaid after 3 years is \$976,540. This will be paid in return for a loan now of \$1m. This constitutes an effective cost of funds of 13.42%. This can be determined as follows:

Inflows	\$	Outflows	\$
Loan funds	976,540	Interest on loan per half-year	68,358
Hedge profit	23,460	Principal to be repaid in	
Total receipts	1,000,000	3 years	976,540

The equation of value is therefore:

$$1,000,000 = 68,358 A_{\overline{6}|i} + 976,540 V^6 \text{ @ } i\%$$

where i = internal rate of return (i.e. the compound rate per half-year).

By an iterative process, i can be found to be 6.5037% per half-year. The annual effective rate is therefore 13.43%, i.e. $[(1.065037)^2 - 1]$.

Effect of transaction costs   Transaction charges for one contract could be \$74, determined as follows:

	\$
Clearing House fee	6
Brokerage	30
Interest forgone on deposit (say 5% forgone on \$1500 deposit, where Clearing House is paying, say, 7% on cash):	
$\frac{0.05}{2} \times 1500$	38
Total	74

$\therefore$ Transaction costs for 10 contracts = \$740

The equation of value now becomes:

$$1,000,000 - 740 = 68,358A_{\overline{6}|i} + 976,540V^6 \ @ \ i\%$$

By an iterative process i can be found to be 6.519% per half-year. The annual effective rate is therefore 13.46%. In other words, transaction costs have increased the cost of funds by approximately 0.03% per annum.

PRACTICAL PROBLEMS

The above examples assume that the physical cash flow synchronises with the futures market. In other words, coupons are received on bond future dates.

Locking in immunises against profits as well as losses. The decision to lock in a particular rate is a policy judgement, and the company must be prepared to accept the guaranteed borrowing rate, even if rates fall. If a company wishes to take advantage of the hedge if rates rise and ignore the hedge if rates fall, this can be achieved via options on bond futures. The initial premium will need to be taken into account in determining the cost of funds.

In a borrowing hedge, a company must ask the question, what will happen if, after 6 months, the funds are not required? As the bond futures contract is non-deliverable, the company would close out the contract and take the hedge profit/loss.

Where a borrowing/investment rate needs to be guaranteed on an instrument other than bonds, the success of the bond-future-matching will depend on rates for the given instrument moving in sympathy with bond rates.

The technique also assumes physical and bond futures availability.

If the loan interest frequency differs from half-yearly, the contracts may need weighting.

BILL OPTIONS

A *call option* is effected by an initial option premium and gives the taker of the option the right to buy a defined good at a specific date in the future. Similarly, a *put option* gives the taker of the option the right to sell in the future.

Consider the abstract of Futures Options quoted in the *Financial Review* dated 26 May 1988 (Table 3). The option prices are quoted, in the case below, at approximately $12 per point. The 'high' value for

Table 3 Futures Options quoted in the *Financial Review* 26 May 1988.

Exercise Price or Strike Price	Prev. Price	Opening Trade	High	Low	Settlement Price	Settlement Change	$ Value of Chg	Open Volume Pos.	

CALL OPTIONS

BANK BILLS—90-day bank bills.

	Exercise Price	Prev. Price	Opening Trade	High	Low	Settlement Price	Change	$ Value of Chg	Volume	Open Pos.
Jun 88	87.00	.51	—	.58	.58	—	—		5	75
Jun 88	87.50	.19	—	.24	.17	—	—		400	1411
Jun 88	88.00	.04	—	.05	.02	—	—		894	2017
Dec 88	88.00	.46	—	.46	.46	—	—		5	40

TOTALS: Volume 1304 Open Position (previous day): 7369.

ALL ORDINARIES SHARE PRICE INDEX—dollar value of 100 times index.

	Exercise Price	Prev. Price	Opening Trade	High	Low	Settlement Price	Change	$ Value of Chg	Volume	Open Pos.
Jun 88	1300.0	183.4	—	—	—	—	—		0	90
Jun 88	1325.0	160.9	—	—	—	—	—		0	12
Jun 88	1350.0	139.5	•—	—	—	—	—		0	63
Jun 88	1375.0	119.4	—	—	—	—	—		0	141
Jun 88	1400.0	100.8	—	—	—	—	—		0	153
Jun 88	1425.0	83.8	—	100.3	100.3	—	—		70	159
Jun 88	1450.0	68.7	—	90.4	90.4	—	—		50	419
Jun 88	1475.0	55.4	—	72.0	52.0	—	—		70	572
Jun 88	1525.0	34.3	—	48.9	45.0	—	—		60	184
Jun 88	1550.0	26.4	—	34.0	34.0	—	—		50	412
Jun 88	1575.0	20.0	—	29.2	29.0	—	—		120	145
Jun 88	1625.0	10.9	—	13.8	13.7	—	—		120	0
Sep 88	1650.0	—	—	36.3	36.3	—	— .		50	0

TOTALS: Volume 590 Open Position (previous day): 3710

TEN YEAR COMMONWEALTH TREASURY BOND.

	Exercise Price	Prev. Price	Opening Trade	High	Low	Settlement Price	Change	$ Value of Chg	Volume	Open Pos.
Jun 88	87.250	.690	—	—	—	—	—		0	130
Jun 88	87.500	.450	—	—	—	—	—		0	640
Jun 88	87.750	.255	—	.270	.270	—	—		300	2890
Jun 88	88.000	.115	—	.150	.120	—	—		1256	6922
Jun 88	88.250	.040	—	.065	.050	—	—		614	8050
Jun 88	88.500	0.10	—	.020	.020	—	—		350	6243
Jun 88	88.750	—	—	—	—	—	—		0	1379
Sep 88	87.750	.390	—	.415	.415	—	—		50	0
Sep 88	88.000	.270	—	.290	.290	—	—		20	697
Sep 88	88.250	.175	—	.200	.200	—	—		5	250
Sep 88	88.500	.110	—	.120	.110	—	—		300	766

TOTALS: Volume 2895 Open Position (previous day): 27967.

AUSTRALIAN DOLLAR—$A100,000 face value;
quotes in US dollars per Australian dollars.

	Exercise Price	Prev. Price	Opening Trade	High	Low	Settlement Price	Change	$ Value of Chg	Volume	Open Pos.
Jun 88	.7300	.0533	—	—	—	—	—		0	10
Jun 88	.7400	.0433	—	—	—	—	—		0	7
Jun 88	.7500	.0333	—	—	—	—	—		0	30
Jun 88	.7600	.0236	—	—	—	—	—		0	66

TOTALS: Volume 0 Open Position (previous day): 221.

option premium for a June 88 with an exercise price of 87 is 0.58 or $696 (58 points × 12).

For the delivery date June '88 there are three exercise prices 87.00, 87.50 and 88.00.

Consider the first exercise price of 87.00 for the call option.

If yields at the date of delivery in June are less than 13% (100 − 87), the taker will exericse the option and buy the bill at the exercise yield of 13%. Alternatively, if yields are higher than 13% at the exercise date,

Table 3 (cont.)

PUT OPTIONS

BANK BILLS—90-day bank bills.

Jun 88	84.00	—	—	—	—	—	—	0	10
Jun 88	87.00	.06	—	.07	.06	—	—	170	1343
Jun 88	87.50	.24	—	.24	.20	—	—	995	4327
¢Jun 88	88.00	.59	—	.58	.50	—	—	170	1951

TOTALS: Volume 1340 Open Position (previous day): 10079.

ALL ORDINARIES SHARE PRICE INDEX—dollar value of 100 times index.

Jun 88	1200.0	.4	—	—	—	—	—	0	1
Jun 88	1250.0	1.5	—	—	—	—	—	0	312
Jun 88	1275.0	2.6	—	—	—	—	—	0	332
Jun 88	1475.0	51.4	—	44.7	44.7	—	—	25	79
Sep 88	1350.0	4.0	—	35.6	35.6	—	—	50	0

TOTALS: Volume 75 Open Position (previous day): 2508.

TEN YEAR COMMONWEALTH TREASURY BOND.

Jun 88	86.000	—	—	—	—	—	—	0	100
Jun 88	86.500	—	—	—	—	—	—	0	250
Jun 88	86.750	—	—	—	—	—	—	0	247
Jun 88	87.000	—	—	—	—	—	—	0	2502
Jun 88	87.250	.005	—	.010	.010	—	—	201	2647
Jun 88	87.500	.030	—	.040	.030	—	—	409	5678
Jun 88	87.750	.085	—	.080	.070	—	—	1316	5486
Jun 88	88.000	.200	—	.200	.160	—	—	1564	5619
Jun 88	88.250	.370	—	.330	.330	—	—	100	3208
Jun 88	88.500	.580	—	.550	.550	—	—	20	203
Sep 88	87.000	.095	—	.065	.060	—	—	300	20
Sep 88	87.250	.150	—	.120	.120	—	—	10	101
Sep 88	87.500	.230	—	—	—	—	—	0	841
Sep 88	87.750	.330	—	.295	.295	—	—	50	100
Sep 88	88.000	.455	—	—	—	—	—	0	696

TOTALS: Volume 3970 Open Position (previous day): 27698.

AUSTRALIAN DOLLAR—$A100,000 face value; quotes in US dollars per Australian dollars.

Jun 88	.7200	—	—	—	—	—	—	0	5
Jun 88	.7300	—	—	—	—	—	—	0	60
Jun 88	.7400	—	—	—	—	—	—	0	151

TOTALS: Volume 0 Open Position (previous day): 963.

AUSTRALIAN FUTURES CONTRACTS

	Prev. Close	Offer	Bid	High	Low	Last	Day's Change	Volume	Open Int
BHP: 10,000 Shares per contract.									
Jul 88	7.77	—	—	—	—	—	—	0	

TOTALS: Volume 0 Open Position (previous day): 3.

the taker will not exercise the option, since it would be cheaper to buy a bill at more than 13% in the open (physical) market.

In either case transaction costs have been incurred. These include Clearing House fees, the option premium, negotiable brokerage and a fixed fee per 'deal' (transaction). No deposit or margins are required.

Assume that one contract of the June '88 is exercised and that cash flows are represented as follows:

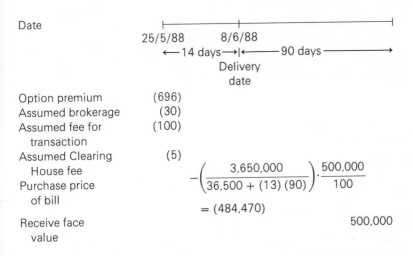

If the interest forgone on initial outlays is at 12% simple per annum then the accumulated initial outlays to 8/6/88 (the Wednesday preceding the second Friday of June) $= 831\left(1 + 0.12 \times \dfrac{14}{365}\right)$

$$= 835$$

The summary of outflows @ 8/6/88 is:

Purchase price	484,470
Accumulated initial outlays	835
	485,305

The annualised return $= \dfrac{500,000 - 485,305}{485,305} \times \dfrac{36,500}{90}$

$$= 12.2802\%$$

The effects of the option premium and transaction costs have reduced the return from the exercise yield of 13% to 10.3826%.

Similarly, for an option premium of between 0.24 (high) and 0.17 (low), 100 face value of a June '88 can be exercised at an index of 87.5 or yield of 12.5%.

If yields on 90-day bills at the exercise date are less than 12.5% the option would be exercised for purchase yield of 12.5%.

Before the exercise date, options may be traded, e.g. a June '88 put for an exercise price of 88 could be sold from 50 to 59 cents per 100 face amount. (Refer to Table 3, ϕ.)

BOND OPTIONS

Call and put options are also available on 10-year bond futures. Call (put) options enable hedging to take place on the purchase (sale) of a physical bond in the future. A sale constitutes a future raising, i.e. borrowing, of cash. A put option can therefore be used to 'lock in' a future maximum borrowing rate.

Consider a September '89 88.000 (exercise index) for a put option, with a premium of $4550 per contract at 2/6/89.

What is the borrowing rate assuming that ten-year bond yields at the exercise date are 13% and that $1m are borrowed on a credit foncier basis for 10 years with payments annual in arrear, based on compound interest of the 10-year bond rate plus 1%?

Assume initial transaction costs are $400 and transaction costs at the exercise date are $100. Interest forgone on the initial cash flows is at a rate of 12% per annum flat. The option premium is $4550(10 × 455).

Solution: Cash flows are:

	2/6/89	15/9/89			
Option premium	(4550)				
Transaction costs	(400)	(100)			
Loan		1 m			
Loan repayment			(P)	(P)	...	(P)

$$\text{Accmulated option premium plus transaction costs} = 4950\left(1 + \frac{105}{365} \times 0.12\right) + 100$$

$$= \$5,221$$

The profit on the bond future is found as follows:

Sale of standard contract @ 12% $= 6A_{\overline{20}|} + 100V^{20}$ @ 6%

$= 100$

less Purchase of standard contract
at market rate of 13% $= 6A_{\overline{20}|} + 100V^{20}$ @ $6\frac{1}{2}\%$
$= 94.4907$

Profit per $100 face amount $= 5.5093$
Profit for $1m (or 10 contracts) $= 55,093$

Summary of cash flows at exercise date:

Loan required	$= 1m$
Deduct bond future profit	$= -55,093$
Add accumulated initial cash flows	$= +5,221$
Loan acquired	$= 950,128$

Annual repayment on loan is found thus:

$$PA_{\overline{10}|14\%} = 950,028$$

$$\therefore P = \$182,152.40$$

The effective borrowing rate i can be determined by equating:

$$182,152.40A_{\overline{10}|i} = 1,000,000$$

i.e. the net cash receipts at the exercise date were the $950,128 + 55,093 - 5,221 = \$1$ m and the future outflows were $\$182,152.40$ per annum for 10 years.

Obtaining i as an IRR gives:

$$i = 12.7065\%$$

i.e. the borrowing rate on $1 m @ $(13 + 1)\%$ has been reduced by the bond future profit and increased by the bond option premium and transaction costs. The resulting rate is 12.7065%.

EXERCISES

1 A bill future is quoted at an index of 88. If 4 contracts are purchased, determine the purchase price.

2 Assume that the data in exercise 1 apply and that the deposit is $1,100 per contract. Clearing House fees of $5 per contract initial and $5 at delivery plus initial brokerage of $30 per contract are assumed. The delivery date occurs in 60 days, and the deposit is refunded on delivery. Determine the annualised rate of return assuming the interest forgone on initial outlays is 12% per annum flat.

3 A client wishes to borrow 18.9 million dollars in 18 months and effects bill future contracts at an index of 87.23. Initial costs amount to $80 per contract and $10 per contract at delivery. Assume a deposit of $1,100 per contract. Required: Find the annualised borrowing rate. Assume interest of 12% flat on the initial outlays.

4 A ten-year bond future is purchased for an index of 87. If yields at delivery (on 10-year bonds) are 14%, determine the bond future profit/loss on 20 contracts. Ignore transaction costs.

5   A client wishes to borrow 2 million of 10-year money in 9 months' time and effects 20 bond future contracts at an index of 88.27. Initial expenses are $1,570 per contract and $20 per contract in 9 months with a refund of $1,500 deposit per contract in 9 months' time.

At the close-out date (in 9 months) 10-year bond physicals are yielding 14%. The client then borrows on the open market for 10 years at a rate of $14\frac{1}{2}$% on a credit foncier basis with equal annual payments in arrear.

Required: Determine the effective annual borrowing rate assuming the initial costs forgo interest at 12% flat.

6   The same information as in exercise 5 is given except that an option is effected at a strike of 88.27. No deposit applies and the option premium is 0.64 per 100 face amount. Determine the effective borrowing rate assuming a 10-year bond rate at exercise of 14% and that a credit foncier loan is acquired @ $14\frac{1}{2}$%. Assume that the interest forgone on initial outlays is 12% flat.

7   A call option on a bill future is effected at a strike of 89 with premium of 0.400 per 100 face value. Twenty contracts are effected and yields at exercise are 10.2%. Initial expenses amount to $90 per contract and $20 per contract at exercise in 60 days' time. There is a deposit of $1,500 per contract refundable at delivery.

Required: (i) Determine the annualised borrowing rate assuming that this rate equals the rate forgone on the initial cash flows.

(ii) What would be your result to (i) if the initial cash flows incurred interest @ 12% per annum flat?

26

Summary and Conclusions

After 25 chapters, what have you learnt? Hopefully, to assess more accurately the feasibility of a borrowing or investment facility!

The decision-making techniques all involve the following basic rules:

(1) Obtain cash inflows and outflows adjusted for tax.
(2) Allow for appropriate timing of taxation.
(3) Equate the present (or accumulated) value of inflows with the present (or accumulated) value of outflows.
(4) Match the cash flow frequency with the interest frequency, i.e. if cash is turning over quarterly, a quarterly effective rate must be used.
(5) Adjust for transaction costs. This may involve initial, renewal, and final expenses expressed as a function of the initial deposit or loan; the renewal interest and/or payments; and the maturing cash flow. Transaction costs could also be fixed in dollar terms.
(6) Where appropriate, adjust cash flows for inflation. This may require valuing some cash flows at real rates and others at nominal rates (e.g. fixed depreciation tax remission is not inflatable and therefore is valued at the gross/nominal rate).
(7) The valuation rate of interest for NPV should reflect the cost of funds of the organisation/company/sole trader/partnership.

In the case of a company the cost of funds consists of a weighted average cost of shares, retained earnings, preference shares and short/long term debt.

The cost of equity can be calculated by $k_e = r_f + \beta(r_m - r_f)$ or by present valuing future income/dividend streams and equating these to current market values.

The cost of debt component must be adjusted for tax savings (if any) on interest.

SOME TRAPS IN PRACTICE

No doubt the traps below are not exhaustive. However, as decision-makers we must be confident of our final answer/decision.

To enhance this prospect we must overcome the following traps:

(1) Checking our solution back in the original expression. Ideally some independent checking mechanism should be employed.
(2) Using too few decimal places in a large transaction.
(3) Assuming that the *IRR* has only one solution. In cases of cash flows with changing signs more than one solution is possible.
(4) Assuming that the *IRR* is the correct reinvestment rate. In fact the actual *IRR* may be in excess of a conservative future reinvestment rate. A holding period analysis with a lower reinvestment rate is therefore recommended.
(5) Comparing instruments using nominal rates, particularly if the cash flow frequencies differ. In this case each instrument should be converted to an effective rate.
(6) Accepting the rate for the *NPV* as unchallengeable. It is the weighted average cost of capital (*WACC*) and this may well alter if future tax rates, the mix of the capital structure, or market value weights, alter. New capital raisings at different levels of market risk (β) will also affect the cost of equity and hence *WACC*.
(7) Making a decision based on the *NPV*/*IRR*/holding period return alone. You may well find that cash flows are affected by economic, political, seasonal and sociological factors. Consider the income of a rubber plantation in New Guinea, exporting rubber expressed in the value of $US. In this case the income could be quite elastic (!). It could be affected by world interest rates, demand for exports, seasonality, the political and economic factors in the host and importing countries, and strikes. The final decision must embrace all these variables. Sensitivity analysis can be employed to vary one or more of the factors to examine the worst/best and other possible scenarios; e.g. rubber prices rise by 1%, 2%, 3%,...—what is the effect on *NPV*?
(8) Forgetting to monitor the decision, once you have implemented a project. Only future cash flows are relevant, e.g. if your project is losing money this fact is irrelevant. Your decision will be based on future cash flows and the problem will be based on selecting the best outcome now.

SUMMARY OF FORMULAE AND SOME MATHEMATICAL RULES

1 Index laws

$$a^m \times a^n = a^{m+n}$$ Add indices when multiplying

$$a^m \div a^n = a^{m-n}$$ Subtract indices when dividing

$$(a^m)^n = a^{mn}$$ Multiply indices when raising from one power to another

$a^{1/n} = n^{th}$ root of a, e.g. $a^{1/3} = $ cube root of $a = \sqrt[3]{a}$

$a^{m/n} = n^{th}$ root of a, raised to the power m, e.g. $a^{2/3} = (\sqrt[3]{a})^2$

$a^{-n} = $ reciprocal of a^n, i.e. $\dfrac{1}{a^n}$, e.g. $a^{-2} = \dfrac{1}{a^2}$

2 Algebraic laws

$\dfrac{a}{c} + \dfrac{b}{c} = \dfrac{a+b}{c}$ e.g. $\dfrac{1}{5} + \dfrac{3}{5} = \dfrac{4}{5}$

$\dfrac{a}{c} - \dfrac{b}{c} = \dfrac{a-b}{c}$ e.g. $\dfrac{3}{5} - \dfrac{1}{5} = \dfrac{2}{5}$

$\dfrac{a}{b} \times \dfrac{c}{d} = \dfrac{ac}{bd}$ e.g. $\dfrac{2}{5} \times \dfrac{3}{7} = \dfrac{6}{35}$

$\dfrac{a}{b} \div \dfrac{c}{d} = \dfrac{a}{b} \times \dfrac{d}{c} = \dfrac{ad}{bc}$ Invert and multiply, e.g. $\dfrac{2}{5} \div \dfrac{3}{7} = \dfrac{2}{5} \times \dfrac{7}{3}$

$a \times \dfrac{1}{b} = \dfrac{a}{1} \times \dfrac{1}{b} = \dfrac{a}{b}$

Multiplying both numerator and denominator of a fraction by the same number gives an equivalent fraction:

e.g. $\dfrac{2}{3} \cdot \boxed{\dfrac{4}{4}} = \dfrac{8}{12}$ $\dfrac{2}{3} \cdot \boxed{\dfrac{2}{2}} = \dfrac{4}{6}$

         $\dfrac{2}{3} \cdot \boxed{\dfrac{3}{3}} = \dfrac{6}{9}$ $\dfrac{2}{3} \cdot \boxed{\dfrac{5}{5}} = \dfrac{10}{15}$

In other words, $\dfrac{2}{3} \equiv \dfrac{4}{6} \equiv \dfrac{6}{9} \equiv \dfrac{8}{12} \equiv \dfrac{10}{15}$

3 Algebraic factors

$$a(b + c) = ab + ac$$

$$(a + b)(c + d) = ac + ad + bc + bd$$

4 Logarithms

$$\text{If } \log_b A = x, \text{ then } A = b^x$$

$$\text{e.g. } \log_{10} 100 = 2 \text{ and } 100 = 10^2$$

$$\ln ab = \ln a + \ln b$$

$$\ln c^n = n \ln c$$

$$\ln \frac{a}{b} = \ln a - \ln b$$

5 Quadratic equation and the discriminant formula
The general formula for a quadratic equation is:

$$ax^2 + bx + c = 0$$

The solution(s) to the quadratic equation can be found by factorising the equation or by using the discriminant formula:

$$x = \frac{-b \pm \sqrt{b^2 - 4ac}}{2a}$$

6 Accumulated value of an amount P

$$AV = P(1 + i)^n$$

$$i = \left(\frac{AV}{P}\right)^{1/n} - 1$$

$$n = \frac{\ln\left(\dfrac{AV}{P}\right)}{\ln(1 + i)} = \frac{\ln AV - \ln P}{\ln(1 + i)}$$

7 Sum of a geometric progression is:

$$\frac{a(1 - r^n)}{1 - r}$$

where $r = \dfrac{\text{term 2}}{\text{term 1}}$

a = first term

n = number of terms

8 Sum of an infinite geometric progression is:

$$\frac{a}{1 - r} \qquad 0 < r < 1$$

9 $V = \dfrac{1}{1 + i}$

10 Present value of a future amount X is:

$$PV = \frac{X}{(1 + i)^n} = XV^n$$

11 $A_{\overline{n}|i} = V^1 + V^2 + V^3 + \ldots V^n$

$$= \frac{1}{(1+i)} + \frac{1}{(1+i)^2} + \ldots \frac{1}{(1+i)^n}$$

$$A_{\overline{n}|i} = \frac{1 - V^n}{i}$$

$$= \frac{1 - \dfrac{1}{(1+i)^n}}{i}$$

12 $S_{\overline{n}|i} = \dfrac{(1+i)^n - 1}{i}$

$$= 1 + (1+i) + (1+i)^2 + \ldots (1+i)^{n-1}$$

13 $\ddot{A}_{\overline{n}|i} = 1 + V^1 + V^2 + \ldots V^{n-1}$

$$= 1 + A_{\overline{n-1}|i} \quad \text{or} \quad (1+i)A_{\overline{n}|i}$$

14 $\ddot{S}_{\overline{n}|i} = (1+i)S_{\overline{n}|i} \quad \text{or} \quad S_{\overline{n+1}|i} - 1$

15 Nominal and effective rates of return

nominal rate	effective rate	nominal rate
12% per annum convertible monthly	$\dfrac{12}{12} = 1\%$ per month	
12% per annum convertible quarterly	$\dfrac{12}{4} = 3\%$ per quarter	
	4% per quarter	$4 \times 4 = 16\%$ p.a.
	2% per month	$2 \times 12 = 24\%$ p.a.

1% per month effective $= (1.01)^{12} - 1\%$ p.a. effective

Convertible half-yearly:

$$\left(1 + \frac{\text{nominal p.a.}}{200}\right)^2 - 1 = \text{effective p.a.}$$

Convertible monthly:

$$\left(1 + \frac{\text{nominal p.a.}}{1200}\right)^{12} - 1 = \text{effective p.a.}$$

16 Real rate of return

$$\text{real rate} = \frac{1 + \text{nominal rate}}{1 + \text{inflation rate}} - 1$$

17 $NPV(1 + i)^n = NTV$

18 The rate i at which NPV or $NTV = 0$ is the IRR.

19 $\infty NPV = \dfrac{NPV}{iA_{\overline{n}|i}}$

$\qquad = \dfrac{EAA}{i}$

$EAA = \dfrac{NPV}{A_{\overline{n}|i}}$

20 After-tax income = before-tax income $(1 - t) +$ tax remission on depreciation

$$M_n = F_n(1 - t) + tD$$

Adjusted for inflation:

$$M_n = F_n(1 - t)(1 + j)^n + tD$$

$$NPV = F_n(1 - t)A_{\overline{n}|k} + tDA_{\overline{n}|i} - \text{outflow}$$

where i = cost of capital

$$k = \dfrac{1 + i}{1 + \text{inflation rate}} - 1$$

21 The price of a bond per 100 face amount is:

$$\text{Price} = \dfrac{\text{coupon}}{2} A_{\overline{n}|i} + 100V^n \text{ @ } i$$

where the coupon is paid half-yearly

and $\qquad\qquad n$ = number of half-years to maturity

22 The price of a bill of exchange per 100 face amount is:

$$\text{Price} = \dfrac{3,650,000}{36,500 + nr}$$

where n = days to run to maturity

$\qquad r$ = yield %

If bills are trading at a discount,

$$\text{Price} = \text{face amount} - \text{discount}$$

$$= 100 - \dfrac{dn}{365}$$

23 Cost of equity $k_e = \text{growth} + \dfrac{\text{dividend}}{\text{market price}}$

$\qquad\qquad\quad = \text{growth} + \text{dividend yield}$

$$k_e = r_f + \beta(r_m - r_f)$$

where r_f = risk-free rate
$\quad\;\, r_m$ = return on market

24 $\beta = \dfrac{\text{covariance } (r_{mt}, r_{st})}{\text{variance } (r_{mt})}$

where r_{mt} = return on market at time t
$\quad\;\, r_{st}$ = return on share/portfolio at time t

25 Covariance $(a, b) = \dfrac{1}{n} \sum\limits_{i=1}^{i=n} (a_i - \bar{a})(b_i - \bar{b})$

$\qquad$ Variance $(a) = \dfrac{1}{n} \sum\limits_{i=1}^{i=n} (a_i - \bar{a})^2$

$$\beta = \frac{\text{covariance } (r_{mt}, r_{st})}{\text{variance } (r_{mt})}$$

$$= \frac{\sum\limits_{t=1}^{t=n} (r_{st} - \bar{r}_s)(r_{mt} - \bar{r}_m)}{\sum\limits_{t=1}^{t=n} (r_{mt} - \bar{r}_m)^2}$$

26 Cost of retained earnings = cost of equity

27 Sigma:

$$\sum_{i=1}^{i=n} i = 1 + 2 + 3 + \dots n$$

28 Loan outstanding = PV of repayments outstanding

29 Weighted average cost of capital:

$$WACC = \sum (\text{cost of capital} \times \text{market value weights})$$

30 Spot ($US/$A) = 0.75 means 0.75 $US exchanges for $A1

$\qquad\qquad$ and $\quad$ $US1 exchanges for A\left(\dfrac{1}{0.75}\right)$

31 Forward premium \$US/\$A $= \dfrac{S(\$US/\$A)n\left(\dfrac{r_A}{365} - \dfrac{r_{US}}{360}\right)}{1 + \dfrac{nr_A}{365}}$

Forward premium £/\$A $= \dfrac{S(£/\$A)\dfrac{n}{365}(r_A - r_{UK})}{1 + \dfrac{nr_A}{365}}$

Forward margin $\approx$ Spot $\times$ Interest differential $\times$ Time fraction

32 Highest annualised yield r_h for a BABF is:

$$r_h = \frac{(S - P)}{P} \cdot \frac{36{,}500}{n}$$

where S = selling price
P = purchase price

33 Price of bond futures contract per 100 face amount is:

$$P = \frac{C}{2} A_{\overline{2n}|i} + 100 V^{2n}$$

where C = annual coupon
n = term in years
i = yield per compound period
$i = \dfrac{r}{m}$ where r = annual yield %
m = number of compound periods per year

Answers to Exercises

1 $A = 5 - (6 \times 3) + (4 \times 2)$

Recall that multiplications and divisions are grouped first.

$\therefore A = 5 - 18 + 8$

$= -13 + 8$

$= -5$

Check using scientific calculator:

$A = \boxed{5} \; \boxed{-} \; \boxed{6} \; \boxed{\times} \; \boxed{3} \; \boxed{+} \; \boxed{4} \; \boxed{\times} \; \boxed{2} \; \boxed{=}$

Check using Hewlett-Packard:

$A = \boxed{5} \; \boxed{\text{ENTER}} \; \boxed{6} \; \boxed{\text{ENTER}} \; \boxed{3} \; \boxed{\times} \; \boxed{-} \; \boxed{4} \; \boxed{\text{ENTER}}$

$\boxed{2} \; \boxed{\times} \; \boxed{+}$

2 $B = \dfrac{12 \div (-6) + 2 - 3 \times 2}{8 \div 4 - 3}$

$= \dfrac{(12 \div -6) + 2 - (3 \times 2)}{(8 \div 4) - 3}$

$= \dfrac{-2 + 2 - 6}{2 - 3}$

$= \dfrac{-6}{-1}$

$= 6$

Check using scientific calculator:

$B = \boxed{12} \; \boxed{\div} \; \boxed{6} \; \boxed{+/-} \; \boxed{=} \; \boxed{+} \; \boxed{2}$ This gives the numerator, -6

$\boxed{-} \; \boxed{3} \; \boxed{\times} \; \boxed{2} \; \boxed{=}$

Add to Memory

$\boxed{8} \; \boxed{\div} \; \boxed{4} \; \boxed{-} \; \boxed{3} \; \boxed{=}$ This gives the denominator, -1

$\boxed{\div} \; \boxed{\text{Memory recall}} \; \boxed{=}$ $-1 \div -6$

$\boxed{\frac{1}{x}}$ Inverts to $-6 \div -1$

Check using the Hewlett-Packard:

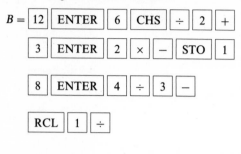

This stores the numerator, -6

This gives the denominator, -1

Recalls numerator and divides by it, $\dfrac{-1}{-6}$

Inverts to give $\dfrac{-6}{-1}$

3   $D = \dfrac{4 \times 3 - (-2) \div (-3) + 3 \times 2}{6 \div 2 + 5}$

$= \dfrac{(4 \times 3) - (-2 \div -3) + (3 \times 2)}{(6 \div 2) + 5}$

$= \dfrac{12 - 2/3 + 6}{3 + 5}$

$= \dfrac{17\frac{1}{3}}{8}$

$= 17\frac{1}{3} \times \dfrac{1}{8}$

$= \dfrac{52}{3} \times \dfrac{1}{8}$

$= \dfrac{52}{24}$

$= \dfrac{13}{6}$

$= 2.1\dot{6}$

Check using a scientific calculator:

This gives the numerator, 17.33

Add to memory

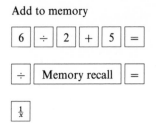

This gives the denominator, 8

Recalls numerator and divides by it

Inverts because division was performed wrong way round

= 2.1$\dot{6}$

Check using the Hewlett-Packard:

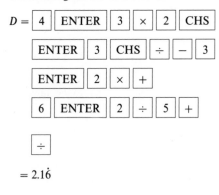

This gives the numerator, 17.33

This gives the denominator, 8

17.33 ÷ 8

= 2.1$\dot{6}$

4 $E = \dfrac{3 \div -1 \times 4 \times 2 - 2 \times 3}{-1 - 7 \times 2}$

$= \dfrac{(3 \div -1 \times 4 \times 2) - (2 \times 3)}{-1 - (7 \times 2)}$

$= \dfrac{(-3 \times 4 \times 2) - 6}{-1 - (14)}$

$= \dfrac{(-12 \times 2) - 6}{-1 - 14}$

$= \dfrac{-24 - 6}{-15}$

$= \dfrac{-30}{-15}$

$= 2$

5 $F = \dfrac{1.912 \times 3.9 - 2.1 \times -3 \div 3}{3.8 \div 2 + 10}$

$ = \dfrac{(1.912 \times 3.9) - (2.1 \times -3 \div 3)}{(3.8 \div 2) + 10}$

Using a scientific calculator:

$F =$ | 1.912 | | $\times$ | | 3.9 | | $-$ | | 2.1 | | $\times$ | | 3 | (numerator, 9.5568)

| +/− | | $\div$ | | 3 | | = |

Add to memory

| 3.8 | | $\div$ | | 2 | | + | | 10 | | = | (denominator, 11.9)

| $\div$ | | Memory recall | | = | $11.9 \div 9.5568$

| $\frac{1}{x}$ | $9.5568 \div 11.9$

$\therefore F = 0.803$ to 3 decimal places

Using the Hewlett-Packard:

$F =$ | 1.912 | | ENTER | | 3.9 | | $\times$ | | 2.1 | (store the numerator, 9.5568)

| ENTER | | 3 | | CHS | | $\times$ |

| 3 | | $\div$ | | $-$ | | STO | | 1 |

| 3.8 | | ENTER | | 2 | | $\div$ | | 10 | | + | (denominator, 11.9)

| RCL | | 1 | | $\div$ | $11.9 \div 9.5568$

| $\frac{1}{x}$ | $9.5568 \div 11.9$

$\therefore F = 0.803$ to 3 decimal places

Using a manual estimation approach:

$F \approx$ (approximately $=$) $\dfrac{(2 \times 4) - (2 \times -3 \div 3)}{(4 \div 2) + 10}$

$ = \dfrac{8 - (-6 \div 3)}{2 + 10}$

$ = \dfrac{8 - (-2)}{12}$

$ = \dfrac{10}{12}$ or $\dfrac{5}{6}$

$\therefore F \approx 0.8\dot{3}$ which is close to 0.803

6   Estimating first, $Q \approx \dfrac{(-3 \div -3) + (6 \times -3) - 4}{-6 + (3 \times -5)}$

$$= \frac{1 + (-18) - 4}{-6 + (-15)}$$

$$= \frac{1 - 18 - 4}{-6 - 15}$$

$$= \frac{-21}{-21}$$

$$\therefore Q \approx 1$$

The answer using a calculator should be close to unity.

Using a scientific calculator:

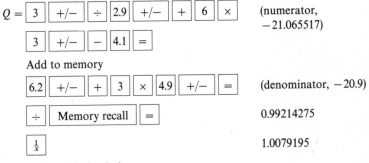

$Q = $ [3] [+/−] [÷] [2.9] [+/−] [+] [6] [×]   (numerator, −21.065517)

[3] [+/−] [−] [4.1] [=]

Add to memory

[6.2] [+/−] [+] [3] [×] [4.9] [+/−] [=]   (denominator, −20.9)

[÷] [Memory recall] [=]   0.99214275

[$\frac{1}{x}$]   1.0079195

$Q = 1.01$ to 2 decimal places

Using the Hewlett-Packard:

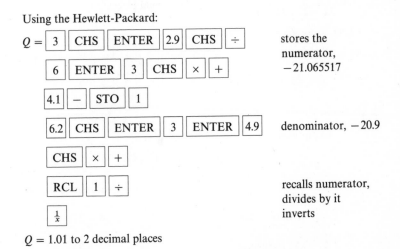

$Q = $ [3] [CHS] [ENTER] [2.9] [CHS] [÷]   stores the numerator, −21.065517

[6] [ENTER] [3] [CHS] [×] [+]

[4.1] [−] [STO] [1]

[6.2] [CHS] [ENTER] [3] [ENTER] [4.9]   denominator, −20.9

[CHS] [×] [+]

[RCL] [1] [÷]   recalls numerator, divides by it

[$\frac{1}{x}$]   inverts

$Q = 1.01$ to 2 decimal places

CHAPTER 2

1 a) $F = 2^3 \times 2^1 = 2^{3+1} = 2^4 = 2 \times 2 \times 2 \times 2 = 16$
   b) $Q = 2^2 \times 2^4 \times 2^{-3} = 2^{2+4-3} = 2^3 = 8$

2 $Y = (2^3 \times 2) + (3 \times 2^2) - (4 \times 2)$
   $= 2^4 + (3 \times 4) - (8)$
   $= 16 + 12 - 8$
   $= 20$

Check using a scientific calculator:

$Y =$ | 2 | y^x | 3 | $\times$ | 2 | + | 3 | $\times$ | 2 | $\times$ | 2 | $-$ | 4 |

| $\times$ | 2 | = |

Check using the Hewlett-Packard:

$Y =$ | 2 | ENTER | 3 | y^x | 2 | $\times$ | 3 | ENTER | 2 |

| ENTER | 2 | y^x | $\times$ | + | 4 | ENTER | 2 | $\times$ | $-$ |

3 $M = \dfrac{(2^{-1} \times 2^2 \div 2^{-1} \times 2^2) + (3 \times 2)}{(2^3 \div 2^{-2}) + 2}$

$= \dfrac{2^{-1+2-(-1)+2} + (6)}{2^{3-(-2)} + 2}$

$= \dfrac{2^4 + 6}{2^5 + 2}$

$= \dfrac{16 + 6}{32 + 2} = \dfrac{22}{34} = \dfrac{11}{17} = 0.6471$ to 4 decimal places

Check using scientific calculator:

$M =$ | 2 | y^x | 1 | +/− | $\times$ | 2 | y^x | 2 | = | $\div$ | 2 | y^x | 1 |

| +/− | = | $\times$ | 2 | y^x | 2 | = | + | 3 | $\times$ | 2 |

| = | (numerator, 22)

Add to memory

| 2 | y^x | 3 | = | $\div$ | 2 | y^x | 2 | +/− |

| = | + | 2 | = | (denominator, 34)

| $\div$ | Memory recall | = | $34 \div 22$

| $\frac{1}{x}$ | Take reciprocal $22 \div 34$

Check using Hewlett-Packard:

$M =$ 2 ENTER 1 CHS y^x 2 ENTER 2 y^x ×

2 ENTER 1 CHS y^x ÷ 2 ENTER 2 y^x ×

3 ENTER 2 × + (numerator, 22)

STO 1

2 ENTER 3 y^x 2 ENTER 2 CHS y^x ÷

2 + (denominator, 34)

RCL 1 ÷ $34 \div 22$

$\frac{1}{x}$ $22 \div 34$

4 a) 1.6 y^x 3 = × 4.1 y^x 2 = ÷ 2.4 y^x 2

+/− =

Answer: 396.597658 (you may have a slight rounding difference on your calculator)

or on the Hewlett-Packard:

1.6 ENTER 3 y^x 4.1 ENTER (numerator)

2 y^x ×

2.4 ENTER 2 CHS y^x (denominator)

÷

Answer: 396.597658

b) $2.3^{3 \times 2} = 2.3^6 = 148.03589$ (to 5 places)

c) $\sqrt[4]{1.7} = 1.7^{1/4} = 1.7^{0.25} = 1.1418583$

5 $D = \dfrac{(2^3 \times 2^{1/2})^3}{2^{1/2} \times (2^4)^{1/3}}$

You will find it easier in examples like this to work in decimals.

$\therefore D = \dfrac{(2^3 \times 2^{0.5})^3}{2^{0.5} \times 2^{4/3 = 1.3}}$

$= \dfrac{(2^{3.5})^3}{2^{1.83}}$

$$= \frac{2^{10.5}}{2^{1.83}}$$

$$= 2^{10.5-1.83}$$

$$= 2^{8.67} \quad \text{(to 2 decimal places)}$$

$$= 407.31468$$

Check using scientific calculator:

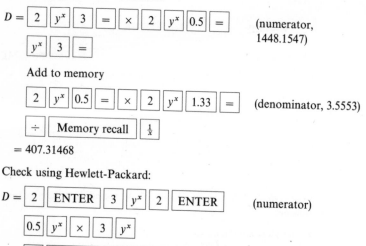

$D =$ [2] [y^x] [3] [=] [×] [2] [y^x] [0.5] [=]   (numerator, 1448.1547)

[y^x] [3] [=]

Add to memory

[2] [y^x] [0.5] [=] [×] [2] [y^x] [1.33] [=]   (denominator, 3.5553)

[÷] [Memory recall] [$\frac{1}{x}$]

$= 407.31468$

Check using Hewlett-Packard:

$D =$ [2] [ENTER] [3] [y^x] [2] [ENTER]   (numerator)

[0.5] [y^x] [×] [3] [y^x]

[2] [ENTER] [0.5] [y^x] [2] [ENTER]   (denominator)

[1.33] [y^x] [×]

[÷]

$= 407.31468$

6 $F = 1.7^{3.1} \times 1.6^{1/3} - 2.1 \times 4^{1/4}$
   $= 1.7^{3.1} \times 1.6^{0.33} - 2.1 \times 4^{0.25}$
   $= 3.0800941$

7 a) $\dfrac{1}{2} \div \dfrac{2}{3} = \dfrac{1}{2} \times \dfrac{3}{2} = \dfrac{3}{4} = 0.75$

   b) $\dfrac{(36^{1/2} - 8^{1/3})^2}{4/5} = \dfrac{(6 - 2)^2}{4/5}$

   $$= 4^2 \div 4/5$$

   $$= 16 \div \dfrac{4}{5}$$

$$= 16 \times \frac{5}{4}$$

$$= 20$$

c) $2^{-2} \div \left(\frac{2}{3}\right)^3 = \frac{1}{2^2} \div \frac{2^3}{3^3}$

$$= \frac{1}{4} \div \frac{8}{27}$$

$$= \frac{1}{4} \times \frac{27}{8}$$

$$= \frac{27}{32} = 0.84375$$

d) $\left(\frac{1}{2}\right)^{-1} = \frac{1}{1/2} = 1 \div \frac{1}{2} = 1 \times 2 = 2$

e) $\left(\frac{4}{5}\right)^{-2} = \frac{1}{\left(\frac{4}{5}\right)^2} = 1 \div \left(\frac{4}{5}\right)^2 = 1 \div \frac{16}{25} = 1 \times \frac{25}{16}$

$$= \frac{25}{16} = 1.5625$$

f) $\dfrac{(2^4 \times 4^{-1} \times 2^{-2})^3}{3^{-2} \times 6^2} = \dfrac{\left(16 \times \frac{1}{4} \times \frac{1}{2^2}\right)^3}{\frac{1}{3^2} \times 36}$

$$= \dfrac{\left(16 \times \frac{1}{4} \times \frac{1}{4}\right)^3}{\frac{1}{9} \times 36}$$

$$= \frac{(1)^3}{4}$$

$$= \frac{1}{4} = 0.25$$

8   Remember to compute inside brackets first.

Scientific calculator:

| 1.07 | y^x | 3 | = | +/− | computes -1.07^3

| + | 1 | = | $-1.07^3 + 1$, i.e. $1 - 1.07^3$

$(1 - 1.07^3)^2$

$(1 - 1.07^3)^2 \div 0.07$

Answer: 0.7235 (to 4 places)

Hewlett-Packard:

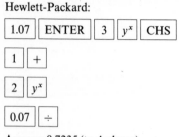

1.07 ENTER 3 y^x CHS	computes -1.07^3
1 +	$-1.07^3 + 1$, i.e. $1 - 1.07^3$
2 y^x	$(1 - 1.07^3)^2$
0.07 ÷	$(1 - 1.07^3)^2 \div 0.07$

Answer: 0.7235 (to 4 places)

9   $\dfrac{[1 - (1.09^2)^3]}{1 - 1.07} \times 41 = \dfrac{1 - 1.09^6}{-0.07} \times 41$

Scientific calculator:

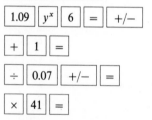

1.09 y^x 6 = +/−	computes -1.09^6
+ 1 =	$-1.09^6 + 1$, i.e. $1 - 1.09^6$
÷ 0.07 +/− =	$(1 - 1.09^6) \div -0.07$
× 41 =	$\dfrac{1 - 1.09^6}{-0.07} \times 41$

Answer: 396.58721

Hewlett-Packard:

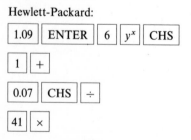

1.09 ENTER 6 y^x CHS	computes -1.09^6
1 +	$-1.09^6 + 1$, i.e. $1 - 1.09^6$
0.07 CHS ÷	$(1 - 1.09^6) \div -0.07$
41 ×	$\dfrac{1 - 1.09^6}{-0.07} \times 41$

Answer: 396.587208

10   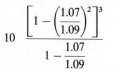 $\dfrac{\left[1 - \left(\dfrac{1.07}{1.09}\right)^2\right]^3}{1 - \dfrac{1.07}{1.09}}$

Scientific calculator:

| 1.07 | ÷ | 1.09 | = |

$$\dfrac{1.07}{1.09}$$

| y^x | 2 | = |

$$\left(\dfrac{1.07}{1.09}\right)^2$$

| +/− |

$$-\left(\dfrac{1.07}{1.09}\right)^2$$

| + | 1 | = |

$$-\left(\dfrac{1.07}{1.09}\right)^2 + 1, \text{ i.e. } 1 - \left(\dfrac{1.07}{1.09}\right)^2$$

| y^x | 3 | = |

$$\left[1 - \left(\dfrac{1.07}{1.09}\right)^2\right]^3$$

Add numerator to memory

| 1.07 | ÷ | 1.09 | = | +/− |

$$-\dfrac{1.07}{1.09}$$

| + | 1 | = |

$$-\dfrac{1.07}{1.09} + 1, \text{ i.e. } 1 - \dfrac{1.07}{1.09}$$

| ÷ | Memory recall | = |

denominator ÷ numerator

| $\frac{1}{x}$ |

numerator ÷ denominator

Answer: 0.00261992

Hewlett-Packard:

| 1.07 | ENTER | 1.09 | ÷ |

$$\dfrac{1.07}{1.09}$$

| 2 | y^x |

$$\left(\dfrac{1.07}{1.09}\right)^2$$

| CHS |

$$-\left(\dfrac{1.07}{1.09}\right)^2$$

| 1 | + |

$$-\left(\dfrac{1.07}{1.09}\right)^2 + 1, \text{ i.e. } 1 - \left(\dfrac{1.07}{1.09}\right)^2$$

| 3 | y^x |

$$\left[1 - \left(\dfrac{1.07}{1.09}\right)^2\right]^3$$

| STO | 1 |

| 1.07 | ENTER | 1.09 | ÷ | CHS |

$$-\dfrac{1.07}{1.09}$$

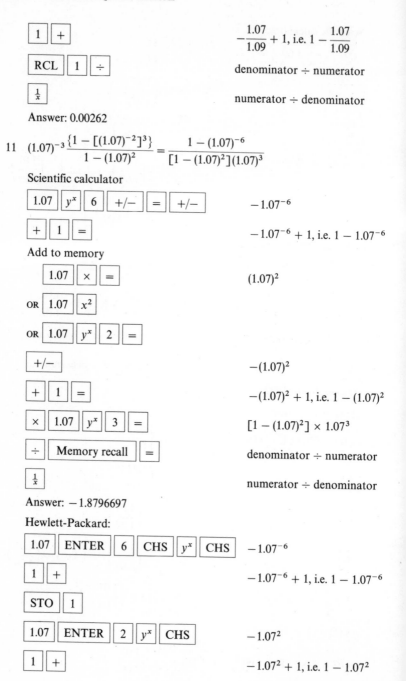

| 1 | + | | $-\dfrac{1.07}{1.09} + 1$, i.e. $1 - \dfrac{1.07}{1.09}$ |

| RCL | 1 | ÷ | denominator ÷ numerator |

| $\frac{1}{x}$ | | | numerator ÷ denominator |

Answer: 0.00262

11   $(1.07)^{-3}\dfrac{\left\{1 - \left[(1.07)^{-2}\right]^3\right\}}{1 - (1.07)^2} = \dfrac{1 - (1.07)^{-6}}{\left[1 - (1.07)^2\right](1.07)^3}$

Scientific calculator

| 1.07 | y^x | 6 | +/− | = | +/− | -1.07^{-6} |

| + | 1 | = | $-1.07^{-6} + 1$, i.e. $1 - 1.07^{-6}$ |

Add to memory

| | 1.07 | × | = | $(1.07)^2$ |

OR | 1.07 | x^2 |

OR | 1.07 | y^x | 2 | = |

| +/− | | $-(1.07)^2$ |

| + | 1 | = | $-(1.07)^2 + 1$, i.e. $1 - (1.07)^2$ |

| × | 1.07 | y^x | 3 | = | $\left[1 - (1.07)^2\right] \times 1.07^3$ |

| ÷ | Memory recall | = | denominator ÷ numerator |

| $\frac{1}{x}$ | | numerator ÷ denominator |

Answer: −1.8796697

Hewlett-Packard:

| 1.07 | ENTER | 6 | CHS | y^x | CHS | -1.07^{-6} |

| 1 | + | $-1.07^{-6} + 1$, i.e. $1 - 1.07^{-6}$ |

| STO | 1 |

| 1.07 | ENTER | 2 | y^x | CHS | -1.07^2 |

| 1 | + | $-1.07^2 + 1$, i.e. $1 - 1.07^2$ |

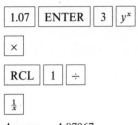

	1.07³
	$(1 - 1.07^2) \times 1.07^3$
	denominator ÷ numerator
	numerator ÷ denominator

Answer: -1.87967

CHAPTER 3

1 a) $\dfrac{3x}{7} = \dfrac{2}{5}$

Divide both sides by $\dfrac{3}{7}$: $x = \dfrac{2}{5} \div \dfrac{3}{7}$

$$= \dfrac{2}{5} \times \dfrac{7}{3}$$

$$= \dfrac{14}{15}$$

Check: LHS $= \dfrac{3}{7} \cdot \dfrac{14}{15}$ $\left(\dfrac{^1\cancel{3}}{_1\cancel{7}} \cdot \dfrac{\cancel{14}^2}{\cancel{15}_5} = \dfrac{1 \times 2}{1 \times 5} \right)$

$$= \dfrac{2}{5} = \text{RHS}$$

b) $\dfrac{-3x}{4} = -2$

Multiply both sides by -4: $3x = 8$
Divide both sides by 3: $x = 8/3$

Check: LHS $= \dfrac{-3}{4} \cdot \dfrac{8}{3} = -2 = \text{RHS}$

c) $\dfrac{-2x}{5} + 3 = -4$

Subtract 3 from both sides: $\dfrac{-2x}{5} = -4 - 3 = -7$

Multiply both sides by -5: $2x = -7 \times -5 = 35$

Divide both sides by 2: $x = \dfrac{35}{2}$

Check: LHS $= \left(\dfrac{-2}{5} \cdot \dfrac{35}{2}\right) + 3 = -\left(\dfrac{^1\cancel{2}}{_1\cancel{5}} \cdot \dfrac{\cancel{35}^7}{\cancel{2}_1}\right) + 3$

$$= -7 + 3$$

$$= -4 = \text{RHS}$$

d) $2(x - 3) = 4(x - 5)$
   $2x - 6 = 4x - 20$

Subtract $4x$ from both sides: $2x - 4x - 6 = 4x - 4x - 20$
                                 $-2x - 6 = -20$

Add 6 to both sides: $-2x - 6 + 6 = -20 + 6$
                                 $-2x = -14$

Divide both sides by -2: $x = 7$

Check: LHS $= 2(7 - 3) = 2(4) = 8$
       RHS $= 4(7 - 5) = 4(2) = 8$

e) $\dfrac{-3}{x} = 4$

Multiply both sides by x: $\dfrac{-3}{\cancel{x}} \cdot \cancel{x} = 4x$

$$-3 = 4x$$

or $4x = -3$ (putting x on LHS)

Divide both sides by 4: $x = \dfrac{-3}{4}$

Check: LHS $= \dfrac{-3}{-3/4} = -3 \div -\dfrac{3}{4} = \dfrac{-^1\cancel{3}}{} \times \dfrac{-4}{\cancel{3}_1}$

$$= -1 \times -4$$

$$= 4 = \text{RHS}$$

f) $\dfrac{2}{3}(x + 6) = \dfrac{-4}{5}(2x - 10)$

Multiply both sides by 15:

$$\dfrac{15 \cdot 2(x + 6)}{3} = \dfrac{15 \cdot -4(2x - 10)}{5}$$

$$5 \cdot 2(x + 6) = 3 \cdot -4(2x - 10)$$

$$10(x + 6) = -12(2x - 10)$$

$$10x + 60 = -24x + 120$$

$$\left[\begin{array}{l} \dfrac{^5\cancel{15} \cdot 2}{\cancel{3}} = 5 \cdot 2 = 10 \\[2mm] \dfrac{^3\cancel{15} \cdot -4}{\cancel{5}} = 3 \cdot -4 = -12 \end{array}\right]$$

Add 24x to both sides:

$$34x + 60 = 120$$

Subtract 60 from both sides:

$$34x = 60$$

$$x = 60 \div 34$$

$$= \frac{60}{34} = \frac{30}{17} = 1.7647059$$

Check: LHS $= \frac{2}{3}(1.7647059 + 6) = \frac{2 \times 7.7647059}{3}$

$$= 5.1764706 \qquad \text{(using calculator)}$$

RHS $= \frac{-4}{5}(2 \times 1.7647059 - 10)$

$$= \frac{-4}{5}(-6.4705882)$$

$$= \frac{4 \times 6.4705882}{5} = 5.1764706 = \text{LHS}$$

g) $\dfrac{365}{365 + 4x} = -2$

Multiply both sides by $(365 + 4x)$:

$$365 = -2(365 + 4x)$$
$$= -730 - 8x$$

Add 8x to both sides:

$$8x + 365 = -730 - 8x + 8x$$
$$8x + 365 = -730$$

Subtract 365 from both sides:

$$8x = -730 - 365$$
$$= -1095$$

Divide both sides by 8:

$$x = \frac{-1095}{8} \quad \text{or} \quad -136.875$$

Check: LHS $= \dfrac{365}{365 + 4\left(\dfrac{-1095}{8}\right)}$ or $\dfrac{365}{365 + 4(-136.875)}$

$$= \frac{365}{365 + \left(\dfrac{-1095}{2}\right)}$$

$$= \frac{365}{365 - 547.5}$$

$$= \frac{365}{365 + (-547.5)}$$

$$= \frac{365}{-182.5}$$

$$= \frac{365}{-182.5}$$

$$= -2 = \text{RHS}$$

$$= -2 = \text{RHS}$$

Your calculator would speed up the checking of this solution.

2   a) $x^2 - 5x + 6 = 0$.

    $a = 1, \quad b = -5, \quad c = 6$

    Using the discriminant formula:

$$x = \frac{-b \pm \sqrt{b^2 - 4ac}}{2a}$$

$$= \frac{-(-5) \pm \sqrt{(-5)^2 - 4(1)(6)}}{2(1)}$$

$$= \frac{5 \pm \sqrt{25 - 24}}{2}$$

$$= \frac{5 \pm \sqrt{1}}{2}$$

$$= \frac{5 \pm 1}{2}$$

$$\therefore x = \frac{5 + 1}{2} = \frac{6}{2} = 3$$

$$\text{and } x = \frac{5 - 1}{2} = \frac{4}{2} = 2$$

    Substituting back into the original equation:

    $x = 3$: $x^2 - 5x + 6 = 3^2 - 5(3) + 6 = 9 - 15 + 6 = 0$
    $x = 2$: $x^2 - 5x + 6 = 2^2 - 5(2) + 6 = 4 - 10 + 6 = 0$

  b) $x^2 - 3x - 10 = 0$

    $a = 1, \quad b = -3, \quad c = -10$

$$x = \frac{-(-3) \pm \sqrt{(-3)^2 - 4(1)(-10)}}{2(1)}$$

$$= \frac{3 \pm \sqrt{9 + 40}}{2}$$

$$= \frac{3 \pm \sqrt{49}}{2} = \frac{3 \pm 7}{2}$$

$$\therefore x = \frac{3 + 7}{2} = \frac{10}{2} = 5$$

$$\text{and } x = \frac{3 - 7}{2} = \frac{-4}{2} = -2$$

Substituting back into the original equation:

$x = 5$: $x^2 - 3x - 10 = 5^2 - 3(5) - 10 = 25 - 15 - 10 = 0$
$x = -2$: $x^2 - 3x - 10 = (-2)^2 - 3(-2) - 10 = 4 + 6 - 10 = 0$

c) $2x^2 - 5x - 8 = 0$

$a = 2, \quad b = -5, \quad c = -8$

$$x = \frac{-(-5) \pm \sqrt{(-5)^2 - 4(2)(-8)}}{2(2)}$$

$$= \frac{5 \pm \sqrt{25 - (-64)}}{4}$$

$$= \frac{5 \pm \sqrt{89}}{4}$$

$$= \frac{5 \pm 9.4339811}{4}$$

$$\therefore x = \frac{5 + 9.4339811}{4} = \frac{14.4339811}{4} = 3.6084953$$

$$\text{and } x = \frac{5 - 9.4339811}{4} = \frac{-4.4339811}{4} = -1.1084953$$

Substituting back into the original equation:

$x = 3.6084953$

$2x^2 - 5x - 8 = \boxed{2} \ \boxed{\times} \ \boxed{3.6084953} \ \boxed{x^2} \ \boxed{=} \ \boxed{-} \ \boxed{5} \ \boxed{\times}$

$\boxed{3.6084953} \ \boxed{=} \ \boxed{-} \ \boxed{8} \ \boxed{=}$

$= 0.00000012$ (slight error caused by rounding)

Use the same procedure for $x = -1.1084953$.

Using the Hewlett-Packard: for $x = 3.6084953$

$2x^2 - 5x - 8 =$ | 2 | ENTER | 3.6084953 | ENTER | 2 | y^x | $\times$

| 5 | ENTER | 3.6084953 | $\times$ | $-$ | 8 | $-$

$= 0.0000002$ (slight error caused by rounding)

d) $5x^2 + 2x = 0$

$a = 5, \quad b = 2, \quad c = 0$

$$x = \frac{-2 \pm \sqrt{2^2 - 4(5)(0)}}{2(5)}$$

$$= \frac{-2 \pm \sqrt{4}}{10}$$

$$= \frac{-2 \pm 2}{10}$$

$$\therefore x = \frac{-2 + 2}{10} = \frac{0}{10} = 0$$

$$\text{and } x = \frac{-2 - 2}{10} = \frac{-4}{10} = \frac{-2}{5} = -0.4$$

Check by substituting the solutions back into the original equation:
$x = 0$: $5x^2 + 2x = 5(0) + 2(0) = 0 + 0 = 0$
$x = -0.4$: $5x^2 + 2x = 5(-0.4^2) + 2(-0.4) = 5(0.16) - 0.8$
$= 0.80 - 0.8 = 0$

e) $x^2 - 1 = 0$

$a = 1, \quad b = 0, \quad c = -1$

$$x = \frac{0 \pm \sqrt{0 - 4(1)(-1)}}{2(1)}$$

$$= \frac{0 \pm \sqrt{4}}{2}$$

$$= \frac{\pm 2}{2}$$

$$= \pm 1$$

$$\therefore x = 1$$

$$\text{and } x = -1$$

Check by substitution:

$x = 1$: $x^2 - 1 = 1^2 - 1 = 1 - 1 = 0$

$x = -1$: $x^2 - 1 = (-1)^2 - 1 = 1 - 1 = 0$

f) $2x^2 - 7x + 4 = 0$

$a = 2$, $b = -7$, $c = 4$

$$x = \frac{-(-7) \pm \sqrt{(-7)^2 - 4(2)(4)}}{2(2)}$$

$$= \frac{7 \pm \sqrt{49 - 32}}{4}$$

$$= \frac{7 \pm \sqrt{17}}{4}$$

$$= \frac{7 \pm 4.1231056}{4}$$

$$\therefore x = \frac{7 + 4.1231056}{4} = \frac{11.1231056}{4} = 2.7807764$$

$$\text{and } x = \frac{7 - 4.1231056}{4} = \frac{2.8768944}{4} = 0.7192236$$

Check by substitution:

$x = 2.7807764$

$2x^2 - 7x + 4 = 2(2.7807764)^2 - 7(2.7807764) + 4$

$\qquad = 15.465435 - 19.465435 + 4$

$\qquad = -4 + 4 = 0$

$x = 0.7192236$

$2x^2 - 7x + 4 = 2(0.7192236)^2 - 7(0.7192236) + 4$

$\qquad = 1.0345652 - 5.0345652 + 4$

$\qquad = -4 + 4 = 0$

3 a) Removing the brackets gives:

$4x^3 + 12x^2 - 24 - 10x^2 - 4x^3 - 2x + 6 = 0$

Collecting like terms:

$(4x^3 - 4x^3) + (12x^2 - 10x^2) - 2x + (-24 + 6) = 0$

$2x^2 - 2x - 18 = 0$

Dividing by 2:

$x^2 - x - 9 = 0$

Now use the discriminant formula to solve for x:

$a = 1$, $b = -1$, $c = -9$

$$x = \frac{-b \pm \sqrt{b^2 - 4ac}}{2a}$$

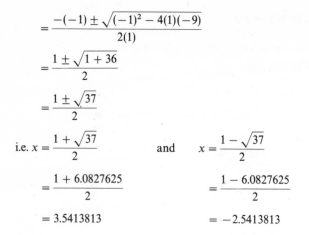

$$= \frac{-(-1) \pm \sqrt{(-1)^2 - 4(1)(-9)}}{2(1)}$$

$$= \frac{1 \pm \sqrt{1 + 36}}{2}$$

$$= \frac{1 \pm \sqrt{37}}{2}$$

i.e. $x = \dfrac{1 + \sqrt{37}}{2}$ and $x = \dfrac{1 - \sqrt{37}}{2}$

$$= \frac{1 + 6.0827625}{2} \qquad\qquad = \frac{1 - 6.0827625}{2}$$

$$= 3.5413813 \qquad\qquad\qquad = -2.5413813$$

Check: Use your calculator to substitute these values back into the original equation.

When $x = 3.5413813$: $4(x^3 + 3x^2 - 6) - 2(5x^2 + 2x^3 + x - 3)$
$= 4[(3.5413813)^3 + 3(3.5413813)^2 - 6]$
$\qquad - 2[5(3.5413813)^2 + 2(3.5413813)^3 + 3.5413813 - 3]$

If you are not confident about doing this in one process on your calculator, proceed bracket by bracket, remembering to compute inner brackets first.

Your calculator should give a result very close to zero, allowing for slight rounding errors.

Use the same method to check $x = -2.5413813$

b) Removing the brackets gives:
$2x^2 - 8x - 6 - 1.4x^2 + 5x + 5.79 = 0$

Collecting like terms:
$(2x^2 - 1.4x^2) + (-8x + 5x) + (-6 + 5.79) = 0$
$0.6x^2 - 3x - 0.21 = 0$

$a = 0.6,\quad b = -3,\quad c = -0.21$

$$x = \frac{-b \pm \sqrt{b^2 - 4ac}}{2a}$$

$$= \frac{-(-3) \pm \sqrt{(-3)^2 - 4(0.6)(-0.21)}}{2(0.6)}$$

$$= \frac{3 \pm \sqrt{9 + 0.504}}{1.2}$$

$$= \frac{3 \pm \sqrt{9.504}}{1.2}$$

$$= \frac{3 \pm 3.0828558}{1.2}$$

$$\therefore x = \frac{3 + 3.0828558}{1.2} = 5.0690465$$

$$\text{and } x = \frac{3 - 3.0828558}{1.2} = -0.06904652$$

4   a) $(x - 1)(x - 2) = x(x - 2) - 1(x - 2)$
$$= x^2 - 2x - x + 2$$
$$= x^2 - 3x + 2$$

b) $(x + 1)(x - 2) = x(x - 2) + 1(x - 2)$
$$= x^2 - 2x + x - 2$$
$$= x^2 - x - 2$$

c) $(2x - 3)(x + 5) = 2x(x + 5) - 3(x + 5)$
$$= 2x^2 + 10x - 3x - 15$$
$$= 2x^2 + 7x - 15$$

d) $(3x - 7)(x^2 + 2x + 9) = 3x(x^2 + 2x + 9) - 7(x^2 + 2x + 9)$
$$= 3x^3 + 6x^2 + 27x - 7x^2 - 14x - 63$$
$$= 3x^3 - x^2 + 13x - 63$$

5   a) $(1 + x)^3 - 1 = 0.07$

Add 1 to both sides:
$$(1 + x)^3 = 1.07$$

Take the cubic (3rd) root of both sides:
$$(1 + x) = \sqrt[3]{1.07} = 1.07^{1/3} = 1.07^{0.\dot{3}}$$

Using $0.\dot{3} = 0.33333333$,
$$(1 + x) = 1.0228091$$
$$x = 0.228091$$

You will use this sort of equation later to find an interest rate.
In this case the interest rate is $0.0228091 \times 100\% = 2.28091\%$

b) $(1 + 4x)^6 - 1 = 0.12$
$$(1 + 4x)^6 = 1.12$$
$$1 + 4x = 1.12^{1/6} = 1.12^{0.1\dot{6}}$$
$$4x = 1.12^{0.1\dot{6}} - 1$$

Using 0.16666667 for $0.1\dot{6}$,
$$4x = 1.0190676 - 1$$
$$= 0.0190676$$
$$\therefore x = 0.00476691$$

Check: $[1 + 4(0.00476691)]^6 - 1 = 1.1200001 - 1 = 0.1200001$

Using scientific calculator:

Using the Hewlett-Packard:

| 4 | ENTER | 0.00476691 | × | 1 | + | 6 | y^x | 1 | − |

CHAPTER 4

1 a) $(3x - 2)(2x + 3) = 3x(2x + 3) - 2(2x + 3)$
$$= 3x(2x) + 3x(3) - 2(2x) - 2(3)$$
$$= 6x^2 + 9x - 4x - 6$$
$$= 6x^2 + 5x - 6$$

b) $(2x - 5)(4x - 3) = 2x(4x - 3) - 5(4x - 3)$
$$= 2x(4x) + 2x(-3) - 5(4x) - 5(-3)$$
$$= 8x^2 - 6x - 20x + 15$$
$$= 8x^2 - 26x + 15$$

c) $(-a + b)(-a - b) = -a(-a - b) + b(-a - b)$
$$= -a(-a) - a(-b) + b(-a) + b(-b)$$
$$= a^2 + ab - ab - b^2$$
$$= a^2 - b^2$$

d) $-2x(x + 3) - 3x(x - 2) = -2x(x) - 2x(3) - 3x(x) - 3x(-2)$
$$= -2x^2 - 6x - 3x^2 + 6x$$
$$= -5x^2$$

2 a) $(x + 2)(x - 2) = 0$
$$\therefore x = 2 \quad \text{and} \quad -2$$

b) $(x + 2)(x + 2) = 0$
$$\therefore x = -2$$

c) $(x - 3)(x - 2) = 0$
$$\therefore x = 2 \quad \text{and} \quad 3$$

d) $(2x - 3)(x + 2) = 0$

$$\therefore x = \frac{3}{2} \quad \text{and} \quad -2$$

e) $6x^2 - 13x + 6 = 0$

This equation is a little more difficult to factorise. Use the short-cut method of multiplying the diagonals and adding:

$$6 \diagdown{-2} \atop 1 \diagup{-3} \qquad 6(-3) + 1(-2) = -18 - 2 = -20 \quad \text{No}$$

$$6 \diagdown{-3} \atop 1 \diagup{-2} \qquad 6(-2) + 1(-3) = -12 - 3 = -15 \quad \text{No}$$

$$3 \diagdown{-2} \atop 2 \diagup{-3} \qquad 3(-3) + 2(-2) = -9 - 4 = -13 \quad \text{Yes}$$

$$\therefore (3x - 2)(2x - 3) = 0$$

$$x = \frac{2}{3} \quad \text{and} \quad \frac{3}{2}$$

f) $(3x - 1)(x - 5) = 0$

$$\therefore x = \frac{1}{3} \quad \text{and} \quad 5$$

3 a) $a = 3, \quad b = -7, \quad c = 4$

$$\therefore i = \frac{-(-7) \pm \sqrt{49 - 4(3)(4)}}{2(3)}$$

$$= \frac{7 \pm \sqrt{1}}{6}$$

$$= \frac{8}{6} \quad \text{and} \quad \frac{6}{6}$$

$$= \frac{4}{3} \quad \text{and} \quad 1$$

b) First simplify the equation.

Let $\dfrac{1}{1 + i} = x$

Then $5 \cdot \left(\dfrac{1}{1 + i} \right) + 7 \cdot \left(\dfrac{1}{1 + i} \right)^2 - 10 = 5x + 7x^2 - 10$

$$\therefore a = 7, \quad b = 5, \quad c = -10$$

$$x = \frac{-5 \pm \sqrt{5^2 - 4(7)(-10)}}{2(7)}$$

$$= \frac{-5 \pm \sqrt{25 + 280}}{14}$$

$$= \frac{-5 \pm \sqrt{305}}{14}$$

$$= \frac{-5 \pm 17.464249}{14}$$

$$x = \frac{-5 + 17.464249}{14} \quad \text{and} \quad x = \frac{-5 - 17.464249}{14}$$

$$= \frac{12.464249}{14} \qquad\qquad = \frac{-22.464249}{14}$$

$$= 0.89030351 \qquad\qquad = -1.6045892$$

$$\therefore \frac{1}{1+i} = 0.89030351 \quad \text{and} \quad \frac{1}{1+i} = -1.6045892$$

Taking reciprocals,

$$1 + i = 1.1232125 \qquad\qquad 1 + i = -0.62321246$$

$$\therefore i = 0.1232125 \quad \text{and} \quad i = -1.62321246$$

4   a) $\frac{1}{2} + \frac{3}{8}$.   Change both fractions to eighths. If you can't see that 8 is the lowest common denominator, work with $2 \times 8 = 16$ and reduce the fractions later.

$$\frac{1}{2} \cdot \boxed{\frac{4}{4}} + \frac{3}{8} = \frac{4}{8} + \frac{3}{8} = \frac{7}{8}$$

$$\text{OR} \quad \frac{1}{2} \cdot \boxed{\frac{8}{8}} + \frac{3}{8} \cdot \frac{2}{2} = \frac{8}{16} + \frac{6}{16} = \frac{14}{16} = \frac{7}{8}$$

b) $\frac{3}{4} - \frac{5}{12} = \frac{3}{4} \cdot \boxed{\frac{3}{3}} - \frac{5}{12}$ (changing to twelfths)

$$= \frac{9}{12} - \frac{5}{12} = \frac{4}{12} = \frac{1}{3}$$

c) $\frac{1}{3} + \frac{7}{12} - \frac{5}{6} = \frac{1}{3} \cdot \boxed{\frac{4}{4}} + \frac{7}{12} - \frac{5}{6} \cdot \boxed{\frac{2}{2}}$ (changing to twelfths)

$$= \frac{4}{12} + \frac{7}{12} - \frac{10}{12}$$

$$= \frac{1}{12}$$

d) $\dfrac{x}{5} - \dfrac{3x}{10} + \dfrac{3x}{5} = \dfrac{x}{5} \cdot \boxed{\dfrac{2}{2}} - \dfrac{3x}{10} + \dfrac{3x}{5} \cdot \boxed{\dfrac{2}{2}}$

$$= \dfrac{2x}{10} - \dfrac{3x}{10} + \dfrac{6x}{10}$$

$$= \dfrac{5x}{10} = \dfrac{x}{2}$$

e) $2 - \dfrac{i}{1+i}$ Make the denominators $(1+i)$

$$2 \cdot \boxed{\dfrac{1+i}{1+i}} - \dfrac{i}{1+i} = \dfrac{2(1+i)}{1+i} - \dfrac{i}{1+i}$$

$$= \dfrac{2 + 2i - i}{1+i}$$

$$= \dfrac{2 + i}{1+i}$$

f) $\dfrac{x^2 - 4}{(x+2)} + 3 = \dfrac{x^2 - 4}{x+2} + 3 \cdot \boxed{\dfrac{x+2}{x+2}}$

$$= \dfrac{x^2 - 4}{x+2} + \dfrac{3x + 6}{x+2}$$

$$= \dfrac{x^2 + 3x + 2}{(x+2)}$$

$$= \dfrac{(x+2)(x+1)}{(x+2)}$$

$$= x + 1$$

An alternative method would be to factorise $x^2 - 4$ at the beginning:

$$\dfrac{x^2 - 4}{x+2} + 3 = \dfrac{(x+2)(x-2)}{(x+2)} + 3$$

$$= (x - 2) + 3$$

$$= x + 1$$

g) $\dfrac{x+3}{x^2 - 9} + \dfrac{2}{x-3} = \dfrac{x+3}{(x+3)(x-3)} + \dfrac{2}{x-3}$

$$= \dfrac{1}{x-3} + \dfrac{2}{x-3}$$

$$= \dfrac{3}{x-3}$$

h) $\dfrac{5}{1+i} + \dfrac{7}{(1+i)^2} - 10 = \dfrac{5}{1+i} \cdot \boxed{\dfrac{1+i}{1+i}} + \dfrac{7}{(1+i)^2} - 10 \cdot \boxed{\dfrac{(1+i)^2}{(1+i)^2}}$

$$= \dfrac{5(1+i)}{(1+i)^2} + \dfrac{7}{(1+i)^2} - \dfrac{10(1+i)^2}{(1+i)^2}$$

$$= \dfrac{5 + 5i + 7 - 10(1 + 2i + i^2)}{(1+i)^2}$$

$$= \dfrac{12 + 5i - 10 - 20i - 10i^2}{(1+i)^2}$$

$$= \dfrac{-10i^2 - 15i + 2}{(1+i)^2}$$

5   a) $\dfrac{3x}{4} - \dfrac{2}{3} = \dfrac{7}{2}$

Change to twelfths:

$$\dfrac{3x}{4} \cdot \boxed{\dfrac{3}{3}} - \dfrac{2}{3} \cdot \boxed{\dfrac{4}{4}} = \dfrac{7}{2} \cdot \boxed{\dfrac{6}{6}}$$

$$\dfrac{9x}{12} - \dfrac{8}{12} = \dfrac{42}{12}$$

Multiply both sides by 12:

$$9x - 8 = 42$$
$$9x = 50$$
$$x = 50/9 = 5\tfrac{5}{9}$$

Check: LHS $= \dfrac{3}{4} \cdot \dfrac{50}{9} - \dfrac{2}{3} = \dfrac{50}{12} - \dfrac{2}{3}$ (cancelling the 3 into the 9)

$$= \dfrac{25}{6} - \dfrac{2}{3}$$

$$= \dfrac{25}{6} - \dfrac{4}{6} = \dfrac{21}{6}$$

$$= \dfrac{7}{2} = \text{RHS}$$

b) $\dfrac{7}{x-2} - \dfrac{2(x^2 - 4)}{x-2} = 3$

Multiply both sides by $(x - 2)$:
$$7 - 2(x^2 - 4) = 3(x - 2)$$
$$7 - 2x^2 + 8 = 3x - 6$$

$$15 - 2x^2 = 3x - 6$$
$$-2x^2 - 3x + 21 = 0$$
$$2x^2 + 3x - 21 = 0$$

Using the discriminant formula:
$$a = 2, \quad b = 3, \quad c = -21$$

$$x = \frac{-3 \pm \sqrt{3^2 - 4(2)(-21)}}{2(2)}$$

$$= \frac{-3 \pm \sqrt{9 + 168}}{4}$$

$$= \frac{-3 \pm \sqrt{177}}{4}$$

$$\therefore x = \frac{-3 + 13.304135}{4} \quad \text{and} \quad x = \frac{-3 - 13.304135}{4}$$

$$= \frac{10.304135}{4} \qquad\qquad = \frac{-16.304135}{4}$$

$$x = 2.5760337 \qquad\qquad x = -4.0760338$$

Check: (i) $x = 2.576$ (to 3 places)

$$\text{LHS} = \frac{7}{2.576 - 2} - \frac{2(2.576^2 - 4)}{2.576 - 2} = \frac{7}{0.576} - \frac{2(6.635776 - 4)}{0.576}$$

$$= \frac{7 - 5.271552}{0.576}$$

$$= 3.0008$$

$$= \text{RHS} \quad \text{(slight rounding error)}$$

Use the same method to check (ii) $x = -4.076$ (to 3 places)

c) $\dfrac{3}{x - 4} + \dfrac{2}{x - 3} = -4$

Make the denominator $(x - 4)(x - 3)$:

$$\frac{3}{x - 4} \cdot \boxed{\frac{x - 3}{x - 3}} + \frac{2}{x - 3} \cdot \boxed{\frac{x - 4}{x - 4}} = -4 \cdot \boxed{\frac{(x - 3)(x - 4)}{(x - 3)(x - 4)}}$$

$$\frac{3(x - 3)}{(x - 4)(x - 3)} + \frac{2(x - 4)}{(x - 3)(x - 4)} = \frac{-4(x - 3)(x - 4)}{(x - 3)(x - 4)}$$

$$\frac{3x - 9 + 2x - 8}{(x - 3)(x - 4)} = \frac{-4(x^2 - 7x + 12)}{(x - 3)(x - 4)}$$

Multiplying by $(x - 3)(x - 4)$ gives:

$$3x - 9 + 2x - 8 = -4x^2 + 28x - 48$$
$$4x^2 - 23x + 31 = 0$$

Now use the discriminant formula:
$a = 4, \quad b = -23, \quad c = 31$

$$\therefore x = \frac{-(-23) \pm \sqrt{(-23)^2 - 4(4)(31)}}{2(4)}$$

$$= \frac{23 \pm \sqrt{1025}}{8}$$

$$= \frac{23 \pm 32.015621}{8}$$

$$x = 6.877 \text{ and } -1.127 \qquad \text{(to 3 places)}$$

Check by substituting these values (one at a time) back into

$$\frac{3}{x - 4} + \frac{2}{x - 3} = -4 \quad \text{or into} \quad 4x^2 - 23x + 31 = 0.$$

CHAPTER 5

1 a) 0.1   b) 0.12   c) 0.125   d) 0.07   e) 0.0525

2 a) 15%   b) 18.5%   c) 2%   d) 2.3%   e) 0.34%

3 $P = 25,000, \quad i = 4\% = 0.04, \quad n = 25$

$\therefore AV = 25,000(1.04)^{25} = 25,000 \times 2.6658363$
$\qquad = \$66,645.91$

4 $P = 100, \quad AV = 300, \quad n = 15$

$$\therefore 300 = 100(1 + i)^{15}$$
$$(1 + i)^{15} = 3$$
$$1 + i = 3^{1/15} = 3^{0.066667} = 1.07599$$
$$i = 0.07599$$
$$= 7.599\%$$

5 Let the initial investment be P.
Then $AV = 2P$ (since the investment doubles)
$n = 10$ years $= 120$ months

$$\therefore 2P = P(1 + i)^{120} \qquad \text{where } i = \text{monthly compound rate}$$

$$(1 + i)^{120} = \frac{2P}{P} = 2$$

Taking the 120th root:

$$1 + i = 2^{1/120} = 2^{0.0083333} = 1.005793 \quad \text{(to 6 places)}$$
$$\therefore i = 0.005793 = 5.793\%$$

Check: LHS $= (1 + i)^{120} = 1.005793^{120} = 2 =$ RHS

Exercises 2 and 3 could both be answered by direct substitution into the formula

$$i = \left[\frac{AV}{P}\right]^{1/n} - 1$$

6   a) $\ln 80 = 4.382$

b) $\ln(2.6)(7.4) = \ln 2.6 + \ln 7.4 = 0.95551144 + 2.00148$
$$= 2.957$$

c) $\ln 65^2 = 2\ln 65 = 2(4.1743873) = 8.349$

d) $\ln \dfrac{99}{4} = \ln 99 - \ln 4 = 4.5951199 - 1.3862944$
$$= 3.209$$

e) $\ln 3(1.1)^4 = \ln 3 + \ln(1.1)^4 = \ln 3 + 4\ln 1.1$
$$= 1.0986123 + 4(0.09531018)$$
$$= 1.480$$

f) $\dfrac{\ln 150}{\ln 120} = \ln 150 \div \ln 120 = 5.0106353 \div 4.7874917$
$$= 1.047$$

7   Let n = investment period in years
P = initial investment, $AV = 3P$, $i = 10\% = 0.1$

$$\therefore P(1 + i)^n = AV$$
$$P(1.1)^n = 3P$$
$$(1.1)^n = 3$$
$$\ln(1.1)^n = \ln 3$$
$$n\ln(1.1) = \ln 3$$

$$n = \frac{\ln 3}{\ln 1.1} = 11.5267 \quad \text{(to 4 places)}$$

Check: $(1.1)^{11.5267} = 2.9999987 = 3$

$\therefore$ The investment period is 11 years and 193 days (rounding to next day).
$(0.5267 \times 365 = 192.2455)$

8   $AV = P(1.12)^5(1.1)^5 = 20,000(1.12)^5(1.1)^5$
$$= \$56,765.38$$

9   The \$80,000 accumulates for 5 years @ 10%, giving $80,000(1.1)^5$.

The lump sum payment, say X, accumulates for only 1 year, giving $X(1.1)$.
The two amounts added together give $200,000.
Thus $80,000(1.1)^5 + X(1.1) = 200,000$

$$128,840.8 + X(1.1) = 200,000$$
$$X(1.1) = 200,000 - 128,840.8$$
$$= 71,159.2$$
$$\therefore X = 71,159.2 \div 1.1$$
$$= \$64,690.18$$
$$= \text{capital (lump) sum required after 4 years}$$

10   This time the $80,000 accumulates to $80,000(1.1)^2(1.09)^3$ and the lump sum payment accumulates to $X(1.09)$.

$$\therefore 80,000(1.1)^2(1.09)^3 + X(1.09) = 200,000$$
$$125,358.81 + X(1.09) = 200,000$$
$$X(1.09) = 74,641.193$$
$$X = \$68,478.16$$

CHAPTER 6

1   By trial and error, $1.04^{24} = 2.5633$
$$1.04^{25} = 2.6658 \quad \text{(to 4 places)}$$

1.04^n	2.5633	2.6		2.6658

| n | 24 | $\triangle$ | 25 |

Let $\triangle$ = the interpolated value for n
The distance between 24 and $\triangle$ is $2.6 - 2.5633 = 0.0367$
The distance between $\triangle$ and 25 is $2.6658 - 2.6 = 0.0658$
The total distance is $0.0367 + 0.0658 = 0.1025$

$$\longleftarrow \text{ } 0.1025 \text{ } \longrightarrow$$
$$\longleftarrow 0.0367 \rightarrow | \longleftarrow 0.0658 \longrightarrow$$
$$\triangle$$

Converting to a strip length of unity,

$$\text{first distance} = \frac{0.0367}{0.1025} = 0.358$$

$$\text{second distance} = 1 - 0.358 = 0.642$$

	0.358	0.642	
24		$\triangle$	25

$\therefore$ The weights are 0.358 and 0.642.

$$\triangle = 0.642(24) + 0.358(25) = 15.408 + 8.95$$
$$= 24.358$$

The interpolated value for $n = 24.358$

Check by substituting back into $1.04^n = 2.6$
$$1.04^{24.358} = 2.5995494$$
$$\approx 2.6$$

2 (i) Let the rate of interest (as a decimal) $= i$
$$10,000(1 + i)^2 + 20,000(1 + i) = 36,000$$
Using trial and error, first try $i = 10\% = 0.1$:
LHS $= 10,000(1.1)^2 + 20,000(1.1) = 34,100$
Then try $i = 11\% = 0.11$:
LHS $= 10,000(1.11)^2 + 20,000(1.11) = 34,321$
Still too small, so try $i = 15\% = 0.15$:
LHS $= 10,000(1.15)^2 + 20,000(1.15) = 36,225$
Too big, try $i = 14\% = 0.14$:
LHS $= 10,000(1.14)^2 + 20,000(1.14) = 35,796$

$\therefore$ The rate of interest lies between 14% and 15%.

| LHS | 35,796 | 36,000 | 36,225 |

$\therefore \triangle = 0.476(15) + 0.524(14)$
$$= 14.476$$

$\therefore$ The compound annual rate of return is 14.476%
$$i = 0.14476$$

(ii) The quadratic equation is
$$10,000(1 + i)^2 + 20,000(1 + i) = 36,000$$
Divide by 1,000 and move constant term to LHS:
$$10(1 + i)^2 + 20(1 + i) - 36 = 0$$

Let $x = 1 + i$

$$10x^2 + 20x - 36 = 0$$

Using the discriminant formula,

$$a = 10, \quad b = 20, \quad c = -36$$

$$x = \frac{-20 \pm \sqrt{20^2 - 4(10)(-36)}}{2(10)}$$

$$= \frac{-20 \pm \sqrt{400 + 1440}}{20}$$

$$= \frac{-20 \pm 42.895221}{20}$$

$$= 1.1447611 \quad \text{and} \quad -3.1447611$$

We can disregard the second solution.

$$\therefore x = 1 + i = 1.1447611$$
$$i = 0.1447611 = 14.47611\%$$

3 $(1 + i)^{10} = 2$
Trial and error (to 4 places):
$1.06^{10} = 1.7908$
$1.07^{10} = 1.9672$
$1.08^{10} = 2.1589$
Now interpolate between 1.07 and 1.08:

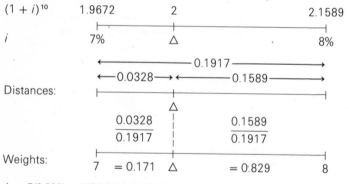

$\triangle = 7(0.829) + 8(0.171) = 7.171\%$

Check $(1 + i)^{10} = (1.07171)^{10} = 1.9988$ (slight error due to interpolation and rounding)

CHAPTER 7

1   $n = 1\frac{1}{2}$ years = 6 quarters, $i = 4\% = 0.04$

$\therefore$ Present Value $(PV) = \dfrac{25,000}{(1.04)^6} = \$19,757.86$

2 $PV = \dfrac{500,000}{(1.1)^7} = \$256,579.06$

3 $n_1 = 4$ years = 8 half-years, $i_1 = 5\frac{1}{2}\% = 0.055$
   $n_2 = 7$ years = 14 half-years, $i_2 = 5\frac{1}{2}\% = 0.055$

$$PV = \frac{70,000}{(1.055)^8} + \frac{90,000}{(1.055)^{14}}$$

$$= 45,611.92 + 42,531.24$$

$$= \$88,143.16$$

Using scientific calculator:

| 70,000 | $\div$ | 1.055 | y^x | 8 | $=$ | Put into memory | 90,000 |

| $\div$ | 1.055 | y^x | 14 | $=$ | $+$ | Memory recall | $=$ |

Using the Hewlett-Packard:

| 70,000 | ENTER | 1.055 | ENTER | 8 | y^x | $\div$ | 90,000 |

| ENTER | 1.055 | ENTER | 14 | y^x | $\div$ | $+$ |

4 Interest $\longleftarrow$————— $5\frac{1}{2}\%$ —————$\longrightarrow$ $\longleftarrow$———— 5% ————$\longrightarrow$
   Half-year   0   8   14

   Cash flow   \$70,000   \$90,000

For the \$70,000 cash flow, $i = 5\frac{1}{2}\% = 0.055$
                            $n = 8$ half-years.

$$\therefore PV = \frac{70,000}{(1.055)^8}$$

For the \$90,000 cash flow, $i = 5\%$ for 3 years
                            $= 0.05$ for 6 half-years
                    and $i = 5\frac{1}{2}\%$ for 4 years
                            $= 0.055$ for 8 half-years

$$\therefore PV = 90,000 \cdot V^6 \text{ @ } 5\% \cdot V^8 \text{ @ } 5\frac{1}{2}\%$$

$$= \frac{90,000}{(1.05)^6(1.055)^8}$$

$$\therefore \text{Price of bond} = \frac{70,000}{(1.055)^8} + \frac{90,000}{(1.05)^6(1.055)^8}$$

$$= 45,611.92 + 43,760.98$$

$$= \$89,372.90$$

5   Let i = annual compound rate, FV = future value

$$PV = \frac{FV}{(1 + i)^n}$$

$$70 = \frac{100}{(1 + i)^5}$$

$$70(1 + i)^5 = 100$$

$$(1 + i)^5 = \frac{100}{70}$$

$$= 1.4285714$$

$$1 + i = (1.4285714)^{1/5}$$

$$= 1.4285714^{0.2}$$

$$= 1.0739409$$

$$\therefore i = 0.0739409$$

$$= 7.39409\%$$

The bond earns 7.39409% per annum compound.

6   Let the annual rate of appreciation = j
Let the $PV = V$
  Then $FV = 2V$

$$\therefore V = \frac{2V}{(1 + j)^{10}}$$

$$V(1 + j)^{10} = 2V$$

$$(1 + j)^{10} = \frac{2V}{V} = 2$$

$$1 + j = 2^{1/10} = 2^{0.1}$$

$$= 1.0717735$$

$$j = 0.0717735$$

$$= 7.17735\%$$

The annual rate of appreciation is 7.17735%

7   n = 4 years and 120 days
What fraction of a year is 120 days?

Answer: $\frac{120}{365} = 0.32876712$

$$\therefore\ n = 4.328767 \quad \text{(to 6 places)}$$

$$\therefore\ PV = \frac{100}{(1.11)^{4.328767}}$$

$$= \frac{100}{1.5710594}$$

$$= \$63.65$$

8   Let the windscreen price = P
Then $PV = P, \quad FV = 2P, \quad i = 11\% = 0.11$

$$\therefore\ P = \frac{2P}{(1.11)^n}$$

$$P(1.11)^n = 2P$$

$$(1.11)^n = \frac{2P}{P} = 2$$

Taking logarithms of both sides:

$$\ln(1.11)^n = \ln 2$$

$$n \ln 1.11 = \ln 2$$

$$n = \frac{\ln 2}{\ln 1.11} = \frac{0.69314718}{0.10436002}$$

$$= 6.6418846 \text{ years}$$

Now $0.6418846 \times 365 = 234.28788 = 235$ days
$\therefore$ The price of the windscreen will double in 6 years and 235 days.

CHAPTER 8

1

Year n	$(1 + i)^n$ $= (1.1)^n$	V^n $= (1.1)^{-n}$	$A_{\overline{n}|10\%}$
I	II	III	IV
1	1.1000	0.90909	0.90909
2	1.2100	0.82645	1.73554
3	1.3310	0.75131	2.48685
4	1.4641	0.68301	3.16986

Notes: a) Column III is the reciprocal of column II
   b) Column IV is the cumulative sum of column III
      e.g. $A_{\overline{2}|} = V^1 + V^2 = 0.90909 + 0.82645$
      $A_{\overline{3}|} = V^1 + V^2 + V^3 = A_{\overline{2}|} + 0.75131$

2   $A_{\overline{4}|10\%} = \dfrac{1 - V^4}{i} = \dfrac{1 - \dfrac{1}{(1.1)^4}}{0.1}$

   $= 3.16987$ (slight rounding difference)

Scientific calculator:

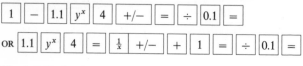

OR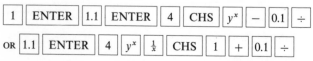

Hewlett-Packard:

| 1 | ENTER | 1.1 | ENTER | 4 | CHS | y^x | − | 0.1 | ÷ |

OR | 1.1 | ENTER | 4 | y^x | $\frac{1}{x}$ | CHS | 1 | + | 0.1 | ÷ |

3   The total of the $A_{\overline{n}|i}$ column is 8.30134.
   This represents $A_{\overline{1}|} + A_{\overline{2}|} + A_{\overline{3}|} + A_{\overline{4}|}$

$$= \frac{1 - V^1}{i} + \frac{1 - V^2}{i} + \frac{1 - V^3}{i} + \frac{1 - V^4}{i}$$

$$= \frac{1}{i}[1 - V^1 + 1 - V^2 + 1 - V^3 + 1 - V^4]$$

$$= \frac{1}{i}[1 + 1 + 1 + 1 - (V^1 + V^2 + V^3 + V^4)]$$

$$= \frac{1}{0.1}[4 - A_{\overline{4}|10\%}]$$

$$= 10[4 - 3.16986]$$

$$= 8.3014 \quad \text{(slight difference due to rounding)}$$

4   PV (in 000's) $= \underbrace{40V^3 + 40V^4 + 40V^5 + 40V^6}_{\text{annuity}} + 30V^6$

$$= 40(V^3 + V^4 + V^5 + V^6) + 30V^6 \text{ @ } 11\%$$

Now $A_{\overline{6}|i} = V^1 + V^2 + V^3 + V^4 + V^5 + V^6$

and $A_{\overline{2}|i} = V^1 + V^2$

Subtracting, we get:

$$A_{\overline{6}|i} - A_{\overline{2}|i} = V^3 + V^4 + V^5 + V^6$$

$$= V^2(V^1 + V^2 + V^3 + V^4)$$

$$= V^2 A_{\overline{4}|i}$$

$$\therefore PV = 40(V^3 + V^4 + V^5 + V^6) + 30V^6$$

$$= 40V^2 A_{\overline{4}|i} + 30V^6 \text{ @ } 11\%$$

Using $A_{\overline{n}|i} = \dfrac{1 - \dfrac{1}{(1 + i)^n}}{i}$

$$A_{\overline{4}|i} = \frac{1 - \dfrac{1}{(1.11)^4}}{0.11} = 3.102446$$

$$\therefore PV = 40 \times \frac{1}{(1.11)^2} \times 3.102446 + \frac{30}{(1.11)^6}$$

$$= 100.720591 + 16.039225$$

$$= 116.759816 \quad \text{(in 000's)}$$

$$\therefore PV = \$116,759.82 \text{ or } \$116,760 \text{ to nearest dollar}$$

Alternatively, $PV = 40(V^3 + V^4 + V^5 + V^6) + 30V^6$

$$= 40(A_{\overline{6}|} - A_{\overline{2}|}) + 30V^6$$

$$= 40(4.23054 - 1.71252) + \frac{30}{(1.11)^6}$$

$$= 116.760025 = \$116,760$$

5    $\ddot{A}_{\overline{n}|} = 1 + V^1 + V^2 + \dots V^{n-1}$

$A_{\overline{n-1}|} = \quad V^1 + V^2 + \dots V^{n-1}$

$\therefore \ddot{A}_{\overline{n}|} = 1 + A_{\overline{n-1}|}$

6
Year	0	1	2	3	4	5	6	7	8	9	10
Cash flows (000's)		50	50	50	50	50	100	100	100	100	100

$$PV = 50,000(V^1 + V^2 + V^3 + V^4 + V^5)$$

$$+ 100,000(V^6 + V^7 + V^8 + V^9 + V^{10}) \text{ @ } 12\%$$

$$= 50,000 A_{\overline{5}|12\%} + 100,000(A_{\overline{10}|12\%} - A_{\overline{5}|12\%})$$

OR $PV = 50{,}000 A_{\overline{5}|12\%} + 100{,}000 V^5(V^1 + V^2 + V^3 + V^4 + V^5)$

$\qquad = 50{,}000 A_{\overline{5}|12\%} + 100{,}000 V^5 A_{\overline{5}|12\%}$

Now $A_{\overline{5}|12\%} = \dfrac{1 - \dfrac{1}{(1.12)^5}}{0.12} = 3.60478$

$V^5 A_{\overline{5}|12\%} = \dfrac{1}{(1.12)^5} \times 3.60478 = 2.04545$

$\therefore PV = 50{,}000(3.60478) + 100{,}000(2.04545)$

$\qquad = \$384{,}783.68$

$\qquad = \$384{,}784$ to nearest dollar

7   PV in 000's $= 20V^1 + 20V^2 + 20V^3 + 20V^6 + 20V^7 + 20V^8$

$\qquad = 20 A_{\overline{3}|i} + 20(A_{\overline{8}|i} - A_{\overline{5}|i})$

$\qquad = 20 A_{\overline{3}|i} + 20 V^5 A_{\overline{3}|i}$

$A_{\overline{3}|1.2\%} = \dfrac{1 - \dfrac{1}{(1.012)^3}}{0.012} = 2.929415$

$V^5 A_{\overline{3}|1.2\%} = (1.012)^{-5} \times 2.929415 = 2.759804$

$\therefore PV = 20(2.929415) + 20(2.759804)$

$\qquad = \$113{,}784$ to nearest dollar

8   Month

The first three cash flows represent an annuity at 1.2%

$$\text{i.e.} \quad PV = 20 A_{\overline{3}|1.2\%}$$

Now look at the second lot of cash flows. They represent an annuity due with valuation date at month 6 and interest rate 1%, i.e. $20\ddot{A}_{\overline{3}|1\%}$
To bring $20\ddot{A}_{\overline{3}|1\%}$ back to zero, present-value the amount back 6 months at 1.2% interest,

$$\text{i.e.} \quad \ddot{A}_{\overline{3}|1\%} \times V^6 \text{ @ } 1.2\%$$

$\therefore$ Total $PV = 20 A_{\overline{3}|1.2\%} + 20\ddot{A}_{\overline{3}|1\%}(V^6 \text{ @ } 1.2\%)$

$$A_{\overline{3}|1.2\%} = \frac{1 - \dfrac{1}{(1.012)^3}}{0.012} = 2.929415$$

$$\ddot{A}_{\overline{3}|1\%} = A_{\overline{2}|1\%} + 1 \quad \text{(as proved in exercise 5)}$$

$$A_{\overline{2}|1\%} = \frac{1 - \dfrac{1}{(1.01)^2}}{0.01} = 1.970395$$

$$\therefore \ddot{A}_{\overline{3}|1\%} = 2.970395$$

$$V_{1.2\%}^6 \ddot{A}_{\overline{3}|1\%} = \frac{2.970395}{(1.012)^6} = 2.765229$$

$$\therefore PV = 20(2.929415) + 20(2.765229) \quad \text{(in 000's)}$$

$$= 113.892885$$

$$\therefore PV = \$113,893 \text{ to nearest dollar}$$

CHAPTER 9

1   a) $S_4 = 4 + 8 + 16 + 32$

$$r = \frac{2\text{nd term}}{1\text{st term}} = \frac{8}{4} = 2$$

Multiply S_4 by 2:

$$2S_4 = \quad 8 + 16 + 32 + 64 \qquad (1)$$

$$S_4 = 4 + 8 + 16 + 32 \qquad\qquad (2)$$

Subtract (1) − (2):

$$2S_4 - S_4 = 64 - 4$$

$$S_4 = 60$$

Check: $4 + 8 + 16 + 32 = 60$

b) $A_{\overline{3}|10\%} = \dfrac{1}{1.1} + \dfrac{1}{(1.1)^2} + \dfrac{1}{(1.1)^3}$

Multiply $A_{\overline{3}|}$ by 1.1:

$$1.1A_{\overline{3}|10\%} = 1 + \frac{1}{(1.1)} + \frac{1}{(1.1)^2} \qquad (3)$$

$$A_{\overline{3}|10\%} = \frac{1}{(1.1)} + \frac{1}{(1.1)^2} + \frac{1}{(1.1)^3} \qquad (4)$$

Subtract (3) − (4):

$$0.1A_{\overline{3}|10\%} = 1 - \frac{1}{(1.1)^3}$$

$$\therefore A_{\overline{3}|10\%} = \frac{1 - \dfrac{1}{(1.1)^3}}{0.1}$$

$$= 2.486852$$

Check: $A_{\overline{3}|10\%} = \dfrac{1}{1.1} + \dfrac{1}{(1.1)^2} + \dfrac{1}{(1.1)^3}$

$$= \frac{1}{1.1} + \frac{1}{1.21} + \frac{1}{1.331}$$

$$= 0.909091 + 0.826446 + 0.751315$$

$$= 2.486852$$

2 a) $S = 1.05 + (1.05)^3 + (1.05)^5 + \ldots (1.05)^{19}$

$a = 1.05$

$$r = \frac{(1.05)^3}{1.05} = \frac{T_2}{T_1} = (1.05)^2$$

Looking at terms and powers:

Term	Power
1	1
2	3
3	5
n	19

The power is obtained by doubling the term number and subtracting 1.

$$\therefore 2n - 1 = 19$$
$$2n = 20$$
$$n = 10$$

$$\therefore S = \frac{a(1 - r^n)}{(1 - r)}$$

$$= \frac{1.05[1 - (1.05^2)^{10}]}{1 - (1.05)^2}$$

$$= \frac{1.05[(1.05)^{20} - 1]}{(1.05)^2 - 1} \qquad \left(\text{multiplying by } \boxed{\frac{-1}{-1}}\right)$$

$$= 16.93622$$

Scientific calculator:

$$\boxed{1.05} \; \boxed{y^x} \; \boxed{20} \; \boxed{=} \; \boxed{-} \; \boxed{1} \; \boxed{=} \; \boxed{\times} \; \boxed{1.05} \; \boxed{=}$$

Store numerator

$$\boxed{1.05} \; \boxed{y^x} \; \boxed{2} \; \boxed{=} \; \boxed{-} \; \boxed{1} \; \boxed{=} \; \boxed{\div} \; \boxed{\text{Memory recall}} \; \boxed{=} \; \boxed{\frac{1}{x}}$$

Hewlett-Packard:

$$\boxed{1.05} \; \boxed{\text{ENTER}} \; \boxed{20} \; \boxed{y^x} \; \boxed{1} \; \boxed{-} \; \boxed{1.05} \; \boxed{\times} \; \boxed{\text{STO}} \; \boxed{1}$$

$$\boxed{1.05} \; \boxed{\text{ENTER}} \; \boxed{2} \; \boxed{y^x} \; \boxed{1} \; \boxed{-} \; \boxed{\text{RCL}} \; \boxed{1} \; \boxed{\div} \; \boxed{\frac{1}{x}}$$

b) $S = \dfrac{1}{(1.04)^3} + \dfrac{1}{(1.04)^4} + \cdots \dfrac{1}{(1.04)^{10}}$

$a = \dfrac{1}{(1.04)^3}$

$r = \dfrac{1}{1.04}$

$n = 8$ (by counting)

$$\therefore S = \frac{\dfrac{1}{(1.04)^3} \left[1 - \left(\dfrac{1}{1.04}\right)^8\right]}{1 - \dfrac{1}{1.04}}$$

Looking at the denominator:

$$1 - \frac{1}{1.04} = \frac{1.04}{1.04} - \frac{1}{1.04}$$

$$= \frac{1.04 - 1}{1.04}$$

$$= \frac{0.04}{1.04}$$

$$\therefore S = \frac{1}{(1.04)^3} \left[1 - \frac{1}{(1.04)^8}\right] \div \frac{0.04}{1.04}$$

$$= \frac{1}{(1.04)^3}\left[1 - \frac{1}{(1.04)^8}\right] \times \frac{1.04}{0.04}$$

$$= \frac{\frac{1}{(1.04)^2}\left[1 - \frac{1}{(1.04)^8}\right]}{0.04}$$

$$= \frac{(1.04)^{-2}[1 - (1.04)^{-8}]}{0.04}$$

$$= 6.224801$$

When using your calculator, work the square bracket first.

Scientific calculator:

Hewlett-Packard:

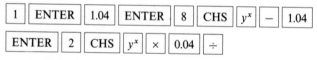

c) $S = \dfrac{1}{(1.04)^3} + \dfrac{1}{(1.04)^6} + \cdots \dfrac{1}{(1.04)^{24}}$

$a = \dfrac{1}{(1.04)^3}$

$r = \dfrac{1}{(1.04)^3}$

$n = 8$

$\therefore S = \dfrac{\dfrac{1}{(1.04)^3}\left[1 - \left(\dfrac{1}{(1.04)^3}\right)^8\right]}{1 - \dfrac{1}{(1.04)^3}}$

$= \dfrac{\dfrac{1}{(1.04)^3}}{1 - \dfrac{1}{(1.04)^3}} \times \left[1 - \dfrac{1}{(1.04)^{24}}\right]$

Ignoring the square bracket for a moment:

$$\frac{1}{(1.04)^3} \div 1 - \frac{1}{(1.04)^3} = \frac{1}{(1.04)^3} \div \frac{(1.04)^3 - 1}{(1.04)^3}$$

$$= \frac{1}{(1.04)^3} \times \frac{(1.04)^3}{(1.04)^3 - 1}$$

$$= \frac{1}{(1.04)^3 - 1}$$

$$\therefore S = \frac{1}{(1.04)^3 - 1} \times \left[1 - \frac{1}{(1.04)^{24}} \right]$$

$$= \frac{1 - \dfrac{1}{(1.04)^{24}}}{(1.04)^3 - 1}$$

$$= 4.884342$$

3 a) $a = \dfrac{1}{1.05}$

$r = \dfrac{1}{1.05}$ $0 < r < 1$

$r^n = \dfrac{1}{(1.05)^n}.$ As $n \to \infty, r^n \to 0$

$\therefore \text{Sum} = \dfrac{a}{1 - r}$

$$= \frac{\dfrac{1}{1.05}}{1 - \dfrac{1}{1.05}}$$

$$= \frac{1}{1.05} \div \left(1 - \frac{1}{1.05} \right)$$

$$= \frac{1}{1.05} \div \left(\frac{1.05}{1.05} - \frac{1}{1.05} \right)$$

$$= \frac{1}{1.05} \div \frac{1.05 - 1}{1.05}$$

$$= \frac{1}{1.05} \times \frac{1.05}{1.05 - 1}$$

$$= \frac{1}{1.05 - 1}$$

$$= \frac{1}{0.05}$$

$$\text{Sum} = 20$$

b) $$a = \frac{1}{(1.05)^3}$$

$$r = \frac{1}{(1.05)^3}$$

$$\text{Sum} = \frac{a}{1-r} \quad \text{since } r^n \to 0 \text{ as } n \to \infty$$

$$= \frac{1}{(1.05)^3} \div \left[1 - \frac{1}{(1.05)^3} \right]$$

$$= \frac{1}{(1.05)^3} \div \frac{(1.05)^3 - 1}{(1.05)^3}$$

$$= \frac{1}{(1.05)^3} \times \frac{(1.05)^3}{(1.05)^3 - 1}$$

$$= \frac{1}{(1.05)^3 - 1}$$

$$= 6.344171$$

4 Year

$$PV = \frac{20,000}{(1.1)^2} + \frac{20,000}{(1.1)^4} + \frac{20,000}{(1.1)^6} + \cdots$$

$$a = \frac{20,000}{(1.1)^2}$$

$$r = \frac{1}{(1.1)^2}$$

$$\therefore \text{Sum} = \frac{a}{1-r} \quad \text{since } r^n \to 0 \text{ as } n \to \infty$$

$$= \frac{20,000}{(1.1)^2} \div \left[1 - \frac{1}{(1.1)^2} \right]$$

$$= \$95,238.10$$

i.e. a lump sum of \$95,238.10 is required to establish the biennial perpetuity of \$20,000.

5 Value of firm $= \dfrac{8}{(1.1)} + \dfrac{8}{(1.1)^2} + \cdots \dfrac{8}{(1.1)^{10}} + \dfrac{4}{(1.1)^{11}} + \dfrac{4}{(1.1)^{12}} + \cdots$
   (in 100,000's)

Break the RHS into two parts.

The first part is $\dfrac{8}{(1.1)} + \dfrac{8}{(1.1)^2} + \cdots \dfrac{8}{(1.1)^{10}}$

This is a finite GP, where $a = \dfrac{8}{1.1}$, $r = \dfrac{1}{1.1}$, $n = 10$

$$\therefore S_{10} = \frac{\dfrac{8}{1.1}\left[1 - \dfrac{1}{(1.1)^{10}}\right]}{1 - \dfrac{1}{1.1}}$$

$$= 49.156537$$

The second part is $\dfrac{4}{(1.1)^{11}} + \dfrac{4}{(1.1)^{12}} + \cdots$

This is an infinite GP, where $a = \dfrac{4}{(1.1)^{11}}$, $r = \dfrac{1}{1.1}$

$$\text{Its sum} = \frac{a}{1 - r}$$

$$= \frac{4}{(1.1)^{11}} \div 1 - \frac{1}{1.1}$$

$$= 15.421732$$

$\therefore$ Total value of firm $= 49.156537 + 15.421732$
$$= 64.578269$$
$$= \$6,457,826.90$$

CHAPTER 10

1 a) $AV = 4S_{\overline{4}|10\%}$

$$= \frac{4[(1.1)^4 - 1]}{0.1}$$

$$= 18.564$$

   Check: $AV = 4(1.1)^3 + 4(1.1)^2 + 4(1.1) + 4$

   or $AV = 4 + 4(1.1) + 4(1.1)^2 + 4(1.1)^3$

$$\text{Sum} = \frac{a(1 - r^n)}{1 - r} \qquad \text{where} \quad a = 4, \quad n = 4, \quad r = 1.1$$

$$= 18.564$$

b) $AV = 4\ddot{S}_{\overline{4}|10\%}$
$= 4(S_{\overline{5}|10\%} - 1) \quad \text{or} \quad 4S_{\overline{4}|10\%}(1.1)$
$= 20.4204$

Check: $AV = 4(1.1)^4 + 4(1.1)^3 + 4(1.1)^2 + 4(1.1)$
$= 4(1.1) + 4(1.1)^2 + 4(1.1)^3 + 4(1.1)^4$
$a = 4(1.1), \quad n = 4, \quad r = 1.1$

$$\text{Sum} = \frac{4(1.1)[1 - (1.1)^4]}{1 - 1.1}$$

$$= \frac{4(1.1)[(1.1)^4 - 1]}{1.1 - 1}$$

$$= 4S_{\overline{4}|10\%}(1.1)$$

c) $AV = 4S_{\overline{3}|10\%} = \dfrac{4[(1.1)^3 - 1]}{0.1}$

$$= 13.24$$

Check: $AV = 4(1.1)^2 + 4(1.1) + 4$

$$= 4 + 4(1.1) + 4(1.1)^2$$

$$a = 4, \quad n = 3, \quad r = 1.1$$

$$AV = \frac{4[1 - (1.1)^3]}{1 - 1.1}$$

$$= \frac{4[(1.1)^3 - 1]}{0.1} = 4S_{\overline{3}|10\%} = 13.24$$

2   $AV = 20,000S_{\overline{20}|6\%}$

$$= \frac{20,000[(1.06)^{20} - 1]}{0.06}$$

$$= \$735,711.83$$

3   $AV = 20,000\ddot{S}_{\overline{20}|6\%}$

$$= 20,000S_{\overline{20}|6\%}(1.06)$$

$$= \$779,854.54$$

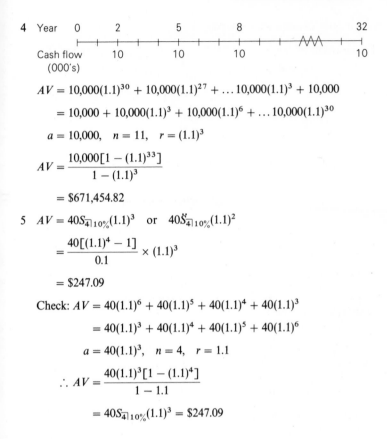

4 Year   0   2   5   8   32

Cash flow   10   10   10   10
(000's)

$AV = 10,000(1.1)^{30} + 10,000(1.1)^{27} + \ldots 10,000(1.1)^3 + 10,000$

$= 10,000 + 10,000(1.1)^3 + 10,000(1.1)^6 + \ldots 10,000(1.1)^{30}$

$a = 10,000, \quad n = 11, \quad r = (1.1)^3$

$AV = \dfrac{10,000[1 - (1.1)^{33}]}{1 - (1.1)^3}$

$= \$671,454.82$

5 $AV = 40S_{\overline{4}|10\%}(1.1)^3 \quad \text{or} \quad 40S_{\overline{4}|10\%}(1.1)^2$

$= \dfrac{40[(1.1)^4 - 1]}{0.1} \times (1.1)^3$

$= \$247.09$

Check: $AV = 40(1.1)^6 + 40(1.1)^5 + 40(1.1)^4 + 40(1.1)^3$

$= 40(1.1)^3 + 40(1.1)^4 + 40(1.1)^5 + 40(1.1)^6$

$a = 40(1.1)^3, \quad n = 4, \quad r = 1.1$

$\therefore AV = \dfrac{40(1.1)^3[1 - (1.1)^4]}{1 - 1.1}$

$= 40S_{\overline{4}|10\%}(1.1)^3 = \$247.09$

CHAPTER 11

1 Let P = monthly instalment

$$70,000 = PA_{\overline{120}|1.2\%}$$

$$A_{\overline{120}|1.2\%} = 63.419391$$

$$\therefore P = \$1,103.76$$

2 Year   0   1   2   3   4   5   6   7   8

Cash   40   40   40   40   X   X   X   X
inflows   60,000
(000's)

Cash   600,000
outflow

Present value of outflows = 600,000

Present value of inflows = $40,000A_{\overline{4}|10\%} + XA_{\overline{4}|10\%}V^4 + 60,000V^8$

$$\therefore 600,000 = 40,000A_{\overline{4}|10\%} + 60,000V^8 + XA_{\overline{4}|10\%}V^4$$

$$= 40,000(3.169865) + 27,990.44281 + 2.16506X$$

$$2.16506X = 445,214.9394$$

$$X = \$205,636.31$$

The yearly inflow for years 5 to 8 inclusive is \$205,636.31.

3   Present value of outflows = 210,000 + 2000 (stamp duty)
                              + 1000 (initial legal cost)
                              + $1000V^{52}$ (legal cost at year end)
                              + $30A_{\overline{52}|i}$ (weekly outgoings)

Present value of inflows = $200A_{\overline{52}|i}$

$$\therefore 213,000 + 1,000V^{52} + 30A_{\overline{52}|i} = 200A_{\overline{52}|i}$$

4   $XS_{\overline{12}|0.01} = 3000$ where X = monthly instalment
$S_{\overline{12}|0.01} = 12.682503$
$\therefore X = \$236.55$

5        $Y\ddot{S}_{\overline{16}|2.5\%} = 120,000$ where Y = quarterly instalment
$Y[S_{\overline{17}|2.5\%} - 1] = 120,000$
$S_{\overline{17}|0.025} = 20.86473$
$Y = \$6,040.86$

6   Let Z = capital sum required
$Z = 2000A_{\overline{60}|1\%}$
$A_{\overline{60}|0.01} = 44.955038$
$\therefore Z = \$89,910.08$

CHAPTER 12

1   $AV = 40,000(1.1)^{10}(1.09)^5$
$= \$159,631.77$

Scientific calculator:

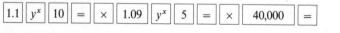

Hewlett-Packard:

2    $PV = 50,000 V_{12\%}^4 V_{11\%}^2 V_{10\%}^{19}$
$= \$4216.88$

Scientific calculator:

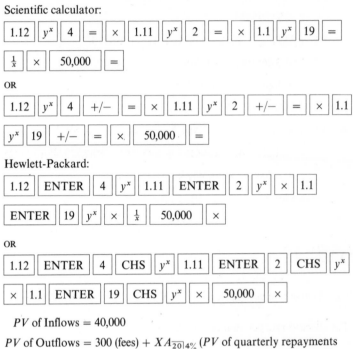

OR

Hewlett-Packard:

OR

3   PV of Inflows $= 40,000$

PV of Outflows $= 300$ (fees) $+ XA_{\overline{20}|4\%}$ (PV of quarterly repayments over first 5 years $= 20$ quarters) $+ XA_{\overline{40}|4.3\%} V_{4\%}^{20}$
(PV of quarterly repayments over next 10 years)
$+ 0.02X A_{\overline{20}|4\%} + 0.02X A_{\overline{40}|4.3\%} V_{4\%}^{20}$

∴ Equation of value is

$$40,000 = 300 + X(1.02)[A_{\overline{20}|4\%} + A_{\overline{40}|4.3\%} V_{4\%}^{20}]$$

4    $60,000 = X A_{\overline{2}|11\%} + X A_{\overline{5}|12\%} V_{11\%}^2$ where $X =$ annual instalment
$= X(A_{\overline{2}|11\%} + A_{\overline{5}|12\%} V_{11\%}^2)$
$= X(1.712523 + 2.925717)$
∴ $X = \$12,935.94$

5   Let $Y =$ monthly instalment

$Y \ddot{S}_{\overline{24}|1.2\%}(1.01)^{36} = 2$ years' instalments @ 1.2% accumulated forward 3 years (36 months) @ 1%

$Y \ddot{S}_{\overline{36}|1\%} = 3$ years' instalments @ 1%

∴ $Y \ddot{S}_{\overline{24}|1.2\%}(1.01)^{36} + Y \ddot{S}_{\overline{36}|1\%} = 200,000$

Using $\ddot{S}_{\overline{24}|i} = S_{\overline{24}|i}(1 + i)$ or $\ddot{S}_{\overline{24}|i} = S_{\overline{25}|i} - 1$:

$Y(27.954206)(1.430769) + Y(43.507647) = 200,000$

$\therefore Y = \$2,395.10$

6    $PV = 50A_{\overline{4}|6\%} + 10V_{6\%}^3 + 60\ddot{A}_{\overline{4}|5\%}V_{6\%}^5 + 20V_{5\%}^3 V_{6\%}^5$

$= 50(3.465106) + 8.39619 + 60(3.723248)(0.747258)$

$+ 20(0.863838)(0.747258)$

$= \$361.50$

OR $PV = 50A_{\overline{5}|6\%} + 10V_{6\%}^3 + 10V_{6\%}^5 + 60A_{\overline{3}|5\%}V_{6\%}^5 + 20V_{5\%}^3 V_{6\%}^5$

$= 50(4.212364) + 8.396193 + 7.472582 + 60(2.723248)(0.747258)$

$+ 20(0.863838)(0.747258)$

$= \$361.50$

CHAPTER 13

1   The effective rate per quarter $= \dfrac{12}{4} = 3\%$

The effective rate per annum $= (1.03)^4 - 1$
$= 12.5509\%$

2   12% p.a. nominal convertible monthly $= 1\%$ per month effective
$= (1.01)^{12} - 1$ per annum effective
$= 0.126825$

If the nominal rate convertible quarterly $= \square\%$,

then the effective rate per quarter $= \dfrac{\square}{400}$ (as a decimal)

and the effective rate per annum $= \left(1 + \dfrac{\square}{400}\right)^4 - 1$

So $\left(1 + \dfrac{\square}{400}\right)^4 - 1 = 0.126825$

$\left(1 + \dfrac{\square}{400}\right)^4 = 1.126825$

$1 + \dfrac{\square}{400} = 1.126825^{1/4} = 1.030301$

$$\frac{\square}{400} = 0.030301$$

$$\square = 12.120397\%$$

The nominal rate convertible quarterly is 12.120397%.

3 16% per annum nominal convertible half-yearly = 8% per half-year effective or $(1.08)^2 - 1$ per annum effective.

If the nominal rate p.a. convertible monthly = $\square$

$$\text{then the effective rate per month} = \frac{\square}{1200}$$

$$\text{and the effective rate per annum} = \left(1 + \frac{\square}{1200}\right)^{12} - 1$$

$$\therefore \left(1 + \frac{\square}{1200}\right)^{12} - 1 = (1.08)^2 - 1$$

$$\left(1 + \frac{\square}{1200}\right)^{12} = 1.1664$$

$$1 + \frac{\square}{1200} = 1.1664^{0.08\dot{3}} = 1.012909$$

$$\therefore \square = 1200(0.012909)$$

$$= 15.491348\% \text{ nominal p.a. convertible monthly}$$

4 Security 1: effective half-yearly rate = 6%
effective annual rate $= (1.06)^2 - 1$
$= 12.36\%$

Security 2: effective monthly rate $= \frac{11.6}{12} = 0.966667\%$
effective annual rate $= (1.0096667)^{12} - 1$
$= 12.2371\%$

$\therefore$ Security 1 is superior.

5 $PV = 20{,}000V^4 + 20{,}000V^7 + 20{,}000V^{10} + \ldots @ \text{rate } i$

$$i = \frac{12}{12} = 1\% \text{ per month effective}$$

$$= (1.01)^{12} - 1 \text{ p.a. effective}$$

$$= 12.6825\%$$

Using $\dfrac{a}{1 - r}$ as the sum of a perpetuity (provided $r^n \to 0$ as $n \to \infty$):

$a = 20{,}000V^4$ and $r = V^3$

$$\therefore PV = \frac{20,000V^4}{1 - V^3} \text{ @ } 12.6825\%$$

$$= \frac{12,405.209}{0.301075}$$

$$= \$41,203.05$$

6   PV of inflows $= 200\ddot{A}_{\overline{52}|i\%} + 260,000V_{i\%}^{52}$

PV of outflows $= 250,000 + 200A_{\overline{4}|j\%} + 600\ddot{A}_{\overline{2}|k\%}$

i = effective rate per week
j = effective rate per quarter
$\quad = (1 + i)^{13} - 1$ (13 weeks in a quarter)
k = effective rate per half-year
$\quad = (1 + i)^{26} - 1$

$\therefore$ The equation of value is:

$$200\ddot{A}_{\overline{52}|i} + 260,000V^{52} \text{ @ } i = 250,000 + 200A_{\overline{4}|} \text{ @ } [(1 + i)^{13} - 1]$$
$$+ 600\ddot{A}_{\overline{2}|} \text{ @ } [(1 + i)^{26} - 1]$$

7   Let X = quarterly instalment.

Then $X\ddot{S}_{\overline{20}|i} + 10,000(1 + i)^{16} + 10,000(1 + i)^{12} = 200,000$

where i = effective rate per quarter

The effective rate per half-year $= 6\%$
$\quad \therefore$ The effective rate per year $= (1.06)^2 - 1$
$$= 0.1236 \quad \text{or} \quad 12.36\%$$

$$\text{Now } (1 + i)^4 - 1 = 0.1236$$
$$\therefore 1 + i = 1.1236^{0.25}$$
$$i = 0.029563$$

$\therefore X[(1 + i)S_{\overline{20}|i}] + 10,000(1 + i)^{16} + 10,000(1 + i)^{12} = 200,000$

$$X\left[(1.029563)\left\{\frac{(1.029563)^{20} - 1}{0.029563}\right\}\right] + 10,000(1.029563)^{16}$$

$$+ 10,000(1.029563)^{12} = 200,000$$

$$X(27.542097) + 15,938.47725 + 14,185.18879 = 200,000$$
$$\therefore X = \$6,167.88$$

The quarterly instalment is $6,167.88.

8   The daily rate of interest $= \dfrac{10.7\%}{365} = 0.029315\%$
$$= 0.00029315$$

Let the initial investment $= Y$

$Y(1.00029315)^{365 \times 3} - \frac{1}{2}Y =$ balance in fund after 3 years,
immediately after $\frac{1}{2}Y$ is withdrawn

This balance is accumulated for 2 years.

i.e. $[Y(1.00029315)^{365 \times 3} - \frac{1}{2}Y](1.00029315)^{365 \times 2} = 50,000$

$[Y(1.37844 - \frac{1}{2}Y](1.238583) = 50,000$

$[Y(1.37844 - 0.5)](1.238583) = 50,000$

$Y(0.87844)(1.238583) = 50,000$

$Y(1.088021) = 50,000$

$\therefore Y = \$45,954.99$

The initial investment required $= \$45,955$.

CHAPTER 14

1   a) NPV (in 000's) $= 30A_{\overline{5}|10\%} - 50V_{10\%}^{3} - 80$ (1)

This assumes a stream of inflows for 5 years and an outflow of 50 in year 3.

Alternatively, $NPV = 30A_{\overline{2}|} - 20V^{3} + 30A_{\overline{2}|}V^{3} - 80$ (2)

Using (1):

$$NPV = 30(3.790787) - 50(0.751315) - 80$$
$$= -3.842137 \quad \text{(in 000's)}$$
$$\therefore NPV = -3,842$$

The project is therefore not viable.

b) NTV (in 000's) $= 30S_{\overline{5}|10\%} - 50(1.1)^{2} - 80(1.1)^{5}$
$$= 30(6.1051) - 60.5 - 128.8408$$
$$= -6.1878$$
$$= -6,188$$

Check: $NPV(1.1)^{5} = -3,842(1.1)^{5} = -6,188 = NTV$

2   NPV (in 000's) $= 30A_{\overline{2}|10\%} + 30A_{\overline{2}|11\%}V_{11\%}^{1}V_{10\%}^{2} - 20V_{11\%}^{1}V_{10\%}^{2} - 80$
(i.e. amounts after year 2 must be brought first to year 2 @ 11% then back to inception @ 10%)

$$= 30(1.735537) + 30(1.712523)(0.900901)(0.826446)$$
$$- 20(0.900901)(0.826446) - 80$$
$$= -4.573239$$
$$\therefore NPV = -4,573$$

The project is still not feasible.

$$NTV \text{ (in 000's)} = 30S_{\overline{2}|10\%}(1.11)^3 + 30S_{\overline{2}|11\%}$$
$$- 20(1.11)^2 - 80(1.1)^2(1.11)^3$$
$$= 30(2.1)(1.367631) + 30(2.11) - 24.642 - 132.386681$$
$$= -7.567928$$
$$\therefore NTV = -7,568$$

Check: $NPV(1.1)^2(1.11)^3 = -4573(1.1)^2(1.11)^3$
$$= -7,567.5$$
$$= NTV$$

3	Cash flow item	PV formula	Effective rate of interest i	Value
	Purchase price	$-280,000$	Not applicable	$-280,000$
	Rent income	$900\ddot{A}_{\overline{24}|i}$	$1\% = 0.01$	$19,310.24$
	Levies	$-200A_{\overline{8}|i}$	$(1.01)^3 - 1$ (3 months in a quarter, $i = 1\%$ per month)	$-1,402.16$
	Water and Sewerage	$-350A_{\overline{8}|i}$	$(1.01)^3 - 1$	$-2,453.78$
	Insurance	$-300\ddot{A}_{\overline{2}|i}$	12.6825%	-566.23
	Sale price	$350,000V^{24}$	$1\% = 0.01$	$275,648.14$
				$10,536.21$

$\therefore NPV = \$11,102.44$

The project is therefore viable, based on the assumptions provided.

4	Cash flow item	PV formula	Effective rate of interest i	Value
	Purchase price	$-100,000$	—	$-100,000$
	Interest	$6,000A_{\overline{6}|i}$	$(1.03)^2 - 1$ (3% per quarter, 2 quarters in a half-year)	$29,420.70$
	Sale price	$106,000V^{12}$	$3\% = 0.03$	$74,346.27$
				$NPV = 3,766.97$

The investment is feasible because $NPV > 0$.

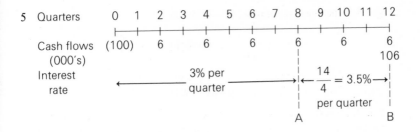

First accumulate cash flows to point A:
The 6's accumulate for 4 half-years @ half-yearly rate of interest $= (1.03)^2 - 1$,
i.e. 3% per quarter for 2 quarters.
The 100 accumulates for 8 quarters @ 3%.

$$\therefore AV \text{ to point A} = 6S_{\overline{4}|} @ [(1.03)^2 - 1] - 100(1.03)^8$$
$$= 6S_{\overline{4}|0.0609} - 100(1.03)^8$$
$$= -100.39424$$

Accumulate this amount to point B:
$$= -100.39424(1.035)^4$$
$$= -115.204701$$

Now accumulate the cash flows between A and B:

i.e. $6S_{\overline{2}|} @ [(1.035)^2 - 1] + 106 = 6S_{\overline{2}|0.071225} + 106$
$$= 118.42735$$

$$\therefore NTV \text{ (in 000's)} = 118.42735 - 115.204701 = 3.222649$$
$$NTV = \$3,223$$

The project is still feasible as $NTV > 0$

CHAPTER 15

1   $40 = 30V^1 + 20V^2$ @ rate $i = IRR$
Divide both sides by 10, then subtract 4 from both sides:

$$2V^2 + 3V^1 - 4 = 0$$

Using the discriminant formula,
$a = 2, \quad b = 3, \quad c = -4$

$$\text{So} \quad V = \frac{-3 \pm \sqrt{3^2 - 4(2)(-4)}}{2(2)}$$

$$= \frac{-3 \pm \sqrt{41}}{4}$$

Ignoring the negative solution, $V = 0.850781$

$$\therefore \frac{1}{1+i} = 0.850781$$

Taking reciprocals, $1 + i = 1.175391$
$$\therefore i = 17.5391\% = IRR$$

Thus the assumed reinvestment rate is 17.5391%. This can be demonstrated by calculating the NTV, i.e. AV of inflows minus AV of outflows. The IRR, or reinvestment rate, equates the AV of inflows and outflows, thus at 17.5391% the NTV should equal zero.

Reinvesting the $30 for 1 year @ 17.5391% gives:
$$AV \text{ of inflows} = 30(1.175391) + 20$$
$$= 55.26173$$

The interest forgone on the $40 for 2 years gives:
$$AV \text{ of outflows} = 40(1.175391)^2$$
$$= 55.26176 \quad \text{(small rounding difference)}$$
$$\therefore NTV = 0$$

2   Approximate IRR = (accounting rate of return)
    + (annual capital growth $\div$ 92)

$$= \left(\frac{12}{92} \times \frac{100}{1}\right) + \left(\frac{8/5}{92} \times 100\right)$$

$$= 14.78\%$$

Thus a 'first guess' for the IRR is 15% and a more accurate answer is found by interpolating between 14% and 15%.

The equation of value is:

$$92 = 12A_{\overline{5}|IRR} + 100V_{IRR}^5$$

At 14%, RHS = 93.134
At 15%, RHS = 89.944

RHS   93.134   92   89.944
         ├──────────┼──────────────┤
IRR   14%   IRR   15%

(You can, of course, use $NPV = 12A_{\overline{5}|} + 100V^5 - 92 = 0$ as your equation of value. You would still interpolate between 14% and 15%, putting the IRR at zero.)

Now $93.134 - 89.944 = 3.19$
and $93.134 - 92 \quad = 1.134$

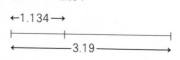

$\therefore$ The first weight is $\dfrac{1.134}{3.19} = 0.355$

and the second weight $= 1 - 0.355 = 0.645$

$\therefore IRR \approx 0.645(14) + 0.355(15)$
$\approx 14.355\%$

Using the Hewlett-Packard:

| f | CL x | clears registers |

92 CHS g CFo   outlay of 92 made negative

12 g CFj   first interest payment

4 g Nj   number of times this cash
flow occurs consecutively

112 g CFj   final cash flow

f IRR $IRR = 14.349895$
$= 14.350\%$ (to 3 places)

3 PV of inflows $= PV$ of outflows

$$76V^1 = 60 + 10V^2 \ @ \ i = IRR$$

$\therefore 10V^2 - 76V^1 + 60 = 0$ (you can divide throughout by 2 if you wish)
$a = 10, \quad b = -76, \quad c = 60$

$$\therefore V = \frac{76 \pm \sqrt{(-76)^2 - 4(10)(60)}}{2(10)}$$

$$= \frac{76 \pm 58.103356}{20}$$

$$= 6.705168 \quad \text{and} \quad 0.894832$$

When $V = \dfrac{1}{1+i} = 6.705168,$

$$i = 0.149139 - 1$$

$$= -0.850861 \quad \text{or} \quad -85.0861\%$$

Ignore this solution.

When $V = \dfrac{1}{1+i} = 0.894832$,

$$i = 1.117528 - 1$$

$$\therefore IRR = 0.117528 \quad \text{or} \quad 11.7528\%$$

4 $55{,}000 = 2{,}000 A_{\overline{4}|} + 56{,}000 V^4$ @ the *IRR* effective per half-year
Divide both sides by 1000:

$$55 = 2A_{\overline{4}|} + 56V^4$$

Approximate *IRR* = (half-yearly accounting rate of return)
                   + (half-yearly capital growth ÷ 55)

$$= \frac{2}{55} \times \frac{100}{1} \quad + \quad \frac{\dfrac{56-55}{4}}{55} \times \frac{100}{1}$$

$$= 4.09\%$$

$\therefore$ Let *IRR* = 4% be your 'first guess' and interpolate between 4% and 4.1%.
At *IRR* = 4%,   RHS = 55.1288
At *IRR* = 4.1%,   RHS = 54.928

```
    55.1288              55              54.928
    ├───────────────────┼──────────────────┤
    4%                  IRR               4.1%
        ←──55.1288 − 54.928 = 0.2008──→
```

$\therefore$ Weights are $\dfrac{0.1288}{0.2008} = 0.641$

   and $1 - 0.641 = 0.359$

$\therefore IRR \approx 0.641(4.1) + 0.359(4)$
    $\approx 4.0641\%$ effective per half-year

$\therefore$ The effective annual return $= (1.040641)^2 - 1$
                   $= 0.082934 \quad \text{or} \quad 8.2934\%$

Using the Hewlett-Packard:

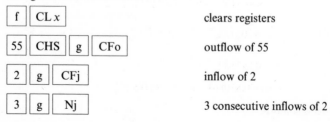

f	CL *x*			clears registers
55	CHS	g	CFo	outflow of 55
2	g	CFj		inflow of 2
3	g	Nj		3 consecutive inflows of 2

last inflow of 58 (56 + 2)

$IRR = 4.064119\%$ per half-year

5 $$60 = 30A_{\overline{3}|} + 10V^1 \text{ @ rate } i = IRR$$

Using the Hewlett-Packard, $IRR = 32.723219\%$

Check: $NTV = 30S_{\overline{3}|0.32723} + 10(1.32723)^2 - 60(1.32723)^3$
$= 122.6631 + 17.6154 - 140.2781$
$= 0.0004 \quad$ (slight rounding difference)
The assumed reinvestment rate $= 32.7232\% = IRR$.
This rate is unlikely to be achieved given the expected range of interest rates.

6 AV of inflows @ $10\% = 30S_{\overline{3}|0.1} + 10(1.1)^2$
$\qquad\qquad\qquad\qquad = 111.4$
Let j = annual rate of return
$60(1 + j)^3 = 111.4$
$(1 + j)^3 = 111.4 \div 60 = 1.856667$
$1 + j = \sqrt[3]{1.856667} = 1.229074$
$\therefore j = 0.229074 = 22.9074\%$
A more conservative reinvestment rate has reduced the rate of return to a more realistic level.

CHAPTER 16

1 $NPV_A = 49A_{\overline{2}|0.1} - 80 = 5.0413$
$NPV_B = 28A_{\overline{4}|0.1} - 82 = 6.7562$

Replicating A once so its life is also 4 years gives:

$$NPV_A = 49A_{\overline{4}|0.1} - 80 - 80V^2$$

$$\text{or} \quad NPV_A = NPV + NPV \cdot V^2$$

$$= NPV + \frac{NPV}{(1.1)^2}$$

$$= 5.0413\left[1 + \frac{1}{(1.1)^2}\right]$$

$$= 9.207664$$

$$> NPV_B$$

$\therefore$ Project A is superior.

Alternatively, value in perpetuity:

Project A

Year	0	1	2	3	4	5	6	

Cash flows: 49 49 49 49 49 49 ... ; -80 -80 -80 -80

$$\infty NPV_A = (49V^1 + 49V^2 + 49V^3 + \ldots) - 80 - 80V^2 - 80V^4 - \ldots$$
$$= (49V^1 + 49V^2 + 49V^3 + \ldots) - (80 + 80V^2 + 80V^4 + \ldots)$$

i.e. the ∞NPV_A is the subtraction of two infinite GPs.

$\therefore$ Use $\dfrac{a}{1-r}$ to find each sum, then subtract.

$$\therefore \infty NPV_A = \left(\frac{49V^1}{1-V^1}\right) - \left(\frac{80}{1-V^2}\right) @ \ i = 0.1$$

$$= 490 - 460.952$$

$$\infty NPV_A = 29.048$$

Project B

Year	0	1	2	3	4	5	6	

Cash flow: 28 28 28 28 28 28 ... ; -82 -82

$$\infty NPV_B = (28V^1 + 28V^2 + \ldots) - (82 + 82V^4 + 82V^8 + \ldots)$$

Using $\dfrac{a}{1-r}$,

$$\infty NPV_B = \left(\frac{28V^1}{1-V^1}\right) - \left(\frac{82}{1-V^4}\right) @ \ i = 0.1$$

$$= 280 - 258.686$$

$$\infty NPV_B = 21.314$$

Since $\infty NPV_A > \infty NPV_B$, project A is superior.

2   Year: 0 1 2 3 ... 10 11 12 13 ...

After-tax cash inflows (10,000's): 52 52 52 ... 52 30 30 30

$$PV = 52A_{\overline{10}|0.1} + 30(V^{11} + V^{12} + V^{13} + \ldots)$$

$$= 52A_{\overline{10}|0.1} + \frac{30V^{11}}{1-V^1} \quad \left(\text{using } \frac{a}{1-r} \text{ for the infinite GP}\right)$$

$$= 319.517 + 115.663$$

$$= 435.18$$

$\therefore$ Value of the firm $= \$4,351,800$

3   Year   0   1   2   3   4   5

Cash flow $\vdash\!\!-\!\!+\!\!-\!\!+\!\!-\!\!+\!\!-\!\!+\!\!-\!\!+\!\!-\!\!-$ $\cdots$

(000's)   20   20

$\longleftarrow\!10\%\longrightarrow\!\longleftarrow\!-\!\!-\!\!-\!\!-9\%\longrightarrow$ $\cdots$

Bringing the cash flows back to year 2 gives:

$$PV \text{ (in 000's)} = 20V^1 + 20V^3 + \ldots @ \, i = 9\%$$
$$= 20(V^1 + V^3 + \ldots)$$

Bringing this amount back to inception gives:

$$PV \text{ in (000's)} = [20(V^1 + V^3 + \ldots) @ \, 9\%]V^2_{10\%}$$

$$= V^2_{10\%} \cdot 20[(V^1 + V^3 + \ldots) @ \, 9\%]$$

$$= (0.826446)(20)\left[\frac{V^1}{1 - V^2} @ \, 9\%\right]$$

$$= (0.826446)(20)(5.79479)$$

$$= 95.78162$$

$\therefore$ Capital sum required $= \$95,781.62$

4   a) $5 = \dfrac{(0.4)(1.025)}{(1 + j)} + \dfrac{(0.4)(1.025)^2}{(1 + j)^2} + \ldots$

Taking the RHS, $a = \dfrac{(0.4)(1.025)}{1 + j}$

$$r = \frac{1.025}{1 + j}$$

As $n \to \infty$, $r^n \to 0$ if $j > 2\frac{1}{2}\%$

$$\therefore \frac{a}{1 - r} = \frac{(0.4)(1.025)}{1 + j} \div 1 - \frac{1.025}{1 + j}$$

$$= \frac{(0.4)(1.025)}{1 + j} \div \left[\frac{1 + j}{1 + j} - \frac{1.025}{1 + j}\right]$$

$$= \frac{(0.4)(1.025)}{1 + j} \div \frac{1 + j - 1.025}{1 + j}$$

$$= \frac{(0.4)(1.025)}{1 + j} \times \frac{1 + j}{j - 0.025}$$

$$= \frac{(0.4)(1.025)}{j - 0.025}$$

$$\therefore 5 = \frac{0.41}{j - 0.025}$$

Multiply both sides by $(j - 0.025)$:

$$5(j - 0.025) = 0.41$$
$$5j - 0.125 = 0.41$$
$$5j = 0.535$$
$$\therefore j = 0.107 = 10.7\% \text{ per half-year}$$

$$\therefore \text{ Effective rate per annum} = (1.107)^2 - 1$$
$$= 0.225449$$
$$= 22.5449\%$$

5 $$PV = \frac{P}{(1 + i)} + \frac{P}{(1 + i)^2} + \frac{P}{(1 + i)^3} + \dots$$

$$\therefore a = \frac{P}{1 + i} \quad \text{and} \quad r = \frac{1}{1 + i}$$

$$\therefore \frac{a}{1 - r} = \frac{P}{1 + i} \div \left[1 - \frac{1}{1 + i} \right]$$

$$= \frac{P}{1 + i} \div \left[\frac{1 + i}{1 + i} - \frac{1}{1 + i} \right]$$

$$= \frac{P}{1 + i} \div \frac{1 + i - 1}{1 + i}$$

$$= \frac{P}{1 + i} \div \frac{i}{1 + i}$$

$$= \frac{P}{1 + i} \times \frac{1 + i}{i}$$

$$\therefore PV = \frac{P}{i}$$

6 $i = 10\%$ per annum nominal convertible half-yearly
   $= 5\%$ effective per half-year
   $= (1.05)^2 - 1$ effective per annum
   If the effective rate per quarter $= j$,
   then the effective rate per annum $= (1 + j)^4 - 1$

$$\therefore (1 + j)^4 - 1 = (1.05)^2 - 1$$
$$(1 + j)^4 = (1.05)^2$$
$$= 1.1025$$

$$1 + j = 1.1025^{0.25}$$
$$= 1.024695$$
$$\therefore j = 0.024695$$

The equation of value @ rate j per quarter is:

$$1\,\text{m} = 10{,}000V^8 + XV^9 + XV^{10} + \ldots$$
$$= 10{,}000V^8 + X(V^9 + V^{10} + \ldots) \quad @ \text{ rate } j$$

In the infinite GP $(V^9 + V^{10} + \ldots)$, $a = V^9$ and $r = V^1$

$$\therefore \frac{a}{1-r} = \frac{V^9}{1 - V^1} = 33.314556$$
$$\therefore 1\,\text{m} = 10{,}000V^8 + X(33.314556)$$
$$= 8{,}227.029668 + X(33.314556)$$
$$X(33.314556) = 1\,\text{m} - 8{,}227.029668$$
$$= 991{,}772.9703$$
$$\therefore X = \$29{,}769.96$$

CHAPTER 17

1   real rate of return $= \dfrac{1.18}{1.11} - 1$

$$= 0.063063$$
$$= 6.3063\%$$

2   Real returns

Japan $\dfrac{1.041}{1.009} - 1 = 3.1715\%$

Australia $\dfrac{1.11}{1.062} - 1 = 4.5198\%$

U.K. $\dfrac{1.072}{1.03} - 1 = 4.0777\%$

Australia has the superior real rate of return in this case. This situation in fact occurred around January 1988.

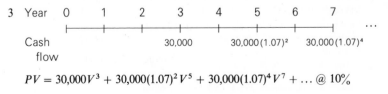

3   Year   0   1   2   3   4   5   6   7   ...

Cash flow   30,000   30,000$(1.07)^2$ 30,000$(1.07)^4$

$$PV = 30{,}000V^3 + 30{,}000(1.07)^2 V^5 + 30{,}000(1.07)^4 V^7 + \ldots \quad @ \, 10\%$$

Using $\dfrac{a}{1-r}$, $a = 30{,}000V^3$ and $r = (1.07)^2 V^2$ @ 10%

$$\therefore PV = \frac{30,000 V^3}{1 - [(1.07)^2 V^2]} \ @ \ 10\%$$

$$30,000 V^3 = \frac{30,000}{(1.1)^3} = 22,539.44403$$

$$1 - [(1.07)^2 V^2] = 1 - \frac{1.07^2}{1.1^2} = 0.053802$$

$$\therefore PV = \$418,935.90$$

The required outlay for the perpetuity is $418,936.

4   Year

Cash inflow: 250,000   250,000(1.06)   250,000(1.06)⁴

The equation of value is:

Project outlay $= 250,000[V^1 + (1.06)V^2 + \ldots (1.06)^4 V^5] \ @ \ 12\%$

$$= \frac{250,000}{1.06} \left[\frac{1.06}{1.12} + \frac{(1.06)^2}{(1.12)^2} + \ldots \frac{(1.06)^5}{(1.12)^5} \right]$$

$$= \frac{250,000}{1.06} A_{\overline{5}|r}, \quad \text{where } r = \frac{1.12}{1.06} - 1$$

$$= 0.056604$$

$$= \frac{250,000}{1.06}(4.251567)$$

$$= \$1,002,727.98$$

The maximum project outlay is therefore $1,002,728.

5   Amount invested in shares $= 40\% \times 300,000 = 120,000$
    Amount invested in IBDs $= 60\% \times 300,000 = 180,000$

Balance in fund at beginning of period = $300,000

Balance in fund at end of first year:

Market value of shares = 120,000(1.04)	=	124,800
Market value of IBDs = 180,000(1.1)	=	198,000
Deduct interest paid on IBDs = 0.10(180,000) =		(18,000)
Deduct withdrawal of 20,000		(20,000)
Total market value or fund balance =		$284,800

or Balance $= 120,000(1.04) + 180,000 - 20,000$
The interest on the IBDs is not included in the formula because it is spent.
The same applies to the share dividends.

Balance in fund at end of year 2:

Market value of shares = 120,000(1.04)²   = 129,792

Market value of IBDs = (180,000 − 20,000)1.1 = 176,000

Deduct interest paid on IBDs = (0.1)(160,000) = (16,000)

Deduct withdrawal of 20,000(1.07)   = (21,400)

         Total market value or fund balance = 268,392

Note that the IBD balance at end of first year is $180,000 - 20,000 = 160,000$. At the end of the second year the IBD balance is $160,000 - 20,000(1.07) = 138,600$.

∴ Balance in fund = $120,000(1.04)^2 + 180,000 - 20,000 - 20,000(1.07)$

Balance in fund at end of year 3:

Market value of shares = 120,000(1.04)³   = 134,983.68

Market value of IBDs = 138,600(1.1)   = 152,460

Deduct IBD interest   = (13,860)

Deduct IBD withdrawal = 20,000(1.07)²   = (22,898)

      Total market value or fund balance   = 250,685.68

IBD balance = 115,702

          = $180,000 - 20,000 - 20,000(1.07) - 20,000(1.07)^2$

The balance of the fund after 3 years is $250,685.68.

b) Market value of shares after 3 years = $120,000(1.04)^3$

   Market value of IBDs after 3 years = $180,000 - 20,000$
$$- 20,000(1.07) - 20,000(1.07)^2$$

(The 10% interest on the IBDs is irrelevant as it is spent by the retiree.)

∴ Total market value = $120,000(1.04)^3 + 180,000$
$$- 20,000[1 + (1.07) + (1.07)^2]$$
$$= 120,000(1.04)^3 + 180,000 - 20,000S_{\overline{3}|7\%}$$
$$= \$250,685.68$$

c) Balance of fund after n years = $120,000(1.04)^n + 180,000 - 20,000S_{\overline{n}|7\%}$

6   Let X = first monthly instalment.

Then second instalment = $X(1.005)$

Third instalment   = $X(1.005)^2$

Last instalment (after 120 months) = $X(1.005)^{119}$

The equation of value is:

$$100,000 = \frac{X}{1.01} + \frac{X(1.005)}{(1.01)^2} + \ldots \frac{X(1.005)^{119}}{(1.01)^{120}}$$

(since 12% p.a. nominal convertible monthly = 1% per month effective)

$$= \frac{X}{1.005}\left[\frac{1.005}{1.01} + \frac{(1.005)^2}{(1.01)^2} + \dots \frac{(1.005)^{120}}{(1.01)^{120}}\right]$$

$$= \frac{X}{1.005}A_{\overline{120}|j} \quad \text{where} \quad j = \frac{1}{1.005/1.01} - 1$$

$$\text{i.e.} \quad j = \frac{1.01}{1.005} - 1$$

$$= 0.004975$$

$$\therefore 100,000 = \frac{X}{1.005}(90.195799)$$

$$X = \$1,114.24$$

The first monthly instalment is \$1,114.24

7   Let Y = first monthly instalment.
$i = 1\%$ per month effective
The first 12 instalments in advance = $Y\ddot{S}_{\overline{12}|1\%}$
This amount is then accumulated forward 48 more months @ 1%.
i.e. accumulation of first year's instalments = $Y\ddot{S}_{\overline{12}|1\%}(1.01)^{48}$

Each monthly instalment during the second year is $Y(1.06)$.
These 12 instalments = $Y(1.06)\ddot{S}_{\overline{12}|1\%}$ and this total amount is accumulated forward 36 more months.
i.e. accumulation of second year's instalments = $Y(1.06)\ddot{S}_{\overline{12}|1\%}(1.01)^{36}$

Each monthly instalment during the third year = $Y(1.06)^2$.
These 12 instalments = $Y(1.06)^2\ddot{S}_{\overline{12}|1\%}$ and this total amount is accumulated forward 24 months.
i.e. accumulation of third year's instalments = $Y(1.06)^2\ddot{S}_{\overline{12}|1\%}(1.01)^{24}$

Similarly, accumulation of fourth year's instalments
$$= Y(1.06)^3\ddot{S}_{\overline{12}|1\%}(1.01)^{12}$$

The last year's instalments are each $Y(1.06)^4$ and the sum $Y(1.06)^4\ddot{S}_{\overline{12}|1\%}$ does not have to be accumulated forward.

$\therefore$ The equation of value is

$$20,000 = Y\ddot{S}_{\overline{12}|1\%}(1.01)^{48} + Y(1.06)\ddot{S}_{\overline{12}|1\%}(1.01)^{36}$$
$$+ Y(1.06)^2\ddot{S}_{\overline{12}|1\%}(1.01)^{24} + Y(1.06)^3\ddot{S}_{\overline{12}|1\%}(1.01)^{12}$$
$$+ Y(1.06)^4\ddot{S}_{\overline{12}|1\%}$$
$$= Y\ddot{S}_{\overline{12}|1\%}[(1.01)^{48} + (1.06)(1.01)^{36} + (1.06)^2(1.01)^{24}$$
$$+ (1.06)^3(1.01)^{12} + (1.06)^4]$$
$$= YS_{\overline{12}|1\%}(1.01)(7.160058) \quad \text{using } \ddot{S}_{\overline{12}} = S_{\overline{12}}(1 + i)$$

$\therefore$ 20,000 = $Y(12.809328)(7.160058)$

$Y = \$218.07$

The first twelve monthly instalments are each \$218.07.

Alternatively, this problem can be solved using an S-function.
Let Y = first monthly instalment

$Y(1.01)^{60} + Y(1.01)^{59} + \ldots Y(1.01)^{49}$ = accumulation of first
year's instalments

$1.06\,Y[(1.01)^{48} + (1.01)^{47} + \ldots(1.01)^{37}]$ = accumulation of second
year's instalments

$(1.06)^2\,Y[(1.01)^{36} + (1.01)^{35} + \ldots(1.01)^{25}]$ = accumulation of third
year's instalments

$(1.06)^3\,Y[(1.01)^{24} + (1.01)^{23} + \ldots(1.01)^{13}]$ = accumulation of fourth
year's instalments

$(1.06)^4\,Y[(1.01)^{12} + (1.01)^{11} + \ldots(1.01)]$ = accumulation of fifth
year's instalments

$\therefore\; Y(S_{\overline{61}|i} - S_{\overline{49}|i}) + 1.06\,Y(S_{\overline{49}|i} - S_{\overline{37}|i}) + (1.06)^2\,Y(S_{\overline{37}|i} - S_{\overline{25}|i})$
$+ (1.06)^3\,Y(S_{\overline{25}|i} - S_{\overline{13}|i}) + (1.06)^4\,Y(S_{\overline{13}|i} - S_{\overline{1}|i}) = 20{,}000$ @ $i = 1\%$

i.e. $Y(83.48637 - 62.83483) + 1.06\,Y(62.83483 - 44.50765)$
$+ (1.06)^2\,Y(44.50765 - 28.2432) + (1.06)^3\,Y(28.2432 - 13.80933)$
$+ (1.06)^4\,Y(13.80933 - 1) = 20{,}000$

$Y(20.65154 + 19.42681 + 18.27474 + 17.19097 + 16.17148) = 20{,}000$
$Y(91.71554) = 20{,}000$
$\therefore\; Y = \$218.07$

The first twelve monthly instalments will each be \$218.07.

CHAPTER 18

1 | Before-tax cash inflow | 400,000 |
Depreciation	200,000
Assessable income	200,000
Tax payable (49% of 200,000)	98,000

$\therefore$ Cash inflow after tax = 400,000 $-$ 98,000
= 302,000

Alternatively, the after-tax inflow can be found from:
$400{,}000(1 - t) + tD = 400{,}000(0.51) + 0.49(200{,}000)$
$= 302{,}000$

The $NPV = 302,000 A_{\overline{5}|10\%} - \$1\,m$
$= \$144,817.60$

$\therefore$ The project is feasible.

2 $NPV = 400,000(1-t)\left[\dfrac{1.06}{1.1} + \dfrac{(1.06)^2}{(1.1)^2} + \cdots \dfrac{(1.06)^5}{(1.1)^5}\right]$

$\quad + (0.49)(200,000) A_{\overline{5}|10\%} - \$1\,m$

$\quad = 204,000 A_{\overline{5}|k} + 98,000 A_{\overline{5}|10\%} - \$1\,m$

where $k = \dfrac{1.1}{1.06} - 1 = 0.037736$

$\therefore NPV = 204,000(4.480279) + 98,000(3.790787) - 1\,m$
$= \$285,474.02$

The project again is feasible.

3    $NPV = 400,000 A_{\overline{5}|k}$ $(PV$ of before-tax inflows$)$

$\quad - 0.49(400,000)\left[\dfrac{(1.06)}{(1.1)^2} + \dfrac{(1.06)^2}{(1.1)^3} + \cdots \dfrac{(1.06)^5}{(1.1)^6}\right]$

$\quad + 0.49(200,000) A_{\overline{5}|}V^1 \; @ \; 10\% - 1\,m$

$k = \dfrac{1.1}{1.06} - 1 = 0.037736$

$\therefore NPV = 400,000(4.480279) - \dfrac{0.49(400,000)}{1.1}\left[\dfrac{1.06}{1.1} + \cdots \dfrac{(1.06)^5}{(1.1)^5}\right]$

$\quad + 98,000 A_{\overline{5}|10\%}V^1_{10\%} - 1\,m$

$\quad = 1,792,111.60 - \dfrac{196,000}{1.1} A_{\overline{5}|k} + 98,000(3.790787)\left(\dfrac{1}{1.1}\right) - 1\,m$

$\quad = 1,792,111.60 - 798,304.26 + 337,724.66 - 1\,m$

$\quad = \$331,532$

Alternatively, the after-tax cash flows can be calculated each year and present-valued thus:

| | Years | | | | |
	1	2	3	4	5
Before-tax cash flow (inflation-adjusted) (000's)	424.0000	449.4400	476.4064	504.9908	535.2902
Depreciation (000's)	200.0000	200.0000	200.0000	200.0000	200.0000
Assessable income	224.0000	249.4400	276.4064	304.9908	335.2902
Tax @ 49%	109.7600	122.2256	135.4391	149.4455	164.2922

Year	0	1	2	3	4	5	6
Cash flow (000's)	(1,000)	424	449.44	476.4064	504.9908	535.2902	
Tax			(109.76)	(122.2256)	(135.4391)	(149.4455)	(164.2922)
Net cash flows	(1,000)	424	339.68	354.1808	369.5517	385.8447	(164.2922)
PV @ 10%	(1,000)	385.45	280.73	266.10	252.41	239.58	(92.74)

$NPV = \$331,530$ (slight rounding error)

4   The equation of value based on half-years is:

$$PV \text{ of outflows} = PV \text{ of inflows}$$

$$8 + (0.49)(2 \times 0.5)(V^4 + V^6 + V^8) = 20V^6 - 0.49(20 - 8)V^8 + 0.5A_{\overline{6}|}$$

These cash flows can be represented on a number line thus:

Half-year	0	1	2	3	4	5	6	7	8
Purchase price	(8)								
Dividends		0.5	0.5	0.5	0.5	0.5	0.5		
Tax on dividends				(2×0.5)0.49		(2×0.5)0.49		(2×0.5)0.49	
Sale of share							20		
Tax on capital gain									(20−8)0.49
Net cash flows	(8)	0.5	0.5	0.5	0.01	0.5	20.01	0	(6.37)

Using the Hewlett-Packard or interpolation,

$$IRR = 14.895\% \text{ effective per half-year after tax}$$

The annualised effective after-tax return $= (1.14895)^2 - 1$
$$= 32.01\%$$

Check: The accounting after-tax rate of return per half-year
$$\approx \frac{0.5}{8} \times \frac{100}{1} \times 0.51$$
$$\approx 3.19\%$$

The after-tax capital accretion expressed as a half-yearly rate
$$\approx \frac{(20 - 8)(1 - 0.49)}{6} \div 8 \times \frac{100}{1}$$
$$\approx 12.75\%$$

The all-up rate per half-year $\approx 3.19 + 12.75 \approx 15.94\%$
This is very approximate as we have not deferred tax or adjusted for the time value of money.

5   The cash flows are as follows:

Half-year	0	1	2	3	4	5	6
After-tax dividend		(0.5) (0.51) =0.255	0.255	0.255	0.255	0.255	0.255
Purchase price	(8)						
Sale price after tax							20−(12×0.49) =14.12
Net cash flows	(8)	0.255	0.255	0.255	0.255	0.255	14.375

Using the Hewlett-Packard,

$$IRR \text{ per half-year} = 12.4968$$
$$\therefore IRR \text{ effective per annum} = (1.124968)^2 - 1$$
$$= 26.56\%$$

6   Let purchase price $= X$
The equation of value is:

$$PV \text{ of outflows} = PV \text{ of inflows}$$

$$\underbrace{X + (0.4)(1.5)A_{\overline{40}|i}V^4}_{\substack{\text{(tax on interest for} \\ \text{40 quarters)}}} + \underbrace{(100 - X)(0.2)V^{44}}_{\substack{\text{tax on capital} \\ \text{gain}}} = 1.5A_{\overline{40}|i} + 100V^{40}$$

The effective after-tax rate $= i$ per quarter

$$\therefore (1 + i)^4 = 0.1$$
$$(1 + i)^4 = 1.1$$
$$1 + i = 1.1^{0.25} = 1.024114$$
$$\therefore i = 0.024114 = 2.4114\%$$
$$\therefore X + (0.4)(1.5)(25.48152)(0.90909) + (100 - X)(0.2)(0.35049)$$
$$= 1.5(25.48152) + 100(0.38554)$$
$$X + 13.89899 + (100 - X)(0.07010) = 38.22228 + 38.554$$
$$X + 13.89899 + 7.010 - 0.07010X = 76.77628$$
$$X(1 - 0.07010) = 76.77628 - 13.89899 - 7.010$$
$$= 55.86729$$
$$\therefore X = 60.079$$
$$\therefore \text{ The purchase price} = \$60.08 \text{ per } \$100 \text{ face amount.}$$

CHAPTER 19

1   Let $P = $ the monthly instalment

$$50,000 = PA_{\overline{240}|i} \qquad \text{where } i = \frac{18}{12} = 1\tfrac{1}{2}\%$$

$$\therefore P = \frac{50,000}{A_{\overline{240}|1.5\%}}$$

$$= \frac{50,000}{64.79573}$$

$$P = \$771.66$$

2 Immediately after the 4th payment there are 236 payments outstanding.

$\therefore$ Loan outstanding $= 771.66 A_{\overline{236}|1.5\%}$
$= \$49,911.68$

Checking with a loan schedule we have:

Instalment number	Loan outstanding before instalment is paid	Interest content	Principal content	Loan outstanding immediately after payment
1	50,000.00	750.00	21.66	49,978.34
2	49,978.34	749.68	21.98	49,956.36
3	49,956.36	749.35	22.31	49,934.05
4	49,934.05	749.01	22.65	49,911.40 (slight rounding difference)

3 Let P = monthly instalment
$$30,000 = P A_{\overline{36}|1.5\%} + P A_{\overline{48}|1.6\%} V^{36}_{1.5\%}$$
$$= P(27.660684) + P(33.326937)(0.58509)$$
$$\therefore P = \$636.13$$
The loan outstanding immediately after the 20th payment
$$= P A_{\overline{16}|1.5\%} + P A_{\overline{48}|1.6\%} V^{16}_{1.5\%}$$
$$= P[A_{\overline{16}|1.5\%} + A_{\overline{48}|1.6\%} \cdot V^{16}_{1.5\%}]$$
$$= 636.13[14.131264 + (33.326937)(0.788031)]$$
$$= \$25,695.79$$

4 a) Let P = first annual loan repayment
$$100,000 = P A_{\overline{2}|15\%} + P A_{\overline{2}|16\%} V^2_{15\%} + 20,000 V^3_{16\%} V^2_{15\%}$$
$$= P[1.625709 + (1.605232)(0.756144)]$$
$$+ 20,000(0.640658)(0.756144)$$
$$= P(2.839495) + 9,688.584854$$
$$\therefore P = \$31,805.45$$

b) Loan outstanding after the second payment
$$= P A_{\overline{2}|16\%} + 20,000 V^3_{16\%}$$
$$= 31,805.45(1.605232) + \frac{20,000}{(1.16)^3}$$
$$= \$63,868.28$$

Annual payment	Loan outstanding before payment	Interest rate	Interest content	Principal content	Loan outstanding immediately after payment
1	100,000.00	15	15,000.00	16,805.45	83,194.55
2	83,194.55	15	12,479.18	19,326.27	63,868.28
3	63,868.28	16	10,218.93		

c) From the loan schedule, interest content of 3rd payment = \$10,218.93

Alternatively,

$$\frac{\text{interest content of}}{3^{rd} \text{ payment}} = \frac{\text{interest}}{\text{rate}} \times \frac{\text{loan outstanding}}{\text{immediately before } 3^{rd} \text{ payment}}$$

$$\frac{\text{Loan outstanding immediately}}{\text{before } 3^{rd} \text{ payment}} = PA_{\overline{2}|16\%} + \frac{20,000}{(1.16)^3}$$

$$= \$63,868.28 \quad \text{(from part b)}$$

$$\therefore \text{ Interest content} = (63,868.28)(0.16)$$

$$= 10,218.92$$

5 a) Let $Y(1.015) = $ first instalment

Interest on the loan $= \dfrac{14}{4} = 3.5\%$ per quarter

$$\therefore 72,000 = \frac{Y(1.015)}{1.035} + \frac{Y(1.015)^2}{(1.035)^2} + \dots \frac{Y(1.015)^{40}}{(1.035)^{40}}$$

$$= YA_{\overline{40}|j} \quad \text{where } j = \frac{1.035}{1.015} - 1$$

$$= 0.019704 \quad \text{or} \quad 1.9704\%$$

$$\therefore Y = 72,000 \div A_{\overline{40}|1.9704\%}$$
$$= 72,000 \div 27.498026$$
$$= 2,618.369781$$

$$\therefore \text{ The first instalment} = 2,618.369781(1.015)$$
$$= \$2,657.65$$

b) Loan outstanding $= \dfrac{Y(1.015)^{16}}{(1.035)} + \dfrac{Y(1.015)^{17}}{(1.035)^2} + \dots \dfrac{Y(1.015)^{40}}{(1.035)^{25}}$

$$= Y(1.015)^{15}\left[\frac{1.015}{1.035} + \frac{(1.015)^2}{(1.035)^2} + \dots \frac{(1.015)^{25}}{(1.035)^{25}}\right]$$

$$= Y(1.015)^{15} A_{\overline{25}|1.9704\%}$$

$$= (2,618.369781)(1.015)^{15}(19.59147)$$

$$= \$64,134.04$$

6   Effective rate per month for loan A $= \dfrac{14}{12} = 1.166667\%$

∴ Effective rate per annum for loan A $= (1 + 0.011667)^{12} - 1$
$$= 14.9342\%$$

Effective rate per annum for loan B $= \left(1 + \dfrac{14.4}{200}\right)^2 - 1$
$$= 14.9184\%$$

Loan B has the lower cost of funds and is therefore superior.

CHAPTER 20

1   Price $= 7A_{\overline{22}|} + 100V^{22}$ @ 6.05%
$$= 83.9258 + 27.4641$$
$$= \$111.39$$
The discrepancy of $111.61–$111.39 = $0.22 is due to the fact that the two prices are at different valuation dates.
The $111.61 is set at the day preceding the release in the *Financial Review* on 22/4/88.

2   After one year the projected sale price (based on future cash flows) is:

Sale price $= 7A_{\overline{20}|} + 100V^{20}$ @ $5\frac{1}{2}\%$
$$= 83.6527 + 34.2729$$
$$= 117.93$$
Accumulated coupons $= 7 + 7(1.05)$
$$= 14.35$$

Sale price + accumulated coupons $= 132.28$

Horizon return $= \dfrac{132.28 - 111.39}{111.39} \times \dfrac{100}{1}$

$$= 18.75\%$$

3   Price @ 12.1% = $111.39
Price @ 13.1% $= 7A_{\overline{22}|} + 100V^{22}$ @ 6.55%
$$= 80.4047 + 24.7642$$
$$= 105.17$$

Volatility $= \dfrac{111.39 - 105.17}{111.39} \times \dfrac{100}{1}$

$$= 5.584\%$$

4   Loss for a 1% increase in yields (interest rates) = 3% of 200,000
$$= \$6,000$$

$$\text{Loss for a } 1.6\% \text{ increase in yields} = 1.6 \times 6{,}000$$
$$= \$9{,}600$$

5   Yield = 3% per quarter and coupon = 3.5 per quarter

$$\therefore \text{Price} = 3.5 A_{\overline{16}|3\%} + 100 V_{3\%}^{16}$$
$$= 43.9639 + 62.3167$$
$$= \$106.2806$$

6   Price $= \dfrac{3}{1.05} + \dfrac{3(1.025)}{(1.05)^2} + \ldots \dfrac{3(1.025)^7}{(1.05)^8} + \dfrac{100}{(1.05)^8}$

$$= \dfrac{3}{1.025}\left[\dfrac{1.025}{1.05} + \ldots \dfrac{(1.025)^8}{(1.05)^8}\right] + \dfrac{100}{(1.05)^8}$$

$$= \dfrac{3}{1.025} A_{\overline{8}|j} + \dfrac{100}{(1.05)^8} \qquad \text{where } j = \dfrac{1.05}{1.025} - 1$$
$$= 0.02439$$

$$= 21.0405 + 67.6839$$

$$= \$88.7244$$

7   Price of one-year bond $= 6A_2 + 100V^2$ @ $5\tfrac{1}{2}\%$
$$= 11.0779 + 89.8452$$
$$= 100.9231$$

Sell the one-year coupon @ yield $j\%$.

Sell the six-month coupon @ yield 10% $= \dfrac{6}{1.05}$
$$= 5.7143$$

$$100.9231 = \dfrac{6}{1.05} + \dfrac{106}{(1+j)^2}$$

$$95.2088 = \dfrac{106}{(1+j)^2}$$

$$(1+j)^2 = \dfrac{106}{95.2088}$$

$$= 1.1133$$

$$1+j = 1.05515 \qquad (= \sqrt{1.1133})$$

$$j = 0.05515$$

$$= 5.515\% \text{ per half-year}$$

The price of the 18-month bond $= 6A_{\overline{3}|} + 100V^3$ @ 6%
$$= 100$$

Let the zero half-yearly yield for the third (18-month) coupon and face amount = $w\%$.

Then $100 = \underbrace{\dfrac{6}{1.05}}_{\substack{\text{6-month} \\ \text{yield}}} + \underbrace{\dfrac{6}{(1.05515)^2}}_{\substack{\text{12-month} \\ \text{yield}}} + \underbrace{\dfrac{106}{(1+w)^3}}_{\substack{\text{18-month} \\ \text{yield}}}$

$$100 - \frac{6}{1.05} - \frac{6}{(1.05515)^2} = \frac{106}{(1+w)^3}$$

$$88.8965 = \frac{106}{(1+w)^3}$$

$$(1+w) = \left(\frac{106}{88.8965}\right)^{1/3}$$

$$= 1.06041$$

$$\therefore w = 0.06041$$

$$= 6.041\% \text{ per half-year}$$

The zero coupon annual nominal yields convertible half-yearly are:

6 months	10%	
12 months	11.03%	(i.e. 2 × 5.515%)
18 months	12.082%	(i.e. 2 × 6.041%)

8   Effective yield on first debenture $= \left(1 + \dfrac{14}{1200}\right)^{12} - 1$

$$= 14.9342\%$$

Effective yield on second debenture $= \left(1 + \dfrac{14.6}{200}\right)^2 - 1$

$$= 15.1329\%$$

$\therefore$ The second debenture is superior.

CHAPTER 21

1   Purchase price $= \dfrac{3,650,000}{36,500 + (90)(12)}$

$$= 97.1261$$

a)   Selling price after 10 days $= \dfrac{3,650,000}{36,500 + (80)(12)}$

$$= 97.4373$$

$$\therefore \text{ Annualised holding period return} = \frac{97.4373 - 97.1261}{97.1261} \times \frac{36,500}{10}$$

$$= 11.695\%$$

b)
$$\text{Selling price after 50 days} = \frac{3,650,000}{36,500 + (40)(12)}$$

$$= 98.7020$$

$$\therefore \text{ Annualised holding period return} = \frac{98.702 - 97.1261}{97.1261} \times \frac{365}{50} \times \frac{100}{1}$$

$$= 11.844\%$$

c)
$$\text{Selling price after 90 days} = 100$$

$$\therefore \text{ Maturity return} = \frac{100 - 97.1261}{97.1261} \times \frac{365}{90} \times \frac{100}{1}$$

$$= 12\%$$

Conclusion: The annualised holding period yield increases as holding period increases. It also approaches the purchase yield as the holding date approaches maturity.

2   Purchase price $= \dfrac{3,650,000}{36,500 + (13)(180)}$

$$= 93.9753$$

Selling price $= \dfrac{3,650,000}{36,500 + (15)(130)}$

$$= 94.9285$$

$$\therefore \text{ Annualised holding period return} = \frac{94.9285 - 93.9753}{93.9753} \times \frac{100}{1} \times \frac{365}{50}$$

$$= 7.404\%$$

3   Purchase price $= 100 - \left(\dfrac{d}{100} \times \dfrac{n}{365} \times 100 \right)$

$$= 100 - \left(\frac{12}{100} \times \frac{90}{365} \times 100 \right)$$

$$= 100 - 2.958904$$

$$= 97.041096$$

Selling price after 10 days $= 100 - \left(\dfrac{12}{100} \times \dfrac{80}{365} \times 100 \right)$

$$= 97.369863$$

$\therefore$ Annualised holding period return $= \dfrac{97.369863 - 97.041096}{97.041096} \times \dfrac{36,500}{10}$
(AHPR)

$$= 12.36589\%$$

Selling price after 50 days $= 100 - \left(\dfrac{12}{100} \times \dfrac{40}{365} \times 100 \right)$

$$= 98.684932$$

$\therefore$ AHPR $= \dfrac{98.684932 - 97.041096}{97.041096} \times \dfrac{365}{50} \times 100$

$$= 12.36589\%$$

Selling price after 90 days $= 100$

$$\text{AHPR} = 12.36589\%$$

Conclusion: When a bill is bought and sold at the same discount, the AHPR is constant. In fact, the AHPR is the purchase yield,

i.e. $\quad \dfrac{100 - 97.041096}{97.041096} \times \dfrac{365}{90} \times 100 = 12.36589\%$

4 Purchase price $= \dfrac{3,650,000}{36,500 + (150)(12)}$

$$= 95.300261$$

2 days of interest @ 11% on purchase price (PP)

$$= PP \times 0.11 \times \dfrac{2}{365}$$

$$= 95.300261 \times 0.11 \times \dfrac{2}{365}$$

$$= 0.057441$$

PP + interest $= 95.357702$

Let break-even sale yield $= x\%$

$\therefore \quad \dfrac{3,650,000}{36,500 + (x)(148)} = 95.357702$

$$3,650,000 = 95.357702(36,500 + 148x)$$

$$= 3,480,556.132 + 14,112.9399x$$

$$14,112.9399x = 3,650,000 - 3,480,556.132$$

$$= 169,443.868$$

$$\therefore x = 12.006277\%$$

The break-even selling yield is 12.006277%.

5 Selling price of bond on compound basis $= \dfrac{106}{(1.063)^1}$

$$= 99.718$$

Purchase price of bond $= 6A_{\overline{2}|i} + 100V^2 \ @ \ i = 6\frac{1}{2}\%$

$$= 99.090$$

The seller receives the 6-month coupon as well as the selling price of the bond.

$$\therefore \text{The AHPR} = \frac{(6 + 99.718) - 99.090}{99.090} \times \frac{365}{183} \times 100$$

$$= 13.341\%$$

The break-even '183' day bill rate is therefore 13.341%.

6 PP on discount basis $= 100 - \left(\dfrac{d}{100} \times \dfrac{n}{365} \times 100 \right)$

PP on yield basis $= \dfrac{3,650,000}{36,500 + yn}$

where y = yield % and d = discount %
Equating these:

$$\frac{3,650,000}{36,500 + yn} = 100 - \frac{dn}{365}$$

$$= \frac{36,500}{365} - \frac{dn}{365}$$

$$= \frac{36,500 - dn}{365}$$

$$3,650,000(365) = (36,500 + yn)(36,500 - dn)$$

$$= (36,500)^2 - dn(36,500) + yn(36,500) - ydn^2$$

Now $3,650,000(365) = (36,500)^2$

$$\therefore 0 = -dn(36,500) + yn(36,500) - ydn^2$$

$$dn(36,500) + ydn^2 = yn(36,500)$$

Divide throughout by n:

$$36,500d + ydn = 36,500y$$

$$d(36,500 + yn) = 36,500y$$

$$\therefore d = \frac{36,500y}{36,500 + yn}$$

Using exercise 3, when $d = 12\%$ and $n = 90$, the yield is $y = 12.36589\%$. If $y = 12.36589\%$ and $n = 90$ are substituted into the formula for d above, the result should be $d = 12$.
In fact this is the case.

CHAPTER 22

1   Let j = effective quarterly after-tax cost of debt

$$PV \text{ of inflows} = PV \text{ of outflows}$$

$$100 + (0.49)(3)A_{\overline{32}|j} = 3A_{\overline{32}|j} + 100V_j^{32}$$

$$100 = 3(1 - 0.49)A_{\overline{32}|} + 100V^{32} \ @ \ j$$

$$= 1.53A_{\overline{32}|j} + 100V^{32} \ @ \ j$$

This can be rewritten as:

$$100 = 1.53A_{\overline{31}|j} + 101.53V^{32} \ @ \ j$$

i.e. the cash flows are 1.53 for 31 quarters and 101.53 for the 32nd quarter.
Using the Hewlett-Packard,

$$j = 1.53\%$$

The effective annual after-tax cost of debt $= (1.0153)^4 - 1$
$$= 6.26\%$$

2   $100 = 3A_{\overline{32}|j} - (0.49)3V^4A_{\overline{32}|j} + 100V^{32} \ @ \ j$

Quarter	0	1	2	3	4	5		32	33		36
Cash flows	100	(3)	(3)	(3)	(3)	(1.53)		(1.53) (100)	1.47		1.47

i.e. for the first year, $3 is paid out each quarter. From quarter 5 till the end of the debenture, $3 is paid out and $(0.49)3 = 1.47$ tax remission flows in. For the next 4 quarters the tax remission flows in.

$$\therefore j = 1.6216\%$$

The effective cost per annum $= (1.016216)^4 - 1$
$$= 6.646\%$$

3   $2 = \dfrac{0.2}{1+i} + \dfrac{0.2(1.03)}{(1+i)^2} + \cdots$ where i = half-yearly cost of equity
The RHS is a perpetuity.

Using $\dfrac{a}{1-r}$, $a = \dfrac{0.2}{1+i}$ and $r = \dfrac{1.03}{1+i}$

$$\therefore \frac{a}{1-r} = \frac{0.2}{1+i} \div \left(1 - \frac{1.03}{1+i}\right)$$

$$= \frac{0.2}{1+i} \div \left(\frac{1+i}{1+i} - \frac{1.03}{1+i}\right)$$

$$= \frac{0.2}{1+i} \div \left(\frac{1+i-1.03}{1+i}\right)$$

$$= \frac{0.2}{1+i} \div \frac{i-0.03}{1+i}$$

$$= \frac{0.2}{1+i} \times \frac{1+i}{i-0.03}$$

$$= \frac{0.2}{i-0.03}$$

$$\text{LHS} = 2$$

$$\therefore 2 = \frac{0.2}{i-0.03}$$

$$2i - 0.06 = 0.2$$

$$2i = 0.26$$

$$i = 0.13$$

$\therefore$ The effective annual cost of equity $= (1.13)^2 - 1$
$$= 27.69\%$$

4

Week	Share price	Return % r_{st}	Dispersion $(r_{st} - \bar{r}_s)$
1	10		
2	14	40.000	19.137
3	16	14.286	−6.577
4	18	12.500	−8.363
5	21	16.667	−4.196

$$\bar{r}_s = 20.863$$

Week	'All Ords' index	r_{mt} %	$r_{mt} - \bar{r}_m$	$(r_{mt} - \bar{r}_m)^2$
1	1000			
2	1200	20.000	7.404	54.819
3	1300	8.333	−4.263	18.173
4	1500	15.385	2.789	7.779
5	1600	6.667	−5.929	35.153
		$\bar{r}_m = 12.596$		115.924

$$\therefore \text{ variance } (r_m) = \frac{115.924}{4} = 28.981$$

Cross-products:

$$(19.137)(7.404) = 141.690$$
$$(-6.577)(-4.263) = 28.038$$
$$(-8.363)(2.789) = -23.324$$
$$(-4.196)(-5.929) = \underline{24.878}$$
$$171.282$$

$$\therefore \text{ covariance } (r_{st}, r_{mt}) = \frac{171.282}{4} = 42.821$$

$$\beta = \frac{\text{covariance } (r_{st}, r_{mt})}{\text{variance } (r_{mt})}$$

$$= \frac{42.821}{28.981}$$

$$= 1.478$$

$$\therefore \text{ Cost of equity } = r_f + \beta(r_m - r_f)$$

$$= 11 + 1.478(14 - 11)$$

$$= 15.43\%$$

Shortcomings:
   (i) sample data too small;
   (ii) need ex ante data;
   (iii) project length may not be 15 years. Hence 15-year bond rate may not be appropriate;
   (iv) market return in the future may not be 14%.

$$5 \quad 2 = \underbrace{\frac{2}{(1+i)^8}}_{\substack{PV \text{ of} \\ \text{principal}}} + \underbrace{\frac{0.12 \times \frac{8}{12} \times 2}{(1+i)^8}}_{\substack{PV \text{ of 8 months'} \\ \text{interest @ 12\%}}} - \underbrace{\frac{\left(0.12 \times \frac{8}{12} \times 2\right) \times 0.49}{(1+i)^{12}}}_{\substack{PV \text{ of tax remission} \\ \text{on interest payments}}}$$

where i = effective monthly after-tax cost.

$$\text{i.e.} \quad 2 = \frac{2.16}{(1+i)^8} - \frac{0.0784}{(1+i)^{12}}$$

$$i = 0.51066\%$$

The effective annual rate $= (1 + 0.051066)^{12} - 1$
$$= 6.303\%$$

6   a) $\sum_{i=4}^{i=7} (i^2 - 1) = (4^2 - 1) + (5^2 - 1) + (6^2 - 1) + (7^2 - 1)$
$$= (16 - 1) + (25 - 1) + (36 - 1) + (49 - 1)$$
$$= 15 + 24 + 35 + 48$$
$$= 122$$

b) $\sum_{t=2}^{t=4} (3t + 2)(t - 1) = (3 \times 2 + 2)(2 - 1) + (3 \times 3 + 2)(3 - 1)$
$$+ (3 \times 4 + 2)(4 - 1)$$
$$= (8)(1) + (11)(2) + (14)(3)$$
$$= 8 + 22 + 42$$
$$= 72$$

c) $\sum_{t=1}^{t=3} (t^3 - 2) = (1^3 - 2) + (2^3 - 2) + (3^3 - 2)$
$$= -1 + 6 + 25$$
$$= 30$$

7   a) $\sum_{i=3}^{i=5} x_i^2$

b) $\sum_{i=3}^{i=5} (x_i - \bar{x})^2$

c) $\sum_{i=1}^{i=3} (r_{is} - \bar{r}_s)$

d) $\sum_{i=3}^{i=5} (r_{is} - \bar{r}_s)(r_{im} - \bar{r}_m)$

8   *WACC* for existing structure is:

$$WACC = \left(\frac{20}{100} \times 9.2\right) + \left(\frac{20}{100} \times 8.7\right) + \left(\frac{50}{100} \times 14.6\right) + \left(\frac{10}{100} \times 14.6\right)$$

$$= 12.34$$

Cost of equity for new project $= r_f + \beta(r_m - r_f)$
$$= 11 + 1.7(14 - 11)$$
$$= 16.1$$

Capital class	Cost of capital %	Market value (millions)
Existing structure	12.34	100
New project	16.1	30
(financed by shares)		130

$$\therefore WACC \text{ for new structure} = \left(12.34 \times \frac{100}{130}\right) \times \left(16.1 \times \frac{30}{130}\right)$$

$$= 13.21\%$$

$$\therefore NPV = 5A_{\overline{4}|i} + 20V^5 - 30 \ @ \ i = 13.21\%$$
$$= 14.808 + 10.755 - 30$$
$$= -4.437$$

The new project is therefore not feasible.

CHAPTER 23

1   Let the loan repayment $= P$
Then $PA_{\overline{120}|1\%} = 50,000$
$$P = 50,000 \div 69.700522$$
$$= \$717.35$$

The equation of value adjusted for transaction costs is:
$$200V^{120} + 717.35A_{\overline{120}|i} + 900 = 50,000 \ @ \ i$$

Using the Hewlett-Packard to find i:

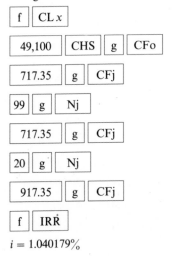

| f | CLx |

| 49,100 | CHS | g | CFo |

| 717.35 | g | CFj |

| 99 | g | Nj |

| 717.35 | g | CFj |

| 20 | g | Nj |

| 917.35 | g | CFj |

| f | IRR |

$i = 1.040179\%$

The nominal annual rate $= 1.040179 \times 12 = 12.4821\%$
The effective annual rate $= (1.01040179)^{12} - 1 = 13.2216\%$

2   Price on 90-day bill per \$100 face value $= \dfrac{3,650,000}{36,500 + (90)(14)}$

$$= \$96.663136$$

$\therefore$ Price on \$60,000 face value $= \$96.663136 \times 600$
$$= \$57,997.88$$

Initial funds received $= 57,997.88 - 600$
$$= \$57,397.88$$

Annualised cost of funds $= \dfrac{60,000 - 57,397.88}{57,397.88} \times \dfrac{36,500}{90}$

$$= 18.3858\%$$

3   Let P = half-yearly premium.
Then $\qquad P\ddot{A}_{\overline{10}|5\%} = 50,000V^{10}_{5\%} + 500 + 0.07P + 0.015PA_{\overline{9}|5\%}$
$P(\ddot{A}_{\overline{10}|5\%} - 0.07 - 0.015A_{\overline{9}|5\%}) = 50,000V^{10}_{5\%} + 500$
$P(8.107822 - 0.07 - 0.106617) = 30,695.66268$
$$P(7.931204) = 31,195.66268$$
$$\therefore P = \$3,933.29 \quad \text{(rounding up)}$$

The half-yearly premium is \$3,933.29.

4   End benefit $= 30,000(0.97)(1.1)^7 - \left(\dfrac{0.1}{100} \times 30,000\right)S_{\overline{6}|10\%}$
$$= 56,707.67 - 231.47$$
$$= \$56,476.20$$

Let the effective return adjusted for transaction costs $= j$.
$30,000(1 + j)^7 = 56,476.20$
$(1 + j)^7 = 1.88254$
$1 + j = 1.88254^{1/7}$
$\qquad\quad = 1.88254^{0.142857}$
$\qquad j = 9.4584\%$

5   Interest content at maturity $= \$26,476.20$
   Tax @ 20\% on 26,476.20 = 5,295.24
Let i = the after-tax rate per annum after transaction costs.
The equation of value becomes:

$$30,000(0.97)(1.1)^7 - 5,295.24V^1_i - \dfrac{0.1}{100} \times 30,000S_{\overline{6}|10\%} = 30,000(1 + i)^7$$

i.e. $56,476.20 - 5,295.24V^1 = 30,000(1 + i)^7$

Multiply both sides by $(1 + i)^7 = V^7$ @ rate i:

$$56,476.20V^7 - 5,295.24V^8 = 30,000$$

or Year 0   outlay of $30,000

Year 7   receipt of $56,476.20

Year 8   tax payment of $5,925.24

Using the Hewlett-Packard:

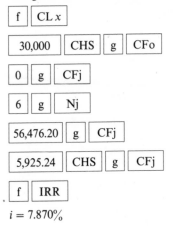

$i = 7.870\%$

The effective after-tax rate adjusted for transaction costs is 7.87%.

6 Days

	0	4	12

Cash flow   (10 m)   10 m   Interest paid

$$\text{Interest} = 10 \text{ m} \times \frac{11.2}{100} \times \frac{4}{365}$$

$$= \$12,273.97$$

The interest rate forgone on the $12,273.97 is assumed to be 11.2%.

$$PV \text{ of } 12,273.97 \text{ to day } 4 = \frac{12,273.97}{1 + \frac{11.2}{100} \times \frac{8}{365}}$$

$$= 12,243.9137$$

$$\text{Annualised flat return} = \frac{12,243.9137}{10 \text{ m}} \times \frac{36,500}{4}$$

$$= 11.17257\%$$

CHAPTER 24

1   $A receipts $= \dfrac{10 \text{ m}}{0.7} = 14{,}285{,}714$

   Interest on loan $= 10 \text{ m} \times \dfrac{8}{100} \times \dfrac{90}{360}$

   $= 200{,}000$

   Amount required to repay loan in $A $= \dfrac{10.2 \text{ m}}{0.69}$

   $= 14{,}782{,}609$

   Cost of funds annualised $= \dfrac{14{,}782{,}609 - 14{,}285{,}714}{14{,}285{,}714} \times \dfrac{36{,}500}{90}$

   $= 14.1063\%$

   $\therefore$ The cost of hedging the principal and interest is 14.107%.

2   Amount required to repay $10.2 m US $= \dfrac{10.2}{0.6875}$

   $= 14{,}836{,}364$

   $\therefore$ Annualised cost of funds $= \dfrac{14{,}836{,}364 - 14{,}285{,}714}{14{,}285{,}714} \times \dfrac{36{,}500}{90}$

   $= 15.6323\%$

When the forward exchange rate worsens, the landed cost rises, in this case from 14.1063% to 15.6323%.
The reduction in the forward exchange rate will increase domestic interest rates to an equilibrium of 15.6323%.

3
$$S(\$US/\$A) = 0.7000 = S \qquad (1)$$

$$\therefore P_A \times S = P_{US}$$

where P_{US} = price in US
   P_A = price in Australia
In one year's time,

$$P_A(1 + j_A)F = P_{US}(1 + j_{US}) \qquad (2)$$

where F = forward exchange rate
   j_{US} = inflation rate in the US
   j_A = inflation rate in Australia
Divide (2) by (1):

$$\frac{F(1 + j_A)}{S} = 1 + j_{US}$$

$$\therefore F = \frac{S(1 + j_{US})}{1 + j_A}$$

$$= \frac{0.7(1.045)}{(1.065)}$$

$$= 0.6869$$

∴ The projected exchange rate is 0.6869.

4 £100 = $240

$$P_{UK} . S(\$A/£) = P_A \tag{3}$$

After one year,

$$P_{UK}(1 + j_{UK})F(\$A/£) = P_A(1 + j_A) \tag{4}$$

Divide (4) by (3):

$$\frac{(1 + j_{UK})F(\$A/£)}{S(\$A/£)} = 1 + j_A$$

$$F(\$A/£) = \frac{(1 + j_A)S(\$A/£)}{(1 + j_{UK})}$$

$$= \frac{1.065}{1.04}(2.4000)$$

$$= 2.4577$$

The exchange rate in 2 years will be:

$$F = \frac{(1.065)^2}{(1.04)^2}(2.4000)$$

$$= 2.5168$$

The exchange rate in 3 years will be:

$$F = \frac{(1.065)^3}{(1.04)^3}(2.4000)$$

$$= 2.5773$$

The after-tax cash flows in $A are:
End of year 1:   200,000 × 2.4577 = 491,540
End of year 2:   200,000 × 2.5168 = 503,360
End of year 3:   200,000 × 2.5773 = 515,460
PV of these cash flows @ 10% is:

$$PV = \frac{491,540}{(1.1)} + \frac{503,360}{(1.1)^2} + \frac{515,460}{(1.1)^3}$$

$$= \$1,250,127.27$$

The break-even purchase price = \$1.25 m A.

5    $100\left(1 + \frac{r_A \cdot n}{365}\right) = 100\frac{S}{F}\left(1 + \frac{r_{US} \cdot n}{360}\right)$

where $S = S(\$US/\$A)$
$F = F(\$US/\$A)$

$$\therefore F = S\left(\frac{1 + r_{US} \cdot n}{360}\right) \div \left(1 + \frac{r_A \cdot n}{365}\right)$$

$$= 0.7\left(1 + \frac{(0.07)(90)}{360}\right) \div \left(1 + \frac{(0.12)(90)}{365}\right)$$

$$= \frac{0.71225}{1.029589}$$

$$\therefore F = 0.6918$$

6   Issue price per £100 face amount = $5A_{\overline{10|}} + 100V^{10}$ @ 6%
$$= 36.8004 + 55.8395$$
$$= £92.6399$$

$$\text{Fee} = \frac{0.2}{100} \times 100 = £0.2000$$

Net proceeds in sterling per £100 = £92.4399
Net proceeds for £50 m = £46,219,950
Net proceeds in \$A = 46,219,950 × 2.4
$$= \$110,927,880.$$

CHAPTER 25

1   Yield = 100 − 88
$$= 12\%$$

$$\text{Purchase price} = \frac{3,650,000}{36,500 + (12)(90)}$$

$$= \$97.126131$$

The face value for 4 contracts = 4 × 500,000
$$= \$2 \text{ m}$$

∴ The purchase price for $2 m face value is:

$$\frac{2\,m}{100} \times 97.126131 = \$1,942,523$$

2

Days	0	60	150

Deposit	(1,100 × 4)		
Clearing House fees	(20)	(20)	
Brokerage	(120)		
	4,540		
Refund of deposit		1,100 × 4	
Bill purchase price		(1,942,523)	
Receive face value			$2 m

Accumulating the initial outlays for 60 days @ 12% per annum flat gives:

$$4,540\left(1 + 0.12 \times \frac{60}{365}\right) = \$4,629.56$$

Thus the cash flows are:

Days	60	150

Accumulated initial outflow	(4,629.56)	
Bill purchase price	(1,942,523)	
Clearing House fee	(20)	
	(1,947,172.56)	
Refund of deposit	4,400	
	(1,942,772.56)	
Receive face value		$2 m

∴ The annualised rate of return is

$$\frac{2\,m - 1,942,772.56}{1,942,772.56} \times \frac{36,500}{90} = 11.946\%$$

The existence of transaction costs has reduced the yield from 12% to 11.946%.

3   Yield $= 100 - 87.23$
$$= 12.77\%$$

$$\text{Purchase price per \$100} = \frac{3{,}650{,}000}{36{,}500 + (12.77)(90)}$$

$$= 96.947354$$

$$\text{Purchase price per contract} = 96.947354 \times \frac{500{,}000}{100}$$

$$= \$484{,}736.77$$

$$\text{Number of contracts required} = \frac{18.9}{484{,}736.77}$$

$$= 39$$

Initial costs:

$$\begin{array}{r}
\text{Deposit} = 1{,}100 \times 39 = 42{,}900 \\
\text{Other initial costs} = 80 \times 39 = \underline{3{,}120} \\
46{,}020
\end{array}$$

$$\text{Accumulated initial costs} = 46{,}020(1 + 0.12 \times 1.5)$$
$$= \$54{,}303.60$$

Outlays in 18 months:

$$\text{Purchase price} = 39 \times 500{,}000 \times \frac{96.947354}{100}$$
$$= (18{,}904{,}734)$$

$$\text{Transaction cost @ delivery} = 10 \times 39$$
$$= (390)$$

$$\text{Accumulated initial transaction costs} = (54{,}303.60)$$

$$\text{Deduct deposit refund} = \frac{42{,}900}{18{,}916{,}527.60}$$

$$\text{Receipts on redemption} = 39 \times 500{,}000$$
$$= 19.5 \text{ m}$$

$$\text{Annualised rate of return} = \frac{19.5 \text{ m} - 18{,}916{,}527.6}{18{,}916{,}527.6} \times \frac{36{,}500}{90}$$
$$= 12.509\%$$

4   Purchase price on standard bond $= 6A_{\overline{20}|} + 100V^{20}$ @ $6\frac{1}{2}\%$
$$= 94.4907$$
Close out by opposite transaction @ 14%,

i.e. sell @ $6A_{\overline{20}|} + 100V^{20}$ @ $7\% = 89.4060$

$$\text{Profit per } 100 = 94.4907 - 89.4060$$
$$= 5.0847$$

Profit on 20 contracts, each $100,000 is:

$$\text{Profit} = 2\text{ m} \times \frac{5.0847}{100}$$

$$= \$101,694$$

5 Sale yield $= 100 - 88.27$
   $= 11.73\%$

Sell standard contract at:

$$6A_{\overline{20}|} + 100V^{20} \text{ @ } \frac{11.73}{2}\% = 101.5656$$

Purchase standard contract at 14%:

$$6A_{\overline{20}|} + 100V^{20} \text{ @ } 7\% = 89.4060$$

$$\text{Profit per } 100 \text{ face value} = 101.5656 - 89.4060$$
$$= 12.1596$$

$$\text{Profit on 20 contracts} = 12.1596 \times \frac{2\text{ m}}{100}$$

$$= \$243,192$$
$$\text{Initial costs} = 1,570 \times 20$$
$$= 31,400$$
$$\text{Accumulated initial costs} = 31,400(1 + 0.12 \times 0.75)$$
$$= 34,226$$

Loan acquired

Loan required =	2,000,000
less Bond future profit =	−243,192
plus Transaction costs =	400
plus Accumulated initial expenses =	34,226
less Refund of deposit =	−30,000
	$1,761,434

Annual loan repayment X @ 14.5% is found from the equation of value:

$$1,761,434 = XA_{\overline{10}|14.5\%}$$
$$\therefore X = \$344,305.28$$

The effective borrowing rate can be determined by equating the actual loan repayment of 344,305.28 with the 2 million (she/he received 1,761,434 − 34,226 − 400 + 243,192 + 30,000 = 2 m):

$$\therefore 2\text{ m} = 344,305.28 A_{\overline{10}|j}$$

By an iterative process, $j = 11.3293\%$

6
$$\text{Initial premium} = 2\,m \times \frac{0.64}{100}$$
$$= 12,800$$

Other initial expenses
$$(\text{excluding deposit}) = 70 \times 20$$
$$= 1,400$$
$$\text{Accumulated initial expenses} = (12,800 + 1,400)(1 + 0.12 \times 0.75)$$
$$= 15,478$$

Loan acquired

$$\begin{array}{rr}
\text{Loan required} = & 2,000,000 \\
\text{less Profit on bond future} = & -243,192 \\
\text{plus Accumulated premium} & \\
\text{and initial expenses} = & 15,478 \\
\text{plus transaction costs} = & \underline{400} \\
& 1,772,686
\end{array}$$

10-year credit foncier repayment X @ $14\frac{1}{2}\%$ is found from:

$$XA_{\overline{10}|14.5\%} = 1,772,686$$
$$\therefore X = 346,504.69$$

The effective borrowing rate can be found from:

$$346,504.69A_{\overline{10}|j} = 2\,m$$
By an iterative process, $j = 11.4826\%$

$\therefore$ The effective borrowing rate allowing for the option premium, expenses, and bond future profit, is 11.483%.

7 (i)
$$\text{Option premium} = 0.400 \times 20 \times \frac{500,000}{100}$$
$$= 40,000$$
$$\text{Deposits} = 1,500 \times 20$$
$$= 30,000$$
$$\text{Other expenses} = 90 \times 20$$
$$= 1,800$$
$$\therefore \text{Total initial outflows} = 71,800$$

As the yields at exercise are less than $100 - 89$, the bill is purchased at 11% (i.e. the option is exercised).

$$\text{Purchase price} = \frac{3,650,000}{36,500 + (11)(90)} \times \frac{10\,m}{100}$$
$$= \$9,735,929.58$$
$$\text{Expenses at delivery} = 20 \times 20$$
$$= 400$$
$$\text{Total outflows in 60 days' time} = 9,736,329.58$$

Deduct deposit refund = $-30,000$
$\therefore$ Outflows in 60 days = $\underline{9,706,329.58}$

Inflows in 150 days = \$ 10 m

The cash flows can be summarised on a time line:

Day	0	60	150
Outflows	(71,800)	(9,706,329.58)	
Inflows			\$ 10 m

Let i = simple interest rate per annum

$$71,800\left(1 + i \times \frac{150}{365}\right) + 9,706,329.58\left(1 + i \times \frac{90}{365}\right) = 10 \text{ m}$$

i.e. $71,800 + 9,706,329.58 + i\left[\left(71,800 \times \frac{150}{365}\right) + \left(9,706,329.58 \times \frac{90}{365}\right)\right]$

$$= 10 \text{ m}$$

$$i(2,422,848.39) = 221,870.42$$
$$\therefore i = 0.091574$$
$$= 9.157\%$$

(ii) Accumulated initial outflows @ 12% flat

$$= 71,800\left(1 + 0.12 \times \frac{60}{365}\right)$$
$$= 73,216.33$$

Outflows after 60 days $= 9,706,329.58 + 73,216.33$
$$= 9,779,545.91$$

Annualised rate of return $= \dfrac{10 \text{ m} - 9,779,545.91}{9,779,545.91} \times \dfrac{36,500}{90}$

$$= 9.142\%$$